Civil Society and Gender Justice

EUROPEAN CIVIL SOCIETY
Editors: **Dieter Gosewinkel** and **Jürgen Kocka**

Civil society represents one of the most ambitious projects and influential concepts relating to the study of modern societies. It encapsulates their structures and their gradual restructuring as well as their changing polities and cultures. Scholars working in this field aim to secure greater equality of opportunity, democratic participation, individual freedom, and societal self-organization against both the overbearing and overburdening powers of the modern state as well as the social deficits of globalizing neo-liberalism. This series deals with the multiple languages, different layers, and diverse practices of existing and emerging civil societies in Europe. Its leitmotif is to analyse whether and how far the renewed interest in the concept can contribute to the gradual evolution of a larger European civil society.

Volume 1
The Languages of Civil Society
Peter Wagner

Volume 2
Civil Society: Berlin Perspectives
John Keane

Volume 3
State and Civil Society in Northern Europe:
The Swedish Model Reconsidered
Edited by Lars Trägårdh

Volume 4
Civil Society and Gender Justice:
Historical and Comparative Perspectives
Edited by Karen Hagemann, Sonya Michel, and Gunilla Budde

CIVIL SOCIETY AND GENDER JUSTICE
HISTORICAL AND COMPARATIVE PERSPECTIVES

Edited by
Karen Hagemann, Sonya Michel, and Gunilla Budde

Berghahn Books
New York • Oxford

First published in 2008 by
Berghahn Books
www.berghahnbooks.com

©2008, 2011 Karen Hagemann, Sonya Michel, and Gunilla Budde
First paperback edition published in 2011

All rights reserved. Except for the quotation of short passages for the purposes of criticism and review, no part of this book may be reproduced in any form or by any means, electronic or mechanical, including photocopying, recording, or any information storage and retrieval system now known or to be invented, without written permission of the publisher.

Library of Congress Cataloging-in-Publication Data

Civil society and gender justice : historical and comparative perspectives / edited by Karen Hagemann, Sonya Michel, and Gunilla Budde.
 p. cm. -- (European civil society)
 Includes bibliographical references and index.
 ISBN 978-1-84545-437-1 (hbk) -- ISBN 978-0-85745-170-5 (pbk)
 1. Civil society—History. 2. Women's rights—History. 3. Feminist theory. I. Hagemann, Karen. II. Michel, Sonya, 1942– III. Budde, Gunilla-Friederike, 1960–

JC337.C5343 2008
300—dc22

2008026635

British Library Cataloguing in Publication Data

A catalogue record for this book is available from the British Library

Printed in the United States on acid-free paper.

ISBN 978-1-84545-437-1 (hardback)
ISBN 978-0-85745-170-5 (paperback)
ISBN 978-0-85745-421-8 (ebook)

Contents

Acknowledgements   viii

Editors' Preface   ix

Introduction: Gendering Civil Society   1
Karen Hagemann, Sonya Michel, Gunilla Budde

RETHINKING CIVIL SOCIETY AND GENDER JUSTICE

Chapter 1   Civil Society Gendered: Rethinking Theories
and Practices   17
Karen Hagemann

Chapter 2   Dilemmas of Gender Justice: Gendering Equity,
Justice, and Recognition   43
Regina Wecker

EARLY CIVIL SOCIETIES IN THEORY AND PRACTICE

Chapter 3   The Progress of "Civilization": Women, Gender,
and Enlightened Perspectives on Civil Society in
Eighteenth-Century Britain   59
Jane Rendall

Chapter 4   The City and the Citoyenne: Associational
Culture and Female Civic Virtues in
Nineteenth-Century Germany   79
Gisela Mettele

Chapter 5 Feminist Campaigns in "Public Space":
Civil Society, Gender Justice, and the History
of European Feminism 97
Karen Offen

CIVIL SOCIETY AND THE FAMILY

Chapter 6 The Family—A Core Institution of Civil Society:
A Perspective on the Middle Classes in
Imperial Germany 119
Gunilla Budde

Chapter 7 Veiled Associations: The Muslim Middle Class,
the Family, and the Colonial State in Nineteenth-
and Twentieth-Century India 135
Margrit Pernau

Chapter 8 "Only Connect": Family, Gender, and Civil Society
in Twentieth-Century Europe and North America 153
Paul A. Ginsborg

CIVIL SOCIETY, GENDERED PROTEST,
AND NONGOVERNMENTAL MOVEMENTS

Chapter 9 Necessary Confrontations: Gender, Civil Society,
and the Politics of Food in Eighteenth- to
Twentieth-Century Germany 173
Manfred Gailus

Chapter 10 "Good" vs. "Militant" Citizens: Masculinity,
Class Protest, and the "Civil" Public in Britain
between 1867 and 1939 190
Sonya O. Rose

Chapter 11 Civil Society in a New Key? Feminist and
Alternative Groups in 1960s–1970s West Germany 208
Belinda Davis

Chapter 12 Civil Society-by-Design: Emerging Capitalism,
Essentialist Feminism, and Women's
Nongovernmental Organizations in
Postsocialist Eastern Europe 224
Kristen R. Ghodsee

CIVIL SOCIETY, THE STATE, AND CITIZENSHIP

Chapter 13 The Rise of Welfare States and the Regendering
of Civil Society: The Case of the United States   245
Sonya Michel

Chapter 14 Fellow Feeling: A Transnational Perspective on
Conceptions of Civil Society and Citizenship
in "White Men's Countries," 1890–1910   265
Marilyn Lake

Chapter 15 Bringing the State Back In: Civil Society,
Women's Movements, and the State   285
Birgit Sauer

Selected Bibliography   302

Contributors   309

Index   314

ACKNOWLEDGEMENTS

We would like to thank several people who supported the international conference on "Civil Society and Gender Justice: Historical and Comparative Perspectives," which took place in July 2004 at the Social Science Research Center Berlin (WZB), and who have helped make this volume a reality. First and foremost, we thank Jürgen Kocka, the former director of the WZB, and Dieter Gosewinkel, who headed the working group on Civil Society: Historical and Comparative Perspectives. They invited Karen Hagemann in 2004 to join this group as a guest researcher, supported her conference idea from the very beginning, and agreed that the WZB would finance and organize it. We are very pleased that they have included this volume in their series on "European Civil Society." We also would like to thank Dagmar Simon of WZB, who helped bring the conference idea to fruition. For the book itself, we would like to acknowledge the work of Nadja Michel-Herf, who copyedited the original manuscript; Marina Jones, who helped us to proofread it; and Friederike Bruehoefener and Jennifer McAndrew, who helped prepare the index; as well as the careful attention of Kristine Hunt, Ann Przyzycki, and Melissa Spinelli at Berghahn Books. Last but not least, we are grateful to all authors of the volume, who worked so cooperatively with us on revisions.

Chapel Hill, North Carolina, USA; College Park, Maryland, USA; and Oldenburg, Germany
August 2007.

Karen Hagemann
Sonya Michel
Gunilla Budde

Editors' Preface

Is there a "European civil society" which cuts across national borders and spreads, though unevenly, through the continent? Does it help to form a European identity from below? Can it be seen as an answer to the obvious democratic deficit of the European Union?

For two and a half years, more than forty political scientists, sociologists, historians, and other scholars from fifteen research institutions in ten different countries have worked together on the project "Towards a European Civil Society." They were supported within the 5th Framework Programme of the EU. The network was coordinated by the Social Science Research Center Berlin (WZB). The results of the project are published in the five to six volumes of this series, which include studies by other authors as well.

"Civil society" means many things—the concept varies and oscillates. To give a working definition: civil society refers to (a) the community of associations, initiatives, movements, and networks in a social space related to but distinguished from government, business, and the private sphere; (b) a type of social action that takes place in the public sphere and is characterized by nonviolence, discourse, self-organization, recognition of plurality, orientation towards general goals, and civility; (c) a project with socially and geographically limited origins and universalistic claims, which changes while it tends to expand, socially and geographically.

Civil society is a deeply historical concept. For a quarter of a century, it has experienced a remarkable career, in several languages. Having a long tradition of many centuries, it had nearly disappeared during most of the twentieth century before being rediscovered and reinforced in the 1970s and 1980s, when the concept became attractive again in the fight against dictatorship, particularly against communist rule in East Central Europe. But in non-dictatorial parts of the world, the term and its promise responded to widely spread needs as well. Western Europe can be taken as an example.

Civil society as a political concept of our time has come to formulate a critique of a broad variety of problems in contemporary society. To name three tendencies: First, the concept emphasizes social self-organization as well as individual responsibilities, reflecting the widespread skepticism towards being spoon-fed by the state. Second, civil society, as demonstrated by the phrase's use by present-day antiglobalization movements, promises an alternative to the unbridled capitalism that has been developing so victoriously across the world. The term thus reflects a new kind of capitalism critique, since the logic of civil society, as determined by public discourse, conflict, and agreement, promises solutions different from those of the logic of the market, which is based on competition, exchange, and the maximization of individual benefits. Third, civic involvement and efforts to achieve common goals are specific to civil society, no matter how differently the goals may be defined. In the highly individualized and partly fragmented societies of the present time, civil society promises an answer to the pressing question of what holds our societies together at all.

On the basis of broad empirical evidence, the project has analyzed a large number of core problems of civil society, among them the complicated relation between markets and civil society, the impact of a European civil society on a European polity and vice versa, and the importance of family and household for the ups and downs of civil society. The project has dealt with resources, dynamics, and actors of civil society. It has dealt with questions of gender and other forms of inequality. It has compared developments in different European regions. It has begun to open up the perspective towards the non-European conditions, consequences, and correlates of European civil society. It has reconstructed the language of civil society, including different semantic strategies in the context of tradition, ideology, and power, which explain the multiple uses of the concept for different practical purposes. These are some of the topics dealt with in the volumes of this series. The authors combine a long historical perspective with broad and systematic comparison.

What does it mean to speak of a "European" civil society? It implies a certain common European development, a parallel or even convergent trend towards the emergence of civil society in Europe. Such a development may be based on the activities of civil society groups. From the eighteenth to the twentieth century, civil society circles, associations, networks, and institutions largely evolved in local, regional, and national frameworks. However, transnational variants, which might contribute to the emergence of transnational coherence and similarities, remained secondary. It is in the second half of the twentieth century that the quality of the process changed. In this phase, the development of civil society in Europe increasingly assumed transnational, "European," and sometimes global dimensions. This is a basic hypothesis of research in this series of studies. "European Civil Society" will concentrate on transnational dimensions of civil society in Europe, by comparing and by reconstructing interrelations.

The evolution of a European civil society in the process of transnationalization is based on actors as well as on mobile concepts. The ideas and practices of civil society have evolved in a very uneven way, starting to emerge mainly in Western Europe, where it was initially restricted to a few proponents and to specific circles. In the course of its development, civil society spread to other parts of Europe (and into other parts of the world) and gained support within broader social spheres. As they expanded into widening social and spatial environments, the ideas and realities of civil society changed. Thus, the potential of an approach is explored which takes civil society as a geographically and socially mobile phenomenon with a good deal of traveling potential and with the propensity to become a European-wide concept.

"European Civil Society" focuses on Europe in a broad, not merely geographical sense. This includes comparing European developments with developments in other parts of the world, as well as analyzing processes of mutual transfer and entanglement. Europe in this sense transcends the institutional and spatial realm of the European Union. Yet, studying the emergence and dynamics, the perspectives and problems of civil society in Europe may produce insights into the historical process of European integration, which is underway, but far from complete, and presently in crisis.

"European Civil Society" is a common endeavor of European and non-European scholars. It centers on a topic that is the object of both scientific analysis and political efforts. The political success cannot be taken for granted. Scientific analysis, however, may help to work out the conditions under which the utopia of civil society in Europe has a chance of realization.

Dieter Gosewinkel and Jürgen Kocka

Introduction
Gendering Civil Society

Karen Hagemann, Sonya Michel, and Gunilla Budde

The essays in this volume represent the emerging research on gender and civil society. Despite the renewed political and scholarly interest in civil society that began in the 1980s, the gendered nature of the concept and of the entire project of civil society was, until the 1990s, not an important subject for feminist scholars. This has changed over the last ten years, as the international conference on "Civil Society and Gender Justice. Historical and Comparative Perspectives," organized by Karen Hagemann, Gunilla Budde, and Dagmar Simon in July 2004 at the Social Science Research Center Berlin (WZB), indicates. Including the speakers, ninety scholars from ten countries participated. Obviously, many shared the main question posed by the organizers: To what extent is the concept of civil society useful for women, and does it allow them to obtain greater gender equality and gender justice? Or, to frame the question differently: Is civil society a feminist concept? And conversely, does feminism need civil society?

These same questions stand at the center of this volume, which is based on the conference and presents revised versions of selected conference papers together with several newly commissioned articles. We pose these questions not only because civil society and civic engagement have increasingly become topics of discussion on the national and international level, but because a wide variety of hopes have been pinned on civil society by diverse groups and forces—social movements and NGOs critical of globalization as well as party politicians and government representatives. Some anticipate the democratization of both the "big" globalized world and the "small" local world of communities. Others hope that increased commitment on the part of citizens will offset reductions in state provisions, allowing the dismantling of welfare states.

While such reductions are routinely rationalized as cost-saving measures, in practice, they often conceal a neoliberal political effort to offload communal duties onto the shoulders of already disadvantaged individuals and groups—disproportionately women.

We also raise these questions because civil society is key to women's role in the renegotiations of the social division of labor, time, and political participation—and thus of responsibility—that are currently occurring across postindustrial societies. The issues being debated include: Who performs what socially necessary labor in occupational life as well as in the household and family? How should this labor be divided up in future? Which tasks should be delegated to the state and financed by the community? What should be left up to the responsibility of individual citizens? How can solidarity be achieved in societies in the future?

Within these debates, the terms *civil society* and *society of citizens* (in German, *Zivilgesellschaft* and *Bürgergesellschaft*) keep reappearing, but their meanings are politically ambiguous. On the one hand, there is a danger that in the prevailing context of neoliberalism, the slogan "civil society" may end up reinforcing a gender-hierarchical division of labor as states and societies move toward a "refamilialization" of reproduction. The work of caring for children, the sick, and the elderly is again being assigned to women, who are expected to perform this labor at home free of charge and are indeed compelled by prevailing economic and social structures to do so.

On the other hand, mobilizations within civil society are more likely than forms of politics close to the state to facilitate women's political participation. It is easier for women to make their demands and interests public through local, informal, and self-formed advocacy groups and issue-based organizations than in the firmly set, male-dominated institutions of parties and parliaments. It is no coincidence that both the old and new women's movements and organizations became important actors in civil society, since women were and continue to be far better integrated into the voluntary sector outside the parties. Moreover, because of their longstanding association with the work of caring, women have been able to establish political claims on the domain of social policy, and it is there that their voices are most likely to be heard.

The aims of this volume are both analytical and programmatic: to illuminate the project of civil society from the perspective of gender, and to develop a concept of civil society that more systematically integrates gender. The volume proceeds, as did the conference, from the understanding of the term *civil society* that underlies the work of the WZB working group on Civil Society: Historical and Social Scientific Perspectives as well as that of the European Civil Society Network.[1] According to this definition, civil society refers to the "largely self-regulated space of civic engagement between the state, the economy, and the private sphere."

Associated with this is a particular type of individual and collective action characterized by personal initiative, communicative competence, openness and pluralism; the ability to engage in constructive conflict and avoid violence, as well as the systematic linking of particular and universal interests. At the same time, civil society refers to the "future project of human coexistence in the tradition of the Enlightenment, which remains to be realized."[2] All of these dimensions are relevant to the ways in which civil society has become imbricated in current political debates.

The authors of the present volume analyze this many-layered concept of civil society from the perspective of gender. Their aim is not so much to challenge the concept head-on, as it is to tease apart and interrogate its terms and assumptions. What, for example, does it mean to place civil society *outside* the private sphere? How is "universal" defined? What constitutes "communicative competence"? By analyzing the historical genesis of the concept and project of civil society across cultures, these essays reveal not only their gendered limitations but also their conditionality. They also question the transnational and intercultural applicability of the ideas that compose Western understandings of civil society and examine their contemporary global significance.

Until recently, theorists of civil society have paid surprisingly little attention to the gender question. Likewise, theorists of gender have given short shrift to the concept of civil society. We would like to initiate a more intensive interdisciplinary debate on civil society and gender from the dual perspective of civil society *and* gender. By gender, we refer to the knowledge about sexual differences produced by cultures and societies—a knowledge that is neither absolute nor true, but always relative and manufactured in complex discursive contexts. The analysis of civil society from the standpoint of gender is meaningful and appropriate to the subject only when gender is understood as one category of difference among others, which functions only in interaction with these other categories. Apart from (and often intertwined with) gender, social, ethnic, racial, and religious differences are also important. With regard to civil society actors and the scope and forms of their action, sexuality, age, and marital status too come into play. Such a relational and contextual approach makes it possible to analyze as gendered even subjects previously conceived of as gender-neutral and "universal," and thus to deconstruct their implicit valences, assignment to hierarchies, and connotations of relevance.

As the focus for our critical reflections on gender and civil society, we have chosen the relation between civil society and gender justice. This second term refers to unequal and unjust relations between women and men—not just in politics and the economy, but also in the family and society, which have been at the center of feminist critiques since the nineteenth century. The concept of gender justice was and is a feminist utopia derived from the early program of civil society, which promised all individuals a legal claim to equal rights and treatment, to justice and recognition. From this perspective, the women's movement must be recognized as one of the first and most important actors in civil society.

We approach the relationship between civil society and gender justice from multiple angles. The first section of the book sets out in general terms the major concepts, critiques, and themes that subsequent sections address in more concrete and historical terms. The themes of the latter include changing discourses on and practices of civil societies and their culture of associations; the significance of the family for the project of civil society and its underlying gender-specific notions of order, as well as the functions accorded the family in the discourses and practices of civil society; the complex connections between civil society, gendered forms of protest, and nongovernmental movements; and finally, the relation between civil society, the state, and different forms of citizenship—civic, political, and social—and the related processes of inclusion and exclusion. Throughout, the volume seeks to ground feminist critiques of mainstream concepts of civil society in specific historical and contemporary contexts that reveal the ways in which those concepts have both been limited by and served to (re)produce hierarchies of gender.

The opening section "Rethinking Civil Society and Gender Justice," provides an overview of both mainstream concepts and gendered reconsiderations. In twin essays, Karen Hagemann and Regina Wecker analyze theories of civil society and gender justice in a critical-historical context. Hagemann first historicizes classical conceptualizations of civil society, revealing the ways in which they were from the outset circumscribed by prevailing gender conventions, and then reviews feminist critiques that seek both to challenge and extend conventional definitions of civil society so as to make it more available to women. In her rereading of major theoretical literature on civil society and texts underpinning the concept of civil society from a feminist perspective, she uncovers gender biases and implications which to date have not been thoroughly examined. She makes the case that much of this literature has failed to take gender into account in the framing and actual historical practices of civil society, but she also points out that many feminist theorists and women's and gender historians have not much been interested in the topic of civil society either. Thus, she proposes a rethinking of the concept of civil society and sets a new agenda for future research on its concrete historical practices.

Wecker studies the relationship and complexity of justice and equality in concepts such as reciprocity, equity, and recognition. She reflects on their significance for the category of gender and gender relations, critically discussing different meanings of equality in civil society. Her case study focuses on waged work and its gendered valuation of feminist theory: the "equality-difference dilemma," as analyzed by historian Joan Scott, and the "redistribution-recognition dilemma" conceptualized by philosopher Nancy Fraser. To remedy both dilemmas and achieve gender justice, Wecker calls for a rejection of the binary oppositions between equality and difference, and recognition and redistribution.

The next section, "Early Civil Societies in Theory and Practice," traces the evolution of key concepts and practices of civil society in specific historical contexts and sorts out their gendered implications. Jane Rendall offers a close examination of the Enlightenment in the eighteenth-century British Isles, especially Scotland, comparing the gendered meanings of civil society and its related terms, *civility* and *civilization*. She argues that it was the newly coined noun *civilization* (rather than *civil society*) that came to be used most widely to characterize the social institutions and relationships of self-consciously modern and rapidly changing commercial societies. The gender relations associated with this shift held paradoxical implications for women: while regarded as the embodiment of civilization, they could retain this distinction only by remaining closely linked (at least in theory) to domesticity and the private sphere. While some women challenged this linkage, others embraced it, cannily understanding that it could provide them with a source of public power.

This dichotomy helps explain the separate paths Western women's activism took in the nineteenth century. Karen Offen focuses on those who challenged female domesticity—namely, feminists—contending that they were central to the emergence of civil societies in Europe from the Enlightenment to the early twentieth century. The "long nineteenth century," Offen explains, was at once a heyday for the expression of demands for the equality of the sexes and the rights of women, and a significant period for feminist organizing and campaigning. At the same time it witnessed a backlash of enormous proportions on the part of antifeminists, who sought to bar women from the male-dominated civil societies they were attempting to wrest from the illiberal monarchies of the era. Offen's account suggests that while feminists may have failed to attain most of their specific political goals, their struggle nonetheless succeeded in highlighting the political capacities and promise that civil societies held out for women.

Gisela Mettele, by contrast, makes a case for the women who embraced their assignment to home and family but transposed it into public activity. The civic virtues and associational culture they developed were significant not only for themselves, but for civil society writ large. Taking the case of nineteenth-century Germany, Mettele demonstrates that the forms of communication and interaction that came to characterize civil society were rooted in the urban voluntary associations that were the principal sites of middle-class self-organization at this time, many of them founded and run by women. The activities of such associations embodied "true civic spirit." Even if they did not pursue clear political goals, their structures, along with internal elections and set rules of procedure, including speaking rights, as well as their purported openness, regardless of social status, provided a model for civil society.

All three of these chapters demonstrate that, contrary to the usual portrayal of early civil societies as all-male provinces, women were involved from the beginning and, moreover, that their public activities, whether debating the meanings of civilization, demanding equality, or establishing model associations, served to consolidate and expand key political institutions. The section also indicates that the private sphere and civil society were not inimical or opposing spheres, as is commonly assumed, but were in fact mutually imbricated—a theme that receives fuller attention in the section that follows, "Civil Society and the Family."

Gunilla Budde opens the discussion by rejecting the mainstream idea that civil society should be defined in distinction to or apart from the family—a distinction that is, she notes, inherently gendered. For Budde, the family serves as one of the core institutions of civil society, but this, she argues, becomes visible only by using an "action-logical" concept of civil society. Focusing on middle-class women and their families in Imperial Germany, Budde identifies the different ways in which they participated in civil society. As educators of the future members of society, these women could convey outward-looking, civil-society-oriented values and help their children develop appropriate emotional dispositions; by organizing social events they overcame the porous frontier between the public and private spheres, bringing the family into the public and vice-versa. Budde's interpretation not only "brings the family back in" to the public sphere but also suggests another way in which conceptualizations of civil society must take women (and children) into account.

Margrit Pernau also challenges the conventional separation between public and private spheres, and in so doing exposes not only the gendered limitations of mainstream theory, but also its Western biases. In her chapter on the Muslim middle class, the family, and the colonial state in nineteenth- and twentieth-century India, Pernau emphasizes that at any given moment, the boundaries between the public and the private were deeply intertwined. Although the family celebrations and religious events, women's literature, and women's associations that she analyzes were structured by the conventions of female seclusion, these practices and organizations, like their Western counterparts, allowed women to pursue a range of reform efforts, particularly around issues such as health and education. Pernau, like Budde, refuses a concept of civil society based on spaces and spheres, instead preferring an actor-oriented approach. Her focus on the agents and functions of civil society, the generation of social trust, and the horizontal solidarity that characterized this Muslim society moves the concept beyond its narrow Western context and reveals the existence of functional alternatives in other parts of the world.[3]

While Pernau and Budde offer persuasive accounts of ways in which family and civil society may overlap in certain cases, Paul Ginsborg alerts us to the historical contingency of such close relationships. In his chapter on family, gender, and civil society in twentieth-century Europe and North America, he suggests that the fragility of the (post-) modern family may undermine its ability to serve as a core institution of civil society. Ginsborg categorizes families as either "closed" or "open"—those that are basically inward-looking and those that look outward toward civil society. Family attitudes and action in contemporary developed societies, he argues, extend across this spectrum. Looking at developments of leisure occupations in the last decades, he underscores the ways in which television, the Internet, and consumerism deter and distract individuals from participating in civil society. The daily practices of modernity push them back into the home, enclosing them once again in the family. But it is not only mass culture that has altered the contours of family life; unprecedented economic, political, and social shifts have also markedly reconfigured families, with both positive and negative implications for civic activity. On the one hand, feminist demands have led to an uptick of fatherly responsibility, at least in some quarters, but on the other, a declining commitment to marriage (at least among heterosexuals) has swelled the number of single-parent households. While the first trend potentially frees women for civic activities, the second, more than ever, ties down mothers (and fathers) to home and family. Ginsborg's provocative piece does not undermine Budde's and Pernau's claims about the linkages between public and private; rather, it prompts us to specify the conditions under which family life can be conducive to civic participation, particularly for women.

Turning outward, the last two sections in the book move away from civil societies' ties to the (now-reinterpreted) private sphere and toward the kinds of political issues and practices that are more commonly associated with civil society. Section Four, "Civil Society, Gendered Protest, and Nongovernmental Movements," offers an abundance of examples of gendered forms of political participation in civil society, while the final section, "Civil Society, the State, and Citizenship," reminds us that the ultimate goal of protest is most often state transformation. Both draw our attention to the forces that limit civil society's potential as a site for unfettered protest and a model of utopian practice.

Each of the chapters in the fourth section shows that the bourgeois norms associated with civil society can restrict access for certain social groups, but taken together, they also reveal that such norms change over time and space. Manfred Gailus begins by examining the politics of food in Germany from the eighteenth to the twentieth century. Analyzing contentious food politics, he observes a paradox: for nonbourgeois female protestors, the merging of civil society with more formally organized party politics in the second half of the nineteenth century meant a shrinking or even loss of traditional spaces of public action, and thus an erosion of public sociopolitical power. After the turn of the century, however, women found new avenues for dissent in the form of cooperative clubs, boycott movements, and mass demonstrations, which could make powerful interventions into political life, even leading to the overthrow of inactive governments. Although their occasional violence was deemed incompatible with the basic values of civility, these practices and associations acted as a control on civil society by pointing to its lacks and imperfections.

Sonya O. Rose complicates our understanding of the relationship between bourgeois gender norms and civic participation by demonstrating that hegemonic concepts of civil society not only routinely exclude women, but can also bar different groups of men who do not or cannot conform to the preferred masculine ideal. Rose's study of masculinity, class protest, and the "civil public" in Britain between 1867 and 1939 identifies two large groups of men who were left out: those who had neither the time nor the money to participate, and those who did not accept the hegemonic definition of "good citizenship." Analyzing two different hunger marches organized by unemployed men, how they were received, and how they became ensconced in the national memory, she is able to trace changing and multiple ideals of masculinity and show how they affected notions of appropriate public performance and behavior.

Drawing our attention to another instance of change, Belinda Davis examines the case of West Germany, where, in the wake of Nazism, bourgeois gender norms were recast to fit the mood of the postfascist state; now the emphasis was on restrained and "reasoned" interventions on the part of men as well as women. To break through these constraints, the feminist and alternative groups of the 1960s and 1970s that Davis discusses developed a new kind of politics—an intentionally provocative set of practices that deployed "theater," visual as well as verbal communications, humor, and emotionally charged discourse. Though not necessarily specific to men or women, these practices still had significant implications for gender relations because they disturbed existing hierarchies of power. Davis points out that because such alternative forms of action occurred in subcultural and other non- or semipublic realms, they have often been dismissed as a retreat from politics and from universalizing and effectual discussion. Moreover, despite the fact that they were more inclusive and expressed demands that had never been made publicly before, provo and informal politics tend to be excluded from discussions of civil society based on concepts developed in relation to nineteenth-century societies. Davis argues that such discussions uncritically reproduce the bourgeois exclusivity of conventional definitions of civil society, and must be revised if alternative practices are to be accommodated.

In postsocialist Eastern Europe, yet another iteration of bourgeois norms appeared, this time, ironically, in the form of an essentialist feminism exported from West to East. In the final chapter of this section, Kristen Ghodsee examines the impact of this brand of politics, which, along with international aid, was intended to build "civil society" for women after 1989. Ghodsee untangles the ways that certain Western feminists and their local counterparts in the East ignored the complex legacy of communism, which had historically opposed what it called "bourgeois feminism." She does not treat all Western feminists homogeneously, but rather focuses on the "professional feminists" who often work in the gender programs of the United States Agency for International Development, the World Bank, the European Union, and other European and North American nongovernmental organizations. Ghodsee contends that the specific type of feminism these professionals sought to introduce in Eastern Europe may have unwittingly reinforced the neoliberal program responsible for the very decline in general living standards that gave Western feminists their mandate to help East European women in the first place. The NGOs that privileged a gender-based analysis of oppression over one that was more sensitive to class issues legitimized claims that women are somehow naturally less suited than men to free-market economies. This not only lowered their status, but also created a backlash that prevented women from building the kinds of independent organizations that would provide them with a voice in newly emerging civil societies.

The final section of the book extends the analysis of the ways that distinctions, exclusions, and inequalities shape civil societies by showing how civil societies relate to state developments. Sonya Michel, in the first chapter, traces the origins of the American welfare state back to the country's early nineteenth-century voluntary associations, many of them organized and run by middle-class women to address the health and welfare of poor women and children. Like Gisela Mettele, Michel recognizes the political opportunities these early associations afforded certain women, but she also emphasizes the paradoxical nature of their social exclusivity and the fact that middle-class women's "maternalist" ministrations to the "less fortunate" often entailed condescension and moralizing—both contradictions of core civil society values. Bourgeois women's political triumph was, however, short-lived; as a welfare state (however fragile) took shape and their voluntary practices metamorphosed into professional social work, the "amateurs" ended up on the margins, their opportunities for civil society participation greatly constricted. Yet many of the maternalists' biases toward the poor persisted under the veneer of scientific objectivity that supposedly guided modern policies and procedures. Ironically, by the late twentieth century, women's and children's health and welfare once again became an important site for women's civil society organization, only this time, instead of allowing the state to take over policies they had developed, they sought to wrest control of their bodies *from* the state as well as from professional providers. Moreover, unlike their predecessors, women of all classes and races attempted to avoid the pitfalls of maternalism by mobilizing on their own behalf.

Most of the authors in this collection, including Michel, analyze the state and civil society within the parameters of a single nation, but for Marilyn Lake, these matters can only be fully understood by moving beyond the nation. Using this wider lens, her chapter exposes the transnational foundations of conceptions of civil society and citizenship in so-called white men's countries—the immigrant societies of South Africa, North America, and the Antipodes—between 1890 and 1910. As a derivative of the concept of "civilization," Lake emphasizes, the idea of civil society was initially forged within the race relations of colonialism and reshaped by settler societies intent on preserving a white male standard of living and white men's rule. In such contexts, immigration by those deemed "nonwhite"—Chinese, Blacks, Indians, Japanese, Pacific Islanders—was restricted on the grounds that these people did not share the "civilized" attitudes, customs, habits, or traditions necessary for engagement in civil society. When the Chinese, Indians, and Japanese pointed to their own proud civilizations, the Anglo-Saxonists of the New World insisted that civilization be understood in terms of a tradition of self-government and, increasingly, a commitment to a civilized standard of living. While the exclusion of women was more or less taken for granted, men who might have made it in on gender grounds were, in the name of civilization and the requirements of civil society, excluded, expelled, marginalized, or segregated.

Taken together, the chapters in this volume offer a forceful reminder that gender definitions change over time and are rarely unitary; at any given moment, notions of masculinity and femininity may not only be opposed to one another but also arrayed in a same-sex hierarchy that is inflected by race and ethnicity as well as class. Yet there are moments when gender definitions do become unitary, whether at the behest of the state, political movements, or both, and as such, can serve as primary determinants of access to civil society and citizenship as well as the basis for critical assessments of the terms of that access. The rise of second-wave feminism was, according to Birgit Sauer, one of those moments.

In the final chapter of the book, Sauer focuses on the European women's movement, the state, and civil society, emphasizing the importance of a strong state for achieving gender justice. She questions the positive image of a "woman-friendly" civil society opposed to the alienating state, and points out the intricate connection and interplay between civil society and state. Sauer proposes conceptualizing civil society and state not as different spheres, but as different discourses and interactions between social actors with different resources and access to power. For her, civil society is a contested arena and the state a hegemonic compromise between conflicting groups in civil society. Moreover, gender is a "conflicted strategy" of self-definition and definition by others within civil society. It is also a result of the process by which state agencies transform individuals into subjects and then interpellate them. Strategies of gendering in civil society as well as in state policies are characterized by hierarchy and inequality. The gendering of civil society was and is therefore a hegemonic process whereby inequality is reproduced; every gender compromise in civil society shapes gendered state institutions and vice versa. In this sense, Sauer's analysis offers a powerful complement to Regina Wecker's previous discussion of gender justice.

While the five sections focus on specific dimensions of the history and theory of civil society and gender justice, there are many themes that traverse the entire volume, tying the sections together in interesting ways and offering insights upon which other scholars may want to build as they continue to study these issues. For example, the cases of colonial India and postsocialist Eastern Europe expose the ways in which both mainstream and feminist concepts of civil society have been embedded in Western capitalist culture. Without privileging Western models, we need to learn much more about the "functional equivalents" of civil society that have emerged elsewhere, and also about the specific factors on the ground that may make a particular setting more or less congenial to the growth of civil society.[4]

But we must also recognize that those "factors on the ground" do not remain stable; the specific movements, organizations, and social structures that facilitate civic participation at one moment may become transformed or made irrelevant by other historical trends. Consider, for instance, the working-class organizations that tried to make spontaneous mass protest obsolete as Germany moved into the early twentieth century, or the bureaucratization and professionalization that marginalized the kinds of associations that formed the core of early civil societies in both the US and Germany. By the same token, gender norms change over time, and with them, the types of strategies that would-be civic participants develop to gain inclusion, whether they are trying to charm the bourgeoisie, as in the case of *bürger* families, or shock it, as were the provos. We must consider too the social and cultural shifts that can make families more or less open to civic participation; in addition to those discussed by Paul Ginsborg, we should also take into account recent queer challenges to the hegemony of the bourgeois family and its privileged access to the public sphere.[5]

The focus on the family and civil society not only dispels assumptions about their separateness but also explains how it was that "the social" became women's special domain within civil society. While we may celebrate women's cleverness in using their assignment to motherhood as a means of entering the public sphere, we must also recognize the fact that this domain has become a feminized one within the state as well as within civil society. Moreover, while conceding this domain to women symbolically, male-dominated state structures and parties tend to retain political control, resulting in the perpetuation of gender injustice. We must focus more attention on the moments of interface between state and civil society involving social policy in order to understand how it is that women so often lose control of the issues that are most vital to them.

The volume thus offers both a revised history of civil society and a program for expanding it and making it more egalitarian in the future. While often critical of specific historical instantiations, all of the authors collected here nonetheless take seriously the political potential inherent in the concept and project of civil society. Thus they have sought to expose the myriad social, cultural, and political mechanisms whereby specific groups of people—not only women, but also working-class men and members of racial minorities—have been routinely excluded from civil society. Sometimes subtle, sometimes blatant, such mechanisms often rested (and continue to rest) on hitherto unexamined assumptions about criteria for membership and participation in civil society that are based in racialized, gendered, nationalistic, and class-specific values.[6] At the same time, the authors have documented countless instances in which these same groups actively sought entry into civil society by using ingenious, creative, unconventional, and sometimes disruptive means. By focusing on actors and actions as well as formal and informal structures and looking for manifestations of civil society beyond taken-for-granted Western venues, the volume provides a rich, often moving, account of the ways in which marginal groups have perceived—and claimed—the promises embodied in civil society. Such discoveries present intellectual as well as political challenges. Both scholars and political actors must acknowledge that by perpetuating narrow definitions of what constitutes civil society, we run the risk of excluding legitimate participants and ignoring their claims. Only by expanding the concept and project can we extend the political opportunities of civil society to all.

Notes

Because the article "Civil Society Gendered: Rethinking Theories and Practices" by Karen Hagemann in this volume discusses the most important literature, we have limited the number of notes in this introduction.

1. For the WZB working group see: http://www.wz-berlin.de/zkd/; for CiSo-Net see: http://cisonet.wz-berlin.de/.

2. All quotes from Jürgen Kocka, "Civil Society from a Historical Perspective," *European Review* 12, no. 1 (2004): 65–79.
3. For important discussions of women, civil society, and politics more generally in other Muslim societies, see Suad Joseph, ed., *Gender and Citizenship in the Middle East* (Syracuse, NY, 2000); Joseph and Susan Slyomovics, eds., *Women and Power in the Middle East* (Philadelphia, 2001); and Deniz Kandiyoti, ed., *Women, Islam and the State* (Philadelphia, 1991).
4. Good starting points may be found in the collections cited above, as well as in Nira Yuval-Davis and Pnina Werbner, eds., *Women, Citizenship and Difference* (London and New York, 1999); and Yuval-Davis, *Gender and Nation* (London and Thousand Oaks, CA, 1997).
5. Eric O. Clarke, *Virtuous Vice: Homoeroticism and the Public Sphere* (Durham, NC, 2000).
6. In many ways, the critiques advanced in this volume build on important recent advances in the historiography and theory of race and of imperialism and colonialism; in working-class (as opposed to labor) history; and, of course, in the scholarship of gender.

Rethinking Civil Society and Gender Justice

Chapter 1

CIVIL SOCIETY GENDERED
RETHINKING THEORIES AND PRACTICES

Karen Hagemann

In recent years across Western societies, it would have been hard to find a politician's speech, an NGO comment, or a media commentary without at least some reference to civil society. This multipurpose term seems to serve as a sort of panacea for the modern longing for community, solidarity, and more political participation "from below." At the same time, civil society frequently functions in everyday political discourse as a new ersatz institution, making up for the loss of social welfare benefits previously provided mainly by the state. In the historical, political, and social sciences, too, this concept has had a remarkable career during the past two decades, not only as a key category for studying the development of the enlightened public sphere and the profound changes in the political practices of Western Europe and North America in the past, but also for analyzing the processes of political and social transformation in the colonial and postcolonial world, and in Eastern Europe in the present.

It is striking that the term *civil society* is mainly used by mainstream scholars. For the majority of these authors, however, the gender dimension of the subject appears to be nonexistent.[1] Only a few feminist theorists who have written explicitly about civil society and gender.[2] In fact, feminist scholars surprisingly seldom address the subject of civil society at all. As Anne Phillips observed recently in an article on feminism and civil society, the concept plays a "minimal part in the feminist division of the world":

> Feminists do use the phrase: they use it when discussing women's confinement to the family and exclusion from the public activities of the wider worlds, they

use it in discussions of women's citizenship. But while the discussion between public and private spheres [and the discussion about citizenship] has been central to (any) feminist analysis, feminists have remained oddly silent on the subject of civil society. Civil society is not a significant organizing category for feminists, and rarely figures in the feminist taxonomy.[3]

This finding forces us to reflect more precisely not just on these striking reticences but also on the diverse meanings of civil society and their respective gender dimensions. In this chapter, I will thus begin by describing briefly the history and the current usage of the concept of civil society before revealing the fundamental differences and similarities I see among the competing concepts of civil society currently being debated. I then discuss women's and gender studies' central points of criticism regarding these concepts, including the ways in which their embeddedness in Western political thought limits their applicability to non-Western contexts. At the end I propose ways in which the concept of civil society needs to be developed if it is to incorporate gender perspectives more systematically and thereby become more useful for gender studies.

Competing Concepts of Civil Society

Much has been written about the history of civil society, in particular about its invention in seventeenth- and eighteenth-century Europe as a key concept of enlightened political theory. Political theorists and philosophers such as John Locke, Adam Ferguson, and Adam Smith in Britain, Charles de Secondat, Baron de Montesquieu, and Denis Diderot in France, and Immanuel Kant in Germany all discussed intensively concepts of civil society, *société civile*, and *Zivilgesellschaft* or *Bürgergesellschaft*, alongside terms like *civility*, *civilization* and *the public*.[4] In this early modern European discourse, the positive connotation of the term *civil society* was unadulterated. It stood, as historian Jürgen Kocka underlines in his article "Civil Society from a Historical Perspective,"

> for what at the time was a utopian plan for a future civilization in which the people would live together in peace as politically mature, responsible citizens—as private individuals in their families and as citizens in public. They would be independent and free, independently cooperative under the rule of law but without being spoon-fed by an authoritarian state; there would be tolerance for cultural, religious, and ethnic diversity but without great social inequality, in any case without the traditional form of corporate inequality.[5]

This utopian plan was one mainly developed by men for men; women were only marginally involved in the debates as either interlocutors or subjects. The "politically mature, responsible citizen" who acted "independent and free" was without any doubt thought of as a man (even though Kocka, like other mainstream authors, does not discuss this gender bias in the article just cited). The enlightened contemporaries persistently defined civil society in contradistinction to the absolutist state. This antiabsolutist and anticorporatist thrust stood at the center of their utopian plans. They aimed for social self-organization by male individuals whom they defined as "worthy" of inclusion, mainly educated white men of Christian faith from noble or middle-class backgrounds (property owners), and by groups made up of the same.

This early understanding of civil society went through important changes under the influence of the emerging capitalism and nationalism in the nineteenth century. The German philosophers Georg Wilhelm Friedrich Hegel and Karl Marx, as well as the French political theorist Alexis de Tocqueville, all developed the term further. In their writings, civil society became "even more clearly distinguished from the state than it had been." They understood the concept as "a system of needs and works, of the market and particular interests"—even more in the sense of a middle-class (*bürgerliche*) society than as a civil society of (male) citizens (*Staatsbürger*).[6] In the German discourse, as a part of this change, the older terms *Bürgergesellschaft* or *Zivilgesellschaft* were increasingly replaced by the term *bürgerliche Gesellschaft*, which more and more lost the older utopian connotation and was used critically or even polemically. In the English and French discourse, particularly in Tocqueville's writings, the term retained its positive utopian connotations longer, but here too lost its importance during the second half of the nineteenth century.[7]

Much has also been written about how the concept of civil society became marginalized in twentieth-century Western political theory, only to regain prominence in the last two decades of the century. Indeed, since the 1980s it has become a key category in the antidictatorial critique in socialist Eastern Europe, but has also been deployed by liberation movements in Latin America and South Africa.[8] Nowadays the term is widely used in political discourses all over the world by exponents of very different Weltanschauung, such as political centrists, neoliberals and anticolonial leftists, by communitarians and antiglobalization activists.

The existing body of academic literature reflects these developments. For more than two decades, political and social scientists and philosophers like John Ehrenberg, Ernest Gellner, Jürgen Habermas, John A. Hall, John Keane, Charles Taylor, and Michael Walzer have engaged in an intensive debate over civil society, yet the concept remains ambiguous and contested, its definition still unsettled.[9] According to historian Dieter Gosewinkel, two central problems have given rise to the many paradoxes and differences among these thinkers: first, the tensions between the ambiguous use of the concept of civil society as an utopian political norm—a descriptive term for concrete historical practices and an analytical concept; and second, the idea that separate spheres or systems with different and separable logics define civil society.[10] Both problems influence and limit the usefulness of the concept, and not only for feminist scholars. This becomes evident if we examine the three most widespread approaches to define civil society: the "field-logical," "normative," and "action-logical."

According to Jürgen Kocka, in the field-logical approach, civil society refers to the "largely self-regulated space of civic engagement between the state, the economy, and the private sphere." Associated with this is a particular type of individual and collective action in civil society characterized by "personal initiative, communicative competence, openness and pluralism, the ability to engage in constructive conflict and avoid violence, as well as the systematic linking of particular and universal interests."[11] In this definition, civil society includes the self-organized initiatives, associations, federations, movements, and networks that are attributed neither to the state sphere and its institutions nor to the market, and are also not located in the so-called private sphere, which in this approach generally refers to the family. Civil society is understood here as a public, non-private sphere, which is connected with other social spheres.[12] This "in-between" sphere is ruled neither by the economic norms of the market (i.e., by competition and profit maximization), nor by the patronizing and alienating norms of the state (i.e., bureaucratic power and the monopoly of physical violence), nor by the particular interest of the family and the private sphere with its intimate, personal relations.[13] Rather, social order is achieved through cooperation, communication, and deliberation.[14]

The field-logical approach is highly problematic, not only because it generates significant problems of distinction between the three spheres, but also because it does not differentiate clearly enough between the three possible usages of civil society as a descriptive term of historical practices, an analytical concept, and a utopian political norm. One reason for this amalgamation is that the field-logical approach is closely related to the normative approach, which defines civil society "as the core of a draft or project that still has some utopian features."[15] For Kocka, as for many other historians and political and social theorists, involved not only in the research on, but also the current practice of civil society, it refers to the "future project of human coexistence in the tradition of the Enlightenment, which remains to be realized." It is a "promise that has yet to be entirely fulfilled, even if European reality today corresponds much more closely to this plan, this utopia, than it did in the past."[16] For the normative approach, civil society is, in short, a utopian vanishing point for the democratization of states and societies, formed after the Western liberal model. But even this utopianism has its limitations; in particular for the analysis of non-Western civil societies, the inherent "Western-centrism" of the normative approach is highly problematic. As Chris Hann and Elizabeth Dunn demonstrate in their volume *Civil Society: Challenging Western Models*, civil societies do not necessarily operate from the premise of individual liberalism that is the basis of the Western utopia—in particular, in non-Western societies. They propose therefore a broader action-logical approach, which focuses on groups, networks, and communities. For them, civil society is a web of autonomous associations and activities independent of the state, which bind citizens together in matters of common concern and by their existence or actions. This approach allows us to include within civil society a much wider range of associations and initiatives based on family relations, religious groups, and neighborhood networks. It thus helps not only to integrate non-Western civil societies systematically in the analysis, but also to challenge the conventional separation between public and private spheres.[17]

Recent scholarship on civil society prefers in general an action-logical approach, which focuses on the actors of civil society and their types of social action. The characteristics usually associated with civil society in this approach are, first, self-organization and autonomy—i.e., the voluntary commitment of individuals and groups who are free to engage in civil society action—a criterion that in itself implies a whole series of political, economic, and social preconditions. Among other things, it entails an antitotalitarian thrust and presupposes sufficient resources, not least sufficient free time, for such an involvement. The second characteristic is action in public space. This comprises activities requiring communication, the willingness and ability to deal with conflict, and publicity. In ideal-typical terms, it implies the acknowledgment of differences, a variety of opinions, and pluralism. Third, civil society action should be "peaceable," i.e., nonviolent. In the prevailing understanding, this does not mean dispensing with conflicts and protest. On the contrary, from the beginning social and political protests have been important forms of civil society action for women and men alike. It does, however, mean avoiding physical violence and military intervention of all kinds. It is no accident that in enlightened discourse the German term *Zivilgesellschaft* was coined and used as a counterconcept to *Militärgesellschaft* (military society). Fourth, according to the action-logical approach, civil society social action, while proceeding from individual, particular interests and experiences, should at the same time also refer to the so-called common good, however this may be defined by the various actors.

In the action-logical approach, civil society thus refers to a specific form of social interaction that is supposed to be different from others, such as state administration and politics, dominance and all types of hierarchical relationships, violence, fighting and war, exchange and the market, as well as personal relationships in nonpublic spaces. But the action-logical approach also encounters—and this is evident even at first sight—significant problems of distinction, because in the analysis of historical and present-day practice, neither the arenas nor the forms of action of civil society manifest themselves in such an ideal-typical fashion. What we find, rather, are for the most part historically specific and not infrequently ambivalent mixed forms. This is particularly true for non-Western forms of civil society action, as the work of scholars like Margit Pernau, Suad Joseph, and others demonstrate.[18] The normative notion of democratic action in this approach is still in conflict with empirical analysis. Thus, an approach that examines only the content and ideal-typical traits of civil society is as inadequate for historical and systematic analysis as one that looks only at its organizations, their motives for action, and actors.

Instead, it is necessary, as historian Frank Trentmann emphasizes in his recent collection *Paradoxes of Civil Society*, to develop the action-logic approach further in three ways: first, both the ideas and historical practices should be studied in the same conceptual framework, because "civil societies developed in a tension-filled dynamic between inclusion and exclusion, tolerance and paternalism"; second, any "essentialist view" of civil society should be avoided and instead the "diverse meanings and functions of civil society" should be highlighted, not only between different societies, but also within them; and third, the "imperial and international dimensions" woven into the fabric of the histories of civil society need to be integrated.[19]

Scholars working in the field of postcolonial studies have criticized studies of civil society for paying insufficient attention to the "rule of difference"—that is, the interplay of the various categories of difference in both the concept and practice of civil society.[20] This leads to an underestimation not just of the significance of the gender dimension, but also of other differences and their respective meanings for the creation of asymmetries and hierarchies in the concrete historical practice of specific civil societies, in particular religion, race and ethnicity.[21] Hann and Dunn, as well as Shalini Randeria, for instance, challenge the Eurocentric perspective of the European debates on civil society in Latin America, Africa, and India. They point out that the Western model of civil society focuses on the tension between an autonomous individual, usually thought of as male, and the state, and includes only open, secular institutions based on voluntary membership. This understanding of civil society does not do justice to the many forms that social integration, safeguarding civility, and exercising solidarity take in non-European societies; it also excludes female activities within the context of religious institutions, including all types of voluntary charity work. The Western model generalizes the developmental path of a few Western European civil societies or, more precisely, of one social stratum and one sex in these civil societies, as *the* universal developmental path.[22] Chris Hann has thus argued for a comparative and descriptive view of civil society that takes into account differences in social structures, historical experience, and processes of transformation.[23] Such an open and non-normative approach would also be quite fruitful for the analysis of the gender dimension of civil society.

This discussion is in turn related to the critique of mainstream scholarship for paying insufficient attention to the gendered, social, and racialized borders of civil society, in particular to processes of inclusion and exclusion not just in discourses, but also in social, political, and cultural practices. Through processes of inclusion and exclusion, the groups, movements, and organizations active in civil society have also defined, and continue to define in practice, both membership (that is, a person's internal position) and his or her individual identity, creating asymmetries and hierarchies of power[24] not only within, but also between civil societies.[25] Such processes also often entail violence, defined as a "powerful activity, which aims for physical destruction of others." This is, as Sven Reichardt, among others, has emphasized, one of the many paradoxes of civil society.[26] Because of the persistence of violence and the fact that civil society actors have repeatedly used it to assert their interests in the so-called private sphere as well as in public space, or to secure group cohesion, it is necessary to pay far more attention to this central boundary problem of civil society as well as to processes of inclusion and exclusion more generally. Accordingly, as both John Keane and Keith Tester have suggested, we must on the one hand incorporate the "various negative tendencies of civil society" as a necessary object of analysis, and on the other regard civil society itself as a historical project that is never finished and also never fully distinct from its surroundings.[27] Moreover, we must focus on the cultural dimension of the project of civil society, particularly the multifarious discursive and cultural practices that create meaning and shape perception and thus also action—and engender violence.[28]

With such a theoretically informed critical and relational approach, it is no longer possible to conceptualize civil societies primarily as a European achievement or solely as national phenomena; rather, they must be analyzed in their concrete historical contexts. It is also impossible to ignore the gender dimension any longer. In short, it seems to be more productive to analyze civil societies from their boundaries and their displacements. First, however, we need to think a good deal more precisely about these boundaries from a gender perspective.

Gendering Civil Society

Already in the 1980s and 1990s feminist historians were arguing that in the "enlightened past," civil society was never an inclusive and just social sphere poised between the market, the state, and the family, but one that was strictly exclusive.[29] From the very beginning, all women, but also men from lower social classes and from minority racial, ethnic, or religious backgrounds were denied access, because the white male middle-class struggle for civil, political, and social citizenship rights was closely related to the processes of state and nation building.[30] The enlightened distinction between public and private helped to define civil society, like politics in general, as an exclusively male sphere, with the family as the female "other" complementing the state and civil society. This exclusion of women from the public sphere, state institutions, and political rights was consolidated by the introduction of universal conscription, allowing military service to become the precondition for political participation.[31] As political theorist Birgit Sauer has observed,

> the modern state is thus grounded in a gender compromise in civil society that separated the family from other social institutions, organized the hierarchical sexual division of labor, and normalized and naturalized these social divisions through binary gender roles. Although the idea of civil society has been broadened during the twentieth century and slowly come to include more social groups, the concept has remained part of a representational regime that is intrinsically intertwined with the development of capitalism, liberal male-dominated democracy and a patriarchal (welfare) state.[32]

Since the 1980s, feminist research has challenged the different approaches to defining civil society. Early on, it posed the question of whether or not civil society is a potentially "open" project that is simply incomplete and only needs to be fully realized in the future, or if the structures of civil society are inherently exclusive because they are based on a hierarchical gendered division of labor and require the complementary female "other" in order to exist.[33]

Mainstream scholarship on civil society, however, tended to ignore feminist scholarship from the very beginning; at best, essay collections contained one article that treated the subject from the "women's viewpoint," written, "naturally," by a woman.[34] But "gendering" research on civil society entails more than merely looking at women as an additional important group of actors in civil society. If gender is understood as relative and contextual "knowledge" about "sexual" differences produced by culture and society, then gender, in conjunction with other "categories of difference" like class, race, and ethnicity,

- shapes the socially and culturally constructed *images and ideas of civil society* in discourses and cultural practices;
- defines the *possibilities of and limits to participation by individuals and groups in the project of civil society*, that is, it shapes their forms and scope of action, among other things, in relation to and within

civil society, and their legal position as well as opportunities for access to the resources and institutions of civil society;
- produces in various ways *hierarchies and asymmetries within civil society as well as between civil society, the state, the market, and the family* (these hierarchies and asymmetries do not arise only between women and men and within various male and female groups; gender also creates hierarchies of order and power well beyond the realm of gender relations); and
- influences to a high degree *individual and collective identity in the framework of civil society as well as the subjective experience and perception of this identity;* both were and are not merely shaped by the interplay of gender with other categories of difference, but also strongly dependent on context.

Following such an understanding, gender as a "cross-sectional category" needs to be systematically included in the analysis of all projects and tested for its significance for each set of questions and objects of research on civil society. This insight, however, has not yet found its way into the mainstream; civil society continues to be conceptualized as "gender-neutral." As Anne Phillips notes,

> Civil society is often presented in terms that make it seem a place where women are not: this is most apparent when it is presented in contrast to the sphere of nature, or as a middle term between the state and the family. Early social contract theorists employed civil society (usually used synonymously with "political society") as a way of making the transition from a state of nature to one regulated by "man-made" obligations and laws, and in the contrast they drew between a natural state and a civil society, women turned out to be less visible and more subordinated to men in the latter.[35]

Early scholarship by feminist historians and political scientists had already critically deconstructed this relationship and sought to demonstrate how theoretical pioneers such as Locke, Ferguson, Montesquieu, and Kant structurally discriminated against women from the beginning. Their aim was, as Carole Pateman put it in her pathbreaking 1988 book, *The Sexual Contract*, to limit the application of the rhetoric of the universal equality of free and independent citizens in civil society to their own sex. The early theorists thus performed extraordinary contortions in order to admit women in civil society far enough so that they were bound by its laws, yet still ensure that they were sufficiently outside of it to be subordinate to men.[36] Pateman also analyzed how, at a later stage, Hegel employed the concept of civil society to generate a tripartite distinction between the family, civil society, and the state. She concluded that Hegel was even more explicit than his predecessors in placing women in an earlier, "more primitive" and sub-natural stage. Hegel saw man as having his "actual substantive life" in the state, labor, and in struggle with the external world, and women as having "her substantial destiny in the family."[37] Other feminist authors have shown that this highly gendered understanding of civil society was by no means unique to enlightened discourse.[38] "Civil" continued to imply a contrast with natural on the one hand, and private and familial on the other, and these in turn were associated with the female sex. Because of this history, Pateman interpreted the story of civil society as one of "masculine political birth."[39]

But even when the concept of civil society has been made more welcoming towards women and is formulated in seemingly "gender-neutral" terms, the problems it generated still derived from a nonfeminist agenda. Even nowadays, female interests are often defined as particular, above all when they start in the home and the family and are rooted in the gendered division of labor in the so-called private sphere. Therefore, scholars in gender studies have directed their critique at the distinction between public and private and the accompanying gender-hierarchical division of labor that underlies the concept of civil society.

Civil Society, the Public, and the Private

Before I discuss in more detail the feminist critique of the public/private dichotomy that underlies mainstream definitions of civil society, some remarks on the terms *public* and *private* themselves are in order. The words *public* and *private* were and are widely used and occur separately, relationally, or in a binary pair as nouns, adjectives, and adverbs. In Europe these two words—adopted or translated in the seventeenth century from Latin into the national languages—spread increasingly from the eighteenth century on, and with this spreading they changed their meaning. The semantic and semiotic fields associated with the words in the different languages varied significantly from the beginning and still vary today. Thus what is called *the public* in English and *le publique* in French nowadays is *die Öffentlichkeit* in German. In French and English *le publique/the public* also means what in German is called *das Publikum*. All three languages, however, share the words *publication* and *publicist*. We have the same problems with the word *private*. All three languages share the idea of a *Privatleben, la vie privée*, or *private life*. In English, however, this idea is supplemented by the notion of *personal life*, which stands more for the individual life and in opposition to working life. It carries associations of leisure and lifestyle. Personal life can be lived in quite different ways: in public or in one's own home, alone or with others. Personal life can also be expressed in the form of participation in civil society. Bilingual dictionaries offer several German translations for the English word *privacy*: *Privatheit*, *Privatleben*, *Privatbereich*, and *Geheimhaltung.* Privacy, however, is used particularly in the case of personal rights and the protection of individuals from surveillance.[40]

Even the related and seemingly very familiar term *family* had and has different meanings in different historical and national contexts. Is a family only a married couple with children, or also a single mother or father and the child? What is most important for the definition of a family? Is it the relations between the adults, or the fact that children and adults—in whatever relationship—live together and the adults care for the children? Before the trend towards single living and the phenomenon of the patchwork family became increasingly apparent and recognized in Western industrial societies, starting in the 1970s, the family was commonly understood as an institution and group based on legitimate and permanent marriage with a monopoly on sexuality, which ensured that children would be born and raised in wedlock, and that the people belonging to the family would, if possible, live together and be provided with all the necessities of daily life. But this was only one hegemonic middle-class definition of the heterosexual *Normalfamilie*, which during the nineteenth and twentieth centuries became more and more the standard for other social strata. Enlightenment theorists and later politicians conceptualized this "average family" as a "private institution" of great "public" importance. As a result, the state had to care about and control, in one way or the other, families that did not conform to the middle-class norms.[41]

These remarks underscore the problem of drawing boundaries. What makes the whole subject of civil society and the public/private even more difficult is that "public sphere" and "civil society" tend to be equated in the literature. In the Anglophone debate about the "public sphere," this tendency became apparent after the publication of the English translation of Jürgen Habermas' masterpiece *Strukturwandel der Öffentlichkeit* (*The Structural Transformation of the Public Sphere*) in 1989 (initially published in German in 1962).[42] One reason might have been that this debate coincided with the radical transformations in Eastern Europe. In this context, the term *civil society*, too, became more and more popular. In the debate about *Strukturwandel*, authors like sociologist Craig Calhoun and historian Joan B. Landes insisted on the difference between the public sphere and civil society, but others tend to conflate the two.[43] Landes, therefore, in her review of the English edition of Habermas' *Strukturwandel*, underscored the point that he had defined the public sphere as the body of private persons assembled to discuss matters of "public concern" or "common interest,"[44] and thereby isolated the public sphere as a structure *within* civil society:

> Habermas rejects the Greek model of a citizenry acting in common to administer the laws and to ensure the community's military survival. Instead he

locates the specificity of the modern public sphere in the civic task of a society engaged in critical public debate to protect a commercial economy. In contrast to the older *res publica*, he deems the bourgeois public sphere to be the site for the political regulation of civil society, and credits its willingness to challenge the established authority of the monarch.[45]

She emphasized that for Habermas, this public sphere was from the outset both private and political. Another reason for the conflation of civil society and public sphere might have been that in Habermas' thinking, the most important institutions of the Enlightenment's middle-class public sphere were the informal and formal associations of private persons. To him, they formed *the* public sphere, which consists of both a literary-cultural and a political-public sector. These informal and formal associations mediated between, on the one hand, the economy (or sphere of commodity, exchange, and social labor) and the family, and on the other, the state (or the realm of police, state administration, and the court). The confusion seems to be that these self-organized informal and formal associations of private persons were at the same time defined by him and others as the core actors of civil society.[46]

To clarify our own analysis, it is important to differentiate between both the public sphere and civil society, but at the same time, as feminist critiques emphasize, to note that both concepts err in drawing a dichotomy between the public and private spheres. Feminist scholars understand this separation as a cultural construction that arose in the Enlightenment period and aimed to determine inclusion and exclusion from the centers of political power on the basis of gender; women were assigned by "nature" to the private, the household, and the family, while men were assigned to the public.[47]

This gendered distinction between public and private has played a crucial role in liberal theory and continues to influence theories of civil society. "The private" is used to refer to a sphere of social life in which intrusion upon or interference with freedom requires special justification, while "the public" is used to refer to a sphere regarded as "more generally" or more justifiably accessible—at least for propertied and educated men of accepted race and faith. But all too often both terms have been used too with little clarity. Susan Moller Okin points to the two most important ambiguities in Enlightenment theory. The first results from the use of the terminology to indicate at least two major conceptual distinctions, with variations in each. In this instance, "public/private" is used to refer to both the distinction between state and society (as public vs. private ownership, for example), and to the distinction between nondomestic and domestic life. In both dichotomies, the state is paradigmatically public, the family domestic, and intimate, personal life private. The crucial difference between the two is, according to Okin, that the intermediate socioeconomic realm (what Habermas, following Hegel, calls civil society) is in the first dichotomy included in the category of the private, but in the second dichotomy, considered to be public.[48] This ambiguity often tends to be overlooked.

If we focus only on the second and more common usage of the public/private dichotomy as public/domestic, there remains an ambiguity, resulting directly from the patriarchal practices and theories of our past. Fundamental to this dichotomy from its theoretical beginnings has been the division of labor between the sexes. Men—as viewed in the Enlightenment's gender order— are assumed to be chiefly preoccupied with and responsible for the occupations in the sphere of economic and political life, and women with those in the private sphere of domesticity and reproduction. Women were regarded as "by nature" both unsuited to the public realm and rightly dependent on men and subordinated within the family. These assumptions, not surprisingly, have pervasive effects on the structuring of the dichotomy and of both its component spheres.

As feminist scholarship has revealed, from the beginnings of liberalism in the eighteenth century, both political rights and the rights pertaining to the modern liberal conception of privacy and the private have been framed as rights of individuals. These individuals were, however, assumed, and often explicitly stated, to be adult male heads of household. Thus the rights of these individuals to be free from intrusion by the state, or society, were construed to mean that they were also to be free from intrusion as they controlled other members of their private sphere—those who, whether by reason of age, sex, or condition of servitude, were regarded as rightfully subject to them and existing within their sphere of privacy. Within classical liberal thought, there was no notion that subordinate members of households might have privacy rights of their own. In short, the autonomous private individuals presumed to be actors in the public sphere and in civil society were constructed as men who were set free, by virtue of female or servitude labor, from all work in the household and the family, and from all forms of caretaking. They were thereby constructed as independent, but de facto their independence was based on the work of their dependants. These ambiguities are still inherent in common definitions of civil society, in particular the field-logical approach.[49]

Extending this historical argument, historian Geoff Eley contends that gender exclusion was linked in all Western and Central European civil societies to other exclusions rooted in processes of class formation.[50] These exclusions were part of the elaboration of a distinctive culture of civil society and of the associated public sphere. It was implicated in the process of male-dominated bourgeois class formation; its practices and ethos were markers of "distinction" in Pierre Bourdieu's sense—ways of defining an emergent elite, setting it off from the older aristocratic elites, on the one hand, and from the various popular and plebeian strata over which it aspired to rule, on the other.[51] This process of distinction, moreover, helps explain the exacerbation of sexism characteristic of the liberal concept of the public sphere; new gender norms praising female domesticity and a sharp separation between public and private spheres functioned as key signifiers of bourgeois difference from both higher and lower social strata.[52]

Because of all the ambiguities and problems associated with the term public sphere, contemporary gender historians have come to prefer the term public space, meaning any place in which communication relating to the state, the economy, society, and culture occurred. In this sense, such events as evening teas held in "open houses" or convivial family gatherings also are public spaces.[53] They assume, moreover, the existence of competing public spaces, unlike Jürgen Habermas, who focused only one—the male-dominated bourgeois—public sphere, which never was *the* public. Since the late 1980s, research by feminist historians such as Joan Landes and Mary Ryan has demonstrated the existence of competing publics,[54] and political theorist Nancy Fraser speaks about the "multiple publics of civil society."[55] Thus a gendered conceptualization of civil society must not only be historicized, but also include competing civil societies alongside the middle-class one—even within a single national context.[56] Here, Antonio Gramsci's ideas about civil society are also important. He envisioned it as the sphere in which consensus or hegemony is contested and organized.[57] This includes "rebellion against the orthodox as well as the construction of cultural and ideological hegemony."[58] In this view, the social protest and the food riots of the lower classes helped shape civil society along with the associations of the labor movement and the women's movement or the philanthropic initiatives of denominational communities.

Connected with this, feminist scholars have criticized the fact that civil society is so often conjured up as a masculine realm—not just because of the described structural issues, but also because of its concrete historical practice. Historically, the relatively unregulated nature of voluntary associations as the main collective actors of civil society has rendered them more prone to discriminatory behavior than the publicly scrutinized institutions of the state, a tendency that persists to this day. At the same time, voluntary associations and the politics associated with civil society were from the very beginning attractive for feminist activists, first because a feminist perspective is—or at least should be—radically pluralist, and pluralism finds a more welcome home in the associations of civil society than in either the family or the state; and second, because some of the associations that spring up in civil society have a looseness, and even indeterminacy, that makes them particularly hospitable to feminist politics. Feminism is and always has been in some sense about transformation and reform. Thus, from the outset, feminists demanded equal rights in civil society and state politics, and while criticizing all forms of misogynist politics, they became, despite widespread discrimination, active in civil society. For them, engagement in civil society was the first step towards political engagement in the state.[59] At the same time, however, the very looseness of civil society associations and networks—their much-vaunted "private" and independent character—entails the risk of exclusion, the freedom to discriminate against all unwanted "others." Paradoxically, then, in order for a democratic civil society to flourish, it is necessary to have a strong state that will guarantee political equality and basic civil, political, and social citizenship rights for all.

Civil Society, Citizenship, and the State

This brings us back again to the question of whether or not civil society is a potentially open project, or if the structures of civil society are exclusive.[60] Feminist scholars have argued that from a gendered perspective there was from the beginning a structural difference between the gradual inclusion of adult men from the lower classes in the community of citizens active in civil society and state-controlled politics during the nineteenth century, and the abolition of women's exclusion from citizenship rights. Even women's efforts to gain more citizenship rights through increasing participation in civil society differed from those of all men. Political theorist Thomas H. Marshall, who differentiated between civil, political, and social citizenship rights, deduced from his historical analysis of the development of the British and other European welfare states that, in the first instance, civil citizenship rights were necessary, for they secured individual freedom. A second step, which usually followed, was the recognition of the right to political participation, and only as a third step were social citizenship rights awarded.[61] Marshall's distinction between the three forms of citizenship rights is broadly used in feminist studies of the welfare state and citizenship rights, but these studies point to an important gender difference. Marshall's path from civil, to political, to social citizenship rights applies only to men, not to women. For most women, political rights came only *after* social rights, and *then* they finally got the same civil rights as men. In addition to the fundamentally different consequences of the public/private dichotomy, this is, as Ute Gerhard has emphasized, a second important structural difference between men and women in civil society.[62]

Because of the importance of gender as a fundamental means of ordering the economy, society, and politics, and the value attached to the family as a basic institution of the state and the nation, it took more than one hundred and fifty years for women to gain the same civil status as men—despite the persistence of feminist critique and struggle from the late eighteenth century on in most modern Western states. The exclusion of women from politics and their enclosure in the private sphere were, therefore, not accidents of the Enlightenment, but part of an "invented tradition" designed to secure male supremacy not only in the family, but also in the economy, society, and politics. The latter meant that all over Europe after the French Revolution, not only state politics but also major parts of the public sphere and civil society were deeply restricted by gender. The distinction between a literary-cultural and a political-public sphere, which political theorist Iris Marion Young, following Jürgen Habermas, has usefully pointed out, helps us to see ways in which civil societies became gendered and to comprehend all the informal and formal public activities of women that took place in the so-called private sphere.[63] Women were accepted in the literary-cultural but not in the political-public sphere. They were welcomed in the private and civic associations of civil society, but not in the explicitly political ones.

How was it historically possible to lend the program of civil society the veneer of "the universal," at least as a utopia, despite its gender order? Scholars tend to tailor the ambiguous and contradictory history of the development of civil society since the eighteenth century to match its utopian telos. Instead we should ask, what possibilities and means did women have, despite being relegated to nonpresence and noninvolvement in the public sphere, to envision a utopia of equal human beings and fight for its practical realization? Women who devoted themselves very publicly to this project in the nineteenth century were, as Joan W. Scott has shown, well aware of its many "paradoxes," which they could not avoid.[64] They constantly ran the risk of losing their public reputations because these activities appeared to violate the rules of "natural" and well-mannered femininity, something they had to do if they wished to make a political impact. If we ask the above question, it will become even more evident why civil society was from the very beginning attractive for feminist activists.

Frequently, women legitimated their political engagement with the slogan "equal but not the same." They wanted equal rights and vehemently demanded the total abolition of all discrimination against the female sex, whether legal, political, economic, or social. But they justified these demands in terms of both the universal principles of human and civil rights and the difference between, but equal value of, the sexes. They believed—like their male contemporaries—that men and women were different by nature, that woman's primary place in society should be marriage and the family, and therefore they could and should work primarily for a "motherly politics," a politics of maternalism that takes better care of the needs of families, women, and children.[65]

The conflict between women's equality and their relegation to the private sphere re-emerged in the new women's movements of the late 1960s, as Western feminists now publicly cast doubt on the much-trumpeted blessings of familial privacy. They demanded an end to the criminalization of abortion as part of their full right to individual self-determination, initiated a debate on wages for housework, and added new bite to the labor movement's inert and unsuccessful call for "equal pay for equal work." They understood that the conventional distinctions between the state, civil society, and the so-called private sphere pushed domestic life out of the view of politics, and thus they argued that the subordination of women in families, sexual violence against women, and the right to control their own bodies should be regarded as questions of common concern and importance. For them, the struggle for equal rights in marital and family law, particularly the rights to determine one's domicile, dispose of one's own property, or choose one's occupation, as well as to exercise equal parental rights in child-rearing and divorce, affects the regulation of the private sphere but is at the same time eminently political. This struggle has involved not just the women who fought these battles in the women's movement, but also the men who sought to prevent legal equality at all costs. It was fought in the home, in the political sphere, and also in the institutions of the state. Thus from a gender perspective, the boundaries separating civil society and the private sphere—including the family—are highly problematic.[66] This is not only the case for Western societies, but even more so, as recent research demonstrates, for non-Western societies.[67]

Civil Society, the Family, and Gendered Division of Labor

Where does the family stand within a gendered analysis? Iris Marion Young's distinction between a literary-cultural and a political-public sphere helps us to conceptualize the family as an important part—a kind of "private association"—of civil society. It is necessary to integrate the family more systematically in the analysis of civil society because the family and kinship networks are important, not only for the organization of civic and political associations, but also as basic institutions for providing a civic education, bringing up children with all the virtues that civil society actors need, and encouraging them to become engaged in civil society.[68] This is true for Western and non-Western societies alike.[69] Feminist scholars pointed out relatively early that mainstream concepts underestimate the significance of the family for the practice of civil society, which, in conventional formulations, arises in the first instance from the definitional separation between civil society and the family and the assignment of the latter to the so-called private sphere. This assignment reproduces the historically constructed dichotomy of public and private, which obscures our view of both the family's roles within and contributions to the project of civil society and the latter's gender-segregated structure and manner of functioning.[70]

Until now, only a few theorists of civil society—mainly "liberal communitarians"—have recognized the importance of the family for civil society.[71] Apart from Michael Walzer, the work of Jean Cohen and Andrew Arato has been most influential here; in their 1992 book, *Civil Society and Political Theory*, they suggested that scholars need to integrate the family as a "core component" into civil society and urged us to think of the family "as a key institution in civil society,"[72] "one that, if conceived of in egalitarian terms, could have provided an experience of horizontal solidarity, collective identity, and equal participation to the autonomous individuals comprising it—a task deemed fundamental for the other associations of civil society and for the ultimate development of civic virtue and responsibility with respect to the polity."[73] They thus consider the family "the voluntary association par excellence."[74] This position is controversial even among the few feminist theorists of civil society, as Ilona Ostner demonstrated in her 1997 essay on "Family and Civil Society."[75] Following Jean Bethke Elshtain, she distinguished between "ultraliberal," "liberal" and "social liberal" versions of civil society.[76] In her model, the position taken by Cohen and Arato would correspond to the social liberal variant, which stresses the social significance of civil society communities, ranging from families and neighborhood initiatives to large associations, in distinction to the market and the state. This variant differentiates only between the market, the state, and civil society and at the same time demands that the state ensure the political, economic, and social preconditions necessary for the development of civil society.[77] She criticized that this social liberal model conceptualizes the family mainly as a heterosexual institution that follows middle-class norms.

Family historians like Paul Ginsborg also question Cohen and Arato. He criticizes the two authors as well for focusing on the heterosexual middle-class family, and demands that the function of the family for civil society be historicized and contextualized.[78] The middle-class family may, under the ideal conditions of the nineteenth century, have served as "a key institution in civil society" and "the voluntary association par excellence," but for many other family forms and in many other circumstances, this was and is not the case. The communitarian approach is implicitly "heteronormative"; that is, it emanates from the assumption that a family is a heterosexual partnership of a married couple with children—the typical male breadwinner and female housewife and mother family.[79] This approach knowingly ignores the variety of family forms, their very different working and living conditions, and their change in the past and the present.

Queer theorists therefore take issue with the very idea of privileging the family in relation to civil society, since it almost invariably connotes a heterosexual relationship, usually formalized through marriage. This, in turn, is linked to "the proprietary codes that (inappropriately) shape publicity practices" and exclude or marginalize gays and lesbians.[80] As queer literary scholar Eric O. Clarke argues,

> Historically, the greatest impediments to queer public sphere inclusion have been twofold: first, the heterosexist tenor of the bourgeois familial morality defining proper civic personhood and universal humanity; and second, the relegation of erotic experience, which has largely shaped a queer sense of self and collective belonging, to the proprietary privacy of the intimate sphere. Acting together, these two impediments have meant that even as the public sphere both draws upon and legitimates specific forms of intimacy and erotic experience—indeed is saturated by spectacles of intimacy—those that do not conform to a heteronormative standard are demonized and repudiated.[81]

To be sure, here Clarke is discussing the public sphere, not civil society, but it is easy to see how the same restrictions would play out in both. Clarke also points out that when gays and lesbians do gain entry to the public sphere (for example, through gay marriage), it is only by conforming to a "hetero-normative standard." "These heroically bland affirmations pay for admission," he writes, "with immiserating disavowals."[82]

The approach developed by Cohen and Arato moreover elides the very different consequences of the gendered division of labor in family and society, not only for men and women, but also for different groups of women separated by class, race, and ethnic background. The gender-hierarchical division of labor in family and society upon which the project and concept of civil society are implicitly based is yet another structural difference between men and women. The family is not merely a place beyond or even cut off from the "public sphere" in which one can pursue private or personal life. The earlier notion and defense of the private sphere were conceived of in terms of the individual. For nineteenth-century theorists, this individual was always an adult man who returned home from his economic, political, or cultural duties in the public sphere in order to enjoy his private life, or his power, in his home with his family. His wife was responsible for the indispensable daily physical and mental labor of caring for the family and organizing the household.

Mainstream concepts of civil society seem to ignore this and presuppose that people are already adults and have, despite the demands of house and care work and paid employment, sufficient time and energy to act autonomously in the arena of civil society. To that extent, the "sexual contract" was not merely self-evident but also necessary for the civil society project of placing women in the familial, private sphere and assigning them the work of caring for others—all in the name of nature. In Western societies, the production and reproduction of human beings were relegated to the private sphere along with women. But they remained nevertheless the basic precondition for any civil society. That is why, during the nineteenth century, women's public political participation was very often equated with the collapse of morality, family, and household, and in the twentieth, women's aspirations for occupational careers were depicted as "unnatural" and incompatible with their family duties.

In brief, feminists criticize the fact that the project and concept of civil society are still implicitly based upon a gender-hierarchical division of labor because its active subject is in all common definitions the "independent and free private individual."[83] De facto this is the male citizen, who is also independent and free from most household and family responsibilities and thus free to pursue not only his professional work but also every form of political engagement in civil society as well state politics. By conceptually devaluing the private as nonpolitical and therefore irrelevant to the "common good," mainstream theorists of civil society tend to strengthen this gender-hierarchical division of labor in theory and practice. They are inclined not simply to ignore the structural economic and social prerequisites for women's opportunities for equal participation in civil society, but to make these conditions more difficult to meet by removing them from the state and calling for an increase in civic society responsibility. In the past, celebrations of an active citizenry or a vibrant civic culture have signaled policy shifts that seek to move responsibility from the state to the community. As Anne Phillips has noted, all too often this "community" turns out to mean women, who are expected in their capacity as wives, mothers, and daughters to take responsibility for more caring activities within the home. This requisitioning of female labor may not be what most theorists have understood by *civil society*, but the term has undoubtedly come to carry this additional connotation.[84]

Despite many critiques, feminists now look to the state as one of the principal sources of gender justice, believing that public provision of child care, health care, and care for the aged is an intrinsic part of the "feminization" of policy, one that will help to create a sexually egalitarian world and a more just division of labor in the family, society, economy, and politics.[85] While crediting voluntary organizations, including those created by women, for initiating many of the institutions and policies that constitute modern social provision, feminists point to the "limits of civil society" and contend that an active welfare state is necessary to meet the current scale of social needs. This position represents a shift on the part of Western feminists. In the 1970s and 1980s, feminist activists, at least in the German-speaking and Anglophone world (the Scandinavian development was different), were highly critical of the state, which they regarded as a hierarchical, bureaucratic, and male-dominated institution.[86] Instead they looked to grassroots movements to build an oppositional feminist civil society. Such an autonomous sphere promised female independency and agency, self-organization without hierarchies, solidarity, gender democracy, and justice. But in the 1990s, as more and more welfare states were being dismantled, with devastating effects for women with children in particular, feminist scholars began to reconceptualize the state. It was no longer simply seen as "patriarchal" but instead as—in the words of Birgit Sauer—a "forum of competing discourses and powers" that could provide society with the necessary institutions to guarantee more social and gender justice.[87] Neoliberal politicians, disproportionately male, however, continue to celebrate "a vibrant civil society" as an alternative to a strong state.

In addition to their growing awareness of the economic and social limits of civil society, feminists have also begun to decry its limited political potential. It became clear that feminist countercultural or alternative associations were relatively weak, and that the more powerful mainstream associations were, even at the end of the twentieth century, still male-dominated and relatively closed to feminist demands. Furthermore, the experiences of the women's movement showed that domination, heteronomy, exclusion, and injustice—the result of differences among women and women's groups—also make up the reality of feminist associations in civil society. Next to this, one equally important factor was that the restructuring of welfare states came along with shifting relations and boundaries between the state, economy, society, and families. State restructuring rested and rests on the reassignment of former state-run tasks and responsibilities to nonstate actors—for example, to families, neighborhood organizations, and female volunteers. To guarantee their social citizenship—itself a precondition for their political citizenship—women need a strong welfare state.

Conclusion

Feminist critiques of the concept and practice of civil society notwithstanding, I would like to answer the two questions that instigated work on this volume—Does feminism need the concept of civil society? And conversely, is civil society a feminist concept?—with an unambiguous YES! Despite all the caveats and problems, civil society was and is the most important space and form of action for articulating and enforcing feminist demands on the market and the state and for protecting women within the family. But the concept must be modified if we want to integrate the gender dimension more systematically and achieve gender justice. The following points appear to be central:

- First, we need to conceptualize civil society more from its borders. This involves thinking more precisely about these borders as processes of inclusion and exclusion. From a gender perspective, the boundaries between civil society and the private sphere in particular are problematic. The family needs to be recognized as a possible key institution of civil society, albeit with certain caveats about its potential for heteronormativity.

- Second, we not only have to historicize civil societies and analyze them in their historic specific relational context, but also to think of competing civil societies alongside the liberal one—even in a single national context.
- Third, we need to develop a robust non-normative comparative and descriptive perspective on civil society that is open to differences in political and social structures and experiences, and particularly sensitive to the "Western-centeredness" of many common conceptualizations, including those of second-wave feminists.
- Finally, we need to integrate into our analysis the various negative tendencies of civil society and to conceive of civil society as an open historical project.

Notes

I would like to thank Sonya Michel for her critical comments and careful editing.

1. Only one recent example is Dieter Gosewinkel and Jürgen Kocka, eds., *Zivilgesellschaft national und transnational* (Berlin, 2003), in which not a single article discusses gender issues. A good overview of the state of mainstream research is provided by the editors in the introduction (11–26) and the article by Dieter Gosewinkel and Dieter Rucht, "History Meets Sociology. Zivilgesellschaft als Prozess," in ibid., 29–60; and Jürgen Kocka, "Civil Society from a Historical Perspective," *European Review* 12, no. 1 (2004): 65–79; Sven Reichardt, "Civil Society: A Concept for Comparative Historical Research," in *Future of Civil Society*, ed. Annette Zimmer and Eckard Priller (Wiesbaden, 2004), 35–55.
2. See Carole Pateman, *The Disorder of Women. Democracy, Feminism and Political Theory* (Oxford, 1989); Jean Bethke Elshtain, *Power Trips and other Journeys. Essays in Feminism as Civic Discourse*, (Madison, WI, 1990); Nancy Fraser, "Rethinking the Public Sphere: A Contribution to the Critique of Actually Existing Democracy," *Social Text* 25, no. 26 (1990): 65–68; Jodi Dean, "Including Women: The Consequences and Side Effects of Feminist Critique of Civil Society," *Philosophy and Social Criticism* 18, no. 3–4 (1995): 378–406; Anne Phillips, "Does Feminism Need a Conception of Civil Society?" in *Alternative Conceptions of Civil Society*, ed. Simone Chambers and Will Kymlicka (Princeton, NJ, 2002), 71–89; Phillips, "Who Needs Civil Society? A Feminist Perspective," *Dissent* 46, no. 1 (1999): 56–61; Iris Marion Young, "State, Civil Society, and Social Justice," in *Democracy's Value*, ed. Ian Shapiro and Casiano Hacker-Cordón (Cambridge, MA, 1999), 141–162; Young, *Inclusion and Democracy* (New York, 2000); Birgit Sauer, "StaatsbürgerInnenschaft und Institutionen der Zivilgesellschaft," in *Kontinuitäten und Diskontinuitäten der politischen Soziologie*. 1. Arbeitstagung der Sektion 'politische Soziologie' am 12, und 13. Oktober 1995, (Freiburg i. Breisgau, 1996), 183–196; Ilona Ostner, "Familie und Zivilgesellschaft," in *Zivile Gesellschaft: Entwicklung, Defizite und Potentiale*, ed. Klaus M. Schmals and Hubert Heinelt (Opladen, 1997), 369–383; Ute Gerhard, "Atempause: die aktuelle Bedeutung der Frauenbewegung für eine zivile Gesellschaft," in *Feministische Perspektiven der Politikwissenschaft*, ed. Kathrin Braun (Munich, 2000), 293–314. See also: Margit Appel et al., eds., *Zivilgesellschaft – ein Konzept für Frauen?* (Frankfurt/M., 2003); Ruth Klein-Hessling, *Zivilgesellschaft, Frauenorganisationen und Netzwerke* (Bielefeld, 1999); Chet Meeks, "Civil Society and Sexual Politics of Difference," *Sociological Theory* 19, no. 3 (2001): 325–334; Valentine Moghadam, "Engendering Citizenship, Feminizing Civil Society:

The Case of the Middle East and North Africa," *Women & Politics* 25, no. 1–2 (2003): 63–88; Annabelle Sreberny, "Feministischer Internationalismus: zur Imagination und Konstruktion globaler Zivilgesellschaft," in *Globalisierung und Demokratie*, ed. Hauke Brunkhorst and Matthias Kettner (Frankfurt/M., 2000), 289–309. One of the fields of feminist scholarship where the term *civil society* is used most often is gender and politics in postsocialist Eastern Europe—see, for example: Barbara Einhorn and Charlotte Sever, "Gender and Civil Society in Central and Eastern Europe," *International Feminist Journal of Politics* 5, no. 2 (2003): 163–191; Brigitta Godel, *Auf dem Weg zur Zivilgesellschaft: Frauenbewegung und Wertewandel in Rußland* (Frankfurt/M., 2002); Martina Ritter, ed., *Zivilgesellschaft und Gender-Politik in Rußland* (Frankfurt/M., 2001); Britta Schmitt, *Zivilgesellschaft, Frauenpolitik und Frauenbewegung in Rußland: von 1917 bis zur Gegenwart* (Königstein/Taunus, 1997).
3. Philipps, "Does Feminism Need," 71f.
4. See Kocka, "Civil Society"; Mary Kaldor, *Global Civil Society: An Answer to War* (Cambridge, UK, 2003), 2ff. As historical background: Nancy Bermeo and Philip Nord, eds., *Civil Society before Democracy: Lessons from Nineteenth-Century Europe* (Lanham, 2000); Daniel Gordon, *Citizens Without Sovereignty: Equality and Sociability in French Thought 1670–1789*, (Princeton, 1994).
5. Kocka, "Civil Society," 66.
6. Ibid., 67.
7. Ibid.
8. Reichardt, "Civil Society," 35–55.
9. See John Ehrenberg, *Civil Society: The Critical History of An Idea* (New York, 1999); Ernest Gellner, *Conditions of Liberty: Civil Society and its Rivals* (London, 1994); Jürgen Habermas, *The Structural Transformation of the Public Sphere: An Inquiry into a Category of Bourgeois Society* (Cambridge, MA, 1989), 1st German ed., 1962; John A. Hall, *Civil Society: Theory, History, Comparision* (Cambridge, 1995); John Keane, *Civil Society: Old Images, New Visions* (London, 1999); Keane, *Global Civil Society?* (Cambridge, UK, 2003); John Keane, ed., *Civil Society and the State: New European Perspectives* (London, 1988); Michael Walzer, ed., *Toward a Global Civil Society* (Providence, RI, 1995).
10. See Gosewinkel and Rucht, "History Meets Sociology."
11. All quotes from Kocka, "Civil Society," 65–79.
12. See Jürgen Kocka, *Zivilgesellschaft in historischer Perspektive. Unveröffentlichtes Arbeitspapier, WZB Discussion Papers* (Berlin, 2003), 32.
13. Ibid.
14. Gosewinkel, "Einleitung," 12.
15. Kocka,"Civil Society," 68.
16. Kaldor, *Global Civil Society*, 22.
17. See Chris Hann and Elizabeth Dunn, eds., *Civil Society: Challenging Western Models* (London, 1996), in particular 1–26.
18. See Margrit Pernau, *The Passing of Patrimonialism: Politics and Political Culture in Hyderabad 1911–48* (New Delhi, 2000); Suad Joseph, ed., *Gender and Citizenship in the Middle East* (Syracuse, NY, 2000); Beth Baron, *The Women's Awakening in Egypt: Culture, Society, and the Press* (New Haven, CT, 1994).
19. Frank Trentmann, ed., *Paradoxes of Civil Society: New Perspectives on Modern German and British History*, 2nd ed. (New York, 2003), vii.
20. See Shalini Randeria, "Zivilgesellschaft in postkolonialer Sicht," in *Neues über Zivilgesellschaft. Aus historisch-sozialwissenschaftlichem Blickwinkel, WZB Discussion Papers*, ed. Jürgen Kocka et al. (Berlin 2001), 81–103.
21. Ibid.
22. Shalini Randeria, "Kastensolidarität als Modus zivilgesellschaftlicher Bindungen. Gemeinschaftliche Selbstorganisation und Rechtspluralismus im (post)kolonialen Indien," in Gosewinkel et al., *Zivilgesellschaft*, 223–243.
23. Chris Hann, "Political Society and Civil Anthropology," in Hann, *Civil Society*, 1–26.

24. See Randeria, "Zivilgesellschaft; Shalini Randeria and Sebastian Conrad, eds., *Jenseits des Eurozentrismus: (post)kolonial Perspektiven in den Geschichts- und Kulturwissenschaften* (New York, Frankfurt a./M., 2002).
25. See Sven Reichardt, "Gewalt und Zivilität im Wandel. Konzeptionelle Überlegungen zur Zivilgesellschaft aus historischer Sicht," in Gosewinkel et al., *Zivilgesellschaft*, 61–82; Reichardt, "Civil Society and Violence: Some Conceptual Reflections from Historical Perspective," in *Civil Society: Berlin Perspectives*, ed. John Keane (Oxford, 2006), 139–168.
26. Heinrich Popitz, *Phänomene der Macht*, 2nd ed. (Tübingen, 1992), 48; see also: Trutz v. Trotha, "Gewaltforschung auf Popitzschen Wegen," *Mittelweg 36*, no. 6 (2000): 26–36. See recently: Trentmann, *Paradoxes*, in particular his "Introduction. Paradoxes of Civil Society," 3–46; Arnd Bauerkämper, Dieter Gosewinkel, and Sven Reichardt, "Paradox oder Perversion? Zum historischen Verhältnis von Zivilgesellschaft und Gewalt," *Mittelweg 36*, no. 15 (2006): 22–32.
27. John Keane, *Reflections on Violence* (London, 1996), 14; see also Keith Tester, *Civil Society* (London, 1992).
28. On the problematic of the term *culture*, see Thomas Mergel and Thomas Welskopp, eds., *Geschichte zwischen Kultur und Gesellschaft. Beiträge zur Theoriedebatte* (Munich, 1997); Ute Daniel, *Kompendium Kulturgeschichte. Theorien, Praxis, Schlüsselworte* (Frankfurt/M. 2001).
29. Karin Hausen, "Öffentlichkeit und Privatheit: Gesellschaftspolitische Konstruktionen und die Geschichte der Geschlechterbeziehungen," in *Frauengeschichte—Geschlechtergeschichte*, ed. Karin Hausen and Heide Wunder (Frankfurt/M., 1992), 81–88; Karen Hagemann, "Familie – Staat – Nation: Das aufklärerische Projekt der 'Bürgergesellschaft' in geschlechtergeschichtlicher Perspektive," in *Europäische Zivilgesellschaft in Ost und West: Begriff, Geschichte, Chancen*, ed. Manfred Hildermeier et al. (Frankfurt/M., 2000), 57–85.
30. Hagemann, "Familie," 59.
31. Ibid., 64.
32. Birgit Sauer, "Conflict, Compromise and Hegemony: Civil Society, Women's Movement and State Feminism," paper for the conference "Civil Society and Gender Justice: Historical and Comparative Perspectives," Berlin, 9–11 July 2004, Social Science Research Centre (WZB).
33. Hagemann, "Familie," 58.
34. See for example Hildermeier, *Europäische Zivilgesellschaft*; Arnd Bauerkämper, ed., *Die Praxis der Zivilgesellschaft: Akteure, Handeln und Strukturen im internationalen Vergleich* (Frankfurt/M., 2003); Ralph Jessen and Sven Reichardt, eds., *Zivilgesellschaft und historischer Wandel: Studien zum 19. und 20. Jahrhundert* (Berlin, 2004).
35. Phillipps, "Does Feminism Need," 72.
36. Carole Pateman, *The Sexual Contract* (Cambridge, MA, 1988).
37. Georg H. W. Hegel, *The Philosophy of Right* (Oxford, 1967), 166. On Hegel: Pateman, *Sexual Contract*, 100ff.
38. See Paul Ginsborg, "Family, Civil Society and the State in Contemporary European History. Some Methodological Considerations," *Contemporary European History* 4 (1995): 249–273.
39. Pateman, *Sexual Contract*, 102.
40. See Hausen, "Öffentlichkeit und Privatheit," 81–88; Lucian Hölscher, "Öffentlichkeit," in *Geschichtliche Grundbegriffe. Historisches Lexikon zur politisch-sozialen Sprache in Deutschland*, ed. Otto Brunner and Werner Conze (Stuttgart, 1978), 413–467; Lucian Hölscher, *Öffentlichkeit und Geheimnis. Eine begriffsgeschichtliche Untersuchung zur Entstehung der Öffentlichkeit in der frühen Neuzeit* (Stuttgart, 1979).
41. For an overview of the history of the family, see Andreas Gestrich, Jens-Uwe Krause, and Michael Mitterauer, *Geschichte der Familie* (Stuttgart, 2003), esp. 364–652.

42. For more on Habermas see Karen Hagemann, "Gendered Boundaries: Civil Society, the Public/Private Divide and the Family," in *The Golden Chain: Family, Civil Society and the State*, ed. Paul Ginsborg, Jürgen Nautz and Ton Nijhuis, Oxford and New York, 2008 (forthcoming).
43. See Joan B. Landes, "Jürgen Habermas: The Structural Transformation of the Public Sphere. A Feminist Inquiry," *Praxis International* 12 (1992): 106–127, 110; Landes, ed., *Feminism, the Public and the Private* (Oxford, 1998); Craig J. Calhoun, ed., *Habermas and the Public Sphere* (Cambridge, 1992).
44. Habermas, *Structural Transformation*, 27–56.
45. See Landes, "Jürgen Habermas," 110.
46. Habermas, *Structural Transformation*, 29ff.
47. See Fraser, "Rethinking"; Fraser, "Sex, Lies, and the Public Sphere: Some Reflections on the Confirmation of Clarence Thomas," *Critical Inquiry* 18 (1992): 595–612; Jean Bethke Elshtain, *Public Man, Private Woman. Women in Social and Political Though* (Princeton, NJ, 1993); Hausen, "Öffentlichkeit und Privatheit"; Leonore Davidoff, "'Alte Hüte.' Öffentlichkeit und Privatheit in der feministischen Geschichtsschreibung," *L'Homme* 4 (1993): 7–36.
48. See Susan Moller Okin, "Gender, the Public, and the Private," in Landes, *Feminism*, 116–141.
49. See for example Kocka, "Civil Society," 66ff.
50. Geoff Eley, "Nations, Publics, and Political Cultures: Placing Habermas in the Nineteenth Century," in Calhoun, *Habermas*, 289–339.
51. Pierre Bourdieu, *Distinction: A Social Critique of the Judgement of Pure Taste* (Cambridge, 1988).
52. Eley, "Nations," 289–339.
53. See Jörg Requate, "Öffentlichkeit und Medien als Gegenstand der historischen Analyse," *Geschichte und Gesellschaft* 25 (1999): 5–32, 8f.
54. See Mary P. Ryan, *Women in the Public: Between Banners and Ballots, 1825–1880* (Baltimore, MD, 1990); Ryan, "Gender and Public Access: Women's Politics in Nineteenth-Century America," in Landes, *Feminism*, 195–222; Landes, *Women and the Public Sphere in the Age of the French Revolution* (Ithaca, NY, 1988).
55. See Fraser, "Rethinking," 109–142; an alternative concept is the "fragmented public sphere," introduced by Jeffrey Alexander, "The Paradoxes of Civil Society," *International Sociology* 12, no. 2 (1998): 115–133. See also Eyal Rabinovitch, "Gender and the Public Sphere: Alternative Forms of Integration in Nineteenth-Century America," *Sociological Theory* 19, no. 3 (2001): 344–370.
56. On the relation of nation, nationalism, and civil society see Edwards Shils, "Nation, Nationality, Nationalism and Civil Society," *Nations and Nationalism* 1 (1995): 93–118; also: Hagemann, "Familie."
57. See Antonio Gramsci, *Prison Notebooks* (New York, 1991).
58. Michael Edwards, *Civil Society* (Cambridge, UK, 2004), 8.
59. See Phillips, "Does Feminism Need."
60. Hagemann, "Familie," 58.
61. See Thomas H. Marshall, *Citizenship and Social Class* (London, 1992).
62. See Ute Gerhard, "Geschlechterdifferenz, soziale Bewegungen und Recht. Der Beitrag feministischer Rechtskritik zu einer Theorie sozialer Staatsbürgerrechte," in *Differenz und Integration. Die Zukunft moderner Gesellschaften*, ed. Stefan Hradil (Frankfurt/M., 1997), 402–419.
63. See Young, "State"; see also: Young, *Inclusion*.
64. See Joan W. Scott, *Only Paradoxes to Offer: French Feminists and the Rights of Man* (Cambridge, 1996).
65. See Karen Offen, *European Feminism. 1700–1950. A Political History* (Stanford, CA, 2000); Sylvia Paletschek and Bianca Pietro-Ennker, eds., *Women's Emancipation in the*

Nineteenth Century (Stanford, CA, 2004); Gunilla-Friederike Budde, "Harriet und ihre Schwestern. Frauen und Zivilgesellschaft im 19. Jahrhundert," in Jessen, *Zivilgesellschaft*, 326–343; Seth Koven and Sonya Michel, eds., *Mothers of a New World: Maternalist Politics and the Origins of Welfare States* (New York, 1993).

66. See Fraser, "Rethinking"; Fraser, *Justice Interruptus: Critical Reflections on the "Postsocialist" Conditions* (New York, 1997).
67. On the Eastern European and the non-Western development, see for example Godel, *Auf dem Weg zur Zivilgesellschaft*; Joseph, *Gender and Citizenship*; Baron, *Women's Awakening*; Moghadam, "Engendering Citizenship"; Pernau, *Passing of Patrimonialism*; Pernau, "From a 'Private' Public to a 'Public' Private Sphere: Old Delhi and the North Indian Muslims in Comparative Perspective," in *The Public and the Private: Issues of Democratic Citizenship*, ed. Gurpreet Mahajan et al. (New Delhi, 2003), 103–130; Sreberny, "Feministischer Internationalismus."
68. See Young, "State," 145ff. See also Gunilla-Friederike Budde, "Das Öffentliche des Privaten. Die Familie als zivilgesellschaftliche Kerninstitution," in Bauerkämper, *Praxis*, 56–76; Melanie L. Miller, "Male and Female Civility: Towards Gender Justice," *Sociological Inquiry* 72, no. 3 (2002), 456–466; Kocka, "Civil Society," 74ff.
69. See Pernau, *Passing of Patrimonialism*; and Pernau, "From a 'Private' Public."
70. See Kocka, *Zivilgesellschaft*, 17ff.
71. See Christa Schnabel, "(Werte-)Gemeinschaften in der Zivilgesellschaft: Konzepte, Aufgaben und Verortung," in Appel, *Zivilgesellschaft*, 87–111, 92ff.
72. See inter alia Michael Walzer, *Zivile Gesellschaft und amerikanische Demokratie* (Frankfurt/M., 1996), 56; and Walzer, *Global Civil Society*; also Jean L. Cohen and Andrew Arato, *Civil Society and Political Theory*, (Cambridge, MA, 1992), 538; and Cohen, "Theorien der Zivilgesellschaft—Civil Society and Political Theory," *Das Argument* (1994): 577–586.
73. Cohen and Arato, *Civil Society*, 631.
74. Ibid.
75. Ostner, "Familie."
76. See Jean Bethke Elshtain, "The New Eugenics and Feminist Quandaries: Philosophical and Political Reflections," in Elshtain, *Power Trips*, 89–106.
77. See Ostner, "Familie," 378ff.
78. See Paul Ginsborg, *The Politics of Everyday Life* (London, 2005); Paul Ginsborg and Francesco Ramella, eds., *Un'Italia minore: Famiglia, istruzione e tradizioni civiche in Valdelsa* (Florence, 1999).
79. See Eric O. Clarke, *Virtuous Vice: Homoeroticism and the Public Sphere* (Durham, NC, 2000).
80. Ibid., 5.
81. Ibid.
82. Ibid. Other queer theorists such as Lauren Berlant and Michael Warner have been particularly vocal in opposing gay marriage on these grounds; see their "Sex in Public," *Critical Inquiry* 24 (Winter 1998): 547–66.
83. Kocka, "Civil Society," 66.
84. Phillips, "Who Needs Civil Society?" 59f.
85. Ibid.
86. Young, "State," 153ff; see also Carole Pateman, "The Patriarchal Welfare State," in Landes, *Feminism*, 241–274.
87. Birgit Sauer, "Demokratisierung mit oder gegen den Staat? Sieben Thesen zu einer feministischen Revision staatstheoretischer Ansätze," in *Demokratie als Projekt. Feministische Kritik an der Universalisierung einer Herrschaftsform*, ed. Gabriele Abels and Stefanie Sifft (Frankfurt/M., 1999), 79–103.

Chapter 2

DILEMMAS OF GENDER JUSTICE
GENDERING EQUITY, JUSTICE, AND RECOGNITION

Regina Wecker

When the Swiss Parliament discussed the ratification of the Convention on Equal Pay proposed by the International Labor Organization in 1953, Rudolf Mäder, one of its members, explained why he opposed the law. For him the fact that the husband was the family's breadwinner legitimized the difference in the income between men and women. His colleague Paul Brodbeck got to the heart of the question even more precisely when he stated: "The difference in salary might be considered unjust by women, but it is just in the eyes of men."[1] The majority of his fellow members in the exclusively male Swiss Parliament (women's suffrage was only introduced in 1971) obviously agreed with him. Justice, they argued, was not the same for everyone, but differed according to gender, race, or status.

For those advocating equal pay, it was a question of social justice. Nevertheless, they remained a minority. The National Council declined to ratify the convention by a vote of 116 to 28, and the Council of States by 28 to 3. The position of the parliament did not change fundamentally when the issue was once again taken up in the early 1960s, although only one chamber opposed it in this later discussion, and the arguments had slightly shifted by then. Now the male breadwinner was no longer the focus of the argument, and the fact that the percentage of gainfully employed women had increased was duly noted. Nevertheless, female employment was considered transitory, while the desired role for women was still that of housewife and mother, with no paid employment. Supporters of equal pay mentioned that there were certain activities at which women were simply better and which might, therefore, conceivably deserve at least equal pay. But the parliamentarians were eager to show that the alleged difference between men and women and between male and female work meant that women's labor power was less valuable. Even in the 1960s, the lower salary level was considered just, and the convention was not ratified. The change finally took place in 1972, when, at last, the legitimacy of equal pay was no longer challenged—at least not in theory.[2]

One year earlier, Swiss women finally won the right to vote, with a majority of 66 percent of the male voters. The country had implemented principles of civil society very early and extensively, but not for women. Switzerland was among the first countries in Europe to implement universal male suffrage, popular elections, limited government, and free association and expression. The system also provides for maximum private participation in politics through instruments like initiative and referendum: every important political issue from taxes to new laws can be put to a plebiscite, leaving room for political initiative outside established parties and state institutions. Many tasks considered elsewhere in Europe as state duties were (and still are) carried out by voluntary organizations or in collaboration with them, especially in the domain of social security, health insurance, and family politics.[3] Social self-organization and individual responsibility were and are held in high esteem, and the Swiss welfare state is not seen as an interventionist one that "spoon-feeds" its citizens.[4] That is one reason why, in the recent debate over the future of the German welfare state, Swiss approaches to the question of social security were presented as a possible solution for Germany.[5]

For women this extensive participation of "the people" in political decisions was clearly a sham, for women's rights—from the vote to equal pay—always lagged behind. The statement "considered unjust by women, but … just in the eyes of men" seems to be almost ironic—a typical expression of patriarchal ideas that would appear particularly ridiculous coming not from a parliamentarian of some remote era but of the 1950s. Taken as a serious political statement, however, it shows that the term *justice*, whose interpretation, significance, and relation to gender and civil society are the focus of the present volume, encompasses many issues. The example of the debate about "just wages" demonstrates that such factors as demands and burdens, performance, qualifications, experience, society, market, and success must be balanced one against the other.[6] Yet it never occurred to the majority of the Swiss parliamentarians that in assessing women's work as less valuable, they were perpetuating a basic injustice. It is paradoxical, as the political scientist Eva Kreisky rightly emphasizes, that for some, "there are more or less fixed ideas about what is just," while for others it is difficult to define the term precisely. Is it surprising that these differences map onto gender?[7]

Civil society as an emancipatory concept is mostly understood as an antipode to the state or at least to governmental institutions. Closely connected to the civil rights movements against undemocratic, dictatorial tendencies in Eastern European countries at the beginning of its current renaissance, it soon gained acceptance as the solution to problems that Western societies had with bureaucracy, political participation, and elements of the welfare state. The concept promises to create aspects or parts of a society in which citizens can defend their claims to solidarity, common interest, independence, and justice better than in a state context or through governmental institutions. But in this context gender justice has rarely been mentioned. This chapter is concerned with the promise of justice—the question of whether and under what circumstance the promise of a just society will include gender justice. I address question of gender injustice in a historical context, mainly focusing on two dilemmas: the equality-difference dilemma and the recognition-distribution dilemma.

In many ways the ideas and definitions of justice coincide with the principle of equality. Just demands in turn require an assessment that takes into account the needs to be met; just qualifications are based on the precondition that qualifications will have to be assessed equally; just experience requires that experience be the surveyor's rod by which just wages are measured; just distribution requires that each and every individual shall receive a fair share of goods, rights, and obligations within the community. "In order for civil society to develop fully," according to historian Jürgen Kocka, equal access to social initiatives and the political system must be a "central condition."[8] The intertwining of justice and equality is already embodied in the Aristotelian definition of justice as "adequacy," the principle of treating equal questions or persons in the same way.[9] Still under contention, however, are the following questions: who is due this justice, what is equality about, and to what does it refer? These questions stand at the center of this chapter, which analyzes the links and intertwining of justice and equality in concepts such as reciprocity, equity, equality, and recognition, and their significance for the category of gender and gender relations. I focus on the world of work, in particular—as already mentioned in the introductory example—the question of how to value work in terms of wages.

(In)Justice, Inequality, and Reciprocity

Equality and justice do not always run in parallel. Thus the political sociologist Barrington Moore, in his 1978 study *Injustice: The Social Bases of Obedience and Revolt*, links justice in different societies to the "concept of reciprocity, or better, mutual obligation" and deliberately stresses that reciprocity does not imply "equalities of burdens or obligations" but that it is a system of obligations which have been negotiated.[10] They are part of what he calls "the [implicit] social contract" and have, for some time, been accepted, but are constantly contested as well. Violations of that reciprocity are commonplace but may, under certain circumstances, be defined as injustice, and Moore sees them as one of the reasons for unrest and even upheaval.[11] In the context of distributive justice, neither mechanical equality nor inequality is considered just. "Only when persons agree on the value of what they invest in a task by comparison with others can they agree on the scale of rewards."[12] There is much disagreement over the principle of distribution, and it is quite obvious that women have been placed outside the field of mutual obligations, with the result that violations of reciprocity in dealing with them have no destabilizing effects. Why, Moore asks, "have blacks and women been willing to place a lower value on the effort they have invested in a task? And how willing were they?"[13] He doubts their willingness and points to the significance of repressive and self-repressive mechanisms.[14]

Women were—even to a larger extent than now—excluded from formal equality during the period Moore is analyzing. It is true that other societies did not take as long as Switzerland to include women; nevertheless, since the French Revolution, the gradual embodiment of the principle of equality in various constitutions has required dedicated efforts on the part of women's movements. Constitutions had to be expanded to include women, and almost everywhere this expansion required specific provisions. In the United States, a suffrage amendment was ratified in 1920, while in Weimar Germany an entirely new constitution was introduced in 1919. These events reveal that the older dictum of "general" equality in the eyes of the law did not yet include women.

Were these the obvious limitations to the antidiscriminatory principles and the acknowledgment of individual independence inherent in civil society? Jürgen Kocka posed this question in a 2004 article on civil society in a historical perspective.[15] I would argue, apparently so, but this did not mean that they passed unnoticed by women. As early as 1791, Olympe de Gouges structured her *Declaration of the Rights of Women* to parallel the *Declaration of the Rights of Men and Citizens* and reproach the deputies for having "forgotten" women. Similarly, the Seneca Falls *Declaration of Sentiments* of 1848 was modeled on the American Declaration of Independence, and other early feminist declarations sought to integrate women's rights into "sacred" documents that purported to declare universal human rights but, in fact, spoke only of men's rights and of equality among men. Attempts to convey a political right by way of a definition—by defining "all men are equal" as including women—had failed in the United States, in France, and in Switzerland: it required constitutional change.

The Equality-Difference Dilemma

Only after World War II did most European countries amend their constitutions to explicitly guarantee equal rights to women and make gender equality a normative part of the concept of civil society. But experience showed that this formal and legal equality would not translate into justice if it met unequal conditions. Switzerland was by no means the only country, and equal pay by far not the only issue, to foreground the conflict between two principles of justice that have been debated since Aristotle—namely, *justitia commutativa* and *justitia distributiva*, the first demanding that equal things be treated equally, the second that existing differences be taken into account. As historian Carola Sachse showed in her study of the West and East German debates on the *Hausarbeitstag* (one day off per month paid by the employer for women to do their housework), that discussion also centered on the question of "justice."[16] Was that day "unjust," a threat to the constitutional principle of equality because it favored women over men? In one of the first rulings after it was established in 1954, the West German Labor Court decided it was not.[17] It was conceptualized as a means of alleviating the "double burden" of earning women and, therefore, consistent with the constitution. The questions of whether women were "by nature" more inclined to do housework or whether all women really did housework were deemed irrelevant by the court on the grounds that it was a sociological fact that women "usually" did housework, even when they were gainfully employed, while men "usually" did not.[18] According to Sachse, the court's argument made housework a female characteristic; thus women won the day off for their housework, but lost their potential for equality.

Another example—with a different outcome—again reveals the problems created by the embodiment of formal equality in Western law: the suit for equal wages filed against the American corporation Sears in 1979. The historians Alice Kessler-Harris and Joan Scott, among others, have analyzed the significance of this case for the concept of equality in the past and the present of the United States.[19] Sears had been accused of wage discrimination and in court had argued that gender differences in wages could be explained by actual differences between women's and men's behavior. Women, they claimed, had failed to apply for the better paid positions not because of discrimination, but because the jobs had not met their expectations—expectations that were different from those of the men—with regard not only to what they wanted from their jobs but also to their domestic situations and general ambitions. Thus, the court decided, it had not been Sears that discriminated against women, but women who did not seek better jobs because they did not meet their expectations.

Unlike the German court in 1954, the American court held that it was because of "natural differences" between men and women and their different preferences that women failed to apply for better jobs. But neither decision brought women closer to justice. What the court seemed to be saying, according to Scott, was that women must behave the same as men, or else they will lose their claim to higher wages and thus to equality. Scott fully grasped the difficulty of the situation: "When equality and difference are paired dichotomously," she wrote, "they structure an impossible choice. If one opts for equality, one is forced to accept the notion that difference is antithetical to it. If one opts for difference, one admits that equality is unattainable."[20] But, she went on, "Feminists cannot give up 'difference'; it has been our most creative analytical tool. We cannot give up equality, at least as long as we want to speak to the principles and values of a democratic political system."[21]

Although the postulate of gender quality had the power to change the legal system in the twentieth-century Western world, it could not alter the social distribution of power. In spite of legal equality, the factual inequalities remain quite visible. Applying the principle of equality may be essential to eliminating inequalities in an unequal legal system, but for any further realization of equality, it seems more of a hindrance. This is because in its "enlightened form," equality has been interpreted to mean that things may only be dealt with in kind. As each deviation from the male measure is, at the same time, a hierarchical devaluation as well, a claim to equality may succeed only if obviously existing inequalities are declared to be incidental or trivial. They may not be valued as actual deviations from the male measure. Only if women perform exactly the same job, have the same curriculum, the same career pattern, can they claim equal rights or equal pay.

The sociologist and philosopher Andrea Maihofer holds that it is this very definition of equality that prevents women from obtaining social equality in spite of progressive legal systems:

> Thus, women have to either deny their otherness or insist that this difference is merely secondary to their nature in their demand for equality; that they, otherwise, have the same abilities as human beings and the same human reason at their disposal as men. Women may turn and twist in all directions—the measure for their equality in the eyes of the law always is man, his abilities and skills, his knowledge, his ideas of family, life, profession, science, politics, etc. Measured by this rod, their difference is mainly perceived as negative and, thus, in a discriminating manner.[22]

Moreover, this scale is harmful not only with regard to gender differences; national, ethnic, and cultural differences are equally devalued by a deviation from a single dominant measure, be it whiteness or social or sexual norms.[23]

Joan Scott's proposed escape from the equality-difference dilemma and the binary confrontation of both terms is based on the principle that, within the context of a deconstructivist gender theory, *man* and *woman* are not antithetical categories. "There are moments when it makes sense for women (or men) to demand consideration for their social role," but, she argues, using motherhood as an example, conceptualizing "motherhood as womanhood is to obscure the difference that makes choice possible."[24] With regard to what has been socially construed as women's work (and pay), she refers to the concept of *comparable worth*. This concept "does not deny the existence of gender difference, but it does suggest that meanings are always relative to particular constructions in specified contexts."[25] Scott refuses sameness as a prerequisite for equality and pleads for an equality that is based on difference. "Equality, therefore, might well be defined as a deliberate indifference to specified differences."[26] Scott asks for the acknowledgment of "diversity" and "difference" when striving for gender justice. She uses the term *equality* but defines it as *equivalence* under certain conditions: "this presumes a social agreement to consider obviously different people as equivalent for a stated purpose."[27]

The Redistribution-Recognition Dilemma

In her work on the same issue, philosopher Nancy Fraser comes close to Joan Scott's conception. She tackles the "equality-difference dilemma" by introducing the legal term *equity* to replace *equality* and defines "gender equity" as a "complex conception."[28] Gender equity comprises seven distinct normative principles: antipoverty, antiexploitation, income equality, leisure-time-equality principle, equality-of-respect, antimarginalization, and antiandrocentrism. For Fraser, each of these principles is necessary and essential. "No postindustrial welfare state can realize gender equity unless it satisfies them all."[29]

Scott's article on the Sears case was written and rewritten in 1988— one year before the breakdown of the socialist system in Eastern Europe. According to Fraser, this development not only changed the political map of the world but also profoundly influenced the discussion of justice, with deep implications for the very concept. She points out three long-lasting effects of this development—"three constitutive features of the 'post-socialist' condition":

- the loss of a credible vision for an alternative solution to the present capitalist order;
- the shift in claims from redistribution to recognition comprising a shift from socially defined to culturally defined groups;

- the resurgence of economic liberalism (neoliberalism), which favors the shift from redistribution to recognition and leads to a retraction of egalitarian commitments and acceptance of a worldwide and sharply rising inequality.[30]

The concept of recognition she refers to, is, of course, not an invention of the postsocialist era. It draws on the Hegelian model of the fight for recognition. The philosopher Charles Taylor, for instance, has drawn on Hegelian notions to argue that nonrecognition can be a form of oppression, and the philosopher Axel Honneth too seeks to draw on the Hegelian "fight for recognition" to establish a model for a normative social theory. Honneth argues in his article "Integrity and Disrespect,"

> We owe our integrity ... to the receipt of approval or recognition from other persons. [Negative concepts such as "insult" or "degradation"] are related to forms of disrespect, to the denial of recognition. [They] are used to characterize a form of behavior that does not represent an injustice solely because it constrains the subjects in their freedom for action or does them harm. Rather, such behavior is injurious because it impairs these persons in their positive understanding of self—an understanding acquired by inter-subjective means.[31]

Since this does not seem to be all that far from Barrington Moore's concept, it is not surprising that Honneth draws on Moore's implicit social contract as "a system of rules determining the conditions of mutual recognition."[32]

Criticizing those theories, Nancy Fraser rejects not the notion of recognition but rather the *replacement* of redistribution by recognition. Using the examples of the "exploited classes" and "despised sexualities," she shows that, although as a last resort, the remedy might be either redistribution (class) or recognition (homosexual or lesbians), matters become "murkier" once we move away from these extremes because real collectivities are "bivalent" and combine features of the exploited class with the despised sex. Members of such collectivities suffer injustices that are traceable to both political economy and cultural aspects. "Both gender and 'race' are paradigmatic bivalent collectivities," Fraser writes. "Although each has peculiarities not shared by the other, both encompass political-economic and cultural-valuational dimensions. Gender and 'race,' therefore, implicate both redistribution and recognition."[33]

This implication becomes obvious if we return to the example of the 1950s Swiss debate on equal pay, in which the opponents' main argument against equal salaries for women was this: "the difference in salary might be considered unjust by women, but it is just in the eyes of men." On the one hand, gender initially structured the fundamental division between paid and unpaid (domestic) labor, assigning women primary responsibility for the latter and legitimizing unequal pay on that basis.

Despite notable increases in women's paid employment, they still perform more unpaid labor than men. On the other hand, however, gender also structures the division within the labor market between higher-paid male-dominated occupations and lower-paid female occupations. Under these conditions, gender injustice is a form of distributive injustice, and gender an economic differentiation. But gender is also a cultural differentiation, and as such it suffers the devaluation of things coded as "feminine." The political-economic and cultural-valuational aspects are by no means separate, but intertwine and reinforce each other. "Redressing gender injustice, therefore, requires changing both political economy and culture," Fraser asserts;[34] in her view, the future civil society is one that is built on alternative conceptions of redistribution and recognition.

As these examples show, Joan Scott and Nancy Fraser, like many other feminists, reject binary oppositions in the debate on gender. Fraser therefore conceptualizes gender as a transgressive category, or, as she puts it, "as soon as we acknowledge that axes of injustice cut across one another, we must acknowledge crosscutting forms of the redistribution-recognition dilemma."[35] She reproaches the feminist movement for paying too much attention to recognition, including questions of male dominance, identity, status, and losing sight of redistribution, that is, the question of socioeconomic inequality.[36] To be sure, she emphasizes that this was not intentional, because the supporters of the "cultural turn" seem to have expected that feminist politics of identity and difference would automatically synergize with struggles for social equality. "But," she argues, "that assumption fell prey to the larger *Zeitgeist*."[37] For her the timing could not have been worse, for it coincided with the emergence of neoliberalism, sharpening economic inequality and widening the gap between rich and poor. Academic feminist theory was preoccupied with debates about "difference," which served to reveal the exclusionary premises of earlier theories and thus opened gender studies to many new voices. But those voices "tended to remain on the terrain of recognition, where subordination was construed as a problem of culture and dissociated from political economy."[38]

The politics of recognition was, however, not confined to the feminist movement; it became a more general trend: antidiscrimination laws were enacted to overcome politically and culturally defined hierarchical status, but no attention was paid to the fact that economic disparities and thereby also social hierarchies were nevertheless growing. Payments to third world countries were reduced or even stopped in favor of so-called structural adaptations. In response, Fraser writes: "All of us are living in an age of declining security, thanks to neo-liberal pressure to increase 'flexibility' and curtail welfare protections amid increasingly precarious labor markets." But for those less integrated, including immigrants, these tendencies overlap with class inequalities of maldistribution, status inequalities, misrecognition of religion. Today, in a new phase of feminist politics, the relationship between the politics of redistribution and the politics of recognition need to be revisited; the two indispensable dimensions must be reintegrated. Moreover, according to Fraser, the scale of feminist politics must change, for gender injustice cannot be adequately challenged within the frame of the modern territorial state. Decisions in one state affect those outside it, international organizations—both governmental and nongovernmental—influence politics, and transnational public opinion—global mass media and cybertechnology—has become a force. Under these conditions, the state territorial frame has become a major source of gender injustice; thus, claims for redistribution and recognition are increasingly linked to struggles to change the frame.[39]

Fighting misframing makes visible a third dimension of gender justice: representation. Usually understood as ensuring equal political rights, representation, in Fraser's interpretation, is not limited to such "ordinary political" matters but encompasses the "meta-political" question "of how the boundaries of established polities are drawn." In this context justice cannot be discussed and framed in territorial or national terms; instead, "transnational feminism is reconfiguring gender justice as a three-dimensional problem, in which redistribution, recognition, and representation must be integrated in a balanced way."[40]

Conclusion

At present, civil society is undoubtedly an influential political concept, one that has, as Jürgen Kocka notes, gained great popularity over the last fifteen years.[41] There are, however, obvious tensions within the concept itself, between different actors and different interpretations of the concept, at different times as well as in different areas, and these become apparent when measured against concepts of gender equity and gender justice. While the feminist movements of the nineteenth and twentieth centuries should be considered part of civil societies at the international as well as the national level, at the same time elements of the various political systems in which they arose could hinder or postpone the acceptance of equal rights and equal pay. The Swiss example may be somewhat extreme with respect to the vote, but it is by no means so with respect to living conditions and equal pay.

Civil society seems to have been more successful in integrating the concept of recognition than that of redistribution. The fact that the recent popularity of the concept of civil society coincides with the rise of neoliberal thought makes things even more complicated. The goals of neoliberals and those of supporters of the concept of civil society are different, the first relying entirely on the "logic of the market" and the force of individual profit, the second seeking a path between unbridled capitalism and permanent state intervention. But both speak of and defend the "principle of subsidiarity," "flexibility," and "individual initiative and responsibility;" both fight the "interventionist social welfare state" and damn "excessive regulation." This overlap of vocabulary might either blur the difference or cause similar or even joint political action to follow the linguistic rapprochement and reinforce the power of neoliberalism. It leaves some doubt as to whether the reduction of state intervention and the division of tasks between civil society and the state will ultimately favor the well-being of a majority of the people and the states.

The modern Western state has become—however reluctantly—a forerunner of gender justice and gender equality even on the economic level: equal pay and equal opportunity programs started in the public sector. Even today differences in salary between men and women are still smaller in the public sector, and statistics show that women have a better chance of obtaining leadership positions there than in the private sector.[42] Women in top management positions and on the boards of directors of stock corporations and companies are rare; even in the United States, only 13.5 percent of board members are women, while the European average is about 8 percent. Where the percentage of female board members is higher than average, as in Norway, it is the result of legal mandate: 40 percent of board members of Norwegian stock corporations must be women.[43]

Redistribution—through taxes, regulation, or education—is state-centered. Although in theory a strong state is one that concentrates its efforts and leaves a lot to civil society,[44] in practice, it is not easy to distinguish between a reduction of state duties in order to strengthen the state and a neoliberal "logic-of-the-market reduction." At the same time, however, the nation-state often provides an inadequate frame for solving political problems, especially those caused by transnational forces, to which women are especially vulnerable.

Women's chances for equity depend at least as much on processes that transgress the borders of territorial states as on those contained within them. But neither a strong state nor a strong international civil society will automatically guarantee gender justice; it has always needed the extra effort of a strong feminist movement to reframe the concept of justice to include gender justice.

We thus have a somewhat contradictory or ambivalent situation in states that are not able to guarantee gender justice because of their male-centered conceptions of equality and justice. The example of Switzerland shows that even a political system that had implemented elements of civil society very early could be among the last with respect to gender justice. Achieving it required the specific impulse and effort of civil society—of the feminist movement, that is. But for the implementation and sustained development of gender justice, a civil society needs a strong state, including both a legal system that guarantees and courts that achieve and implement gender justice.

It is an illusion to think that because the Swiss state was not willing to implement gender justice or was even hindering its implementation, a reduction of state activities and responsibilities would automatically open up a space for civil society and could guarantee (more) gender justice. Historically the impulse came from feminist critique—from feminist politicians, lawyers, and philosophers. However, the feminist movement alone was not able to reform a legal system strongly rooted in a patriarchal understanding of gender roles and the (ancient) meaning of equality. It needed a strong state to be able and willing to take up those impulses.

Notes

1. Paul Brodbeck, "Die Frau mag diese Differenz als Unrecht empfinden, der Mann findet sie gerecht," quoted in Gaby Sutter, "Parlamentarische Dabatte zum Postulat 'gleicher Lohn für gleichwertige Arbeit,' 1953 und 1960/61," in *Die 'schutzbedürftige Frau': Zur Konstruktion von Geschlecht durch Mutterschaftsversicherung Nachtarbeitsverbot und Sonderschutzgesetzgebung*, ed. Regina Wecker et al. (Zurich, 2001), 209–227, 219; Gaby Sutter, *Berufstätige Mütter: Subtiler Wandel der Geschlechterordnung in der Schweiz (1945–1970)* (Zurich, 2005), 63.
2. The 1972 decision might be connected to the introduction of women's suffrage: although the initiative to discuss the Convention on Equal Pay began before 1971 and the handful of women who gained seats in the first election did not really matter numerically in the vote on the matter, the Swiss parliament had to take into account the fact that women could petition for an initiative and decide a referendum.
3. See Erwin Carigiet et al., eds., *Wohlstand durch Gerechtigkeit: Deutschland und die Schweiz im sozialpolitischen Vergleich* (Zurich, 2006).
4. For the characteristics of the concept of civil society, see Jürgen Kocka, "Civil Society from a Historical Perspective," *European Review* 12, no. 1 (2004): 65–79, 67ff.
5. See Carigiet, *Wohlstand*.
6. See the gender-specific wage study by the University of Basel, 2004.
7. See Eva Kreisky, *Gerechtigkeitsdiskurse: Thesen, Themen und Materialien zur zehnten Vorlesungseinheit*, 15 December 2002. http://evakreisky.at/.
8. Kocka, "Civil Society," 71.
9. This definition was, paradoxically enough, used in many national contexts to deny women—as traditionally "unequals"—political rights.
10. See Barrington Moore, *Injustice: The Social Bases of Obedience and Revolt* (London, 1978).
11. The aim of his study is to find out "why people so often put up with being the victims of their societies and why at other times they become very angry and try with passion and forcefulness to do something about their situation"; see Moore, *Injustice*, xiii.
12. Ibid., 45.
13. Ibid.
14. Ibid., 46.
15. Kocka, "Civil Society," 69.

16. Carola Sachse, *Der Hausarbeitstag: Gerechtigkeit und Gleichberechtigung in Ost und West 1939–1994* (Göttingen, 2001).
17. Sachse, *Hausarbeitstag*, 343.
18. Sachse, *Hausarbeitstag*, 344.
19. Alice Kessler-Harris, "Equal Employment Opportunity vs. Sears, Roebuck and Company: A Personal Account," in *Unequal Sisters: A Multicultural Reader in U.S. Women's History*, ed. Vicki Ruiz and Ellen DuBois (New York, London, 1990), 432–446; Joan W. Scott, "The Sears Case," in *Gender and the Politics of History* (New York, 1988), 167–177.
20. Scott, "Sears Case," 172.
21. Ibid.
22. Andrea Maihofer, "Gleichberechtigung in der Differenz oder Gleichheit und Differenz," in *Differenz und Gleichheit in Theorie und Praxis des Rechts*. Veröffentlichungen des 5. Schweizerischen Juristinnentages 1994 (Basel, 1995), 17–31, 24.
23. See Regina Wecker, "Geschlechtsvormundschaft im Kanton Basel-Stadt: Zum Rechtsalltag von Frauen—nicht nur im 19. Jahrhundert," in *Weiblich–Männlich. Geschlechterverhältnisse in der Schweiz: Rechtsprechung Diskurs, Praktiken*, ed. Rudolf Jaun and Brigitte Studer (Zurich, 1995), 87–101, 99.
24. Scott, "Sears Case," 175.
25. Ibid.
26. Ibid., 176.
27. Ibid., 172.
28. Nancy Fraser, *Justice Interruptus: Critical Reflections on the "Postsocialist" Condition* (New York, 1997), 43ff. The German translation of *Justice Interruptus* did not acknowledge the difference between the two terms, using "Gleichheit" for both. See "Die Gleichheit der Geschlechter und das Wohlfahrtssystem: ein postindustrielles Gedankenexperiment," in: *Politische Theorie, Differenz und Lebensqualität*, ed. Herta Nagl-Docekal and Herlinde Pauer-Studer (Frankfurt/M., 1996), 469–498, 469 ff.; Nancy Fraser, *Die halbierte Gerechtigkeit: Schlüsselbegriffe des postindustriellen Sozialstaats* (Frankfurt/M., 2001), 73 ff.; Alice Kessler-Harris uses "equity" in the same context: Alice Kessler-Harris, *In Pursuit of Equity: Women, Men, and the Quest for Economic Citizenship in 20th-Century America* (Oxford, 2001).
29. Fraser, *Justice Interruptus*, 49.
30. Ibid.
31. Axel Honneth, "Integrity and Disrespect," *Political Theory* 20, no. 2 (May 1992): 188–89; Fraser, *Justice Interruptus*, 14.
32. Axel Honneth, *Kampf um Anerkennung: Zur moralischen Grammatik sozialer Konflikte* (Frankfurt/M., 2003), 268.
33. Fraser, *Justice Interruptus*, 19.
34. Ibid., 21.
35. Ibid., 33.
36. Nancy Fraser, "Mapping the Feminist Imagination: From Redistribution to Recognition to Representation," *Constellations* 12, no. 3 (2005), 296–307. See also "Für eine dreidimensionale Gerechtigkeit," *Die Wochenzeitung*, 30 March 2005, 15–16, shortened German version of a paper given at the international conference "Gender in Motion: New Perspectives in Gender Studies" of the Swiss Graduate Program in Gender Studies in Basel, 3–4 March 2005. An extended German version was published in the conference proceedings in 2007.
37. Fraser, "Mapping the Feminist Imagination," 299.
38. Ibid.
39. Ibid., 304.
40. Ibid., 305.

41. Kocka, "Civil Society," 65.
42. Rita Bose, "Sind Geschlechterquoten für Verwaltungsräte von Publikumsgesellschaften legitim?" (Zürich, 2004), 3. http://www.ethik.unizh.ch/asae/downloads/diplomarbeiten/MASAE_Bose.pdf.
43. In Sweden a similar law has been discussed. Ibid., 3.
44. Ibid., 72

EARLY CIVIL SOCIETIES
IN THEORY AND PRACTICE

Chapter 3

THE PROGRESS OF "CIVILIZATION"
WOMEN, GENDER, AND ENLIGHTENED PERSPECTIVES ON CIVIL SOCIETY IN EIGHTEENTH-CENTURY BRITAIN

Jane Rendall

In the dramatic modern revival of the concept of civil society, the experience of eighteenth-century Britain has been an important point of reference. Jürgen Habermas identified its lively civil society, its print culture and coffee houses, its commercial activity and public spaces, as the precondition for the growth of a "bourgeois public sphere."[1] Over the last two decades social and political historians of eighteenth-century Britain have explored the spaces of urban life, the proliferation of voluntary associations and the extension of political interests in a spirit which, if not explicitly Habermasian, has certainly enhanced our knowledge of that social world.[2] And many historians of women and gender in this period, though critical of Habermas's gender-blindness, have identified sites of mixed sociability inside and outside the home as well as women's agency in the expanding world of print, and used these to challenge any simple notion of a gendered division between public and private worlds.[3] Some commentators have gone so far as to write of "the birth [of civil society] in eighteenth-century Britain," others of "the peculiarities of the English," as a starting point for that concept.[4] Most, in tracing the history of the concept, have looked at significant developments in the period between the publication of John Locke's *Second Treatise on Government* (1689) and Adam Ferguson's *Essay on the History of Civil Society* (1767).[5]

The term *civil society* was frequently employed in Britain from the late seventeenth century to the early nineteenth century, in political theory and debate, in religious writings and sermons, and in conversation and polite letters. Yet, as for other areas of Europe, there are fundamental differences between eighteenth-century usage in Britain and the meanings normally attributed to civil society at the end of the twentieth century.[6] This chapter will focus on the Enlightenment in Britain, and especially Scotland, but will draw upon French and German comparative perspectives where appropriate, to consider the gendered meanings of *civil society* and its related terms, *civility* and *civilization*. I examine eighteenth-century British usages, discuss the two alternative strands of writing on civil society in the Scottish Enlightenment, briefly compare the situation in France and Germany, and consider the impact of the French Revolution on these terms. I suggest that although the long-established term *civil society* remained in use in Britain throughout the eighteenth century, it was the newly coined noun *civilization* that became more widely used to characterize the social institutions and relationships—including the gender relations—of a self-consciously modern and rapidly changing commercial society.

"Civil Society" and "Civility": Eighteenth-Century Contexts

The English *civil society*, the French *société civile*, and the German *bürgerliche Gesellschaft* shared to some degree a common root in the Latin *societas civilis*. The emergence of these vernacular terms across Europe in the sixteenth century was stimulated by the revival of natural law theory. The first systematic writer on civil society in England was the theologian Richard Hooker, who, in his *Of the Laws of Ecclesiastical Polity* (1593), validated the position of the national church, the Church of England. He wrote of a civil society, as opposed to a "natural society," as the institutions of government exercising authority over individuals who had given a rational consent to that authority. This view of civil society brought together institutions that included the established national church, natural law and the positive requirements of the particular nation. Through its good order such a society facilitated sociability, not only between its members, but internationally. Hooker's perspective continued to influence Anglican writing into the eighteenth century and beyond.[7]

Like Hooker, Thomas Hobbes, in *Leviathan* (1660) and *De Cive* (The Citizen) (1651) also identified civil society with an effective form of government, in this case one to which men subjected themselves from fear and the desire for protection. Even more influentially, in John Locke's *Two Treatises of Government* (1689), civil society implied a form of government to which individual heads of households had given their consent, to ensure protection of their lives and property. But Locke did suggest the possibility that such a civil society might, briefly, through the strength of its institutions, survive a dissolution of government. For all these writers, civil society assumed and was built upon the good order of individual households, an order epitomized through the hierarchical relationships of husbands and wives, parents and children, and masters and servants.

The eighteenth-century British consumer of print culture might have encountered the concept of civil society in different but related genres of writing, which drew upon and at times strengthened the force of earlier usages. Throughout the eighteenth century, British clergy of the established churches of England and Scotland in their writings and sermons constantly reminded their readers and congregations of the relationship between government and religion in an ordered civil society.[8] Similarly, in the frequently reprinted works of John Locke, as in the works of eighteenth-century British and translated European writers on natural law, including Thomas Rutherforth, Jean-Jacques Burlamaqui, and Johann Heineccius, the familiar association of civil society with political institutions and ordered households, for the collective good, was maintained.[9] In his commentaries on Hugo Grotius, Rutherforth defined the origin and nature of civil society: "A civil society or, as we usually call it, a state has already been defined to be a complete assembly of men of free condition, who are united together for the purposes of maintaining their rights, and of advancing a common good. These two purposes, which civil society has in view, point out to us the mutual claims of such society, and of its several members."[10] By the early eighteenth century, however, there were also significant shifts in perspective, as "civil society" came to overlap with "civility" and "politeness" in both Britain and France. Popular manuals, sometimes translated from the French, offered "maxims for civil society."[11] This advice was directed towards those participating in new forms of sociability. These included not only the mainly masculine coffee houses, but also the places—theaters, pleasure gardens, assemblies, salons, and households—where such sociability would include mixed genders. Yet "civility" was also opposed to "vulgarity." As historian Amanda Vickery has pointed out, the new sites of politeness and civility, of public display and commercialized leisure, sought to attract less a growing middle class than the men and women of the fashionable world and the gentry. The assembly rooms built in many provincial towns from the late 1720s onwards were designed for socially exclusive, but mixed-gender, gatherings.[12] Gentlewomen like Elizabeth Shackleton of Lancashire drew upon the language of civility, of Joseph Addison and Richard Steele in the periodicals the *Tatler* (1709–11) and the *Spectator* (1711–12), as well as the novels of Samuel Richardson, to distinguish between truly polite and superior behavior, most likely to come from those of superior birth, and that of the vulgar, unworthy, and ill-mannered.[13] The vocabulary of civility was relevant to the social interactions that took place both in public settings and in households that encouraged mutual visiting, entertainment, and conversation. The diaries of Elizabeth Shackleton and of Katherine Plymley of Shropshire, as well as the better-known culture of the London salons of "bluestocking" women like Elizabeth Montagu and Sarah Scott, all illustrate the significance of that vocabulary.[14]

Civility had also to do with the growing exchange and consumption of material goods appropriate to new levels of politeness, about which Bernard de Mandeville wrote in *The Fable of the Bees* (1714). Mandeville argued that civil society functioned not through a conscious awareness of the public good, but through the unintended consequences of the "private vices" of greed, vanity, and self-interest, though he emphasized also that such a society depended on its laws and governments for survival.

These issues were most systematically addressed in the course of the eighteenth century by the theorists of the Scottish Enlightenment. They were influenced particularly by the strength of the natural law tradition in Scottish universities, as well as by the inheritance of Protestant Christianity, ambivalence about the complexities of Scottish national identity, and eighteenth-century interest in ethnography and the primitive. Fully aware of the older usages of *civil society*, they deployed that term in slightly different ways, drawing upon related but not identical themes of *civility, civilization,* and the *civic* (or *public* or *common*) *good*. They directed attention away from the divine ordering of civil society, towards its secular and social grounding. There were, however, tensions and contradictions between the two major strands of thinking among these theorists, the first stressing the civic concerns of civil society, the second the processes of civilization.[15]

The Scottish Enlightenment and Civil Society: Adam Ferguson's *Essay on the History of Civil Society*

Adam Ferguson's *Essay on the History of Civil Society* (1767) is the only major work of the Scottish Enlightenment in which the term *civil society* appears in the title. It was an attempt to redefine that term from a civic humanist perspective.[16] He wrote in response both to his French contemporaries Baron de la Montesquieu and Jean-Jacques Rousseau, and to his Scottish friends, David Hume and Adam Smith, whose focus was rather on the history, material context, and polite sociability of commercial societies. Ferguson was the only member of the Scottish literati from a Highland background, and he served for a period as military chaplain to a Highland regiment before entering the circles of the leading men of letters in Edinburgh in 1756. With other members of the literati there he actively sympathized with the campaign for a Scottish militia from 1756 on. In the *Essay on the History of Civil Society* Ferguson identified civil society with a particular kind of polity, one that allowed the full participation and consequently fulfillment of the citizen, for "it is in conducting the affairs of civil society, that mankind find the exercise of their best talents, as well as the object of their best affections."[17]

In doing this he used the typology of governments of Montesquieu's *De l'esprit des lois* (*The Spirit of the Laws*) (1749) with particular reference to the types that encouraged political freedom, the mixed monarchy, and the republic. In Ferguson's "civil society," the word *civil* opposed not *natural*, but *rude*. He had no sympathy with hypotheses that depended upon an original contract, and his work directly responded to Rousseau's *Discours sur l'origine et les fondements de l'inegalité parmi les hommes* (*Discourse on the Origins of Inequality*) (1755). He rejected its notion of the individual in the state of nature, on whom the chains of civil society (the term used in contemporary English translations) were imposed with the coming of property. For Ferguson the bonds of society were, from their beginning, natural, since "mankind are to be taken in groups, as they have always subsisted."[18] Civil society, defined by its possession of political institutions that facilitated men's civic engagement, evolved gradually, accidentally, in unintended directions, from such earlier social formations. But Ferguson desired to retain the values he saw in primitive communities—values that modern commercial societies appeared to be in danger of losing, and that emerged from men's identification with a larger whole, whether tribe, people, or nation, and its military defense. Ferguson may well have been influenced by Rousseau's emphasis on the importance of the active civic life as well as by earlier Scottish defenders of civic ideals, like the opponent of the Union with England, Andrew Fletcher of Saltoun, and the moral philosopher Francis Hutcheson.

Although Ferguson recognized that social development from the rude to the civil state also brought changing relations between men and women, he was fundamentally not very interested in the situation of women. He occasionally refers to what were to become the familiar elements in a narrative of women's history. He asserted that among the American Indian tribes, the women who labored while their men idled, hunted, and fought were in effect "the slaves and the helots of their country."[19] The seraglios of tropical climates were emblems of despotism incompatible with civil establishments.[20] He acknowledged the importance of the coming of chivalry, which, "uniting with the genius of our policy, has probably suggested those peculiarities in the laws of nations, by which modern states are distinguished from nations."[21] But nowhere did he consider women's place within such a modern state, in which men were to find their fulfillment in an active civic life. Indeed, his occasional references to domesticity were satirical. He mocked the ladies who "never look abroad," who suggest to their bored husbands that they learn to sew and knit; and men who have no occupation, who "cultivate a taste for gardening, building, drawing, or music," and merely "endeavor to fill up the blanks of a listless life," losing the chance of a greater satisfaction in civic fulfillment.[22] Neither domesticity nor sociability has much place in Ferguson's *Essay*. Historian Fania Oz-Salzburger suggests that "human nature, in this text, is synonymous with playful, aggressive masculinity" and notes that the term *civil society* appears more often in a military context than in any other in the *Essay*, though that perhaps underestimates the extent to which Ferguson looked forward to the extended participation of active male citizens in their state.[23] This canonical text does not, then, directly yield an interpretation of civil society that can be related to the growth of the "bourgeois public sphere" Habermas described.

The Scottish Enlightenment: Women, Gender, and the Progress of "Civilization"

An examination of the alternative strand of Scottish thinking, with which Ferguson was in dialogue, suggests different possibilities, not always explicitly described in terms of civil society. Adam Smith and David Hume were to redefine the language of politeness and refinement as the moral sentiments appropriate to an advanced commercial society, characterized by the contractual relationships of individuals. Scottish historians like Lord Kames, William Robertson, and others simultaneously chronicled and expanded the ethnographic and historical evidence on which that narrative rested. It was to be this approach that placed gender difference explicitly at its heart, as did William Alexander when he wrote of women's condition as an index to "the exact point in the scale of civil society" to which any people might have attained.[24]

The term *civilization* was to convey the dynamic force of material and social change more effectively than *civil society*, though the two were also sometimes used synonymously, as William Alexander tended to do. Historian Lucien Febvre has noted that, although in both French and English the verb *civiliser* (to civilize) and the participle *civilisé* (civilized) had a much longer history, the first use of the French noun *civilisation* may have been in 1766, and that it was used in the singular, implying a universal concept of the direction of progress.[25] The digitization of eighteenth-century printed material in English, in Eighteenth Century Collections Online, enables a crude quantitative measure of the works in which "civil society" and "civilization" occur in eighteenth-century English texts, by decade. The rapid growth in the use of the latter from the 1760s onwards is, as Table 3.1 shows, very clearly indicated.

There were, however, clearly significant continuities in usage among these philosophers and historians. When Hume wrote that "liberty is the perfection of civil society, but still authority must be acknowledged essential to its very existence," he was drawing upon the familiar European

Table 3.1 Full-text search for works in which "civil society," "civilization" and "civilisation" occur (in the Eighteenth Century Collections Online)

Years	"civil society"	"civilization"	"civilisation"	total "civiliz/sation"
1700–10	380	1	0	1
1711–20	365	0	0	0
1721–30	461	0	0	0
1731–40	499	0	1	1
1741–50	616	17	3	20
1751–60	611	2	2	4
1761–70	911	105	8	113
1771–80	1273	628	20	648
1781–90	1315	1234	68	1302
1791–1800	2477	2741	177	2918

Note: The data indicate the number of works, including multiple editions, in which these terms occur; they do not show the number of occurrences within each work. The collection includes approximately 150,000 works.

Source: Eighteenth Century Collections Online, February 2005 edition, National Library of Scotland, through a search at http://infotrac.galegroup.com/itweb/nlibscot, accessed 11 August 2005.

assumptions about the institutions of ordered civil society.[26] Smith and John Millar built upon the framework of natural law in their lectures on civil law, lectures from which Millar published his *Observations Concerning the Distinction of Ranks in Society* (1771). Political institutions were an integral part of their histories. Nevertheless these writers translated the "civil society" of the natural lawyers into something different: a theory of stages underlying evolving and progressive histories of different societies, histories of the gradual and unintended effects of material change, of the "civilizing process" that had at its apex their own Western "civilization." The societies of which they wrote were defined in material terms, through the four stages of hunting, pastoral, agricultural, and commercial life, but also seen in their totality, in terms of their manners, customs, laws, and polity. This included the historicization of the hierarchical relationships sketched by the natural lawyers, of husbands and wives, parents and children, and masters and servants.[27] Such histories drew, comparatively, on many sources, including classical and biblical writings, legal codes, and modern travel accounts of many different parts of the world, to reconstruct a sequence of development assumed to be applicable to the European distant past as to contemporary conditions elsewhere.

David Hume and Adam Smith were however concerned not only with such an historical framework but also with moral strategies for a commercial society. The adjective *civil* in their ideas not only served to legitimate political and legal institutions but also, in its association with "civility" and "civilization," suggested the kind of politeness and refinement that would characterize the relationships of individuals in such a society. They used the language of civility and sociability that was simultaneously being employed in the social practices of an elite, as suggested above. But they also turned to moral philosophy and psychology to explore the interaction between environmental forces and the individual self, and the relationship between the senses, feeling, and reason. David Hume's skeptical philosophy suggested not only that knowledge must rest on experience and custom, rather than reason, but that human actions were shaped by feelings rather than by reason, though that could also include reflection and calculation on the overall desirability or utility to society of particular actions. The implications were different for women and for men, as in what he had to say of the "artificial" and the "natural" virtues. So, to Hume, both justice and chastity were artificial virtues, based originally on self-interest but strengthened through sympathy with the sentiments of (masculine) others. But he also identified the existence of the "natural virtues" among men and women, including the love of relations and those close to us, pity, benevolence, meekness, and generosity.[28] And both natural and artificial virtues were rooted in the sympathy of individuals with the feelings of others. Passions and feelings in both sexes could be destructive to society, yet, when ordered and regulated, provided the basis of the social virtues. Hume wrote in his essays of the ways in which, with a growing refinement in the arts and the easy mixed sociability of the urban environment, "*industry, knowledge* and *humanity* are linked together by an insoluble chain," and one beneficial to the public.[29]

Adam Smith elaborated on Hume's concept of sympathy in successive editions of his *Theory of Moral Sentiments* (1759). He believed that propriety and morality were founded on the mutual exchange of sympathy between individuals, an exchange to be regulated and controlled by the "impartial spectator" who could take a sufficiently detached position to bring such sympathies into harmony. Moral cultivation depended on sociability and "complacency," here meaning the ability to take part in sympathetic exchanges in a moral community. If, in the *Wealth of Nations* (1776), Smith appears to ground modern civil society firmly on the "propensity to truck, barter and exchange" and to link individual self-interest to the common good through the mechanism of the "invisible hand," he did not cease to be equally preoccupied with the appropriate ethical behavior for such a society. His revision of the *Theory of Moral Sentiments* in 1790 significantly shifted his emphasis towards the Stoic self-command required by the "impartial spectator" in 1790. It is not clear whether Smith believed that women could reach such a high degree of detachment: "The fair sex, who have commonly much more tenderness than ours, have seldom so much generosity."[30]

The concept of sensibility drew upon medical, sentimental, and philosophical roots; it was part of the enlightened analysis of sexual difference and the "natural" attributes of women and men. What came to be emphasized by eighteenth-century Scottish moralists following Hume and Smith was that both sensibility and "complacency" were exhibited to a higher degree by women than men. They had a particular role to play in the cultivation of a morality with its roots in sensibility, that is, in the sociable exchanges of a modern commercial society, as when David Hume asked, "what better school for manners than the company of virtuous women?"[31] This "virtuous discourse" of late eighteenth-century Scotland sought to create moral and social strategies for the elite men and women of a modernizing society.

Women's condition was central to these strategies and was represented in ways that were both aspirational and prescriptive, defined through contrast and exclusion. Smith's successor, the Scottish historian and philosopher John Millar, first wrote systematically of the "natural progress from ignorance to knowledge, and from rude to civilized manners, the several stages of which are usually accompanied with peculiar laws and customs." The first chapter of Millar's account of that progress was "Of the Rank and Condition of Women in Different Ages." Lord Kames included in his *Sketches of the History of Man* (1774) a lengthy chapter on "The Progress of the Female Sex." William Robertson described what he regarded as the degradation of American Indian women in his *History of America* (1777).

To Millar, Kames, and Robertson, in the early stages of society women were subordinate laborers and slaves who provided rapid satisfaction of sexual desires. Only the later stages of material development, and particularly the acquisition of private property, brought with them inequality of property and rank, higher status for women, and a degree of leisure and tranquility that allowed the male imagination to focus on women as objects of desire. Millar, like Robertson, regarded chivalric ideals as bringing a new reverence, if sometimes an extravagant one, for women, with lasting effects on European manners. Yet not until the emergence of commercial society did "women become, neither the slaves, nor the idols of the other sex, but the friends and companions," in the modern and domesticated family, divided by labor but united by "esteem and affection," according to Millar.[32] William Alexander's *History of Women* drew extensively on their discussions. It has been strongly argued that these improvements in the condition of women reflected changes in the refinement and sexual behavior of men, rather than any degree of female agency. Yet at the same time in commercial society, women's developing influence both in the household and more widely was perceived to have a civilizing force. For Millar and others, however, commercial society was still liable to moral corruption through its pursuit of luxury and self-interest. If the republic or commonwealth was no longer to be the site of public virtue, as Ferguson desired, then it was women's influence that would preserve the household as the site of moral virtue and maternal inspiration, while also shaping a wider society.[33]

Women's appropriate role in commercial societies, in these histories, was clearly differentiated from their situation in earlier stages of development. When he traced a brief but very influential portrait of the American Indian woman, William Robertson wrote, "to despise and degrade the female sex, is the characteristic of the savage state in every part of the globe."[34] A view of the "savage" woman as drudge, laborer, slave, and servant became a familiar trope of eighteenth-century European commentary. In "savage" and "barbarian" societies, it was suggested, women were bought and sold in marriage, treated as slaves or servants, excluded from the succession of property, and forced to do heavy laboring work. "Nothing can exceed the dependence and subjection in which they are kept or the toil and drudgery, which they are obliged to undergo," Millar wrote.[35] The one significant exception to this, for Millar and Kames, lay in ancient Scotland. They found in a series of volumes of Highland verse, supposedly written by the ancient Scottish bard Ossian and published by the young James Macpherson between 1759 and 1762, evidence for the high status of the women of ancient Caledonia, a point surely made in the Scottish national interest. Similarly, from the perspective of Montesquieu's typology, the corrupting effects of wealth and luxury might be seen at their unchanging worst in the seraglios and harems of Eastern societies. This literature used the stereotypes of eighteenth-century orientalism, as Ferguson had done, to demonstrate the dangers of the corruption of female manners in a modern society.

Writers and preachers like Hugh Blair, James Fordyce, and John Gregory strove to encourage the kind of social and moral sensibility appropriate to a modern commercial society. For them such a sensibility also reflected the "natural" attributes of women.[36] The most popular of these writers was Dr. John Gregory, a distinguished Scottish physician. In *A Father's Legacy to His Daughters* (1774) he attempted to write of "the peculiar propriety of female manners" and therefore stressed: "I want to know what Nature has made you, and to perfect you on her plan." In the preface Gregory referred to "a little Treatise of mine just published," in which he had considered women "not as domestic drudges or the slaves of our pleasures, but as our companions and equals; as designed to soften our hearts and polish our manners."[37] This treatise was his *Comparative View of the State and Faculties of Man with those of the Animal World* (1764 and later editions), in which he wrote about Rousseau's admiration of an early state of society for showing mankind to its best advantage, though the loss of the virtues of that early stage, in a society which pursued wealth through commerce and industry, was inevitable. Gregory advocated uniting "the peculiar advantages of these several stages." That meant recognition of the importance of women's domestic, social, and educative role: "We should either improve the women or abridge their power."[38] He also wrote of the ways in which women were superior to men, including their "sensibility of heart, sweetness of temper, and gentleness of manners.... They have a more lively fancy, and a greater delicacy of taste and sentiment." They were also distinguished as "peculiarly susceptible to the feelings of devotion."[39]

Class and race, as well as gender, defined the sexual attributes through contrasts and exclusions. Henry Mackenzie, the Scottish novelist and man of letters, explicitly stated that he, like Gregory and others, wrote for "all above the lower ranks, of all who claim the station or the feeling of the gentleman," to the professional and middling classes as well as to the landed.[40] The women for whom these moralists wrote were clearly not the laboring women of industrializing Scotland, as women's labor came to be associated with an earlier stage of society, in spite of the absurdities of this position. In focusing on the differences between peoples, a few Scottish historians, like Lord Kames, adopted a polygenist theory of human origins assuming divinely created racial differences—differences that included and were shown as especially evident in the relationship between the sexes in non-European peoples. The representation of racial and physical differences, as well as of national particularities, could limit the apparent universalism of the theory of stages.[41] The history of women in European civilization was also the history of the progress of white Western elites.

Comparative Perspectives

The debate about the nature of a modern civil society took place across eighteenth-century Europe, sometimes in dialogues between its men and women of letters. The Scots had responded directly to the writings of Montesquieu and Rousseau, and their own rapidly translated works were read with considerable interest in France and Germany. In France similar shifts in vocabulary had taken place as men of letters attempted to map the relationship between the political institutions of absolute monarchy and the social interactions. Historian Daniel Gordon has traced the rapid increase in the use of *société* by the mid-eighteenth century and the emergence of the term *sociabilité* from its first use in the early eighteenth century from natural jurisprudence. In Diderot's *Encyclopédie* (1751–54), the articles on *société* and *sociabilité* appeared to suggest a secular approach to conceptualizing the ethical relations of equal individuals.[42]

And historian Dena Goodman has demonstrated how the sociable and convivial practice of the salons came to exemplify the degree of French civilization. The civilizing rule of the *salonnière* was accepted in the regulation of polite conversation.[43] To the Abbé Morellet, "the free commerce of the two sexes [is] one of the most powerful principles of civilization and of the improvement of sociability."[44] In the writings of another enlightened man of letters, Paul-Henri Thiry, Baron d'Holbach, politeness and the art of conversation were brought together with a discussion of the social virtues to be practiced in civil behavior outside the legal and political sphere, as individuals pursued their own quest for happiness.[45]

Attention was also paid to the historical framework of such *civilisation*.[46] In the early 1750s, in a fragment unpublished in his lifetime, "On History," the economist and later finance minister Anne-Robert-Jacques Turgot constructed his own three stage view of the history of societies, suggesting also the significance of unintended actions and conflicts. He wrote, if briefly, of domestic slavery and women's subjection in the earliest societies, and of polygamy as being established with the growth in large and wealthy empires.[47] Jean-Baptiste Suard's translations of the works of Scottish historians were very well received. He was particularly praised for the French version of Robertson's *History of the Reign of Emperor Charles V* (1769, French trans. 1771), and he himself greatly admired the account of the emergence of refinement in the introductory section, "The Progress of Society in Europe." In this he translated "refinement" as *civilisation*, and was able to show through this account the development, through the coming of commerce, of a sphere of sociable exchange, removed from both the absolute monarchy and democratic republican virtue.[48]

Antoine-Léonard Thomas' *Essai sur la caractère, les moeurs, et l'esprit des femmes dans les differens siècles* (Essay on the Character, Manners, and Genius of Women in Different Ages) (1771) circulated and roused controversy across Europe. Thomas surveyed the different situation of women in savage societies, classical households, and despotic regimes, as well as in modern commercial society. He juxtaposed the natural attributes of women against environmental and historical influences, and he called, in a Rousseauist spirit, for a return to the natural order, exemplified for him in women's primarily domestic role. He stressed the dangers of unrestricted material growth and the effects of luxury in morally corrupting women.[49] In France, Denis Diderot criticized Thomas for failing to recognize women's capacity for both feeling and knowledge, and "the advantages of the commerce of women for a man of letters" in his *Sur les femmes* (On Women) (1772). Mme d'Épinay wrote critically of Thomas's work: "He attributes to nature what is so evidently due to education and social institutions."[50] In Britain, the translation of the *Essai* by William Russell, a Scottish printer, included substantial passages from Adam Ferguson and John Millar on the treatment of savage women and the rise of chivalry, and also combined Hume's *History of England* (1754–62) with George Ballard's *Memoirs of Several British Ladies* (1752) to produce an alternative account of the progress of British society that had the progress of women—especially learned women—at its heart.[51]

The Scottish historians found a ready readership in Germany, where their work was also quickly translated. There, although the concept of civil society had a similar jurisprudential genealogy to that in Britain and France, the vernacular term *bürgerliche Gesellschaft* did not necessarily imply the possibility of participation by citizens in government, nor were eighteenth-century German men of letters as likely to participate in a lively political culture as the Scottish literati.[52] The rapid translation and wide circulation of Ferguson's *Essay on the History of Civil Society* did much to renew interest in the term. Fania Oz-Salzberger points out that the concept of a civil society that preceded the state was already "in the air" in Germany from the 1770s, and that Ferguson might well be given some credit for increasing the circulation of the phrase, although his intentions in writing the *Essay* were misunderstood. Oz-Salzberger demonstrates the difficulties that German translators and readers of the German text faced and suggests the extent to which German pietism came to gloss Ferguson's text.[53] His civil society had been a civic concept, not dependent on the natural law tradition or easily translated into the German context. And given that the German language lacked a term that, like the adjective *civil* in English and French, brought together political society and civilization, the "civilizing process" conceptualized on this linguistic basis by French and Scottish philosophers could not be smoothly translated into German terms.[54] However, Adam Smith's economic principles were, from the 1790s onwards, to make a considerable impact in Germany, and their influence on the Hegelian concept of civil society has of course been closely examined.[55]

The French Revolution: The Politics of "Civil Society" and "Civilization"

The impact of the French Revolution saw the terms *civil society* and *civilization* used with sharper political associations. At the same time, the condition of women became part of the political conflicts generated across Europe, in which women were themselves participants. The relationship between religion and society remained a critical theme. In the sharply polarized atmosphere of Britain in the 1790s, *civil society* was used in defense of the association of established religion with social and political order. Edmund Burke, in his *Reflections on the Revolution in France* (1790) wrote: "We know, and what is better, we feel inwardly, that religion is the basis of civil society, and the source of all good and of all comfort."[56] He used the term *civilization* much less frequently, and only to emphasize the contribution of Christianity to the improvement of manners. In his allusion to the desirability of recovering a spirit of chivalry and his use of the familiar figures of savagery in his description of the Parisian women of the crowds, he demonstrated familiarity with the work of the Scottish historians.[57] Ministers of the established churches also continued to emphasize their commitment to political order in their sermons and their writings.[58] When Hannah More referred to infidels as directing their attacks "principally ... against the female breast" because they were "conscious of the influence of women in civil society" in her *Strictures on Female Education* (1799), she was writing in the same spirit.[59] It was important to her conservative argument to stress that civil society, as well as the domestic setting, was the site of women's influence. More's own philanthropic interventions, in the name of order and of Christianity, have been seen as an important starting point for upper- and middle-class women's evangelical activism, directed especially towards poor women, in Britain.[60]

"Civil society" could be turned to radical purposes, as the American Thomas Paine did in his *Rights of Man* (1791–2), although his future society, dependent on minimal government and natural rights, assumed a preindustrial economy. By the mid-1790s, many Whigs and radicals had come to find this unsatisfactory.[61] But supporters of the French Revolution, for whom political change meant a radical, voluntaristic intervention in the political process, were also ambivalent in their responses to histories of the civilizing process. Mary Wollstonecraft shared that ambivalence. Her few references to "the constitution of civil society" and to its damaging effects are negative, suggesting that it was the present state of civil society that rendered women "weak if not vicious."[62] "Civilization" occurs much more frequently in the *Vindication of the Rights of Woman* (1792) and, especially, in her *Historical and Moral View of the French Revolution* (1794). Wollstonecraft strongly rejected the nostalgia of Rousseau for an earlier stage of society, yet she also saw her own world as one of "partial civilization." She was unequivocally in favor of the potential benefits of "a civilization founded on reason and morality," associated with increasing knowledge of the arts and sciences, a growing industry, domestic happiness, and social virtues. "True civilization" had, however, not yet been achieved, and could not be while hierarchical institutions survived, as in Britain, where "the pestiferous purple ... renders the progress of civilization a curse." It would be for her also very much a European civilization, to be differentiated from the condition of savages and that of the confined Eastern woman.[63] Looking at the French Revolution, she saw a disjunction between economic, political, and cultural developments, as France, the first country to achieve civilization of manners, remained hampered by the legacy of the past, the absence of a sufficiently large middling rank, and consequent failures in political science. She had further doubts about the direction of economic growth and the division of labor. Good government, actively intervening, remained necessary to maintain the progressive direction of civilization.[64]

But the fate of the French Revolution indicated the difficulties of political and social reform in a commercial society. And it became increasingly difficult for women writers to associate themselves with the politics of reform and revolution. The counterrevolutionary reaction in Britain to women's activism in the Parisian crowds and clubs, and to the defense of sexual freedom in William Godwin's *Memoirs of Mary Wollstonecraft* (1798) and Wollstonecraft's posthumous novel, *Maria, or the Wrongs of Women* (1798), inhibited radical and reformist analyses of the condition of women. Nevertheless, some possibilities for rewriting the situation of women in a modern commercial society still remained. For instance, Priscilla Wakefield, an active and reformist Quaker, drew upon Adam Smith's political economy when she referred to his assertion that every individual not contributing their fair share of productive labor would become a burden on society:

> The Doctor ... does not absolutely specify, that both sexes, in order to render themselves beneficial members of society, are equally required to comply with these terms; but since the female sex is included in the idea of the species, and as women possess the same qualities as men, though perhaps in a different degree, their sex cannot free them from the claim of the public for their proportion of usefulness.[65]

An educationalist, very active in the philanthropic Society for Bettering the Condition of the Poor and in defending the education and employment of women of the middle and lower middle classes, Wakefield argued: "Civilization would be advanced by bestowing such a rational mode of education upon this order of the sex, as shall teach them just notions of their duties and offices, and of the proper place they hold in society."[66] Where Hannah More had advocated philanthropy in the defense of a hierarchical civil society, Wakefield mobilized "the claim of the public" and of "civilization" in the cause of improvement. Across their political and religious differences, marked by contrasting vocabularies, both More and Wakefield shared an acceptance of sexually differentiated roles, yet also of educational practice, religion, and philanthropy as providing appropriate forms of influence and activism for women in a commercial society.

In France, women's role in the culture of the prerevolutionary court and in salons meant that their public role tended to be associated with the corruption of the civilization of the ancien régime, and few revolutionary leaders suggested such a role could be combined with republican virtue. The Marquis de Condorcet, who clearly shared the view that women's position in society was an important determinant of the level of civilization of that society, made the case for admitting women to full citizenship. Yet it was Rousseau's view of the purely domestic functions of women within a republican state that influenced revolutionary regimes, and the legacy of a secular republicanism in France to future generations contained no indication that a wider social role for women was desirable.[67] In Germany, Theodor von Hippel's *Über die bürgerliche Verbesserung der Weiber* (On Improving the Status of Women) (1792) called for women to recover their original rights, lost with the progress of civilization: "The female sex was deprived of its human rights through no fault of its own, but merely through the great strides forward taken by all human activity and affairs in their advancement toward civilization." Influenced rather by German pietism, he chose to stress the complementary qualities of men and women and the extent to which "women have God *in their hearts.*"[68]

Conclusion

We need more historically and linguistically specific discussions of these vocabularies to continue these investigations. For Britain, historian José Harris has described how the usage of *civil society* began to dwindle from the 1820s, remaining as "little more than a conventional synonym for civilization, the constitution, or the 'rule of law,'" though there were some contexts, notably the relationship between church and state, in which it retained some significance. After 1918 the term largely disappeared from use altogether. But the Eurocentric, complacent, and dynamic noun *civilization* continued to carry a powerful charge, especially in the context of Britain's expanding imperial role, and rule over subjected peoples.[69] Yet as the term *civil society* faded from use, so, paradoxically, the print culture, the world of literature, and the expanding associational movement, with its political pressure groups and philanthropic organizations that characterize the twentieth-century meaning of the "bourgeois public sphere," thrived. So too, very significantly, did the voluntarism of sects, chapels, and churches. The early nineteenth century saw a steady expansion of women's participation in such activities, even if in ways clearly marked out by gender differences. The nineteenth-century language used to describe middle-class women's social role centered on the domestic setting but extended their influence beyond, to the sociability of the household and the philanthropic and religious structures in which its members participated. The narrative of women's history inherited from the Enlightenment was one that retained a powerful hold in nineteenth-century Britain. But it was not the older form of *civil society* but the "progressive" implications of *civilization* that were to be employed, in print and in association, in both philanthropic and feminist causes.[70]

Notes

1. Jürgen Habermas, *The Structural Transformation of the Public Sphere: An Inquiry into a Category of Bourgeois Society*, trans. Thomas Burger (Oxford, 1989), 57–88.
2. See, for instance, Peter Borsay, *The English Urban Renaissance: Culture and Society in the Provincial Town, 1660–1770* (Oxford, 1989); John Brewer, *The Pleasures of the Imagination: English Culture in the Eighteenth Century* (London, 1997); Kathleen Wilson, *The Sense of the People: Politics, Culture and Imperialism in England, 1715–1785* (Cambridge, 1995).
3. Amanda Vickery, *The Gentleman's Daughter: Women's Lives in Georgian England* (New Haven, CT, London, 1998); Elizabeth Eger et al., eds., *Women, Writing and the Public Sphere 1700–1830* (Cambridge, 2001).
4. James Van Horn Melton, *The Rise of the Public in Enlightenment Europe* (Cambridge, 2001), 19–44; Frank Trentmann, "Introduction: Paradoxes of Civil Society," in *Paradoxes of Civil Society: New Perspectives on Modern German and British History*, ed. Frank Trentmann (2nd ed., New York, Oxford, 2003), 4.
5. See Adam B. Seligman, *The Idea of Civil Society* (Princeton, NJ, 1992), 59–101; John Ehrenberg, *Civil Society: The Critical History of an Idea* (New York, 1999), 83–109; John Dunn, "The Contemporary Political Significance of John Locke's Conception of Civil Society," in *Civil Society: History and Possibilities*, ed. Sudipta Kaviraaj and Sunil Khilnani (Cambridge, 2001), 39–57; Fania Oz-Salzberger, "Civil Society in the Scottish Enlightenment," in Kaviraj and Khilnani, *Civil Society*, 58–83.
6. José Harris, ed., *Civil Society in British History: Ideas, Identities, Institutions* (Oxford, 2003).
7. José Harris, "From Richard Hooker to Harold Laski: Changing Perceptions of Civil Society in British Political Thought, Late Sixteenth to Early Twentieth Centuries," in Harris, *Civil Society*, 15–17.
8. José Harris, "Introduction: Civil Society in British History: Paradigm or Peculiarity?" in Harris, *Civil Society*, 25.
9. J. J. Burlamaqui, *The Principles of Political Law: Being a Sequel to the Principles of Natural Law* (London, 1752); Thomas Rutherforth, *Institutes of Natural Law: Being the Substance of a Course of Lectures on Grotius, De jure belli et pacis* (Cambridge, 1754–56); Johann Gottlieb Heineccius, *A Methodical System of Universal Laws* (London, 1763).
10. Rutherforth, *Institutes*, 2, 22ff.
11. Abbé de Bellegarde, *Reflexions upon the Politeness of Manners; with Maxims for Civil Society* (London, 1707).
12. Vickery, *Gentleman's Daughter*, 240.
13. Ibid., chap. 6: "Civility and Vulgarity," 195–224.
14. Ibid.; Kathryn Gleadle, "'Opinions Deliver'd in Conversation': Conversation, Politics and Gender in the Late Eighteenth Century," in Harris, *Civil Society*, 61–78; Gary Kelly, "Bluestocking Feminism," in Eger et al., *Women*, 163–180.
15. See Colin Kidd, *Subverting Scotland's Past: Scottish Whig Historians and the Creation of an Anglo-British Identity, 1689–1830* (Cambridge, 1993), 107–122; David Allan, *Virtue, Learning, and the Scottish Enlightenment* (Edinburgh, 1993); Ronald Meek, *Social Science and the Ignoble Savage* (Cambridge, 1976).
16. See Oz-Salzberger, "Civil Society," 59; Duncan Forbes, introduction to *Essay on the History of Civil Society*, by Adam Ferguson (Edinburgh, 1966), xiii–xli.

17. Adam Ferguson, *An Essay on the History of Civil Society*, ed. Fania Oz-Salzberger (Cambridge, 1995), 149; Fania Oz-Salzburger, *Translating the Enlightenment: Scottish Civic Discourse in Eighteenth-Century Germany* (Oxford, 1995), 148.
18. Ferguson, *Essay*, 10.
19. Ibid., 82ff.
20. Ibid., 73, 112ff.
21. Ibid., 191–193.
22. Ibid., 45, 58.
23. Oz-Salzberger, introduction to Ferguson, *Essay*, xviii; Oz-Salzberger, "Civil Society," 75.
24. Alexander, *History of Women*, 1 n. 151.
25. Lucien Febvre, "*Civilisation*: Evolution of a Word and a Group of Ideas," in *A New Kind of History from the Writings of Febvre*, ed. Peter Burke (London, 1973), 219–257; see also Raymond Williams, *Keywords: A Vocabulary of Culture and Society* (London, 1988).
26. David Hume, "Of the Origin of Government," in *Essays Moral, Political and Literary*, ed. Eugene F. Miller (Indianapolis, IN, 1987), 41.
27. Knud Haakonssen, *Natural Law and Moral Philosophy: From Grotius to the Scottish Enlightenment* (Cambridge, 1996); Mary Catherine Moran, "'The Commerce of the Sexes:' Civil Society and Polite Society in Scottish Enlightenment Historiography," in Trentmann, *Paradoxes*, 61–84, 61–69; Jane Rendall, "Virtue and Commerce: Women in the Making of Adam Smith's Political Economy," in *Women in Western Political Philosophy*, ed. Ellen Kennedy and Susan Mendus (Brighton, UK, 1987), 44–77.
28. David Hume, *A Treatise of Human Nature*, ed. Ernest C. Mossner (Harmondsworth, UK, 1969), 629–631.
29. David Hume, "Of Refinement in the Arts," in *Essays*, 268–80, 271.
30. Adam Smith, *Theory of Moral Sentiments*, ed. D. D. Raphael and A. L. Macfie (Oxford, 1976), IV.ii.10; see also Henry C. Clark, "Women and Humanity in Scottish Social Thought: The Case of Adam Smith," *Historical Reflections/Réflexions Historique* 19 (1993): 335–361; Nicholas Phillipson, "Adam Smith as Civic Moralist," in *Wealth and Virtue*, ed. Istvan Hont and Michael Ignatieff (Cambridge, 1983), 179–203, 181–91; John Dwyer, *Virtuous Discourse: Sensibility and Community in Late Eighteenth Century Scotland* (Edinburgh, 1987), 52–65, 168–85.
31. David Hume, "Of the Rise and Progress of the Arts and Sciences," in *Essays*, 111–137, 134.
32. Millar, *Observations Concerning the Distinction of Ranks in Society* (London, 1771), 63–65.
33. Moran, "Commerce of the Sexes," 79–80; Rendall, "Virtue and Commerce," 7ff.
34. *The Works of William Robertson D.D.: History of America* (London, 1817), 9 n. 103.
35. John Millar, *Observations*, 18ff.
36. John Dwyer, *Virtuous Discourse*, 117–140; Dwyer, "Clio and Ethics: Practical Morality in Enlightened Scotland," *The Eighteenth Century* 30 (1989): 45–72.
37. John Gregory, *A Father's Legacy to His Daughters* (Dublin, 1790), in *The Young Lady's Pocket Library, or Parental Monitor*, ed. Vivien Jones (Dublin, 1790; repr., Bristol, UK, 1995), 3, 22; see Mary Catherine Moran, "Between the Savage and the Civil: Dr John Gregory's Natural History of Femininity," in *Women, Gender and Enlightenment*, ed. Sarah Knott and Barbara Taylor (Houndmills, UK, 2005), 8–29; Jane Rendall, "Clio, Mars and Minerva: The Scottish Enlightenment and the Writing of Women's History," in *Eighteenth Century Scotland: New Perspectives*, ed. T. M. Devine and J. R. Young (Edinburgh, 1998), 134–151.
38. John Gregory, *A Comparative View of the State and Faculties of Man with Those of the Animal World* (Edinburgh, 1764, 1788), xvi–xviii, 18–19, 121–122.

39. Gregory, *Father's Legacy*, 5f; Moran, "Between the Savage and the Civil," 22, 24.
40. Henry Mackenzie, *The Lounger: a Periodical Paper* (Edinburgh, 1787), 102, quoted in Dwyer, *Virtuous Discourse*, 113.
41. Silvia Sebastiani, "'Race,' Women and Progress in the Scottish Enlightenment," in Knott and Taylor, *Women*, 75–96.
42. Daniel Gordon, *Citizens Without Sovereignty: Equality and Sociability in French Thought 1670–1789* (Princeton, NJ, 1994), 6, 51–54, 64–65; see also Keith M. Baker, "Enlightenment and the Institution of Society: Notes for a Conceptual History," in Kaviraj and Khilnani, *Civil Society*, 84–104.
43. Dena Goodman, *The Republic of Letters: A Cultural History of the French Enlightenment* (Ithaca, NY, 1994), 3–7.
44. Morellet, "De la conversation," in *Mélanges de littérature et de philosophie du 18e siècle* (Paris, 1818), quoted in ibid., 130.
45. Gordon, *Citizens*, 65–71.
46. Sylvana Tomaselli, "The Enlightenment Debate on Women," *History Workshop Journal* 20 (1985): 101–125.
47. Ronald Meek, ed., *Turgot on Progress, Sociology and Economics* (Cambridge, 1973), 69, 80–82.
48. Gordon, *Citizens*, 129–176, here especially 150–160; Febvre, "Civilisation," 223–224.
49. On Thomas, see Jane Rendall, *The Origins of Modern Feminism: Women in Britain, France, and the United States, 1780–1860* (Basingstoke, UK, 1985), 28–30; Goodman, *Republic of Letters*, 10ff.; Mary Catherine Moran, "L'Essai sur les femmes / Essay on Women: An Eighteenth-Century Transatlantic Journey," *History Workshop Journal* 59 (2005): 19–22.
50. Mónica Bolufer Peruga, Isabel Morant Deusa, "On Women's Reason, Education and Love: Women and Men of the Enlightenment in Spain and France," *Gender & History* 10 (1998): 183–216.
51. William Russell, *Essay on the Character, Manners and Genius of Women in Different Ages* (Edinburgh, 1773), section VII: "Of the Progress of Society in Britain, and of the Character, Manners and Talents of British Women"; Moran, "L'Essai sur les femmes," 22–28.
52. Oz-Salzberger, *Translating*, 40, 144.
53. Ibid., 256.
54. Ibid., 152.
55. Norbert Waszek, *The Scottish Enlightenment and Hegel's Account of Civil Society* (Dordrecht, Neth., 1988); Gareth Stedman Jones, "Hegel and the Economics of Civil Society," in Kaviraj and Khilnani, *Civil Society*, 105–130.
56. Edmund Burke, *Reflections on the Revolution in France* (London, 1790), 134.
57. See J. G. A. Pocock, introduction to *Reflections on the Revolution in France*, by Edmund Burke (Indianapolis, IN, 1987), xxii–iiii; Pocock, "The Political Economy of Burke's Analysis of the French Revolution," in *Virtue, Commerce and History*, ed. J. G. A. Pocock (Cambridge, 1985), 193–214; Tom Furniss, "Gender in Revolution: Edmund Burke and Mary Wollstonecraft," in *Revolution in Writing: British Literary Responses to the French Revolution*, ed. Kelvin Everest (Milton Keynes, UK, 1991), 65–100.
58. Harris, "From Richard Hooker," 25.
59. Hannah More, *Strictures on Female Education* (London, 1799), 1 n. 62.
60. See for instance Kathryn Sutherland, "Hannah More's Counter-revolutionary Feminism," in Everest, *Revolution in Writing*, 27–64; Eileen Yeo, *The Contest for Social Science: Relations and Representations of Gender and Class* (London, 1996), 3–31.
61. John Keane, "Despotism and Democracy: The Origins and Development of the Distinction between Civil Society and the State," in *Civil Society and the State: New European Perspectives*, ed. John Keane (London, 1988), 35–69, 48–50; Gregory Claeys,

"The French Revolution and British Political Thought," *History of Political Thought* 11 (1990): 59–80.

62. Mary Wollstonecraft, *Vindication of the Rights of Woman* (1792) in *The Works of Mary Wollstonecraft*, ed. Marilyn Butler and Janet Todd, 7 vols. (London, 1989), 5 n. 116; see also 5 n. 76, and *Vindication of the Rights of Men* (1790), in Butler and Todd, Works, 5 n. 46.
63. Wollstonecraft, *Vindication*, 82–84, 87; Wollstonecraft, *A Historical and Moral View of the Origin and Progress of the French Revolution....* (1794) in Butler and Todd, *Works*, 6 n. 111.
64. Jane Rendall, "The Grand Causes which Combine to Carry Mankind Forward: Wollstonecraft, History and Revolution," *Women's Writing* 4 (1997): 155–172; Joyce Zonona, "The Sultan and the Slave: Feminist Orientalism and the Structure of *Jane Eyre*," *Signs* 18 (1993): 592–617.
65. Priscilla Wakefield, *Reflections on the Present Condition of the Female Sex; with Suggestions for its Improvement* (London, 1798), 1–2.
66. Ibid., 155f.
67. Rendall, *Origins*, 42–54; Joan Landes, *Women and the Public Sphere in the Age of the French Revolution* (Ithaca, NY, 1988), 203–6; Dorinda Outram, "Le Langage Mâle de la Vertu: Women and the Discourse of the French Revolution," in *The Social History of Language*, ed. Peter Burke and Roy Porter (Cambridge, 1987), 120–136.
68. Theodor Gottlieb von Hippel, *Über die bürgerliche Verbesserung der Weiber* (1792), trans. and ed. Timothy F. Sellner, *On Improving the Status of Women* (Detroit, 1979), 120, 138.
69. Harris, "From Richard Hooker," 26ff; George Stocking, *Victorian Anthropology* (New York, 1987), 8–46 and passim.
70. For one discussion of its relevance to the case for women's suffrage, see Jane Rendall, "Citizenship, Culture and Civilization: The Languages of British Suffragists 1866–74," in *Suffrage and Beyond: International Feminist Perspectives*, ed. Melanie Nolan and Caroline Daley (Auckland, 1994), 127–150.

Chapter 4

THE CITY AND THE *CITOYENNE*
ASSOCIATIONAL CULTURE AND FEMALE CIVIC VIRTUES IN NINETEENTH-CENTURY GERMANY

Gisela Mettele

On 26 December 1867, Therese Schaaffhausen died in Cologne at the age of ninety. The obituary published by her relatives had the following to say about her:

> It was those truly rare qualities of heart and mind, the upright and religious life she led, her unflagging, considerate and strongly supportive dedication to all that was beneficial and to the common good which earned our dear departed one the undivided affection and respect of all those circles with whom she came into contact during her long and active life.[1]

The circles with which Therese Schaaffhausen had been associated all her life quite obviously reached far beyond her family. Her relatives emphasize the commitment to the "common good" that had earned her great distinction as a citizen of her city. In 1800, Therese deMaes had moved from the Dutch town of Roermond to Cologne, where she married Abraham Schaaffhausen, a banker and merchant. In 1814, she first took an active part in the city's civic affairs, joining the patriotic women's association. Ten years later she collected money for the War of Liberation in Greece. She became one of the founders of the Cologne Association for Poor Girls' Schools, and served as its chair until 1859. She had also belonged to the city's Arts Society since its foundation in 1838. And as a widow she was a financial benefactor of Cologne's newly built theater house.[2]

Such an impressive range of public activities is perhaps not typical of all women of her time, but Therese Schaaffhausen was also not an isolated case. Indeed, the scope of her activities exemplifies the spectrum of the public involvement of German middle-class women during the nineteenth century. This essay will examine the role these female public activities played within the general context of an emerging civil society that was itself unfolding first and foremost as an increasingly tight-knit network of voluntary associations. In particular, I argue that the women's associations, through their specific forms of interaction, contributed to an essentially democratic civic activism.[3]

The activities of middle-class women were significant because the project of civil society, at least in Germany until the end of the nineteenth century, was closely connected to the culture and aspirations of the middle classes (*Bürgertum*). The reality of women's lives in other social classes was quite different, both as far as their specific social background was concerned and with regard to opportunities for women to express themselves in public. The class bias of civil society remained intact for a long time during the nineteenth century, and this holds true even for a gender-sensitive notion of civil society. The Prussian Law of Associations (*Preußisches Vereinsgesetz*) of 1850 did not allow women and juveniles to become a member of any "political association"; this law was not abolished before 1908. Only adult men won universal suffrage in 1869 in the Northern German Federation (*Norddeutscher Bund*), and in 1871 in the newly founded German Empire, women were excluded from this right till 1919.

City and Civil Society

For several reasons, this essay uses a local, more specifically urban, perspective. First, it was in the cities that new forms of communication and interaction that led to the development of a civil society were initially established. In nineteenth-century Germany, citizens' primary field of action was the city. The middle classes were for the most part not involved in governmental decision-making processes, yet they did not withdraw into a private "domestic idyll" but instead became politically active in various ways outside the home. It was in the domain of the city that the middle classes took their affairs into their own hands. Indeed, for liberals the city even became the prototype for civil society as a whole. Within a local framework, the middle classes demanded the right of cultural and political self-determination, and in this process gained the self-confidence to demand a voice in structuring the territorial state and the wider society as well. Hence, activities on the local level were not necessarily parochial, but rather served as local manifestations of issues that were significant in the territorial states and the nation.[4]

Second, the shift of perspective from the nation and the state to the city is important precisely with regard to women, since they were active primarily on a local level.[5] And third, a perspective on civil society that refers back to the community may be more adaptable than a national perspective to current questions concerning the transnational or global dimensions of civil society. Since this perspective puts the focus on agency and active participation rather than on institutions, it points toward the possibility of a multilayered conceptualization of citizenship that loosens its ties with the nation-state.[6]

Citizenship and Personal Independence

According to Immanuel Kant's famous definition, a *citoyen* was "he who has been enfranchised." The "sole" prerequisite for this status, "aside from the natural one (that he not be a child, nor a woman)," was "that he be his own lord and master ... which is to say, own some form of property ... which provides for his subsistence."[7] Explicitly this is a deeply gendered notion of citizenship. For Kant as for his contemporaries, personal independence was the decisive criterion for participation with other citizens in self-government. It established the middle-class male as a mature individual and responsible political subject. Since women were economically and legally dependent, they were—"naturally," as Kant put it—excluded from political participation and the institutional nexus. And they were excluded on principle.

The German liberal constitutional movement may have believed in the broad integration of politically and socially disadvantaged lower-class men into what the historian Lothar Gall calls a future "classless society of middle-income bracket citizens"—of course not instantly, but by improving their conditions up to the point where they could meet the requirements of an independent "housefather."[8] As far as women were concerned, however, there was no comparable anticipation of eventual emancipation and integration; enfranchised women were not even included in the long-term liberal agenda.[9] Citizenship and civil society were not universal projects in the first place; the referent for the "free and individual actor" was always the independent paterfamilias, and this was not a hidden agenda but obvious to Kant and his contemporaries.[10] In this sense, society and family were closely interconnected. At the core of the concept of civil society in nineteenth-century Germany was not an abstract notion of single males, but families whose male heads represented the entire household in the political sphere.[11]

In middle-class political ideology, men's worlds and women's worlds constituted two separate spheres, but in the everyday reality of city life women did not necessarily conform to this conceptual model. Actual relations between the sexes deviated from the normative ideals of liberal middle-class theorists. The lack of formal, political rights by no means prevented women from becoming involved in the emerging middle-class public sphere.[12] Indeed, one might argue that women helped to create this sphere through their very actions. Thus I want to propose a broader concept of personal independence that is based on agency and the autonomy that derives from it. In accordance with political theorist Ruth Lister and others, I want to conceptualize citizenship not only as status but also as a *practice* that considers the interests of the wider community.[13] Of course, full citizenship would have to include both status and practice. But since status can develop out of practice, it seems to be justified to focus on practice first, especially in an attempt to create a more inclusive notion of citizenship.

Free Association and Civic Spirit

In the nineteenth century, the idea of "civic spirit" (*Bürgersinn*) stood at the center of the German discourse on civil society. This key slogan referred not only to political self-determination, but in a more comprehensive and quite practical sense, to the commitment to supraindividual goals and tasks—in other words, to a sense of civic duty. This meant a concept of life that was not limited to professional or materialistic interests, but also found its expression in participation in society and orientation toward the "common good" (which was of course always defined within the confines of a middle-class perspective on reality). Only thus was it possible to prove one's citizenship (*Bürgerlichkeit*) in relation to what was understood by the notion at the time.

The concept of civic spirit had strong roots in a tradition of civic republicanism in German cities that was marked by a "cooperative" spirit (*genossenschaftlicher Sinn*)—i.e., it was based on the self-government and self-regulation of a political community composed of independent householders with equal rights.[14] In the nineteenth century this term became a by-word for those traditions, (re-)interpreted in an emancipatory manner. In particular, activities in voluntary associations became a characteristic of "true civic spirit."[15] The principle behind the concept of association was the notion of self-organization and hence self-determination. Through its emphasis on voluntary participation, the concept of civic spirit directly opposed both the paternalistic or bureaucratic state as well as the traditional corporate structure of society. Society, according to the new middle-class ideal, should be formed by the free association of (male) equals, without regard to their social status, origin, and occupation. This was obviously a somewhat idealistic self-perception, but it nevertheless represented a powerful mental concept that held huge potential for dynamism and adaptability.

In the nineteenth century, associations became a main structural principle of society and the crucial arenas where the middle class's claim to social emancipation unfolded and new forms of social interaction were developed. As historian Thomas Nipperdey has noted, "all middle-class activity was organized in voluntary associations."[16] Concert associations held regular musical performances; the municipal theaters were often financed and run by theater societies; art societies organized exhibitions and supported artists by purchasing their works. Important art galleries and museums, orchestras, and theaters emerged from these activities of the urban middle classes, for example, the *Leipzig Gewandhaus* Orchestra, the Senckenberg Research Institute in Frankfurt-Main, or the Wallraf-Richartz Museum in Cologne. Numerous social, economic, and political reform initiatives were carried out by associations or at least initiated and co-financed by them, creating institutions such as hospitals, institutes for the deaf and dumb, and the like.[17]

The activities of the individual associations did not stand isolated from one another, but formed a kind of network. Members of individual associations within a city formed tight-knit personal connections and frequently interacted with one another in a variety of associational and social contexts. This close social contact guaranteed middle-class cohesion and made the abstract analytical term *civil society* something that citizens could experience first-hand in their daily lives in the *bürgerliche Gesellschaft* (middle-class society). In everyday life it underlined the right of the middle classes to social emancipation. Even if the associations did not pursue any clear political goals, their structure alone, with internal elections and set rules of procedure on speaking rights and the postulated openness over and above social status, demonstrated that here the ideal of a future society was to be modeled and shaped.[18]

Women in "General" Associations

In contrast to the female-dominated informal sociability that characterized private middle-class homes, the more formal associations, clubs, and societies were fashioned to a large extent as a form of male culture. Even though the culture of the open houses continued to a certain extent in the nineteenth century, it ceded its dominant role in the building of a civil society to the associations.[19] Women were granted limited membership in some theater and art societies and also in some choir societies, where female participation was desirable if only for purely musical reasons—to increase, as one source says, the "diversity" of the singing. As a rule, however, the female members did not possess the same rights to vote or have any direct influence in matters relating to the associations themselves.[20] With respect to women's participation, the "general" associations can be divided into two groups: If associations were intended to promote the moral and aesthetic refinement and "ennoblement" of life, then women were involved to a certain degree. If, on the other hand, an association (for example, the male choir society or the gymnastic society) was thought to be a place for informal social interaction free from social constraints—a counterbalance to an increasingly formal and more refined middle-class life—then the contemporaries could or would not imagine the presence of women. Here the "fraternal bonds underpinning civil society" become most apparent.[21] The same was true with Masonic sociability, where male friendship and bonding stood at the center of activities.[22]

Another reason for women's limited participation in the "general" associations was that their activities were always connected with money. The establishment of a club, the purchase of, for example, a piano, or the cost of construction of a theater building were mostly financed by the members of the association on a shared basis. The opportunity for (married) women to own any property and thus make contributions was, however, very limited in the nineteenth century. For that reason alone, women's participation was mostly restricted to some wealthy widows and single ladies. Thus the "general" associations remained, in most cases, men's clubs.[23]

Women were also absent when things turned political because, in the eyes of the middle-class contemporaries, politics (in the narrow sense of the word) was a men's affair. This can be seen in the example of the men's choir and gymnastic societies, as well as in most of the liberal and middle-class democratic associations that arose during and after the Revolution of 1848, all of which barred female members.[24] Only the republican-socialist associations and some dissenting religious groups opened their doors to full female membership.[25] After the revolution, female public political activity was often banned, as for example in Prussia by the 1850 association law. It was not until 1908 that the law of the German empire permitted female membership in political associations.

Women's Associations

At an early date women were already organizing themselves in their own voluntary associations. The work of women's organizations was usually associated with charity. In the area of social welfare in particular, women were developing a broad spectrum of activities in the nineteenth century, beginning with the patriotic women's associations in 1813–14, maternal care associations, poor girls' schools, and the like.[26] Charity work is a classic example of the tasks assigned to women but—and this is often neglected—in the nineteenth century it was also a main concern of an emerging civil society. Throughout the century care for the poor was an important part of local self-government. In some cities poor-law administration even formed the largest municipal department. The urban welfare system had its roots in the traditions of the early modern city. In the nineteenth century it became regarded as an expression of civic spirit and of the middle-class capacity to organize civil society independent of the territorial and federative state. The state's influence on these levels was seen as an infringement on citizens' freedom, and until the state took over welfare responsibilities around the end of the nineteenth century, poor-law administration in Germany remained largely within the confines of local authorities.[27] Through their specific welfare activities, middle-class women not only participated in the building of civil society; by adding the needs of women and children to the agenda of communal charity and generating and implementing specific welfare policies, they also expanded and transformed its scope.[28]

Voluntary social work by female citizens was not linked, as it was for male citizens, to any political rights or positions within institutions of local self-government, yet in the charitable societies women acquired public influence that they did not otherwise have in the middle-class public sphere. In this way, the boundaries between private and public became blurred. Moreover, through their associations, middle-class women often acquired social power over women of the lower classes. Indeed, it can even be said that women's charity was an important and constituent part of middle-class domination in the cities.[29] If civil society is both a sphere of emancipation and, as Antonio Gramsci has argued, the arena in which cultural and social hegemony is contested, women's charitable associations are a prime example of the middle-class struggle for emancipation and domination—acted out in the language of the "common good."

Being active for the common good of the community—as the middle classes understood it—was the ultimate goal of the women's associations. They organized along the same lines of the "general" associations of the time, with statutes, internal elections, and set rules of procedure on speaking rights. In Cologne's Poor Girls' School Association, which I take here as an example of women's multifaceted charity activities, women who wished to join were nominated by two members and accepted on the basis of a simple majority. The president and executive committee were elected in a regular two-year cycle. Each member was authorized to enter proposals and motions, and resolutions were passed by a majority of votes.[30]

The statutes of most women's associations were cast in broadly inclusive terms, commonly welcoming "all well-intentioned fellow lady citizens" (*Bürgerinnen*) to participate. Of course the social openness of the women's associations often existed more in theory than in practice. The women's associations were—just like most "general" associations—characterized by a considerable measure of social exclusivity.[31] The social spectrum of the members remained limited, usually centered in the upper and (to a lesser extent) the educated middle-class milieu. The combination of inclusive rhetoric and exclusive reality, which was so typical of civil society in the nineteenth century, had its reflection in the women's associations as well. In merchant cities like Cologne, for example, women from the wealthiest merchant families dominated the associations and, not surprisingly, acted primarily as members of their class, not on the basis of universal female solidarity.[32]

Within their associations, these women defined their own goals and were responsible for all aspects of associational life. In Cologne's Poor Girls' School Association, for example, the women oversaw all aspects of the schools' organization and handled inspections, bookkeeping, and accounting. They saw to the maintenance and renewal of furniture, equipment, and materials as well as procurement of clothing for the girls. In addition, they took the liberty of making personal visits to parents, claiming the right, "in the event of recurring mistakes by children or negligence on the part of the parents the association ... [to] summon the children and the parents to the monthly association meetings."[33] This is but one example of the ways in which middle-class women exercised social power over lower-class women (and men).

The association depended on private donations to keep up the schools. Since most women owned no property, there was no provision for membership fees, but members were bound by the statutes to support the association's work through their own voluntary contributions.[34] Therese Schaaffhausen donated a thousand thalers to this association in 1841 and left the same amount to the association in her will;[35] others acted similarly. To secure the continuous inflow of funds, women's associations actively sought outside sources and thus developed a specifically new form of civic "fundraising" culture. The Cologne association, for example, collected money from friends and acquaintances and organized benefit concerts and charity balls or raffles of women's handicraft work.[36] They launched calls for donations in the city's newspapers, which usually met with considerable success. In addition to donations from private individuals they often also received contributions from other associations, such as the Cologne Freemason's Lodge and the music-lovers' society, which donated the proceeds from a concert.[37]

These exchanges reveal how closely women worked together with their male fellow-citizens (*Mitbürger*) and the extent to which the men acknowledged their work. This in turn calls into question some historians' assumptions of a separate women's political culture arising from women's public activities.[38] Indeed, the women's success depended upon close integration into a network of personal relations, friendships, and kinship within the middle classes. Far from trying to create a separate female "counterculture," these women collaborated with their male counterparts in establishing a common civic culture.

Women's methods of self-financing their work had been tried and proven since 1813–14, the first instance in which they took sides by establishing associations of "Patriotic Women and Maidens." These associations were founded in many German cities in the course of the so-called Wars of Liberation in order to ensure that volunteers had the necessary equipment and to care for wounded soldiers. Records indicate that there were 258 such associations in Prussia alone.[39] It was not until the 1830s that the number of newly founded "general" associations reached a similar peak.

Women's work within the patriotic associations expanded their individual horizons well beyond the city walls. Although local in scope, the projects were national in outlook. Women spoke the language of charity but often shared the anti-French tone of the German nationalist movement, a tone that became increasingly aggressive. One announcement published by the Cologne Association of Patriotic Women and Maidens in October 1813 stated, "In the battle for Freedom and Fatherland ... the unruly, perfidious and notorious French people shall be trodden underfoot once and for all by obedience, loyalty and steadfast courage."[40] Here the women were speaking in a clearly politicized language; they saw themselves as part of the German nationalist movement, and the women's associations of 1813–14 can be regarded as among its first organizations. Women, as Karen Hagemann has recently emphasized, were also involved in the aggressive anti-French course taken by this movement and in the close linking of the idea of a German nation and war, a trope that would continue to play a role in German history.[41]

Only a few years later, the organizational experiences women had acquired in the wars of liberation were transformed into renewed sociopolitical commitment. When the liberal Leipzig University professor Wilhelm Traugott Krug launched the first public appeal for support for the Greek cause in 1821, the response was overwhelming. In August 1821, the *Augsburger Allgemeine* reported the great success of the campaign, noting that women in particular had quickly organized themselves in groups "after the model of those who saw the birth of the German war of liberation."[42] The philhellenic movement was to become the broadest social movement in Germany of the period between the Carlsbad Decrees (1819) and the French July Revolution (1830).[43] As historian Christoph Hauser has pointed out, German support for the Greek struggle for freedom against the Ottoman Empire was at the same time an expression of the Germans' own aspirations for freedom, which, under the repressive political conditions of the 1820s and 1830s, could only be expressed covertly with regard to a situation outside Germany.[44] The philhellenic movement, like support for the Polish liberation struggles that followed in 1830–31, relied heavily on women, and through their associations women continued to play an active role in liberal politics.[45] To the extent that scholars acknowledge female participation at all, they usually regard women's philhellenic associations as having purely humanitarian motives and thus exclude them from the political context. Although closer examination reveals that the arguments advanced by men were not much more "political" than the women's, historians attribute the lack of explicitly political arguments in the men's philhellenic associations—but not in the women's—to the conditions of censorship.[46] Here clearly the argumentation becomes somewhat tautological. In applying a double standard for male and female actions, scholars define women out of the political context. As historian Jean Quataert points out, "only male actions are considered as political and through this prism, nationalism indeed becomes a debate among German men."[47] Thus scholars fail to analyze women's role in shaping civic identity.

But regardless of how one wishes to assess the fact that women's work was "limited" to providing humanitarian aid, their involvement meant taking a stand—and a public one at that—on a contemporary political event. Before becoming actively involved in a cause as far removed from their own lives as the Greek or Polish freedom struggles seemed to be, these women had to participate in the middle-class public sphere by, for example, reading the newspaper. It can therefore be assumed that the women were just as (well or poorly) informed about the overall context of solidarity with Greece as were their male contemporaries.

The activities of Cologne's philhellenic women met with considerable financial success. Several Cologne associations made donations, and a local painter put the earnings from an art exhibition at their disposal. In addition, donations came from nearby communities, funds were raised by private individuals, and the net proceeds from a concert organized by the singing club were donated as well. (Incidentally, many Cologne women were active in the singing club.) The largest portion of the funds came from the proceeds of the raffle of women's handicraft work.[48]

German involvement ultimately had no impact on the outcome of the struggles for liberation in Greece or in Poland, but it was significant as an expression of middle-class self-organization vis-à-vis the state: "Overshadowed by the bans ... in the crypto- and semipolitical sphere," Nipperdey has noted, "the middle-class movement and public sphere nevertheless managed to establish themselves."[49] What historian Wolfgang Hardtwig terms the "latent politicization" of society that was generated by philhellenism consisted for the most part of the experiences that were acquired in the organizations themselves.[50] To a large extent, it was women who accumulated these experiences.

In Cologne many of the women active in the association of Patriotic Women and Maidens in 1813–14 also participated in the philhellenic movement some years later. Women's civic engagement was thus too diverse to warrant the general conclusion, articulated by historian Nancy Reagin and others, that the middle-class women's movement in nineteenth-century Germany was politically conservative.[51] This assessment does not do justice to the complex mix of traditional and modern elements in women's activities and in German civil society more generally during the nineteenth century.

Conclusion

Taking as a standard such social situations and constellations in which civil society presents itself as a concrete context of action, the women's associations are a prime example of the process through which civil society constituted itself. For women and men alike, sociability was an important fermenting agent in the process of developing civic awareness. Through their associations, women learned the civil society's "grammar of conduct": self-organization, self-determination, orientation toward the "common good." And they attached great value to the forms of social interaction associated with civil society: a democratic internal organization, refined discourse, and the purported openness of its doors and activities to all classes of society.

Women's associations were not inward-turning circles that simply adopted a self-satisfied attitude; instead, they brought their influence to bear in strong measure on the society in which they lived. Women's public activities profoundly influenced their cities in many ways, whether through the sociopolitical impact of the activities themselves or the events that were necessary to finance these activities, such as raffles, concerts, and balls. Women accumulated organizational experience and experience in dealing with the public. They expressed themselves self-confidently within a framework of public action and had no qualms about regularly launching public appeals. However, as the annual reports they published in local newspapers reveal, their self-confidence in demanding the support of their fellow citizens was matched by the sense of responsibility they felt toward their communities. Women's associations were integrated in the social network that constituted the city's public life, and with their work they gained the recognition of their fellow citizens. They understood themselves to be participating in the establishment of a common civic culture, not creating a separate female counterculture.

Women's activities usually met with broad-based support, and criticism was rare. Thus it was unusual when, in 1815, the *Westfälischer Anzeiger*, the daily gazette of Westphalia, denounced women's patriotic involvement on the grounds that "it is only appropriate for German women to work for the good cause quietly, modestly and unassumingly."⁵² Even here, women defended themselves with spirit:

> It is so disgraceful doing good that we have to conceal it? Should the better of us consort with those who work in the shadows? ... No, when the house is on fire we are not afraid to pull out the hoses in public, and to climb on the roof for everyone to see; and when the fatherland is in danger, we have no reservations about taking our place shoulder to shoulder with others to save the day under the eye of our fellow citizens. Soldier with soldier in the field, men's federation with men's federation at home, women's association with women's association.⁵³

Both women and men did their civic duty in a specific way, according to their own understanding of themselves and their roles. Thus I would like to propose a concept of civil society that is based on a plurality of families in which matres- and patresfamilias *both* had public duties to fulfill. As male householders' sense of community expanded in the course of the unfolding civil society, so too did that of women, who transformed their housewife identity into a concept of civic motherhood.⁵⁴ This is not to say there were no gender differences; indeed, these were deeply inscribed into the associational culture of nineteenth-century civil society. But within, and through, their own associations, women nevertheless participated in shaping civil society. Their associations were important in individual and collective processes of identity formation as citizens, and there they built up reservoirs of "social capital"—shared beliefs and values. Moreover, we should understand civil society not only as a set of social practices but also as the process of learning a particular form of social behavior. Women, by taking part in associational life, developed the habit of working together for common purposes and learned to see with a collective vision. And they learned to take for granted the citizen's right to participate in the polity. The social attachments, codes of conduct, and public distinction that the associations provided supported the self-respect that gave rise to a strong sense of individual agency. Women might not have had the legal status of citizens, but they acted as citizens and thus fulfilled the potential of that status: personal independence.

As U.S. historian Nancy Isenberg reminds us, middle-class women did not encounter difficulties in becoming publicly active; rather, they had to contend with a political culture that defined their public activities as essentially and necessarily nonpolitical. Although their significant contributions to civil society through charitable associations were widely recognized by their male fellow citizens, women could not assume that this would turn them into political agents.⁵⁵ Nevertheless, the lines between charity and rights of citizenship began to blur, and by the end of the nineteenth century, women were making political demands based on their activities. Middle-class feminists argued that women's work in welfare associations gave them the right to vote and hold municipal posts; indeed, they argued, honorary activity in the local welfare system qualified women as citizens with independent political rights. In 1904, the feminist and politician Helene Lange asked,

> Why [is] the topic "the woman as a citizen" ... of practical interest today [?] The answer would be: because today the woman actually is a citizen; because the woman ... has already begun on the area of social work to take on board those tasks which officially fall to society as a whole.... If this development is to be a blessing for herself and society at large, then the system of laws for public life must also acknowledge her as a citizen.[56]

Lange's argument sums up what the concept of citizenship meant to her contemporaries even at the beginning of the twentieth century: independence in a material but also in a figurative sense, proved by the honorary work for the "common good" and consequently the right to a voice in the political decision-making processes. In other words, since women were already performing the duties of citizens, they deserved the formal status of citizenship as well.

Notes

1. Historical Archives City of Cologne (HStAK), Family archives Schaaffhausen, Best. 1296, C 10.
2. Ibid.
3. An extensive review of the literature on women's associations in the nineteenth century can be found in Rita Huber-Sperl, ed., *Organisiert und engagiert: Vereinskultur bürgerlicher Frauen im 19. Jahrhundert in Westeuropa und den USA* (Königstein/Taunus, 2002). Recent publications often focus on the ways in which female public activities contributed to the construction of state and nation; see particularly Jean Quataert, *Staging Philanthropy: Patriotic Women and the National Imagination in Dynastic Germany, 1813–1916* (Ann Arbor, MI, 2001). Quataert stresses the importance of dynastic patronage for the patriotic women's associations and the essentially conservative, dynastic conception of state the women helped to solidify through their work. But she examines the patriotic women's associations isolated from the overall context of civil society and does not take into account the fact that women were engaged in a variety of communal public activities.
4. The importance of the local level for the self-mobilization of German civil society is common sense among scholars of the German middle classes; see for example Paul Nolte, *Gemeindebürgertum und Liberalismus in Baden, 1800–1850* (Göttingen, 1994); Wolfgang Kaschuba, "Zwischen deutscher Nation und deutscher Provinz: Politische Horizonte und soziale Milieus im frühen Liberalismus," in *Liberalismus im 19. Jahrhundert: Deutschland im europäischen Vergleich*, ed. Dieter Langewiesche (Göttingen, 1988), 83–108. Also Brigitte Meier and Helga Schultz, eds., *Die Wiederkehr des Stadtbürgers: Städtereformen im europäischen Vergleich 1750 bis 1850* (Berlin, 1994).
5. For a recent overview see: Adelheid von Saldern, "Die Stadt und ihre Frauen: Ein Beitrag zur Gender-Geschichtsschreibung," in *Informationen zur modernen Stadtgeschichte*,

no. 1 (2004): 6–16; see also Kerstin Wolff, *"Stadtmütter:" Bürgerliche Frauen und ihr Einfluss auf die Kommunalpolitik im 19. Jahrhundert (1860–1900)* (Königstein/Taunus, 2003); Günter Hödl et al., eds., *Frauen in der Stadt* (Linz, 2003). Anke Ortlepp examines the patterns of German women publicly taking sides in the different political framework of the American society in *"Auf denn, Ihr Schwestern!" Deutsch-amerikanische Frauenvereine in Milwaukee, Wisconsin, 1844–1914* (Stuttgart, 2003). For the American context in general, see also: Sarah Deutsch, *Women and the City: Gender, Space and Power in Boston 1870–1940* (Oxford, 2000); Nancy A. Hewitt, *Southern Discomfort: Women's Activism in Tampa, Florida 1880s–1920s* (Urbana, IL, 2001).
6. See for example Michael Walzer, ed., *Toward a Global Civil Society* (Providence, RI, 1995); Jan Jindy Pettman, "Globalisation and the Gendered Politics of Citizenship," in *Women, Citizenship and Difference*, ed. Nira Yuval-Davis and Pnina Werbner (London, 1999), 207–220; Emilios A. Christodoulidis, ed., *Communitarianism and Citizenship* (Aldershot, UK, 1998).
7. "Derjenige nun, welcher das Stimmrecht in dieser Gesetzgebung hat, heißt ein Bürger.... Die dazu erforderliche Qualität ist außer der natürlichen (das es kein Kind, kein Weib sei) die einzige: Daß er sein eigener Herr ... sei, mithin irgend ein Eigenthum habe..., welches ihn ernährt," Immanuel Kant, *Vom Verhältnis der Theorie zur Praxis im Staatsrecht* (1793) (Berlin, 1923) 7, 295 (translation G.M.).
8. Lothar Gall, "Liberalismus und 'bürgerliche Gesellschaft,'" in *Liberalismus* (Königstein/Taunus, 1985), 162–186, 176.
9. See Andrea Löther, "Unpolitische Bürgerin: Frauen und Partizipation in der vormodernen praktischen Philosophie," in *Bürgerschaft: Rezeption und Innovation der Begrifflichkeit vom Hohen Mittelalter bis ins 19. Jahrhundert*, ed. Klaus Schreiner and Reinhart Koselleck (Stuttgart, 1994), 239–273; Ulrike Spree, "'Die verhinderte "Bürgerin?' Ein begriffsgeschichtlicher Vergleich zwischen Deutschland, Frankreich und Großbritannien," in Schreiner, Koselleck, eds., *Bürgerschaft*, 274–308; Ursula Vogel, "Patriarchale Herrschaft, bürgerliches Recht, bürgerliche Utopie: Eigentumsrechte der Frauen in Deutschland und England," in *Bürgertum im 19. Jahrhundert: Deutschland im europäischen Vergleich*, ed. Jürgen Kocka (Munich, 1988), 406–438: Claudia Opitz et al., eds., *Tugend, Vernunft und Gefühl: Geschlechterdiskurse der Aufklärung und weibliche Lebenswelten* (Münster, 2000).
10. See Erna Appelt, *Geschlecht, Staatsbürgerschaft, Nation: Politische Konstruktionen des Geschlechterverhältnisses in Europa* (Frankfurt/M., 1999), especially the chapter "Vermännlichung der Politik," 61–72; Carole Pateman, *The Sexual Contract* (Stanford, CA, 1988); Jean Bethke Elshtain, *Public Man, Private Women: Women in Social and Political Thought* (Princeton, NJ, 1981), especially chapter 3, "Patriarchalism and the Liberal Tradition." On the gendered notions of citizenship in the twentieth century see also the special issue "Gender, Citizenships and Subjectivities," ed. Kathleen Canning and Sonya O. Rose, *Gender & History* 13, no. 3 (2001).
11. Gall, "*Liberalismus*," 176. See also: Karen Hagemann, "Familie—Staat—Nation: Das aufklärerische Projekt der 'Bürgergesellschaft' in geschlechtergeschichtlicher Perspektive," in *Europäische Zivilgesellschaft in Ost und West. Begriff, Geschichte, Chancen*, ed. Manfred Hildermeier et al. (Frankfurt/M., 2000), 57–84.
12. The separation of public and private spheres has a long orthodoxy in nineteenth-century women's history, which has been questioned and considerably qualified in the last years. References to the literature can be found in Katharina Rennhak and Virginia Richter, eds., *Revolution und Emanzipation: Geschlechterordnungen in Europa um 1800* (Cologne, 2004). However, as the historian Lynn Abrams has argued, during the first decades of the nineteenth century the discourse of feminine domesticity was newly and forcefully articulated and widely disseminated across classes and cultures throughout Europe. But she also reminds us that "we should remain skeptical of the

degree to which the ideology of domesticity was internalized." Lynn Abrams, *The Making of Modern Woman: Europe 1789–1918* (London, 2002), 44, 64. Jane Rendall too examines in her article "Women and the Public Sphere," *Gender & History* 11, no. 2 (1999): 375–488, some of the ways in which twentieth-century commentators have attempted to categorize the contrast between private and public.

13. Ruth Lister, *Citizenship: Feminist Perspectives*, 2nd ed.; (Houndsmill, UK, 2003); see also Will Kymlicka and Wayne Norman, "Return of the Citizen: A Survey of Recent Work on Citizenship Theory," in *Theorizing Citizenship*, ed. Ronald Beiner (Albany, NY, 1995), 283–322.

14. As, for example, Paul Nolte points out, the distinctions between liberal theory and civic republicanism were not clear cut in nineteenth-century political theory and practice; Paul Nolte, "Bürgerideal, Gemeinde und Republik: 'Klassischer Republikanismus' im frühen deutschen Liberalismus," *Historische Zeitschrift* 254 (1992): 609–656. Regarding Victorian liberalism, Eugenio F. Biagini shows that its popularity was based above all on a "communitaristic" rhetoric of civic republicanism in his *Liberty, Retrenchment and Reform: Popular Liberalism in the Age of Gladstone, 1860–1880* (Cambridge, 1992). For the communal assessment of Victorian liberalism in general, see also Biagini, ed., *Citizenship and Community: Liberals, Radicals and Collective Identities in the British Isles, 1865–1931* (Cambridge, 1996); James Vernon, *Politics and the People: A Study in English Political Culture, 1815–1867* (Cambridge, 1993); Vernon, ed., *Re-Reading the Constitution: New Narratives in the Political of England's Long Nineteenth Century* (Cambridge, 1996).

15. Thomas Nipperdey, "Verein als soziale Struktur in Deutschland im späten 18. und frühen 19. Jahrhundert," in *Geschichtswissenschaft und Vereinswesen im 19. Jahrhundert*, ed. Hermann Heimpel (Göttingen, 1972), 1–44; see also Otto Dann, *Vereinswesen und bürgerliche Gesellschaft in Deutschland* (Munich, 1984); Etienne François, *Sociabilité et Société Bourgeoise en France, en Allemagne et en Suisse, 1750–1850* (Paris, 1986). For the most recent overview of literature and research documents see Heinrich Best, ed., *Vereine in Deutschland: Vom Geheimbund zur freien gesellschaftlichen Organisation* (Bonn, 1993); Wolfgang Hardtwig, *Genossenschaft, Sekte, Verein in Deutschland*, vol. 1, *Vom Spätmittelalter bis zur Französischen Revolution* (Munich, 1997).

16. Nipperdey, "*Verein als soziale Struktur*," 3.

17. Lothar Gall, *"Der hiesigen Stadt zu einer wahren Zierde und deren Bürgerschaft nützlich": Städel und sein "Kunst-Institut"* (Frankfurt/M., 1992), 13.

18. Many scholars of recent questions of civil society also regard voluntary associations as the "cement" of civil society. In their view, associations enhance social connectedness and provide the possibility of forming deep interpersonal bonds among constituents as important prerequisite for the democratic process, see for example: Robert D. Putnam, *Making Democracy Work: Civic Traditions in Modern Italy* (Princeton, NJ, 1993); Putnam, *Bowling Alone: The Collapse and Revival of American Community* (New York, 2000); Michael Walzer, "The Civil Society Argument," in *Theorizing Citizenship*, ed. Ronald Beiner (Albany, NY, 1995), 153–174; Sigrid Rossteutscher, ed., *Democracy and the Role of Voluntary Associations: Political, Organizational and Social Contexts* (London, 2005); for a more critical view of voluntary associations: Frank Trentmann, ed., *Paradoxes of Civil Society: New Perspectives on Modern German and British History* (New York, 2000).

19. See Gisela Mettele, "Der private Raum als öffentlicher Ort: Geselligkeit im bürgerlichen Haus," in *Bürgerkultur im 19. Jahrhundert*, eds. Dieter Hein, Andreas Schulz (Munich, 1996), 155–169; Brigitte Schnegg, "Soireen, Salons, Sozietäten: Gechlechtsspezifische Aspekte des Wandels städtischer Öffentlichkeit im Ancien Régime am Beispiel Berns," in *Frauen in der Stadt: Les femmes dans la ville*, ed. Anne-Lise Head-König and Albert Tanner (Zurich, 1993), 163–184 ; Ulrike Weckel, "Der 'mächtige'

Geist der Assoziation: Ein- und Ausgrenzung bei der Geselligkeit der Geschlechter im späten 18. und frühen 19. Jahrhundert," in *Archiv für Sozialgeschichte* 38 (1998): 57–77; Verena von der Heyden-Rynsch, *Europäische Salons: Höhepunkte einer versunkenen weiblichen Kultur* (Düsseldorf, 1997).

20. Carola Lipp, "Frauen und Öffentlichkeit: Möglichkeiten und Grenzen politischer Partizipation im Vormärz und in der Revolution 1848/1849," in *Schimpfende Weiber und patriotische Jungfrauen: Frauen im Vormärz und in der Revolution 1848/49*, ed. Carola Lipp et al. (Bühl-Moos, 1986), 270–307, 272.

21. Kathleen Canning and Sonya O. Rose, "Gender, Citizenship and Subjectivity: Some Historical and Theoretical Considerations," *Gender & History* 13, no. 3 (2001): 427–443, 429.

22. Stefan-Ludwig Hoffmann has pointed out the significance of male friendship as an important presupposition for civility and a "brotherhood of man." Masonic secrecy made possible a form of sociability that allowed men to experience intimate relations with each other: Stefan-Ludwig Hoffmann, "Civility, Male Friendship, and Masonic Sociability in Nineteenth-Century Germany," *Gender & History* 13, no. 2 (2001): 224–248; Hoffmann, *Die Politik der Geselligkeit: Freimaurerlogen in der deutschen Bürgergeselligkeit* (Göttingen, 2000).

23. Vogel, *"Patriarchale Herrschaft"*; Ute Gerhard, "Die Rechtsstellung der Frau in der bürgerlichen Gesellschaft des 19. Jahrhunderts: Frankreich und Deutschland im Vergleich," in Kocka, *Bürgertum*, 167–196.

24. See, for example, Dieter Langewiesche, "Die schwäbische Sängerbewegung in der Gesellschaft des 19. Jahrhunderts—ein Beitrag zur kulturellen Nationsbildung," *Zeitschrift für württembergische Landesgeschichte* 52 (1993): 257–301.

25. Sylvia Paletschek, *Frauen und Dissens: Frauen im Deutschkatholizismus und in den freien Gemeinden 1841–1852* (Göttingen, 1990); Catherine M. Prelinger, *Charity, Challenge and Chance: Religious Dimensions of the Mid-Nineteenth-Century Women's Movement in Germany* (New York, 1987).

26. The history of female welfare activities has been a vital field of research since the 1990s. See for example Gisela Bock and Pat Thane, *Maternity and Gender Policies: Women and the Rise of the European Welfare States 1880s–1950s* (London 1994); Elisabeth Meyer-Renschhausen, *Weibliche Kultur und Sozialarbeit: Eine Geschichte der Frauenbewegung am Beispiel Bremens 1810–1927* (Cologne, 1989); Christoph Sachße, "Social Mothers: The Bourgeois Women's Movement and Welfare-State Formation, 1890–1929," in *Mothers of a New World: Maternalist Politics and the Origins of Welfare States*, ed. Seth Koven and Sonya Michel (New York, 1993), 136–158.

27. See Jürgen Reulecke, "Formen bürgerlich-sozialen Engagements in Deutschland und England im 19. Jahrhundert," in *Arbeiter und Bürger im 19. Jahrhundert*, ed. Jürgen Kocka (Munich, 1986), 261–285, 281. The welfare system in the German cities was modernized in the nineteenth century, i.e., systematic and preventive measures such as schools for the poor and improvements of the infrastructure were introduced as an alternative to simply helping in acute situations of need. But this new concept was still connected to the traditions of the old burgher cities; see Dieter Langewiesche, "'Staat' und 'Kommune'. Zum Wandel der Staatsaufgaben in Deutschland im 19. Jahrhundert," *Historische Zeitschrift* 248 (1989): 621–635, 623f.; Jürgen Reulecke, "Die Armenfürsorge als Teil der kommunalen Leistungsverwaltung und Daseinsvorsorge im 19. Jahrhundert," in *Kommunale Leistungsverwaltung und Stadtentwicklung vom Vormärz bis zur Weimarer Republik*, ed. Hans Heinrich Blotevogel (Cologne, 1990), 71–80. See also Ludovica Scarpa, *Gemeinwohl und lokale Macht: Honoratioren und Armenwesen in der Berliner Luisenstadt im 19. Jahrhundert* (Berlin, 1995); Thomas Küster, *Alte Armut und neues Bürgertum: Öffentliche und private Fürsorge in Münster von der Ära Fürstenberg bis zum Ersten Weltkrieg (1756–1914)* (Münster, 1995); Su-

sanne F. Eser, *Verwaltet und verwahrt: Armenpolitik und Arme in Augsburg vom Ende der reichsstädtischen Zeit bis zum Ersten Weltkrieg* (Sigmaringen, 1995). As a study of care (in an even broader sense of the word) as element of citizenship see Paul W. Kershaw, *Carefair: Rethinking the Responsibilities and Rights of Citizenship* (Vancouver, BC, 2005).
28. See Sonya Michel and Seth Koven, "Womanly Duties: Maternalist Politics and the Origins of Welfare States in France, Germany, Great Britain, and the United States, 1880–1920," *American Historical Review* 95, no. 4 (1990): 1076–1108.
29. See also Dietlind Hüchtker, *"Elende Mütter" und "liederliche Weibspersonen": Geschlechterverhältnisse und Armenpolitik 1770–1850 in Berlin* (Münster, 1999).
30. HAStK 403-XII-1-732, Statutes §§ 14 u. 17.
31. The research project "The City and the Middle Classes in the Nineteenth Century," which was carried out at the University of Frankfurt from 1989 to 1996, has shown that this finding is true in very different types of German cities: see, for example, Susanne Kill, *Das Bürgertum in Münster 1770–1870* (Munich, 2001); Andreas Schulz, *Vormundschaft und Protektion: Eliten und Bürger in Bremen 1750–1880* (Munich, 2002); Frank Möller, *Bürgerliche Herrschaft in Augsburg 1790–1880* (Munich, 1998); Ralf Zerback, *München und sein Stadtbürgertum* (Munich, 1997); Karin Schambach, *Stadtbürgertum und industrieller Aufbruch: Dortmund 1780–1870* (Munich, 1996); Gisela Mettele, *Bürgertum in Köln: Gemeinsinn und freie Association* (Munich, 1998).
32. See Gisela Mettele, "Bürgerliche Frauen und das Vereinswesen im Vormärz," *Jahrbuch zur Liberalismusforschung* 5 (1993): 23–46. The Cologne data applies to other German merchant cities as well; see for example Schulz, *Vormundschaft und Protektion*; Ralf Roth, *Stadt und Bürgertum in Frankfurt am Main* (Munich, 1996). In cities where the court or the university was the main structural feature, the situation was only slightly different: there, the women who dominated the voluntary associations came more from the educated rather than the wealthier ranks of the middle class. In most female associations, aristocratic women were of minor significance and could gain dominance only in the patriotic associations; see for example Kill, *Bürgertum*; Zerback, *München und sein Stadtbürgertum*. The Cologne women's associations were cautious about not letting the Prussian *Landesmütter* gain influence in shaping their associations; nor did they submit to male subordination. The statutes of the Poor Girls' School association, for example, explicitly stipulated that the associated male "consultants"—the priest or parson, the school superintendent, and the two secretaries—could submit expert opinion but did not have the right to vote in the monthly association meetings; HAStK 403-XII-1-732. See also Nancy R. Reagin, *A German Women's Movement: Class and Gender in Hanover 1880–1933* (Chapel Hill, NC, 1995).
33. HAStK 403-XII-1-735.
34. HAStK Chroniken und Darstellungen, 219–227 (1834–1836), 403-XII-1-735 (1846–1852) a. 403-XII-1-732 (1853–1859).
35. HAStK Family Archives Schaaffhausen, Best. 1296, C2 u. C9.
36. HAStK 403-XII-1-735.
37. HAStK 400-III-24C-1.
38. As for example in Kirsten Heinsohn, *Politik und Geschlecht: Zur politischen Kultur bürgerlicher Frauenvereine in Hamburg* (Hamburg, 1997).
39. Luise Scheffen-Döring, *Frauenbewegung und christliche Liebestätigkeit* (Leipzig, 1917), 12. For the German female patriotic associations see also: Quataert, *Staging Philanthropy*; Ute Daniel, "Die Vaterländischen Frauenvereine in Westfalen," in *Westfälische Forschungen* 39 (1989): 158–179; Dirk Reder, *Frauenbewegung und Nation: Patriotische Frauenvereine in Deutschland im frühen 19. Jahrhundert (1813–1830)*, Cologne, 1998. See also Karen Hagemann, who discusses the relation of the cultural construction of national identity and universal conscription and the establishment of a new gender

order in the course of the anti-Napoleonic wars in her *"Mannlicher Muth und teutsche Ehre". Nation, Militär und Geschlecht zur Zeit der antinapoleonischen Kriege Preußens* (Paderborn, 2002).
40. *HAStK* 400-III-24C-1.
41. Karen Hagemann, "Female Patriots: Women, War and the Nation in the Period of the Prussian-German Anti-Napoleonic Wars," *Gender & History* 16, no. 3 (2004): 396–424.
42. Christoph Hauser, *Anfänge bürgerlicher Organisation: Philhellenismus und Frühliberalismus in Südwestdeutschland* (Göttingen, 1990); see also Natalie Klein, *L'humanité, le Christianisme, et la liberté: die internationale philhellenische Vereinsbewegung der 1820er Jahre* (Mainz, 2000).
43. The Carlsbad Decrees were resolutions adopted by the ministers of the German states at a conference in Carlsbad in 1819. They provided for uniform press censorship with the aim of suppressing all liberal agitation against the conservative governments of the German Confederation. The resolutions remained in force until 1848. The period between the Carlsbad Degrees and the March Revolution of 1848 is also called *Vormärz* (literally: "Pre-March").
44. Hauser, *Anfänge bürgerlicher Organisation*.
45. See Lipp, "Frauen und Öffentlichkeit," 284.
46. Andreas Tischler, *Die Philhellenische Bewegung der 1820er Jahre in den preußischen Rheinprovinzen* (Forschheim, 1981), 42. His double standard argumentation is also evident on pages 229, 233, 285, 327.
47. Quataert, *Staging Philanthropy*, 294.
48. Tischler, *Die Philhellenische Bewegung*, 231ff
49. Thomas Nipperdey, *Deutsche Geschichte 1800–1866: Bürgerwelt und starker Staat* (Munich, 1989), 401.
50. Wolfgang Hardtwig, "Strukturmerkmale und Entwicklungstendenzen des Vereinswesens in Deutschland 1789–1848," in *Vereinswesen und bürgerliche Gesellschaft*, ed. Otto Dann (Munich, 1984), 11–50, 29.
51. Reagin, *German Women's Movement*; Quataert, *Staging Philanthropy*, 6. In general, see Christiane Streubel, "Literaturbericht: Frauen der politischen Rechten," in *H-Soz-u-Kult*, 10 June 2003, http://hsozkult.geschichte.hu-berlin.de/rezensionen/2003-2-141. Streubel counts even the confessional associations working for parochial welfare to the political right.
52. "Deutscher Sinn. Die Frauen,"*Westfälischer Anzeiger*, no. 36, 6 May 1815, cited in Dirk Reder, "'Im Felde Soldat mit Soldat, daheim Männerbund mit Männerbund, Frauenverein mit Frauenverein'—Der Patriotische Frauenverein Köln in Krieg und Armenpflege 1813–1826," *Geschichte in Köln* 32 (1992): 53–76, 76.
53. "Entgegnung," *Westfälischer Anzeiger*, no. 40, 20 May 1815, cited in Reder, "Im Felde Soldat," 76.
54. For the significance of the concept of public motherhood for the German feminist movement see Sachße, "*Social Mothers*"; Sachße, *Mütterlichkeit als Beruf: Sozialarbeit, Sozialreform und Frauenbewegung 1871–1929* (Opladen, 1994); Irene Stoehr, "'Organisierte Mütterlichkeit:' Zur Politik der deutschen Frauenbewegung um 1900," in *Frauen suchen ihre Geschichte*, ed. Karin Hausen (Munich, 1983), 221–249.
55. Nancy Isenberg, *Sex and Citizenship in Antebellum America* (Chapel Hill, NC, 1998), 66.
56. Iris Schröder, "Soziale Frauenarbeit als bürgerliches Projekt: Differenz, Gleichheit und weiblicher Bürgersinn in der Frauenbewegung um 1900," in *Wege zur Geschichte des Bürgertums*, Göttingen, eds. Klaus Tenfelde and Hans-Ulrich Wehler (Göttingen, 1994), 209–230, 224; Iris Schröder, *Arbeiten für eine bessere Welt: Frauenbewegung und Sozialreform, 1890–1914* (Frankfurt/M., 2001).

Chapter 5

FEMINISTS CAMPAIGNS IN "PUBLIC SPACE"
CIVIL SOCIETY, GENDER JUSTICE, AND THE HISTORY OF EUROPEAN FEMINISM

Karen Offen

In 1925, an article entitled "What is Feminism?" appeared in *The Woman's Leader and the Common Cause* in England. This article laid out the ambitions of the feminist agenda, insisting that it was not merely about gaining access to male privileges. Instead, the writer (probably the British feminist Eleanor Rathbone) continued:

> the mere throwing open to women of all privileges, political, professional, industrial, social, religious, in a social system designed by men for men is not going to carry us all the way to our feminist ideal. And what that ideal is, becomes clear when we define feminism as *the demand of women that the whole structure and movement of society shall reflect in a proportionate degree their experiences, their needs, and their aspirations.*[1]

The arena in which European women contested the exclusivity of "male privilege," in which they condemned "masculine aristocracy" during a period of several hundred years, was precisely that arena that we are addressing in this volume as "civil society," the space in which the status of citizen is claimed and citizenship practiced; indeed, it is the secular space in which the "nation" is constituted. It was there that women sought to act, by speaking, by publishing, and by organizing—to attain "equal rights" with men—in order to express and incorporate "their experiences, their needs, and their aspirations" and thereby effect desired changes in their societies. The ultimate objective was to end male domination in the family and in society; the effects of such change could be very radical.

As one prescient French feminist, writing in post-1848 France, put it: "We must make it absolutely clear that the abolition of the privileges of race, birth, caste, and fortune cannot be complete and radical unless the privilege of sex is totally abolished. It is the source of all the others, the last head of the hydra."[2]

Restoring Gender to the Concept of Civil Society

The objective of this volume is to "discuss the concept and project of civil society from a gender perspective." It bears remembering that civil society (like democracy) is a *concept*, an *abstraction*, a fiction—one best understood in recent times by those who have no access to its promised benefits, by those who object to absolutism, to authoritarian or totalitarian states, to one-party systems—by those who want to participate in the decision-making process that shapes the societies in which they live but feel they have no way of doing so.[3] Civil society is envisioned as a space, an intermediary arena for negotiating common action, for speech, association, communication, lying somewhere between the state and the family. Throughout history, men in disadvantaged positions have understood this perfectly well. Most men, however, were long oblivious to the fact that women, too, could or would claim inclusion; they viewed women, children, and slaves all as dependents, as inferiors. They aspired to be the lords of households, heads of families, rulers of the roost. Thus, central to the concept of civil society historically (as analyzed by historian Jürgen Kocka and others) is its seemingly implicit, unmarked, long taken-for-granted exclusion of the family, and in particular women, who were long subordinated and silenced as both wives and daughters, enclosed in what has long been called the "private," or more precisely, the "domestic sphere"—the only place where female voices ought to be heard, but where they remained subject to the authority of husbands and fathers.[4] I have finally given up using the terms *public/private* (except between quotation marks), having concluded that these words are not, and never have been, purely descriptive terms. They have all too frequently been used prescriptively and polemically as weapons to contain and silence women.[5]

We now know that the exclusion of women always had to be asserted. Civil society was, historically speaking, a space fundamentally marked by gender struggles; indeed campaigns to include—or exclude—women are central to understanding its history, and should be central to its definition. In fact, gender politics has been a primary feature of theorizing about civil society since antiquity, as the example of Aristotle reminds us. His notion of *koinonia politiké*, or *societas civilis* in the Latin rendering, his own distinctions between "public" and "private," and his consignment of women to the domestic sphere and to passivity (as against men's activity; he was arguing against Plato, the champion of the Spartans' approach to sexual equality) remind us that keeping women (and slaves) out of civil society was central to his political philosophy. This important fact notwithstanding, discussion of its singularity virtually disappeared from the work of political theorists (and their commentators) until feminist political philosophers, beginning with the late Susan Moller Okin and Carole Pateman, drew our attention to it again during the 1980s.[6] Yet even these theorists did not tell the whole story, since their initial discussions were directed toward a mostly Anglo-American canon; they did not then know of, or examine, the contributions to the discussion by European women or male feminist thinkers, which have since been unearthed by gender-conscious women's historians. They did not notice that since the early Renaissance, feminists in various European settings had been contesting such revived Aristotelian thinking, beginning with protests against men's misogynistic writing, the as-then-constituted institution of male-dominated marriage, and the much-neglected education of girls. They were unaware that these early feminists insisted that any inferiority exhibited by women was a product of culture, not of nature. Indeed, the most significant debates of these issues by participants of both sexes took place in the valleys of public opinion that lay in-between the peaks of canonical male political theory (Hobbes, Locke, Montesquieu, Rousseau, Kant, Hegel, Marx, etc.); these contentious debates provided the context for more elegant theoretical treatments of the philosophers.[7] The so-called "woman question" had been a favorite theme for debate in European societies since the advent of print culture. Even the works of the canonical political theorists, we now know, contain significant gender components that had, until recently, gone wholly unanalyzed.

But once women began voicing their own claims (enabled by the advent of literacy and print culture, broadened property rights, educational opportunities, economic expansion, travel, and nation-building), they voiced them as women who aspired to be treated as full-fledged individuals. These claims included objections to the absolutism of male rule, to the authoritarian male-headed household, and to the severe handicaps (legal, economic, political) it placed on wives and daughters. Indeed, the historical tension between family and freedom cannot be exaggerated. Well before 1789, feminists exposed the "sex" of the abstract individual and insisted on the rights of women as sexed, embodied beings with a particular set of needs.[8] Thus did women, with the help of important male allies, stake their claims—on their own terms—to inclusion in the arena called *civil society.*[9]

Such feminist protests had already become frequent by the mid-seventeenth century. What seems remarkable, when one actually examines the debates, is how such critiques set an agenda for the *responses* of the eighteenth-century continental philosophes, some of whom—notably Montesquieu—did begin to grasp (and popularize) the analogy reinforced by seventeenth-century French women writers, including the novelist Madeleine de Scudéry, between the status of women and that of slaves, and the broad claims registered in Cartesian terms on women's behalf by François Poullain de la Barre.[10] Historian Sarah Hanley has shown that French women's awareness of the legalities of the act of marriage itself (in her words, the "framing of the Marital Law Compact") became the linchpin for French women's assertion of an independent legal identity, and that the practice of judicial publicity that arose around the elaboration and enforcement of this body of secular/civil jurisprudence lay at the heart of France's emerging civil society.[11] The English writer Mary Astell contested the ideas of John Locke on marriage.[12] It is well known that Jean-Jacques Rousseau became a major participant in these debates, focusing on the "social contract." Yet until very recently (as in the case of Aristotle) the gendered elements of Rousseau's thinking—which were contested in his own time—passed virtually without comment by twentieth-century political theorists and historians of political thought, who long neglected both *Julie* and *Émile* (with its notorious Book V)—until feminist political theorists and historians began to point out such omissions. Did not the actress and writer Marie-Madeleine Jodin claim, in her *Legislative Views for Women Addressed to the National Assembly* (1790), "And we too are Citizens"?[13] This claim recurs repeatedly throughout the early years of the French Revolution, but it did not originate then.

Thus, the history of European feminisms, of women's efforts to join men in formulating the rules of their societies, to restore a sexual balance of power at the decision-making level, lies at the heart of the history of civil societies (in the plural). It is central to virtually every national history, and it constitutes a core feature of comparative European political, intellectual, social, and cultural history. Knowledge of this history is essential to the proper study of political philosophy and central to the elaboration of civil society. Putting women in, and exploring the evidence on the political workings of gender, totally changes the way we understand narratives of political theory and nation-building, as well as transnational developments.

I do not recall ever having employed the term *civil society* in my research on the comparative history of feminisms.[14] Instead, I made it a practice to stick to terms used by the historical participants I was discussing: *emancipation, liberty, equality, rights, justice, citizenship*. These were the key terms that informed activity as civil societies developed in western and central Europe. All these abstract terms could apply equally well to adult women as to adult men. And that, for those who opposed the emancipation of women, became a problem. Throughout the two-hundred-and-fifty-year span between 1700 and 1950 some European women (and their male allies) made determined efforts to join men in the work of constructing civil societies. They challenged even more concerted efforts orchestrated by men aspiring to their own rights, equality, emancipation, and justice to deny those very same objectives to women, most often in the name of "public utility" as incarnated by the "needs" of the (male-headed) family—or the national interest. Behind the latter's objections lay subterranean fears: antifeminist men worried not only that women would escape from men's control, but also that they would lose their support systems. Contemporary caricatures, editorials, and even parliamentary debates reveal the specifics of the fears: that women might desert their housework, forget to fix their husbands' meals or to salt their soup, and insist that fathers change the diapers or babysit or do the wash while mothers went out to pursue other activities (the list was long: drill with the army, mix with politicians, write books, turn into men, etc.). In short, these men feared the challenge to male hegemony and to the prevailing division of labor (assignment of essential tasks) and space between the sexes. We can speak here of an upsurge of "antifeminism" in response to "feminism" that was completely disproportionate to the size of feminist eruptions.

Throughout the late eighteenth and early nineteenth centuries, feminists in France, England, the German principalities and free cities, the Low Countries, the Italian city states, and some Swiss cantons led the world in entering civil society to formulate claims for gender justice and to demand women's inclusion in budding democracies. Even in areas of Europe where feminist claims were scarcely being voiced, defendants of the male-centered status quo, knowledgeable—and fearful—about what was happening elsewhere, deployed the weapons of satire to resist women's claims to citizenship. Already during the later years of the French Revolution, for example, in the city of Bern, anonymous journalists writing for the *Berner Tagebuch* in 1798 mercilessly ridiculed the arguments of Mary Wollstonecraft and others.[15] The German political philosopher Johann Gottlieb Fichte went so far as to argue in 1796 that the public exercise of rights was incompatible with femininity itself; to act in the public sphere as a woman was to unsex oneself. His colleague Georg Friedrich Wilhelm Hegel wrote women out of his theory of the state. Because of their interests in the personal and the particular, he thought that women could not be trusted to operate in accordance with the dictates of Ideal Universal Reason.[16]

Despite such opposition and ridicule, in 1830, 1848, the 1860s and the 1890s women and men stated and restated these claims in a thousand different ways. In an age in which religious dictates were being seriously questioned, such claims were very hard to refuse or refute, except by resorting to elaborate rationalizations based on "nature," "biology," physiological and mental difference—all of which were invoked in support of male dominance and female subordination. These lay at the heart of what I have called elsewhere the "knowledge wars" of the nineteenth and twentieth centuries, intellectual wars in which attempts to keep women "in their place" (and off men's turf) were countered by increasingly sophisticated feminist arguments—and through the slow entry of women into the learned professions.[17] In what follows, I will examine in more detail the major contributions of feminists to exposing the gender injustice in discourses about emerging civil societies over several centuries of European history.

Mapping Changes in the Political Geography of "Civil Society" and the "Public Sphere"

To firmly grasp the gendered character of civil society over time, we must not only "reveal the gender" embedded in the concept but also map its political geography. Is civil society "public"? Or "private"? Or neither? We must, first, inquire at any given historical moment how the space is divided up, and where the line between public and private is being drawn.[18] We must also ask where the "public space" of communications lies within civil society. Second, we must ask who is included and who is excluded in these arenas when political theorists and others speak in general terms of "the people," "private individuals," and "citizens." Despite the best efforts of feminist political theorists and historians, most of today's contemporary literature on civil society continues to speak in these general (neutral) terms, with the seeming assumption that these are comprehensive terms, applying to all adults, whether male or female.[19]

In fact, in most places, these terms are still not gender-inclusive, nor have they been so in the past. Western societies have become an exception in this regard, but even in our world the exception is of relatively recent origin; indeed, in nineteenth and early twentieth-century England, the question of whether or not women were "people" provoked lawsuits by feminists and attracted attention from progressive legislators, most notably John Stuart Mill.[20] In French history, the question was whether the terms *l'homme* or *tous les français* included women.[21] Indeed, from the outset of the French Revolution, feminist writers of both sexes insisted that "the individual" or "*l'homme*" or "person" must not be implicitly understood to be male. These writers were all too aware of that maneuver from the beginning. Various attempts to clarify the nature of the individual ensued, as for example with the Saint-Simonians, who in the 1830s posited that the "social individual" was constituted by a man and a woman together. Today these issues, which some would dismiss as quarrels over "mere grammar," remain fraught with weighty political consequences—which invariably weigh more heavily on women. Finally, we must acknowledge what a major shift in political thinking has been required (and what an uproar it has created historically) to affirm adult women (both married and unmarried) not as dependents of a male householder, but as sexed, explicitly embodied (not "abstract") individual citizens, perfectly capable and empowered to participate in public debate and decision-making in their own right. In many parts of today's world, we are still witnessing the working-through of that transition.

Historical Phases in the Gendering of Civil Society in Europe

There were roughly three key phases of development in the varied histories of European societies that made possible the realization of feminist claims to participate in civil society. My perspective here will be comparative, but it is important to recognize that conditions that might be seen as historical parallels can differ importantly from one society to another. In what follows, I focus more on the practice than on the theory. I look on the ground for traces of "civil society in motion," and illustrate ways in which gender operated at its core—particularly during the formation of nation-states. Many of my examples here are taken from French history, but comparable examples can be found in a number of different Western societies.

The First Phase

It is absolutely clear from recent work by historians of women that the advancing literacy and the communications revolution (i.e., what the philosopher Jürgen Habermas refers to as "*Öffentlichkeit*," or the "public sphere") provided a broad platform for women's plaints and claims.[22] Although political theorist Carole Pateman has argued that in political philosophy, women were shut out of the social contract by an earlier "sexual contract," in fact, the history of feminisms in western European countries, especially in France and England, reveals a number of significant attempts by seventeenth and eighteenth-century women writers, not only to expose, critique, and annul this sexual contract (by challenging masculine supremacy in the institution of marriage as then controlled by the Catholic Church), but also to assert their full right to participate in public affairs. As I indicated earlier, women used every available means to critique the institution of marriage, to blame any intellectual inferiority on the inadequacy of their education, and to assert their right to equality, or at least to equal *opportunity* with men—economically, socially, and as democratic campaigns advanced, politically. Feminist challenges abound in novels and short stories, as they did in tracts, treatises, legal briefs, periodicals, pamphlets, poetry, and broadsides. Sympathetic male feminists assisted women in this campaign, most notably the seventeenth-century French writer François Poullain de La Barre (whose recent biography by historian Siep Stuurman places his radical feminism fully in the context of his times) and the late eighteenth-century philosopher the Marquis de Condorcet.[23] Far from being squelched by "the Enlightenment," feminists drew freely on Enlightenment language, using it to promote their own goals. Contrary to claims that were made for many years, Mary Wollstonecraft was by no means the "first feminist," not even in England.[24] She had many predecessors as well as plenty of company in articulating her controversial arguments. I have proposed elsewhere that, Rousseau notwithstanding, we need to reclaim the Enlightenment for feminism.[25]

The Second Phase

Writing and publishing were one thing; speaking out and organizing independently in the constricted space between family, church, and state was another. Intermediate bodies were usually subject to the controls of church or state, and sometimes both. The guilds provide an early and interesting perspective on "gendering" the entire society. In her research on the "gender" of social capital, for example, historian Sheilagh Ogilvie draws on early modern archival materials from the Black Forest area of the German state of Württemberg. She demonstrates that male-controlled guilds or corporations, which were central institutions for that community, deliberately and severely disadvantaged women economically.[26] Although theorists of civil society often bracket economics and production as being outside the perimeters of civil society, it was not so in the communities Ogilvie studied. The economic discrimination apparent there would have made it extremely difficult for women to even think about organizing on behalf of their "rights." Indeed, even west of the Rhine, it remained difficult. Not that the possibility had not occurred to some: in eighteenth-century Freemasonry, which was developing as a network of secret organizations in some urban settings, the question of admitting women and allowing their participation in the rituals sparked controversy.[27] From the 1760s on, at least in a few novels and plays, female authors in France were imagining the organization of "separate leagues of women" and "women's clubs," to (as Marie-Anne de Roumier, dame Robert wrote in 1780) "aveng[e] themselves against male injustice."[28] Whether on a local, national, or international level, the possibilities to quest for change through association remained severely limited. The efforts of some women to achieve, exercise, or maintain property rights; to obtain economic security outside the family; and to exercise reproductive control were deliberately curtailed. And yet, when this began to change, it changed fast.

The first four years of the French Revolution offered a particularly effective platform for analyzing gender operations in civil society. A close look at these operations, seen within their context, reveals that women were literally everywhere, and that the lines between the "political" and the "social" were exceptionally fluid; in particular, the economic realm remained tightly joined to both. The issue of citizenship encompassed multiple aspects. Education became part of the mix, as plans for schooling boys and girls became tightly tied to definitions of sex roles, sociopolitical function, and the future of the new republic.

During these early years, in fact, it proved hard for the more radical revolutionaries to hold the lines on questions of citizenship; drawing on old categories, they devised a distinction between "passive" and "active" citizenship—the latter masculine, and between "civil" and "civic" (or political), in order to contain women. Meanwhile, women complained about their lack of representation in the Estates-General; they argued that the female sex should "always enjoy the same liberty, advantages, rights, and honors as does the masculine sex."[29] They insisted that men could not speak for women, and some even called for the abolition of male privilege. Adding to Mademoiselle Jodin's claim for citizenship in 1790, Olympe de Gouges demanded a national assembly of women—composed of mothers, daughters, sisters; she also called for the adoption of a "Declaration of the Rights of Woman and *Citoyenne*," and a new conjugal contract. The very fact that these challenges could be so strongly articulated proves, instead, that these speakers did recognize male domination as provisional, contingent—a sociopolitical construction that was subject to revolutionary revision, in the name of the powerful principles of liberty, equality, and justice. These challenges continued, for more than four years. The women and their allies considered the abstract conception of "the rights of man" to be inclusive of women, and they believed fully in their entitlement to citizenship. It required the invocation of "public utility" by Talleyrand in 1791, qualifying the "rights of man" when applied to women, to provide ammunition for diminishing the role that some women were busily carving out for themselves in the nascent civil society of revolutionary France. "Public utility" was the "escape clause" the revolutionaries had provided for making exceptions to the Declaration of the Rights of Man.[30] My point is this: if, as Joan Landes has claimed, the "bourgeois public sphere" was "essentially, not just contingently masculinist," why then did feminists develop such powerful arguments to the contrary rather than accepting their exclusion as a fact of life?[31]

Political claims and political clubs developed right away, and it could be difficult to tell the difference between such clubs and associations organized for charitable ends (to pick up the work for the poor that had been left in tatters by the disestablishment of the Catholic Church and its institutions). A few deliberately mixed-sex groups, notably the *Cercle Social,* advocated women's rights and civic participation. Single adult women gained legal independence, and secular divorce laws provoked a rash of formal filings by women to end unhappy marriages. Yet, some revolutionary men viewed the springing up of dozens of secular women's clubs in cities throughout France with considerable anxiety; against the feisty publisher of *Révolutions de Paris,* Louis-Marie Prudhomme, who objected to women assembling, taking minutes, and swearing civic oaths, the women's club president from Dijon eloquently spoke to the necessity of women's civic activism:

> Among all forms of government, republican government most closely approaches nature; and in such a government each individual is an integral part of the whole and should cooperate in all that concerns the welfare of the republic; it necessarily follows that women, who are part of society, should contribute, as much as they are able, to the common good.... It is quite natural that the *citoyennes* ... should make themselves useful to the commonweal and offer advice on ways to do so. To accomplish this ... they must meet. For what can individuals accomplish in isolation?[32]

To this, Prudhomme responded: "You take care of your household government, and let us take care of the republic; let the men make the revolution."[33]

The Paris-based organization called the Society of Revolutionary Republican Women extended its civil activities even further in 1793, calling for women's rights, stringent economic measures, and even for women's participation in paramilitary civil defense activities. Its highly conspicuous and vocal activities alarmed the Jacobins. After nearly five years of witnessing women's efforts to include themselves in constructing the new society, the acolytes of Rousseau, of whom Prudhomme was one, succeeded in 1793, at the height of the Terror and a crisis of war, in banishing them from the budding civil—and civic—society fostered by the revolution. The Jacobin men forcibly consigned all women to domesticity, drawing on Rousseau's rehabilitation and reinscription of Aristotelian categories such as the "private," and reinforcing the ban by appeals to "Nature." They mapped the terms *public* and *private* onto *political/domestic* and drew a hard line before the front door. Governments, even revolutionary ones, began to pass laws against associations of women—and workers. It is important to recognize that this was a *defensive* move on their part. The fact was that the notion of women as citizens had become "thinkable"—and, in the eyes of opponents, dangerous. Uppity women cannot be "sent back" to their households—expelled from civil society and political life—unless they are already out there, actively operating in that arena.[34]

I have mentioned the importance of the "public utility" argument used by Talleyrand and others to argue for women's exclusion. But feminists would also embrace the public utility argument in support of their own public activity. The evidence clearly shows that women of the revolutionary era constructed the role of civic motherhood as a *political* role—one that was public, not domestic.[35] One contemporary image from the early 1790s shows a mother reading the Declaration of the Rights of Man to her child; such reading was a political act, far different than reading Aesop's Fables. To misunderstand the civic significance of the citizen-mother, the mother-educator, is to misrepresent the tools available to women who wished to participate fully in both civil and civic society.

Even after their eviction from political life in 1793, Parisian women continued to voice their opinions and demands, especially in print, though they were forbidden to participate in club meetings, to march in the streets, or to assemble in large groups. Indeed, the entire nineteenth century was marked by women's continuing efforts to rejoin civil society and, as democratization efforts continued, carve out a space in political life. Given the extent of the counterrevolution, though, it was a long, slow process for European women, especially married women, to work their way back in, especially since in most countries married women had long been considered legally "covered" (*femmes covertes*) by their husbands and had to obtain their permission to do just about anything that took them beyond the household. The campaigns for married women's property rights of the nineteenth century, first in England, then in France and elsewhere, along with attempts to empower wives so they could open savings accounts, enroll for professional or vocational schooling, claim personal nationality, and travel at will, can all be read as efforts to enable women to participate fully as individuals in civil society. In the interim, women organized "patriotic societies" or other types of charitable and philanthropic groups in a space that became known in some retrospective accounts as "the social"—working with the poor, the sick, and the unfortunate.[36] And then, in democratizing societies, they began to organize on behalf of the vote for women, to formalize their claim to become decision-makers on a par with their menfolk. For them, "democracy without women" was unthinkable.[37]

The Third Phase

I have argued earlier that in the period under consideration here, "civil society" encompassed more types of activity, activities not so clearly differentiated as they subsequently became (at least in the thinking of some theorists). In discussing this third phase, I want to argue that to gender the notion of civil society also requires, briefly, revisiting the history of women's quest for full citizenship: obtaining the vote and office-holding. This became an increasingly important feminist goal, following the insertion of the word *male* in Britain's Reform Act of 1832—a legal move that was consciously copied in a number of other European countries.

The claims of French women for the vote (and for the legalization of divorce) in 1848 were forthright; they contested the idea that a purely masculine suffrage could be called "universal." In various areas of Germany, women activists also laid claim to citizenship (*Bürgerrechte*), only to be disappointed. In Saxony, the journalist and political activist Louise Otto expressed her frustration in verse:

> On men alone rights were conferred
> In the upheavals of the revolution.
> For even though it seemed like changes had occurred
> And like the monarchy was on the brink of dissolution:
> Those new struggles were for the rights of man;
> The rights of women were not part of their plan...
> The free men spoke of fraternization:
> They were citizens, not lords and slaves;
> They sang of their new affiliation
> And considered themselves a reborn race.
> But they viewed their sisters with deprecation—
> There were no rights for half the populace,
> For the cry "for all!" excluded women—
> They were denied the rights of citizens.[38]

Particularly after the failed revolutions of 1848, feminist activists faced off against fearful men who would deny them the right not only to vote but even to speak out, to publish, and to assemble, much less to claim the right to work. In France, some even questioned their right to petition. Throughout Europe in the 1850s, concerned male intellectuals turned to the study and scholarly justification of patriarchal rule. This epoch of reaction was vicious, precisely in the ratio to which the inclusion of women had become "thinkable." And the threat of violence continued for decades, as we are reminded by evidence from the Paris Commune of 1871, where women's participation in the new civil society in formation was brutally foreclosed by military action, and by the violence deployed by British government forces against the militant suffragettes of the WSPU and by the Washington, DC police against Alice Paul's National Women's Party agitation for the vote.[39] Such violence seemed antithetical to the very presuppositions of civil society, most notably peaceable discussion and debate.

It is important to remark that, in the face of the efforts of physician philosophers in France, England, the Germanys and elsewhere, from the immediate postrevolutionary period through the entire nineteenth century, to insist on the weak female bodies (and minds) of women as a means of substantiating their exclusion (the so-called "science of woman"), the demands that many feminists were making for full citizenship, including the vote, were *embodied demands*, based on the strong, maternal bodies of women (countered by the asexuality of mind, and reason).[40] No abstract individuals, these. It was *women's* rights they argued for, "equality-in-difference," in the name of which they mounted a virtually complete critique of the societies in which they lived, ultimately challenging militarism, war, and men's sexual habits, and claiming control over their own bodies, especially over their own fertility.[41] At no time was the aim of most earlier feminists to substitute public patriarchy for private patriarchy, although from the 1880s on, some made appeals to the state to provide financial support for single mothers, most often at the expense of the government budget for war. These feminists drew a strategic parallel between soldiers and mothers.[42] The point was to dispute patriarchy in all its aspects—to challenge male domination, which was no longer thought to be written in stone, and the institutions, ideas, forms, and practices that upheld it. Varied strategies and tactics were used in different national, regional and local settings. But the ultimate goal was to share power, in the interest of creating a better-balanced and woman-friendly civil and political society. Alfred, Lord Tennyson captured this thought nicely in his long poem "The Princess" (1847):

> ...everywhere
> Two heads in council, two beside the hearth,
> Two in the tangled business of the world,
> Two in the liberal offices of life,
> Two plummets dropt for one to sound the abyss
> Of science and secrets of the mind:
> Musician, painter, sculptor, critic, more.[43]

As the women of *Common Cause* underscored (and as feminists repeated over and over again), the vote and office holding were viewed not as ends in themselves, but as means to achieve women's full participation in societal decision-making. And indeed, the vote did count for a lot, particularly in the years immediately following enfranchisement. In 1928, Dr. Aletta Jacobs, the first Dutch woman physician and an ardent suffragist, wrote to Carrie Chapman Catt, former president of the International Alliance for Woman Suffrage, on the topic of whether woman suffrage was worth the fight. "People who ask that," Jacobs said, "are blind for [*sic*] the great change in the world after we have got it. Since ten years ago women are beginning to play a rôle in the building of a new world and men are beginning to look to women more as comrades than as a creature only for their pleasure."[44]

Women without Citizenship Enter Civil Society: The Case of Madame Avril de Sainte-Croix

The road traveled toward the gendering of civil societies in Europe was rocky, full of potholes and obstacles. There were nevertheless women who took the bit in their teeth—and even in the absence of the vote in their home countries, constituted themselves as participants in public, indeed, even governmental, affairs on the international and transnational stages. Such women have been less well studied than those who participated strictly on the national stage, and yet they are very important, precisely because they were carving out new modes of civic action in an international or transnational arena, a new space for civil society. To name a few: Dr. Aletta Jacobs and Rosa Manus in the Netherlands; Dr. Alice Salomon, Dr. Anita Augspurg, and Lida-Gustava Heymann in Germany; Marianne Hainisch in Austria; Pauline Chaix-Chaponnière and Emilie Gourd in Switzerland; Kirsten Hesselgren in Sweden; Ishbel, Lady Aberdeen, longtime president of the International Congress on Women; and Carrie Chapman Catt of the United States. I focus here on Madame Ghénia Avril de Sainte-Croix (1855–1939) of France as a representative of such women.[45]

This intrepid activist inserted herself into France's civil society in the 1890s, in an era when women were still legally barred from exercising the right to the so-called universal but conspicuously restricted to "manhood" suffrage of the French republics. Madame Avril de Sainte-Croix succeeded in participating in civil society without the vote. She exemplifies what women could accomplish by sheer initiative, bravado, and organizing skill during the early twentieth century, and epitomized the "particular type of individual and collective action in civil society, characterized by personal initiative, communicative competence, openness and pluralism, the ability to engage in constructive conflict and to avoid violence as well as the systematic linking of particular and universal interests."[46] As a young unmarried woman, she published short stories and wrote for the French feminist newspaper *La Fronde* as an investigative reporter, highlighting the plight of women prisoners, prostitutes, and working women. Married in 1900 (at the age of 45), the year prior to the passage of the French Association Law, she emerged as an uncrowned queen of associational and public activity.

Never one to surrender "to the age-old notion that women had no concern in public life except to wipe up the mess made by men," as her British contemporary Helena Swanwick put it, Mme Avril de Sainte-Croix intended to change things through organizational means.[47] She first served as the secretary-general of numerous organizations, including the *Conseil National des Femmes Françaises* (National Council of French Women), which she helped found, and the *Oeuvre Libératrice*, an organization she founded and financed, dedicated to saving young women from prostitution. She became a relentless organizer of international feminist congresses as well as editor of their proceedings. She traveled extensively, attending and speaking at all sorts of other congresses in London, Berlin, Geneva, Rome, Kristiania (Oslo), Bucharest, Vienna, Spain, and the United States. Active in the International Abolitionist Federation (which campaigned against government-sanctioned prostitution), she served as organizer of the French branch and attracted the attention of Josephine Butler (subsequently she became known as the Josephine Butler of France). She published many articles, not only in feminist periodicals such as *La Française*, but also in venues such as *La Grande Revue*, and in 1907, her one and only book, a history of feminism; her speeches and editorials were translated into a number of other languages. She spent the last decade (1922–32) of her long life presiding over the National Council of French Women and the Women's Section of the *Musée Social*. Her most triumphant personal moment was undoubtedly the opening of the Estates-General of Feminism, held in Paris in 1929. She also presided over two successive estates-general in 1930 and 1931, devoted respectively to the topics of women's economic activity and women and colonialism.

In the early twentieth century, Madame Avril de Sainte-Croix also served on French government high commissions, one of a very few women named to investigate the morals police, revise the laws governing marriage, challenge government-regulated prostitution, and combat what was then called "the white slave trade," and later "the traffic in women and children" for purposes of prostitution. She subsequently became an international player in this arena, within the framework provided by the International Council of Women. After 1919, when she was in her sixties, she served in official capacities at the League of Nations, representing a coalition of six international women's organizations in an attempt to end the international trafficking and to promote the use of women police agents. Thus, she participated effectively not only in helping build civil society in her own nation, but also in promoting what political scientist Valentine Moghadam calls "global civil society" through the international women's (emancipation) movement.[48] Even in the absence of the vote, an intrepid woman citizen could—and did—make her presence felt. Such women, now largely forgotten, laid the foundation on which women's NGOs (nongovernmental organizations) now stand to influence gender-related policy-making at the United Nations.

Conclusion

The history of European feminisms literally embodies the linked histories of civil society and gender justice during the past three hundred years. It encompasses the passage from the virtually total exclusion of women, through their struggle for inclusion, to their not-yet-completely welcome participation. In European countries, civil society is nowadays nominally ungendered, yet limitations are still placed on women's inclusion owing to prejudice, habit, and (occasionally) sheer bad faith, and women who have contributed enormously to the expansion of civil societies continue to be omitted from the historical record. It is high time that women be fully incorporated. "Citizens" do come in two sexes—female and male—and both sexes (and all genders, ethnicities, etc.) must be welcomed in civil society, bringing their differing perspectives, talents, and wisdom to bear on the weighty problems we face today. Despite many setbacks—and these should not be underestimated—we are still working toward the full inclusion of women's "experiences, needs, and aspirations," this time on a global scale in civil societies, national governments, and international problem-solving initiatives. Our definition of civil society should reflect these aspirations.

Notes

1. "What is Feminism?" *The Woman's Leader and the Common Cause*, 17 July 1925: 195; emphasis in the original.
2. Jeanne Deroin, "Woman's Mission in the Present and Future,"(1849) in *Women, the Family, and Freedom: The Debate in Documents, 1750–1950*, ed. Susan Groag Bell and Karen Offen vol.1 (Stanford, CA, 1983), 263. Translations are by Bell or Offen, unless otherwise indicated.
3. See, on the pre-1989 manifestations of this pent-up desire in eastern European settings, the essays in John Keane, ed., *Civil Society and the State: New European Perspectives* (London, 1988).
4. Most recently, see Jürgen Kocka, "Civil Society from a Historical Perspective," *European Review* 12, no. 1 (2004): 65–74; Huri Islamoglu, "Concept and History of Civil Society," in *International Encyclopedia of the Social and Behavioral Sciences* 3 (2001), 1891–1897; Craig Calhoun, "Civil Society/Public Sphere: History of the Concept," in *International Encyclopedia*, 1897–1903. For the earlier discussions, see Jürgen Habermas, *The Structural Transformation of the Public Sphere: An Inquiry into a Category of Bourgeois Society* (Cambridge, 1989; 1st German ed., 1962); Craig Calhoun, ed., *Habermas and the Public Sphere* (Cambridge, MA, 1992); M. Johanna Meehan, ed., *Feminists Read Habermas: Gendering the Subject of Discourse* (New York, 1995); Joan B. Landes, ed., *Feminism, the Public and the Private* (New York, 1998). For French approaches and interpretations, see: Christine Fauré, *Democracy Without Women: Feminism and the Rise of Liberal Individualism in France* (Bloomington, IN, 1991; 1st French ed., 1985); Alain Corbin et al., eds., *Femmes dans la cité, 1815–1871* (Grâne, 1997); Jean-Paul Barrière, Véronique Demars-Sion, eds., *La Femme dans la Cité* (Lille, 2003); Christiane Veauvy, ed., *Les Femmes dans l'espace public*, special issue of *Le Fil d'Ariane: Cahiers du CEME, Institute d'études européenes* (Winter 2002); Christiane Veauvy, ed., *Les Femmes dans l'espace public: Itinéraires français et italiens* (Paris, 2004); Pierre Rosenvallon, *Le modèle politique français: la société civile contre le jacobinisme de 1789 à nos jours* (Paris, 2004).

5. See Dario Castiglione and Lesley Sharpe, eds., *Shifting the Boundaries: Transformation of the Languages of Public and Private in the Eighteenth Century* (Exeter, UK, 1995).
6. Susan Moller Okin, *Women in Western Political Thought* (Princeton, NJ, 1979); Carole Pateman, *The Sexual Contract* (Stanford, CA, 1988; 1st ed., 1979); Anne Phillips, *Engendering Democracy* (University Park, PA, 1991).
7. See my review of Jean Bethke Elshtain, *Public Man, Private Woman: Women in Social and Political Thought* (Princeton, NJ, 1981), and Elshtain, ed., *The Family in Political Thought* (Amherst, MA, 1982), in *History of European Ideas* 8, no. 6 (1987): 723–725.
8. I am arguing here against the interpretation of Joan Wallach Scott, *Only Paradoxes to Offer: French Feminists and the Rights of Man* (Cambridge, MA, 1996).
9. See Hilda L. Smith and Berenice Carroll, eds., *Women's Political and Social Thought: An Anthology* (Bloomington, IN, 2000).
10. Siep Stuurman, *François Poulain de la Barre and the Invention of Modern Equality* (Cambridge, MA, 2004); Karen Offen, "How (and Why) the Analogy of Marriage with Slavery Provided the Springboard for Women's Rights Demands in France, 1640–1848," in *Women's Rights and Transatlantic Antislavery in the Era of Emancipation*, ed. Kathryn Kish Sklar and James Brewer Stewart (New Haven, CT, 2007).
11. See Sarah Hanley, "Social Sites of Political Practice in France: Lawsuits, Civil Rights, and the Separation of Powers in Domestic and State Government, 1500–1800," *American Historical Review* 102, no. 1 (1997): 27–52; Hanley, "'The Jurisprudence of the Arrêts': Marital Union, Civil Society, and State Formation in France, 1550–1650," *Law and History Review* 21, no. 1 (2003): 1–40.
12. See Evelyne Pisier and Eleni Varikas, "De l'invisibilité du genre dans la théorie politique: Le Débat Locke/Astell," in *Quand les femmes s'en mêlent: Genre et pouvoir*, ed. Christine Bard et al. (Paris, 2004), 64–79.
13. The authoritative translation of this treatise appears in the appendix to Felicia Gordon and Philip N. Furbank, *Marie Madeleine Jodin, 1741–1790: Actress, Philosophe and Feminist* (Aldershot, UK, 2001), 176–206; the quote is on p. 176.
14. Karen Offen, *European Feminisms, 1700–1950: A Political History* (Stanford, CA, 2000). For many of the supporting documents, see also Bell and Offen, *Women, the Family, and Freedom*.
15. Véronique Borgeat-Pignat, "Les droits politiques des femmes durant l'Helvétique: le parti d'en rire," in *Structures sociales et économiques: Histoire des femmes*, ed. Christian Simon, *Dossier Helvétique/Dossier Helvetik* 2 (Basel, 1997), 199–209.
16. See Offen, *European Feminisms*, 72.
17. See ibid., chapter 5; Karen Offen, "'Woman Has to Set her Stamp on Science, Philosophy, Justice, and Politics:' A Look at Gender Politics in the 'Knowledge Wars' of the European Past," in *Geschlecht und Wissen/Genre et Savoir/Gender and Knowledge*, ed. Catherine Bosshart-Pfluger et al. (Zurich, 2004), 379–393. For an edifying example, see Patricia Mazón, *Gender and the Modern Research University: The Admission of Women to German Higher Education, 1865–1914* (Stanford, CA, 2003).
18. The line is drawn differently, depending on which political theorist one reads. For Habermas, it falls between government/the state and what he refers to as "*Öffentlichkeit.*" Thus, paradoxically, this "public sphere" seems to constitute a particular area of communication within civil society, yet both are situated in the domain of the "private." In this configuration, the family and women virtually disappear from sight. By contrast, the French Jacobins and others adopting the Rousseauean schema drew the line at the door of the household; everything else outside it was considered "public"—and "public" was designated as men's territory.
19. See Nancy Bermeo and Philip Nord, eds., *Civil Society before Democracy: Lessons from Nineteenth-Century Europe* (Lanham, MD, 2000). Like many other commentators, Nord situates civil society between the family and its property, on the one hand, and government and public administration on the other; see his introduction to ibid., xiv.

20. According to the 1850 "Act for Shortening the Language Used in Acts of Parliament" (13 & 14 Vic., c. 21), "in all Acts words importing the masculine gender shall be deemed and taken to include females unless the contrary ... is expressly provided." (*Hansard's Parliamentary Debates*, 3rd series 113, no. 21). See also Albie Sachs and Joan Hoff Wilson, *Sexism and the Law: A Study of Male Beliefs and Legal Bias in Britain and the United States* (New York, 1986), especially chapter 1.
21. See Karen Offen, "Women, Citizenship, and Suffrage with a French Twist, 1789–1993," in *Suffrage and Beyond: International Feminist Perspectives*, ed. Caroline Daley and Melanie Nolan (Auckland, 1994), 151–169. For the pre-1848 situation see: Anne Verjus, *Le cens de la famille: Les femmes et le vote, 1789–1848* (Paris, 2002).
22. Two recent works on early nineteenth-century feminist networks emphasize the importance of new developments in communications and transportation in facilitating feminist mobilization across national boundaries: Margaret H. McFadden, *Golden Cables of Sympathy: The Transatlantic Sources of Nineteenth-Century Feminism* (Lexington, KY, 1999); Bonnie S. Anderson, *Joyous Greetings: The First International Women's Movement, 1830–1860* (New York, 2000).
23. Stuurman, *François Poulain de la Barre*.
24. See Karen Offen, "Was Mary Wollstonecraft a Feminist? A Contextual Re-reading of *A Vindication of the Rights of Woman*, 1792–1992," in *Quilting a New Canon: Stitching Women's Words*, ed. Uma Parameswaran (Toronto, 1996), 3–24.
25. Karen Offen, "Reclaiming the European Enlightenment for Feminism: Or, Prologomena to any Future History of Eighteenth-Century Europe," in *Perspectives on Feminist Thought in European History: From the Middle Ages to the Present*, ed. Tjitske Akkerman and Siep Stuurman (London, 1998), 85–103.
26. Sheilagh Ogilvie, "How Does Social Capital Affect Women? Guilds and Communities in Early Modern Germany," *American Historical Review* 109, no. 2 (2004): 325–359.
27. See the conflicting perspectives of Janet Burke and Margaret Jacob, "French Freemasonry, Women, and Feminist Scholarship," *Journal of Modern History* 68, no. 3 (1996): 513–549; and James Smith Allen, "Sisters of Another Sort: Freemason Women in Modern France, 1725–1940," *Journal of Modern History* 75, no. 4 (2003): 783–835.
28. Marie-Anne de Roumier, as quoted in Offen, *European Feminisms*, 48.
29. *Requête des dames à l'Assemblée Nationale* (1789), reprinted in *Les Femmes dans la Révolution française, 1789–1794*, présentés par Albert Soboul 1 (Paris, 1982), unpaginated.
30. On the political use of "public utility," see Offen, *European Feminisms*, chap. 3.
31. See Joan B. Landes, *Women and the Public Sphere in the Age of the French Revolution* (Ithaca, NY, 1988).
32. Mme Blandine Demoulin, in Offen, *European Feminisms*, 62.
33. Ibid., 63.
34. Such exclusion has since been partially rectified by the studies of Dominique Godineau, *The Women of Paris and Their French Revolution* (Berkeley, CA, 1998; 1st French ed.,1989); Suzanne Desan, *The Family on Trial in Revolutionary France* (Berkeley, CA, 2004); on the upsurge in women writers during the later eighteenth century: Carla Hesse, *The Other Enlightenment: How French Women Became Modern* (Princeton, NJ, 2001).
35. For examples: Elke Harten and Hans-Christian Harten, *Femmes, Culture et Revolution* (Paris, 1989; 1st German ed., 1988). It should be pointed out here that the pithy term *republican mother*, introduced by Linda K. Kerber in the 1970s and so frequently employed by subsequent historians, was rarely, if ever, used as such during the revolutionary and postrevolutionary eras. See her subsequent reflections on this point in Linda K. Kerber, *Toward an Intellectual History of Women* (Chapel Hill, NC, 1997), 15–17.

Kerber deserves full credit, however, for pointing out the deliberately political and public character of this mother-educator role.
36. Concerning women's extensive participation in the "public sphere," "civil society," or the "social" in France prior to acquiring formal political rights, see Corbin, *Femmes dans la cité;* Veauvy, *Femmes.* For a broad survey of women's participation in nation-building efforts, see especially Ida Blom et al., eds., *Gendered Nations: Nationalisms and Gender Order in the Long Nineteenth Century* (Oxford, 2000). On the German women's press, see Ulla Wischermann, *Frauenbewegungen und Öffentlichkeiten um 1900* (Königstein/Taunus, 2003); for their early associational activities, see Dirk Alexander Reder, *Frauenbewegung und Nation: Patriotische Frauenvereine in Deutschland im frühen 19. Jahrhundert (1813–1830)* (Cologne, 1998); and the various publications of Karen Hagemann, especially "Female Patriots: Women, War and the Nation in the Period of the Prussian-German Anti-Napoleonic Wars," *Gender & History* 16, no. 3 (2004): 396–424. For the women's press in the Netherlands, see Lotte Jensen, *"Bij uitsluiting voor de vrouwelijke sekse geschikt": Vrouwentijdschriften en journalistes in Nederland in de achttiende en negentiende eeuw* (Hilversum, 2001).
37. See Fauré, *Democracy Without Women;* Yolande Cohen and Françoise Thébaud, *Féminisme et identités nationales: Les processus d'intégration des femmes au politique* (Lyon, 1998); Ute Gerhard, ed., *Feminismus und Demokratie: Europäische Frauenbewegungen der 1920er Jahre* (Königstein/Taunus, 2001); Sylvia Paletschek and Bianka Pietrow-Ennker, eds., *Women's Emancipation Movements in Nineteenth-Century Europe* (Stanford, CA, 2004).
38. Louise Otto, "Für Alle" (1849), trans. S. L. Cocalis and G. M. Geiger, in *The Defiant Muse: German Feminist Poems from the Middle Ages to the Present,* ed. Susan L. Cocalis (New York, 1986), 57.
39. See Gay L. Gullickson, *Unruly Women of Paris: Images of the Commune* (Ithaca, NY, 1996); Carolyn J. Eichner, *Surmounting the Barricades: Women in the Paris Commune* (Bloomington, IN, 2004).
40. On the so-called science of woman, see Sylvana Tomaselli, "Reflections on the History of the Science of Woman," in *A Question of Identity: Women, Science & Literature,* ed. Marina Benjamin (New Brunswick, NJ, 1993); Ludmilla Jordanova, *Sexual Visions: Images of Gender in Science and Medicine between the Eighteenth and Twentieth Centuries* (Madison, WI, 1989); Londa Schiebinger, *Nature's Body: Gender in the Making of Modern Science* (New Brunswick, NJ, 2nd ed., 2004; 1st ed., 1993); Geneviève Fraisse, *Reason's Muse: Sexual Difference and the Birth of Democracy* (Chicago, 1994; 1st French ed., 1989). For the later nineteenth century, see Mary Lynn Stewart, *For Health and Beauty: Physical Culture for Frenchwomen 1880s–1930s* (Baltimore, 2001).
41. See Offen, *European Feminisms.*
42. See Karen Offen, "Depopulation, Nationalism, and Feminism in Fin-de-Siècle France," *The American Historical Review* 89, no. 3 (1984): 648–676; Offen, "Body Politics: Women, Work, and the Politics of Motherhood in France, 1920–1950," in *Maternity and Gender Policies: Women and the Rise of the European Welfare States, 1880s–1950s,* ed. Gisela Bock and Pat Thane (London, 1991), 138–159. Anne Cova, *Maternité et droits des femmes en France (XIXe – XXe siècles)* (Paris, 1997).
43. Alfred, Lord Tennyson, *The Princess, a Medley* (London, 1847); Canto II, lines 155–61.
44. Letter from Aletta Jacobs to Carrie Chapman Catt, 23 October 1928 in *Politics and Friendship: Letters from the International Woman Suffrage Alliance, 1902–1942,* ed. Mineke Bosch and Annemarie Kloosterman (Columbus, OH, 1990), 204.
45. Karen Offen, "'La plus grande féministe de France': Mais qui est donc Madame Avril de Sainte-Croix?" *Bulletin de l'Archives du Feminisme* 9 (2005): 46–54; and Offen, "Madame Ghénia Avril de Sainte-Croix, the Josephine Butler of France," in *Women's History Review* (London), 17, no. 2 (April 2008): 239–255.

46. From the prospectus for the conference on "Civil Society and Gender Justice: Historical and Comparative Perspectives," Berlin, 9–11 July 2004, Wissenschaftszentrum Berlin für Sozialforschung (WZB).
47. Helena Swanick, *I Have Been Young* (London, 1935), 316.
48. Valentine M. Moghadam, "Engendering Citizenship, Feminizing Civil Society: The Case of the Middle East and North Africa," *Women and Politics* 25, no. 1–2 (2003): 63–87, 66.

CIVIL SOCIETY AND THE FAMILY

Chapter 6

THE FAMILY—A CORE INSTITUTION OF CIVIL SOCIETY
A PERSPECTIVE ON THE MIDDLE CLASSES IN IMPERIAL GERMANY

Gunilla Budde

Was early civil society a male project? In our search for the opportunities for and obstacles to female participation in nineteenth-century civil society, is it the obstacles that dominate? That, at least, is what most research on the modish topic of "civil society," whose spectacular renaissance has also included a number of historical studies, would seem to suggest. "Civil society," sociologist Keith Tester notes concisely, "is about what happens when we leave our family and go about our own lives."[1] Even if few of the earlier and current theorists of civil society would agree with such a broad description, most would appear to concur with Tester on at least one point: all attempts to define the term, and as is the case with such elusive concepts, all efforts to pinpoint precisely what civil society is *not*, share a broad consensus that it must be distinguished from the "private sphere." "In most cases," historian Jürgen Kocka concludes, "civil society is defined in distinction to the state, and often in distinction to the economy, but always in opposition to the private sphere."[2]

For the women of nineteenth-century Germany, this definition had dire consequences: they were written out of early civil society as historical agents. The more they were ideologically enclosed in the private sphere of the family from the eighteenth century on, the more clearly they were excluded from the public sphere of civil society. According to this construct, they appeared as actors in civil society only individually in the few organizations open to them under the restrictive law on associations, and later as protagonists of the women's movement in Imperial Germany.[3]

The dichotomy between "private" and "public," which feminist historians have been challenging for some time now and have refuted empirically, appears set for revival in the concept of a civil society strictly separate from the "private sphere."[4] Political scientist Nancy Fraser has objected quite plausibly to the fact that even present-day theorists of civil society risk are taking up a "rhetoric of the private" that was "used in the past to limit the universe of legitimate public debate."[5] In her view, a tenable concept of the public sphere must promote not the exclusion but the inclusion of such interests and problems that a middle-class "masculinist" ideology labels "private."[6]

In order to avoid further fencing off these "separate spheres," I will not focus here on the activities of the women's associations and women's movement, which have already been studied in detail, and which, above all in the Wilhelmine period, impressively demonstrated the self-referential dynamics of the program of civil society by taking its promise of equality at its word. Instead, this chapter will offer reflections on the private side of civil society and the public side of the family. I will begin with an overview of the gender concepts of early civil society that is intended to show that the gender order was by no means a marginal point on the discourse agenda of nineteenth-century civil society, but was instead a kind of liminal area, one that was undergoing constant redefinition and renegotiation. I will then turn my attention to the family and the women who operated within it, arguing that, because of women's function as transmitters of the values and choreographers of the practices of civil society, the family, too, must be considered part of it.

If I focus here solely on middle-class women and families, I do so mainly because of the prominent role that this social formation played as a pillar of eighteenth- and nineteenth-century civil society in Germany. Even if civil society and the behavior associated with it are not fundamentally tied to class—this may be one of the advantages over the German term *bürgerliche Gesellschaft*, which can mean both civil society and middle-class society—it remains true, particularly in a historical retrospective, that families of the educated and propertied bourgeoisie were especially predisposed by wealth, values, and opportunities for leisure to participate in the project of civil society.[7] This article will concentrate on the Wilhelmine period, which, in contrast to the decades that preceded it, many historians believe was characterized by diminishing civility, not least with reference to tendencies towards "social militarization" and a nationalism permeated by racism. As to female actors, I would like examine the extent to which middle-class women in practice represented and passed on values that equipped people to participate in civil society.

The Gender Concepts of Civil Society Discourses

From the eighteenth century on, it was commonly argued that men and women, according to their "natural sex-specific characters," which were conceived as polar but complementary, should operate in different spheres of action and influence, supplementing one another and living in harmonious co-existence. Woman was considered "by nature" to be emotional, passive, and gentle, while man was rationally oriented, active, and volatile. The acceptance of individual plurality and the promotion of functional differentiation belonged to the constitutive and new characteristics of not just ideal but also actually existing civil society, which consciously sought to leave behind the tightly-laced compactness of ancien régime corporative groups.[8]

But with the polarized gender order, society did not merely take on "inequalities"; at the same time it also rooted them in a system of hierarchies. How did the idea of female subordination fit in with civil society's program of universal equality of opportunity and personal development regardless of birth, and thus also of sex? Was the long-denied emancipation of women, which began late and hesitantly and remains incomplete even today, inherent in the central principles of civil society, or did patterns of inequality not adhere to its very foundations? The first assumption seems unlikely in light of the growth rather than diminution of inequalities and their institutionalization in the social, legal, and political arenas towards the end of the nineteenth century, at a time when they could no longer be explained away as mere remnants of the old estate system and tradition. Thus we must sadly accept the second.

This inconsistency also exercised the minds of the pioneers and key thinkers of the affirmative program of civil society, who zealously sought to legitimize the discrepancy. A spate of theological, philosophical, pedagogical, and scientific publications, penned with the sole purpose of supporting and passing on the dualist model of gender relations, flooded the public sphere.[9] Friedrich Herder's *Adrastea* of 1803 provided a pattern of explanation that was apparently adopted by many other authors. According to this work, in which two Freemasons explain to a fictitious female interlocutor why she was refused membership in a lodge, women had no need to distinguish between purely human and civic duties, since as "educators of humanity" they "constantly live in the paradise of domestic society." Man, in contrast, must shoulder the "burdens of civic life" for himself and his family. He must stand his ground in civil society—in public space—while woman could develop in private, "purely human" space. As a consequence, in order to perfect themselves, women had no need of sociability, which seeks to overcome the boundaries of civil society and aspires to the "purely human."[10]

Apparently, these thinkers were reacting not just to the tensions in the intellectual edifice, which they recognized themselves, but also to the gender order that was changing everywhere, and whose real mobility was in need of restriction through domestication. Those voices calling not for justifications of inequality but for its abolition were fainter. Instead, most authors assisted vigorously in bringing "this order safely into civil society and defending it against the dynamic of modern thought and social change."[11] Anthropology, the science of humanity developed since the late Enlightenment, in particular, served as a much-tapped source of argumentation. Irresistibly schematic and thus well suited to the need for simplified notions of order, the gender order became a basic mental model for, above all, bourgeois self-representation, albeit one that radiated far and beyond the boundaries of class.

The spheres assigned to male and female citizens were to correspond to the "natural gender-specific characters" attributed to men and women. According to this model, the sphere of the family, which was constructed as private, was a female sphere, while men moved in the realm of professional, political, and cultural influence, the public sphere of civil society. The key bourgeois thinkers of the eighteenth and nineteenth centuries still took a positive view of the private here, which they celebrated, as it were, as an achievement of civil society. They regarded the private and the family as the very symbolic essence of civil society, not just as a space of emotions and intimacy, far removed from all the competition, profit motive, and demands of a public sphere defined by intellect and reason. It was also a realm outside the enforced infantilization of the authoritarian state, a sphere in which one could find, be, and invent oneself. The necessity for clubs and associations was justified not least in terms of men's need to create their own terrain, which offered them what the family provided to women.

Nevertheless, despite the gender-specific coloring of these spheres, in social practice their margins proved historically highly variable, permeable, and fluid. Even if it is easy enough to locate spheres in history in which either men or women set the tone, these did not exist as free-floating, autonomous male or female islands, but rather were closely linked, interrelated, and thus subject to constant reconstruction by interaction, cooperation, and conflict. Gender and gender difference as products of discursive construction were continually being (re)created in various contexts and in diverse ways with differing consequences. A specifically bourgeois gender order emerged in interplay with normative models and subjective experience. For nineteenth-century middle-class women, too, the private was not a fixed entity, nor was it located outside the realm of engagement in civil society. It was these women who frequently opened it to the outside and decided when their own actions were private and when public.

Present-day theorists of civil society, who treat it as rather stable by definition, often misunderstand this historically observable crossing of the borders between the public and private spheres. By noting a "privatization" of the family in the nineteenth century, in which it increasingly closed itself off from the public sphere, they push the family to the margins of civil society. Looking at social practice instead gives us the opportunity to bring the family back into civil society—and, indeed, to understand it as one if its core institutions.

Women as Transmitters of Civil Society Values

As I have already suggested, this viewpoint goes against the mainstream of thinking on civil societies, according to which the family belongs at best to the "marginal areas of civil society organizations."[12] While the enlightened German philosopher Georg Friedrich Wilhelm Hegel still regarded the "modern family," which was conceptualized as private, as an institution situated outside the civil society that provided the preconditions for it, philosopher Jürgen Habermas constructed it as an explicit countersphere to the state, the economy, and the public sphere.[13] The political scientists Jean Cohen and Andrew Arato are among the few scholars who believe that the family should be integrated into civil society as a "core component."[14] As an institution that brings individuals together on a voluntary basis and with common intent, is based on mutual solidarity and collective identity, and tempers egotism with empathy, they regard the family as a key institution, "the voluntary association par excellence."[15]

This interpretation, while not yet well established in the current discussion on civil society, seems to correspond quite well to the self-understanding of many German middle-class women in the late nineteenth century. If we are to believe their numerous written accounts, they by no means saw themselves as marginal figures in the project of civil society. Confirmed by contemporary discourses in which the upbringing of future male and female citizens became an increasingly important theme, they were well aware of their significance for the socialization of the coming generation. Contemporary educators nourished mothers' confidence in their own childrearing competence.[16] The fact that this task was viewed not as a private female affair but rather as acting in the "public interest" is also confirmed by the diary entries of Helene Eyck, wife of a Berlin merchant and mother of six, in which she reported her conversations with neighbors every evening: "We spoke about just everything, and it goes without saying that children and childrearing did not go unmentioned."[17]

The development of the family into a nuclear family consisting only of parents and children limited the possibilities for an exchange of information on childrearing within the family on the one hand, while on the other also increasing the need to consult experts outside the family circle. The inexhaustible and always available female expertise that the extended family could have offered now had to be sought elsewhere. Apart from informal conversations, the flood of pedagogical handbooks, the wealth of letters to the editors of family magazines, and the extensive correspondences beyond the family circle show that many women of the middle classes chose this route. "Books do so differ," nineteenth-century English novelist Elizabeth Gaskell lamented on behalf of many other women facing widely varying published opinion on contemporary childrearing.[18] By sharing their experiences, often publicly, middle-class mothers contributed significantly to advancing childrearing and family life as topics on the civil society agenda. They by no means appeared solely as passive recipients of ideas, but decisively helped shape the discourse. Through this form of publicizing matters labeled private, they firmly refuted the notion that the "modern" family disappeared from the public sphere as it became privatized.

Women assumed a key position not just in shaping pedagogical discourses on educational theory, but also in practice. It was their job not least to teach their children the values that would equip them to take their proper places in civil society. Helene Eyck, who kept meticulous records on the development of her six daughters and sons between 1876 and 1898, was not unique in her sense of responsibility. "May I succeed, together with my beloved husband, in raising our children to be the sort of people I would so like them to become ... not child prodigies, but simply *useful members of human society*," was how she expressed her educational maxim.[19] She regarded it as her foremost task to make the family a "peaceful place" so that her children might "carry forth the good seed, plant it, and produce good seedlings again."[20] Even if the vocabulary of this mother of six did not include the term *civil society*, as it was not a current phrase of the late nineteenth century, her goals in childrearing, along with those expressed by many of her contemporaries, point to notions that we would generally include in the program of civil society.

Helene Eyck seems to have been very certain of which values she wished to convey to her children as they moved along the path to life as good members of the middle class. Apart from raising them to have a "straightforward, truth-loving character," her pedagogical records emphasize three aspects of development that she was eager to foster.[21] First, she was anxious to awaken, preserve, and nourish her children's curiosity through extensive conversations, conducted in an atmosphere of trust. She never failed to be charmed by the "innocent questions" of her youngest daughter "about the great force that moves the world," and she noted with satisfaction her second son's "lovely thirst for knowledge."[22] "She will never hear anything she does not understand without inquiring into its meaning," she praised another daughter.[23] "Since," she continued, "it is a pleasure to listen to her and she chatters so prettily, one sometimes turns a blind eye to something that might appear a trifle naughty, and yet without indulging her I can manage her quite well, for she can reconcile herself to objections that her understanding accepts."[24] She also met the occasional obstinacy of her second oldest child with consistent patience, since "he always reaches better conclusions on his own, once one takes the time to lead him to the proper path."[25] A thirst for knowledge and interest in the world seemed to her positive traits worth encouraging, as she frequently stressed: "I believe, however, that it is a great good fortune when children ask many questions, and an even greater one when they receive precise answers, which are as close to the truth as possible."[26] Education through conviction was the credo of this middle-class woman.

Whenever her children shone in social exchange outside their own home, Eyck felt herself confirmed in her choice of educational philosophy. She noted with satisfaction her offspring's "talent for charming and pleasing the people around them."[27] What was practiced and negotiated face-to-face at home now had the chance to prove itself in the public eye. After the confirmation of one of her sons, she wrote, "I hope that he will always remember this ceremony and the subsequent celebration at our house as a day on which he was the center and occasion of a large party, in which he, his parents and siblings were frequently celebrated and honored."[28] She appreciated it not just when her children displayed their civil conduct in "nice manners" and "good behavior," but also when they gave evidence of wit, irony, and the capacity for critical thinking.[29] "She [one of her daughters] is not very amiable at the moment, particularly in the company of others, but her observations were acute and she later shared her suspicions and judgments," she commented, quite sympathetically, on a phase her pubescent daughter was going through.[30] Later she wrote enthusiastically of the girl's younger sister: "She can be very cheerful and exuberant, and knows how to respond to a joke!"[31] This Wilhelmine middle-class mother also regarded the ability to "speak in one's own voice," which Nancy Fraser has called the basis of participation in civil society, to be a worthwhile objective of childrearing.[32] The capacity to work out conflicts and tolerate compromise was part of this. Despite reigning contemporary notions of gender, she nurtured communicative traits that fostered the willingness and ability to debate and appreciated good listening on the part of both her sons and daughters.

Eyck never doubted that her children, regardless of sex, should learn independence from an early age. Even if she was constantly compelled to reduce her ambitions for her offspring's achievements, she never gave up the hope "of making capable, independent people of them."[33] It is striking how often she emphasizes the value of independence among the educational goals she set herself. Placing her children in a position from an early age to assume responsibility for their thinking and actions appeared to her the very quintessence of successful childrearing. Moreover, although she herself had never prepared for an occupation, she explicitly wished her daughters to have this opportunity for autonomy. "For it is my wish and my will," she wrote, "that they receive enough training in some field that they might stand on their own two feet and, if necessary, make their way in life!"[34] This openness clearly set Helene Eyck apart from most of her middle-class contemporaries, both male and female. Numerous autobiographical texts, especially from members of the early women's movement, reveal mother-daughter conflicts fought out behind the doors of middle-class houses. While many late nineteenth-century daughters met with the approval of their fathers, and sometimes even with support for their "unwomanly" ambitions for autonomy, middle-class mothers not infrequently threw a spanner in the works of emancipation. But this Berlin merchant's wife was highly practical, and she understood that vocational training would protect her daughters in case they were not able to fulfill their "true" destiny as wives and mothers. Yet by couching her ambitions for her daughter in conditional terms, she avoided challenging contemporary gender norms head-on.

Such debates demonstrate the extent to which the idea of civil society could itself become a medium of self- and other-critique, thus creating the preconditions for reform and change. This self-referential dynamic, mirrored here in the educational process that took place between mothers and daughters, was also reflected in the tensions and indeed paradoxes that were and remain peculiar to civil society. Inclusion and exclusion also determined models of the self and others, and feelings about the self and others such as they existed in the middle-class family.

Helene Eyck also believed that it was very much her duty to foster her children's emotional as well as cognitive abilities and individuality. The role of emotions belongs to the ingredients in civil society that have received little attention up until now. To be sure, such values as "tolerance" and an "orientation towards the common good" have been emphasized as fundamental to a "culture of civility," without however accentuating the emotional components of such a habitus.[35] Sociologist Anthony Giddens has suggested speculativelybut convincingly that "individuals who are at home with their own emotions, and able to sympathize with those of others, are likely to be more effective and engaged citizens than those who lack such qualities."[36] The enlightened Scottish philosopher and historian Adam Ferguson put it more directly: "Joined to the power and deliberation," he emphasized, "our sensibility" constitutes "the basis of a moral nature."[37] Helene Eyck would have agreed with them.

Thus she generally took a benevolent view of the individual characteristics of her six sons and daughters, and encouraged them to appreciate these specific traits as lovable personal advantages. In so doing, she sought to bolster the self-confidence and self-esteem of each child, while also teaching them to accept and appreciate their individuality and differences as siblings. She thus consciously promoted acceptance of "the Other" and the acknowledgment of plurality.

In Eyck's opinion, it was essential for interaction both within and outside the family that autonomy and the self-confidence it produced did not come at the cost of others, and that her children's excessive willfulness be tempered by the readiness and capacity to empathize with others. She observed with pride her oldest daughter's "extraordinary kindness towards her fellow men," in whom she showed a "lively interest."[38] She was no less pleased with her youngest, whose "caring nature and friendliness towards everyone" never failed to impress her.[39] This capacity for empathy and cooperation not only served to cement solidarity within the familybut was also intended to assist in making and cultivating contacts outside it. From their earliest childhood, Eyck sought to convey to her offspring an understanding of other people and a willingness to approach them. "Today," she wrote of her eldest son, "he pleased me greatly and moved me deeply with his gentle heart, which he revealed to me. The children told me of a poor family of whose fate they had learned, and Hans did so with tears in his eyes he could not suppress! He asked me to do something for these people, which I gladly promised him."[40]

But she distinguished carefully between those who deserved her children's sympathy and those whom she wished them to treat as equals, and with whom they were permitted to play, celebrate, and communicate. Indeed, the family's social contacts were limited to rigidly selected circles. While the children were expected to take an interest in "inferiors" and their problems, there was never any question of their sharing any additional interests with these classes of people. On the contrary, Eyck feared that her sons and daughters might fall in with "the wrong circles" at times when the family budget became tight.[41] In making this sharp distinction, Eyck's childrearing practice reflected the paradoxes that characterize the social reality of civil society more generally. On the one hand, she conveyed values that equipped them for life in civil society and helped shape their ideals, while on the other she reinforced notions that ran contrary to an egalitarian concept of civil society. In Wilhelmine Germany, trust and empathy, as emotional and ethical attitudes essential for the functioning of civil society, were still strongly colored and graded by class.[42]

Sociability as Civil Society Practice

What began with guest lists for children's birthday parties continued with the choice of whom to invite to weightier social occasions. Here, too, the supposedly closed space of the family opened itself for those of like mind and status, and did so ever more rapidly and ambitiously during the Wilhelmine period. Many autobiographical documents report on the almost constant stream of visitors to middle-class households, which left little room for the intimate privacy of the nuclear family. Instead, they were caught up in a perpetual round of sociability, which repeatedly brought the husband's "public life" home to the family dinner table in the form of guest lists, seating arrangements, and convivial rituals. Elisabeth Budde, the wife of a district administrator in Wilhelmine Germany, confirmed in her unpublished memoirs the close interconnections between private and public when she described social invitations to private homes as quite suitable contexts for promoting civil society agendas: "On our way home my husband said to me, 'Now I know why we had to dine there. The state subsidy for a doctor for Spiekeroog [an island off the coast of Germany in the North Sea] is a sure thing.' He had sat next to the relevant official from the ministry and described to him the hardship of the population of the island, who could not reach help if they fell ill in winter."[43] Career advancement also affected middle-class men and women equally. The young district administrator learned of his coming promotion from the wife of his superior, who offered a discreet hint. "Give my best to your wife, and tell her she need not wash curtains anymore!"[44]

The choreography of these social events, which rendered the already porous privacy of the family increasingly permeable, was designed and directed mainly by middle-class women. It was their communicative and organizational abilities that helped ease husbands' acceptance as members of civil society.[45] As many memoirs by civil servants attest, rapid career advancement not infrequently depended upon the candidate's possession of a wife who could master the necessary social duties with aplomb. This applied not just to more or less private gatherings, but also to participation in the club and associational life that flourished in the nineteenth century.

The increasing activities of middle-class women in imperial Germany are evidence of the role of sociability in building networks that served not just to advance their husbands' careers and enhance the social prestige of the whole family. Many used "semi-official female sociability," as one wife of a provincial administrator called it, to initiate their own associations, which were dedicated to cultural or more commonly to charitable ends.[46] Some local activists in German middle-class women's associations like Helene Weber and Ida Baumgartner, sisters who were both married to national-liberal-minded civil servants, clearly quite successfully reconciled and linked social duties, philanthropic commitments, and political activities as well.[47] It goes without saying that their familial networks played a role here. After signing the famous petition to the Prussian parliament on the improvement of training for female teachers in 1887, penned by Helene Lange, the chairwoman of the *Allgemeine Deutsche*

Lehrerinnenverband (the professional organization of female teachers), Helene Weber, who lived at this time in Berlin because her spouse was a member of the Prussian House of Deputies, tried to enlist her sister's aid in a letter: "By the way, the petition will probably also go to the Reichstag and signatures from elsewhere would be most welcome then."[48] The sisters' correspondence shows that the two reinforced each other in their activities more generally. They exchanged information, recommended edifying books for the other to read, provided contacts, and reassured each other of their standpoints.[49]

The two sisters, whose social engagement began while they were wives and mothers and intensified in widowhood, were by no means concerned solely with the sort of "female matters" in which middle-class men were not, or were no longer, interested—a description that British historians Leonore Davidoff and Catherine Hall have applied to women's engagement in civil society.[50] "This time it is the dock workers' strike that has hindered me," wrote Ida Baumgartner, apologizing for a delayed letter to her sister. A short time before, she had strongly supported a female garment workers' strike in Berlinand successfully encouraged her sister to do so as well. This support included soliciting donations or, as in the case of Ida Baumgartner, giving the proceeds from her little book *Soziale Bilder* to the families of the striking workers.[51]

Like many of their middle-class female contemporaries, the two women used the emotional monopoly accorded them in order to engage actively in civil society. "For charity many of them are by nature admirably fitted," noted the liberal British philosophers John Stuart Mill and Harriet Taylor Mill in *The Subjection of Women*.[52] In this field, they argued, "women generally excel men" with their "insight into present fact, and especially into the minds and feelings of those with whom they are in immediate contact."[53]

While the distinction between public and private was used in contemporary discourse to restrict and exclude women and stamp their issues and communication forms and forums as private and therefore irrelevant, the female-run relief associations, which generally operated on the municipal level, deployed the leitmotif of "organized motherhood" (*Mütterlichkeit*) in order to subvert this separation without fundamentally challenging it. In the late nineteenth century, as increasing numbers of middle-class women all over Europe were dedicating themselves to philanthropic work, they could expect a positive response to these public activities. After all, they were acting on the special capacity for empathy attributed to them, which seemed to predestine them for the side of civil society devoted to the general well-being. "Everywhere we find that lively, benevolent endeavor from one person to another, that entire widely ramified activity we generally subsume under the name of social assistance; it is there, however valuable and important the collaboration of man may be, that we find the royal domain of the woman of the future," was how Helene Lange, doyenne of the German middle-class women's movement, and in 1894 co-founder and first chairwomen of the *Bund Deutscher Frauenvereine*, the umbrella organization of German middle-class women's associations, described and underlined this female sphere of action.[54]

Middle-class women adopted the call for "emotional openness" that underlay the concept not least in order to demand and enforce their own right of participation, in a sense recasting male projects as female ones. Step by step they expanded their activities in the political realm as well. Plenty of resources were at their disposal. Women's competence in making and cultivating contacts, communicating, and cooperating—in short, in the art of "networking"—rested on years of "private" practice in what Helene Lange called "maternal care in public life."[55] Here, too, the ambivalences of action in civil society could become quite evident. It was precisely the many charitable societies and associations, most of whose members were women, that not infrequently exhibited dogmatic as well as civil traits. The power to define "civility," which these women claimed for themselves, could quickly undermine the idea of tolerance.

Domestic servants working in middle-class households were not the only people to experience this firsthand. In general, members of the middle classes attributed a lack of civility to their social inferiors, which could be compensated for by proper training. Elisabeth Budde recalled the wife of a "colleague" of her spouse, whose missionary zeal revealed this "dark side" of civil society in her memoirs: "[She] did a good deal of work in poor relief. On her bicycle she traversed the working class district of Wilhelmshaven, and could become quite energetic when she noticed that one of the housewives was not at her post and took poor care of her husband. It was said that her bicycle bell could drive any gossiping wife from the street back to her soup pot."[56] Thus on the one hand, for both male and female actors, civil society form corresponded fully to civil society content. On the other, civil society values and ideals, which the middle-class women discussed here represented as mothers or as maternal purveyors of charity, could cancel themselves out if they were presented and transmitted as absolute.

Conclusion

The options for female actors to participate in civil society were varied and ambiguous. As the conveyors of civil society's values they could equip others for civil society but also contributed to the persistence of its tensions and ambivalences. The examples presented here allow us to substantiate the familiar thesis that engagement in civil society helped open paths for middle-class women beyond the family, and thus gradually expanded the radius of female activity. At the same time, these paths by no means took women away from the family. Rather, they used familial networks to bolster and promote their charitable and political activities. In so doing, they testified to the inextricable links between the "public" and "private" spheres—in defiance of contemporary discourses and still prevalent notions that continue to invoke their separation.

The concepts briefly outlined here are intended to show that historical civil society by no means existed solely outside the family, or largely without active female participation. If one generally declares the family to be private and thus excludes it from civil society, one runs the risk of falling back into a polarization between public and private, which the broadened perspective of historical studies has already superseded. On the one hand, the middle-class family offered protection from state interventions as well as providing nurture, security, and intimacy. The fact that families can fulfill these function marks the civility of a society, setting it apart from societies shaped by dictatorship, with their deliberate penetration and thus abolition of the private.

On the other hand, the approach to civil society I have presented here, with its focus on the logic of action, prevents us from defining spaces and spheres as more or less "nonpublic" and thus losing sight of their roles and practices in civil society. Just as civil society itself has no spatial restrictions, action in civil society knows no boundary between private and public spheres. Like the hierarchically structured gender order, the nuclear family wholly isolated from the public sphere is a historical construct that bears little resemblance to the social reality of Wilhelmine Germany. The restriction of female actors to the "narrow circle" that many contemporary political authors wanted, and many historians today still believe existed, fails to recognize the effectiveness and radiant force of the "culture of civility" that, at least in imperial Germany, was generated and transferred through the not-so-narrow circle of the family.

Ideally, even the not very hermetic practice of childrearing could convey outward-looking, civil society-oriented values and emotional dispositions such as confidence in others, oneself, and the world; the capacity for empathy; acknowledgment of difference; and a willingness and ability to communicate. The Eyck family was by no means unique. At the same time, families—and here, too, the Eycks were no exception—could also equip their members with notions that ran counter to the values of civil society. Class- and gender-specific strategies of exclusion, nepotism, and dogmatic definitional claims over the "culture of civility" were but a few facets of the dark side of civil society. And yet the family shared this dual nature with other institutions whose civil society quality is not generally challenged. One need only think of the many clubs and associations that were no less exclusive, no less shielded from the public eye, and scarcely less hierarchically structured than the family.[57] Like them, the family with its positive and negative sides represented *one* core institution of civil society.

Notes

1. Keith Tester, *Civil Society* (London, 1992), 8; Jürgen Kocka, "Zivilgesellschaft als historisches Projekt und Versprechen," in *Europäische Zivilgesellschaft in Ost und West: Begriff, Geschichte, Chancen*, ed. Manfred Hildermeier et al. (Frankfurt/M., 2000), 13–39, 24f.
2. Jürgen Kocka, "Zivilgesellschaft. Zum Konzept und seiner sozialhistorischen Verwendung," in *Neues über Zivilgesellschaft: Aus historisch-sozialwissenschaftlichem Blickwinkel*, WZB Discussion Papers, P 01-801, ed. Kocka et al. (Berlin, 2001), 4–21, 9.
3. Ute Gerhard, "Bürgerrechte und Geschlecht: Herausforderung für ein soziales Europa," in *Staatsbürgerschaft in Europa. Historische Erfahrungen und aktuelle Debatten*, ed. Christoph Conrad and Jürgen Kocka (Hamburg, 2001), 63–91, 79.
4. On the problematic of the categories of "public" and "private," see Gisela Bock, "Changing Dichotomies: Perspectives on Women's History," in *Writing Women's History: International Perspectives*, ed. Karen Offen et al. (London, 1991), 1–23; Karin Hausen, "Öffentlichkeit und Privatheit: Gesellschaftspolitische Konstruktionen und die Geschichte der Geschlechterbeziehungen" in *Frauengeschichte—Geschlechtergeschichte*, ed. Karin Hausen and Heide Wunder (Frankfurt/M., 1992), 81–88; Leonore Davidoff, "'Alte Hüte': Öffentlichkeit und Privatheit in der feministischen Geschichtsschreibung," *L'Homme* 4, no. 1 (1993): 7–36; Gunilla-Friederike Budde, "Das Geschlecht der Geschichte," in *Geschichte zwischen Kultur und Gesellschaft*, ed. Thomas Mergel and Thomas Welskopp (Munich, 1997), 125–150.
5. Nancy Fraser, *Justice Interruptus: Critical Reflections on the "Post-Socialist" Condition* (London, 1996), 76.
6. Ibid., 88.
7. This certainly does not mean that we cannot find female actors or civil society actions in other social strata, but they have been less well studied under the keyword *civil society*. One example is women in the German labor movement and their struggle for the equal right to votes. See for example: Richard J. Evans, *The Feminist Movement in Germany, 1894–1933* (London, 1976); Jean H. Quataert, *Reluctant Feminists in German Social Democracy, 1885–1917* (Princeton, NJ, 1979). An examination of the family's services to civil society in the twentieth century would also doubtless be worthwhile.
8. Paul Nolte, "Zivilgesellschaft und soziale Ungleichheit: Ein historisch-sozialwissenschaftlicher Problemaufriss," in *Neues über Zivilgesellschaft: Aus historisch-sozialwissenschaftlichem Blickwinkel*, WZB Discussion Papers, P 01-801, ed. Jürgen Kocka et al. (Berlin, 2001), 22–44, 25.
9. Karen Hagemann, "Familie—Staat—Nation: Das aufklärerische Projekt der 'Bürgergesellschaft' in geschlechtergeschichtlicher Perspektive," in Hildermeier et al., *Europäische Zivilgesellschaft*, 57–84.
10. Johann Gottfried Herder, "Freimäurer," in *Sämtliche Werke*, ed. Bernhard Suphan, (Hildesheim, 1886; reprint, Berlin, 1997), 126–48, 132; Stefan-Ludwig Hoffmann, *Die Politik der Geselligkeit: Freimaurerlogen in der deutschen Bürgergesellschaft 1840–1918* (Göttingen, 2000), 44.
11. Karin Hausen, "Die Nicht-Einheit der Geschichte als historiographische Herausforderung: Zur historischen Relevanz und Anstößigkeit der Geschlechtergeschichte," in

Geschlechtergeschichte und Allgemeine Geschichte: Herausforderungen und Perspektiven, ed. Hans Medick and Ann-Charlott Trepp (Göttingen, 1998), 15–55, 26.
12. Nolte, "Zivilgesellschaft," 9.
13. Georg Wilhelm Friedrich Hegel, Encyclopädie der Philosophischen Wissenschaften im Grundrisse: Zum Gebrauch seiner Vorlesungen, 3rd ed. (Heidelberg, 1830); Jürgen Habermas, The Structural Transformation of the Public Sphere: An Inquiry into a Category of Bourgeois Society (Cambridge, MA, 1991; 1st German ed., 1962); Jürgen Habermas, The Theory of Communicative Action, vol. 2, Lifeworld and System—A Critique of Functionalist Reason (Boston, 1985; 1st German ed., 1981).
14. Jean Cohen and Andrew Arato, Civil Society and Political Theory (Cambridge, MA, 1992), 538.
15. Ibid., 629. "We nevertheless believe that it would have been better to include the family within civil society, as its first association. ... For then the family could have taken its place as a key institution in civil society, one that, if conceived of in egalitarian terms, could have provided an experience of horizontal solidarity, collective identity, and equal participation to the autonomous individuals comprising it—a task deemed fundamental for the other associations of civil society and for the ultimate development of civic virtue and responsibility with respect to the polity." Ibid., 631.
16. Gunilla-Friederike Budde, Auf dem Weg ins Bürgerleben: Kindheit und Erziehung in deutschen und englischen Bürgerfamilien, 1840–1914 (Göttingen, 1994), 166–192.
17. Diary of Helene Eyck (1876–1898), Eyck private archive, Calgary, Alberta, Canada. 18 October 1888. It is interesting that Helene Eyck, writing about her family, remarks only in one entry that the family is Jewish. This fact seems to have played a very minor role in the daily life of the family. However, as Marion Kaplan suggests in her excellent study of Jewish families in Imperial Germany, it is possible that Helene Eyck laid so much stress on the "civility" of her children and their public appearance because of being confronted with growing anti-Semitism; see Kaplan, The Making of the Jewish Middle Class in Imperial Germany (New York, 1991).
18. Quoted in Budde, Auf dem Weg, 171.
19. Eyck, Diary, 31 December 1884.
20. Ibid., 6 September 1883.
21. Ibid., 4 June 1881.
22. Ibid., 6 September 1883. See also 21 February 1884.
23. Ibid., 6 September 1883.
24. Ibid., 21 February 1884.
25. Ibid., 6 January 1888.
26. Ibid., 26 July 1881.
27. Ibid., 6 July 1897.
28. Ibid., 4 January 1892.
29. Ibid.
30. Ibid., 31 December 1888.
31. Ibid., 4 October 1895.
32. Nancy Fraser, "Toward a Discourse Ethic of Solidarity," Praxis International 5, no. 4 (1986): 425–429.
33. Eyck, Diary, 4 October 1895.
34. Ibid., 29 December 1896.
35. Kocka, "Zivilgesellschaft als historisches Projekt, " 26.
36. Anthony Giddens, "Risk, Trust, Reflexivity," in Reflexive Modernization: Politics, Tradition and Aesthetics in the Modern Social Order, ed. Ulrich Beck et al. (Cambridge, MA, 1994), 184–197, 193.
37. Adam Ferguson, An Essay on the History of Civil Society, ed. Fania Oz-Salzberger (Cambridge, 1995), 36.

38. Eyck, Diary, 2 January 1891.
39. Ibid., 4 October 1895.
40. Ibid., 21 February 1884.
41. Ibid., 26 November 1897.
42. Gunilla-Friederike Budde, "Familienvertrauen—Selbstvertrauen—Gesellschaftsvertrauen: Pädagogische Ideen und Praxis im 19. Jahrhundert," in *Vertrauen: Historische Annäherungen*, ed. Ute Frevert (Göttingen, 2003), 152–184.
43. Elisabeth Budde (1880–1914), Memoirs and Letters, Budde Private Archive (Oldenburg), 123.
44. Ibid., 31.
45. Gunilla-Friederike Budde, "Harriet und ihre Schwestern: Frauen und Zivilgesellschaft im 19. Jahrhundert," in *Zivilgesellschaft und historischer Wandel. Studien zum 19. und 20. Jahrhundert*, ed. Ralph Jessen and Sven Reichardt (Berlin, 2004).
46. Budde, *Memoirs and Letters*.
47. Jean H. Quataert, *Staging Philanthropy: Patriotic Women and the National Imagination in Dynastic Germany, 1813–1916* (Ann Arbor, MI, 2001).
48. Günther Roth, *Max Webers deutsch-englische Familiengeschichte 1800–1950* (Tübingen, 2001), 524.
49. Ibid., 516–19.
50. Leonore Davidoff and Catherine Hall, *Family Fortunes: Men and Women of the English Middle Class* (London, 1987), 434.
51. Roth, *Max Webers*, 524.
52. John Stuart Mill and Harriet Taylor Mill, *The Subjection of Women* (London, 1996; 1st English ed., 1869), 99.
53. Mill and Mill, *Subjection*, 88.
54. Helene Lange, "Intellektuelle Grenzziehungen zwischen Mann und Frau," *Die Frau* 4 (1896/97): 321–34, 322.
55. Helene Lange, "Die Frau im Dienst an der Gemeinde," *Die Frau* 15 (1908), 192.
56. Budde, *Memoirs and Letters*.
57. The Freemasons are merely a particularly obvious example. Hoffmann, *Die Politik*.

Chapter 7

VEILED ASSOCIATIONS
THE MUSLIM MIDDLE CLASS, THE FAMILY, AND THE COLONIAL STATE IN NINETEENTH- AND TWENTIETH-CENTURY INDIA

Margrit Pernau

For the past several years, academic history writing in Germany has not only been expanding its field to include Western and Eastern European history, but it has also been aiming at a truly global perspective. Global history, in turn, needs global concepts in order to constitute a common framework that allows analyzing different phenomena together. It is here, however, that the problems start. The jealousy with which European historians guard their monopoly on defining notions and terms by insisting on their usage as related to a European context is at least matched by the uneasiness with which non-European historians view the intrusion of foreign concepts into their work. Instead of pursuing this battle, this paper will seek to take a small step forward to show how a concept that originates from the European discussion can be transformed through the inclusion of non-European experience and thus reframed in a way that allows historians to use the same language while speaking of two cultures. The existence of difference does not preclude use of a common framework, nor does the framework imply a negation of difference.[1] Indian civil society in the nineteenth century—assuming for a moment

---

This article is dedicated to the memory of Nausheen Jaffry (1972–2004), who started as my research assistant before she became a scholar in her own right. Together we traveled to Hyderabad and searched for most of the Urdu books and journals on which this present article is based, and much fun we had together. She had a brilliant career as a medieval historian before her, when her life was cut short by cancer. I miss a dear friend.

that it existed—will obviously look different from German, English, or American civil society at the same time. What is needed is a concept that is flexible enough to encompass these differences without annihilating them, and to establish a relationship between them.

This task, which we face for every global approach to a problem, is rendered all the more difficult in the case of civil society, as the "civility" that constitutes its fundamental basis combined, from the very beginning, a claim to universal validity and exclusionary practices.[2] Civility was at once a normative standard for all of mankind and the core of the identity of white middle-class men.[3] The civilizing mission embodied in colonialism (as well as in cross-class and cross-gender reform in many metropoles) thus combined a putatively universal moral duty to conform to these values with an implicit assumption that this goal could only be reached by a select few.[4] In other words, civility needed barbarism as its Other. Thus, while a plurality of civilities was excluded, while civil society's most perfect definition could be derived only from Europe's political philosophy and history, while it was Europe that set the goal, this goal had to remain unattainable. If at all, non-European societies could reach a stage of, to vary postcolonial theorist Homi Bhabha's famous saying, "civil society, but not quite."[5] Denial or redefinition of the goal exposed these societies to the charge of barbarism, while their attempts to conform to this standard were derided as mimicry by the colonizers. The colonized people's assimilation had to be demanded and resisted at the same time.[6]

Far from being a promise that would eventually be redeemed, civil society consisted of such a tight intermingling of inclusion and exclusion that the two could not be taken apart without destroying the whole edifice. If, therefore, we allow the concept of civil society to remain as it was initially defined and practiced by those white middle-class men who profited from it, we will never proceed beyond the traditional assertion of deficiency of non-European countries, but instead will perpetuate the power relations this concept helped to build and stabilize.

The fact that the white middle-class men's civility was based not just upon a single identity and its correspondent exclusion, but also upon the categories of race, class, and gender, led to overlapping communities and hence to a crisscrossing of civilizing missions from the nineteenth century on, blurring the boundaries between East and West. It was not only British men who attempted to civilize and dominate India; British women, whose gender role in Britain limited them to the private sphere and excluded them from civil society, also became an important element of civility, civilizing mission, and the spreading of civil society in India.[7] At the same time, Indian men, who were deemed to be in need of civilization by the colonial administrators before they could be admitted to the rights of active citizenship, pursued their own civilizing and excluding agenda towards their wives and daughters, who in turn joined their project, once it came to educating the lower classes.[8]

White middle-class men had excluded from their view the popular classes and especially working-class associational life, women, and families as well as non-European men and women.[9] Bringing these excluded categories back into the framework of civil society and at the same time globalizing it poses a challenge to the concept itself. For some time already, the great advantage of linking the normative and the historical aspects of civil society has been seen in the fact that this permits a historicization of the discussion of norms and thereby reintroduces the historical actors' own perceptions and practices into the debate.[10] The present essay draws on this approach but expands its frame by introducing new actors—those who have historically been excluded by white middle-class men (and by those historians who reproduced their worldview). Once the perceptions and practices of these actors are taken into consideration, the concept of civil society will necessarily change.

Admittedly, such a reworking runs the risk that, in the process, the concept will lose its coherence and hence its analytical value. If, however, we focus less on the forms and more on the functions that civil society was deemed to fulfill, we might be more open to recognizing alternative ways of generating solidarity, trust, and social capital—ways that have been hitherto excluded through an all-too-narrow definition. The first part of this chapter focuses on the competing efforts of the colonial state and middle-class Muslim men to redefine the private sphere and women's place in society. The men's efforts point forward to the entry of women into the new public sphere, which, with its associations and journals, had developed as a result of colonial power, and in which elements of the European concept of civil society can be found. At the same time, they also direct our attention backward to the ways in which women had associated with each other before the breakthrough of the reforms—to forms of solidarity and philanthropy that transcended the extended family, and hence to precolonial varieties of female civil society.

The second part traces women's responses to this project and the way they renegotiated its agenda. Civil society as it was acted out by Muslim women in India from the late nineteenth century on, the argument runs, owes as much to the older forms based on family, neighborhood, and religion, as to the colonial ideas. While civil society may thus be read as referring to any place in which communication relating to the state, the economy, society, and culture occurred, this place will not necessarily be located within the *public* space, but rather in that space which was considered as private, because it was screened off from the gaze of unrelated men and reserved to women. Nevertheless, this sphere was deemed crucial for the formation of civil society by both men and women, both for the civilizing task and for the social work among their sisters that women were deemed to perform.

Women's Reform—A Contested Terrain

The nineteenth century in India saw a radical reconfiguration of the divide between the public sphere and the private. Whereas the private was hardly talked and written about, and women in the outgoing eighteenth century were deemed a subject befitting love poetry but not serious theological, philosophical, and political treatises, a hundred years later, the way women behaved and were treated within the private sphere had become an eminently public and political issue. Women had become the terrain upon which a fierce battle for Indian national and religious identity was fought. Two entangled developments brought about this transformation: on the one hand the politics of the colonial power, which turned its attention to social reform and to the "woman question," and on the other hand the reform movements within Hinduism and Islam. These movements contributed to more sharply drawing the boundaries between the two religious communities; although they brought about much antagonism, their discourse and their policy was astonishingly similar—the behavior that made a Muslim woman a good Muslim was the same that made the Hindu woman a good Hindu.[11] Despite the fact that the present paper for practical reasons focuses on Muslims only, a study on Hindus would in all probability come to quite parallel conclusions.

For the first century and a half of its existence, the East India Company was a trading company, whose aims were restricted to enhancing the efficiency of its trading system and maximize its profits. Even after the Battle of Plassey in 1757 had brought it a semblance of state power with the right to collect land revenue in Bengal and thus forced company officials to give a thought to administrative matters, they still aimed at working within existing state structures. Any attempt to introduce European laws, institutions, or culture was viewed with mistrust by the British administrators. The East India Company aimed neither at state formation for its own sake, nor at a monopoly of legitimate violence, as long as working through allies at different levels—from Rajas and Nawabs down to landowners—was both cheaper and safer.[12] In discussing civil society in India, one should keep in mind that the state had never gone through a phase of absolutism and was therefore much less pervasive than its European counterpart.[13] Much of what in Europe was a contested terrain between state and society, in India belonged to the purview of society—not because of any question of political philosophy, but for lack of an alternative.[14]

The idea that Indian society should be interfered with as little as possible never disappeared completely. However, from the first decades of the nineteenth century on, it was matched by the apparently opposite idea of a British civilizing mission, which led to the establishment of missionary centers, educational projects, and, most important in our context, to the introduction of social reforms, ostensibly aimed at bettering the lot of Indian women. Taking up a widespread European notion, James Mill, in his book on British India, argued that women's position could be used as an indicator of a society's advancement—its civility, we might translate.[15] For the British policy in India, this suggests that the campaign for the abolition of widow immolation and widow remarriage, and the debates around the age of consent (i.e., the minimal age for the consummation of marriage) were not simply aimed at improving women's lives but also served to legitimize the colonial government, both in their own eyes as also hopefully in the eyes of the colonized. At the same time, the British implicitly denied Indian men the basic civility they needed to qualify for membership in a civil society and for citizenship. The woman question thus became a key public site for the struggle over civility and civil society between colonial power and Indian men.[16] Nevertheless, the boundaries between the adversaries were never clearly demarcated according to national criteria. The British reformers relied on the support and at times the initiative of Indian reformers, the most well known among them the Bengali Raja Ram Mohan Roy. Indian orthodox adversaries to social change, on the other hand, found ready encouragement among those British who believed that the differences between the West and the East were so great that they prevented an adaptation of what they saw as British political and moral culture to Indian circumstances.

This discussion intertwined with a second debate, which had begun among Indian Muslim thinkers even before the cultural influence of the colonial power became pervasive, and which aimed at redefining the boundaries between the public and the private. Traditionally, the safeguarding of the Islamic character of a state or community was seen as a central task of the ruler. If he was a Muslim, if he protected and patronized religious scholars and holy men and imparted an Islamic character to the public sphere through certain highly symbolic acts, his territory became an "abode of Islam."[17] Personal piety was certainly decisive for the individual Muslim's salvation or damnation, its lack, however, did not endanger the Islamic character of the community. Women's behavior, especially if it occurred within the confines of the female quarters of the houses, thus had no public importance.

This changed once it became clear that the decline of the Mughal empire was no passing phenomenon, but that Muslim state power in the subcontinent was on the wane, to be replaced by the Hindu Marathas in the north and the British in Bengal and Madras. The new rulers were at best neutral, but certainly no longer the guardians of the community's Islamic identity. Personal piety therefore gained an importance it had never had before. The reform of the individual Muslims' beliefs, the weaning from superstitions, and the return to the pristine purity of the holy texts became the central agenda. The personal and private comportment of Muslims became endowed with the symbolic significance that was once reserved for the ruler's government: it decided on the Islamic or un-Islamic character of the community. Common Muslims, and even more so the respectable classes, were expected to exhort each other to act according to the precepts of the holy scripture and to follow its writ in every particular of their life. Enabling them to live up to this necessity through education, guidance, and legal arbitration became the religious leaders' primary task.[18] This new public and political importance of the private sphere in turn gave prominence to women—to their piety, behavior, and education.

Unlike male education, transmission of knowledge for women had never been formalized. Although the number of girls taught to read the Quran was probably larger than the reformers admitted, teaching of religion and social obligations and of correct behavior and comportment for girls was an exclusively female domain, taking place in the home. To an even larger extent than its male counterpart, it was transmitted orally rather than in a written form, tradition-bound, and changed only slowly. For the reformers this meant that the forms of religion that they had set out to fight in the name of scripturalist Islam—localized and bearing the imprint of the encounter with Hindus and their beliefs—remained entrenched in their own homes. Popular customs and rites, now classified as un-Islamic and superstitious by the reformers, proved much more resilient than expected, and it could be assumed that as long as the power structures within the female quarters remained intact, women would continue to be taught and controlled by their mothers, mothers-in-law, and elder female relatives and not by their young reforming husbands. While there is certainly no call to exalt this "old patriarchy," it is important to see that within the extended family, gender was not the only axis along which power was distributed or withheld, but that it overlapped with the category of age.[19] While the male head of the household might impose his decisions even on the female quarters, it would be very difficult for his younger brothers and most definitely out of question for his sons and nephews, to follow his lead. The debate on female education may thus be read as a struggle over whose right it was to civilize young women: the elder women's, the husband's, or the colonial state's.

This discussion forms the background for one of the most influential books for women, the *Bihishti Zewar* (Heavenly Ornaments) by Ashraf Ali Thanawi (1864–1943).[20] Initially published in the early years of the twentieth century, it saw countless reprints and is still widely available in the Urdu original and in translations and adaptations today. It was said that for several generations, young Muslim brides entered their in-laws' home with the Quran in one hand and the *Bihishti Zewar* in the other; the book certainly formed part of their material and intellectual dowry. Thanawi has been widely acclaimed as a champion of women's rights, as he held that women were not debarred by their intellectual capacities from attaining knowledge, that in fact it was the duty of pious Muslim men to ensure that their daughters and wives acquired the knowledge they needed to follow the precepts of Islam. This implied not only teaching them to read the Quran in the Arabic language, which hardly any of them understood, but enabling them to read and write in Urdu. The danger that they might use their new knowledge to correspond with a potential lover was far outweighed by the access to religious learning it allowed them and which would better protect their virtue than any external safeguards. This, however, should not be read as a call for women's empowerment and equal rights. As the book states, "There is a natural difference between men and women. They are unable to be on par with men. They are less intelligent, their power of endurance is relatively lower, their body-parts are more fragile.... When *Allah Ta'ala* (the Highest) has made you relatively more deficient, what equality do you now lay claim to?"[21]

The alternative to submission to the mother-in-law was not to be the bride's right to think and decide for herself, but obedience to her husband and to the texts he taught her. The new woman is devoted to her husband—the reformist loved quoting a tradition from the Prophet, that if God had allowed prostration before any created being, he would have ordered wives to prostrate before their husbands—and she strictly observes the injunctions of the Quran and the sayings of the Prophet, many of which are recounted in the *Bihishti Zewar*.[22] Education from both these sides transform her into a perfect housewife, into the ideal manager of a middle-class household, struggling to keep up its respectability with restrained means. A pious wife not only manages the intricacies of personal relations within an extended family and its large social network. She also establishes a tight control over the servants and she herself works tirelessly. Under her supervision, neither time nor money are wasted, the house is transformed into an oasis of peace and prosperity.

The *Bihishti Zewar* and the many other texts aimed at reforming Muslim women certainly tightened male control over their lives and penetrated into areas which hitherto had been ruled by women without outside interference. Nevertheless, for young women this "new patriarchy" held an attraction, as it not only allowed them access to education but also provided them with the possibility to play off one patriarchy against the other and thus mitigate the all-powerful empire of the elderly women of the household. While men attacked the reformers for a variety of reasons and on a variety of issues, the most important resistance they themselves pointed to over and again came from women themselves. Younger women were depicted as too lazy, slovenly, or quarrelsome in their habits to submit to this healthy education; many warning stories were written to show them how it led the way to disaster—for themselves, but also for their families and children.[23] But even worse were the older women, who resisted reform not only for themselves but for their daughters and especially their daughters-in-law, fearing to lose their hold over the young women.

Unfortunately, there seem to be few extant documents that portray this female universe, except through its resistance to the reformist ventures. Even from this sketchy and distorted picture, however, some outlines emerge. They point to a world rich in informal networks and association that straddle the boundary lines between the public and the private. Of course no respectable Muslim woman would appear "in public," if that is taken to mean a space accessible to both unrelated men and women. On the other hand, women's relations were by no means confined to the space and concerns of their family. Although they do not match the European concept of a civil society, they did create the social capital and trust necessary for the enactment of a solidarity that neither relied on the state nor limited itself to a narrowly conceived family. If traditional Muslim women would never dream of founding an association for bowling, complete with registration, membership fees, and the election of a president, neither would they dream of bowling alone.

The occasions that brought them together were on the one hand the lifecycle celebrations, from the rites to be performed for a newly born baby and her mother, the ceremony of her weaning, her first solid food, the beginning of her education, and above all marriages and funerals.[24] During these celebrations the roles and obligations of the actors—the bride's sisters, her mother, her sisters-in-law, but also her unmarried or married friends—were fixed by tradition, as were the gifts exchanged between the families and friends. These events were not limited to the extended family living together in one household, but were occasions for meetings with distant relatives who might have migrated to other towns and localities, where the women's natal and marital families joined, and which, depending on the social and economic position of the family, would include at least the neighborhood, possibly the respectable families of the entire town.

The other great occasions for women to get together were religious functions—celebrations at Sufi shrines, female congregational prayers during Ramadan, and the assemblies held in Muharram, commemorating the death of the Prophet's grandson at Karbala—which were not only organized by women, but in which, for reasons of seclusion, women were also the speakers and preachers. These celebrations provided the women with a network of their own, on which they could rely in times of distress. It was here and through women that a large part of the social capital of the families, their prestige and their relations, were built up and maintained. We have hardly begun to investigate the financial transactions by women in the nineteenth century; however, early signs seem to indicate that women did play a role, and possibly even a major role, in pious foundations and charity. It is too soon to say how far these philanthropic activities transcended the limits of the patron-client relationship; however, the fact that charity also served to impart social prestige to the donor should not in itself disqualify these women as protagonists of civil society, any more than it does so for their male (and female) British or American contemporaries.

It was this female world, based on customs, ruled by the elder women, and often transcending the boundaries of class and community, that Thanawi and his allies derided as the den of superstition and wasteful habits and that they wanted to civilize in the name of an Islam, seemingly universal, but in reality fragmented through the prism of male gender and middle-class identity. Although entry into this new and sanitized area was proclaimed as women's moral and religious duty, they would at best remain relatively more deficient than the men who claimed to set up their agenda for them. Albeit the scale was different from the one James Mill had in mind, for the Muslim reformers, too, the woman question appeared to serve as a barometer for the status of a society. Unlike Mill, however, they denied any role to the state in this civilizing mission. The same process of inclusion and exclusion that was taking place between the colonial power and the Indian middle class was thus reproduced, with the included-excluded men becoming includers-excluders in their turn, once they faced their women.[25] In the eyes of the reformers, the fact that the debate on women took place in the public sphere did not imply that women themselves were supposed to leave the privacy of their homes and participate as active citizens. On the contrary, they believed that what was needed was a public discussion of how to keep the private out of the public sphere and how to teach women in the name of Islam to respect an even stricter seclusion than they had ever known before. The politicization of the private and the call for its privatization went hand in hand.[26]

Education and Association: Female Answers to a Male Project

Even more than in European history, Indian women's voices have long been considered elusive, their recovery nearly impossible, with Muslim women deemed even more silent than their Hindu counterparts. Recent studies have shown, however, that even if their voices did not always reach the male-dominated public sphere, women nevertheless forcefully articulated their own opinions, not only in private, but also as speakers at female gatherings and through published articles and books.[27] This second part of the chapter examines women's reactions to the reformers' call, asking whether they at all took part in the debate and how and with which results they rephrased its basic assumptions. To do this, it is necessary to leave behind the all-India perspective and instead focus on a local case study of the women of the upper-middle class in Hyderabad. Hyderabad was the largest of the more than five hundred princely states that made up almost a third of the Indian territory. A highly flexible form of indirect rule permitted the British to reduce their administrative and military costs while at the same time allowing them to interfere in Hyderabad's government whenever they judged imperial interests to be at stake. To ward off British intervention, the state, starting in the 1870s, had embarked on a program of administrative and financial reforms, which in turn triggered a number of educational ventures as well as the import of an elite of highly qualified bureaucrats from northern India. Even before their migration to Hyderabad, many of these men had been linked with one or another group of Islamic reformists. In the setting of the princely state, reformism—a mixture of Islam and Victorian middle-class values—provided them with an additional resource to strengthen their position in the complicated patron-client relations suffusing the administration and social life. This group was among the first to promote education for their daughters—first at home, but already by the last decades of the nineteenth century, in newly founded schools for girls for the upper social classes.[28]

The reformers' view on the appropriate position for respectable Muslim women can be seen clearly in a journal for ladies, the *Teacher of Women* (*Mu'alim-e Niswan*), founded in 1886 by one of these migrants, Muhibb Husain. While he fought every bit as energetically as Thanawi against the evils of a separate women's world where superstitions and un-Islamic and degrading social customs could evolve, his remedy lay in convincing women that they should no longer sit idly in "shameful solitary confinement."[29] Instead, it behooved them to improve their minds through "social intercourse" with their equals and the integration into "civil society," (terms left in English in the text).[30] Islam, so his argument ran, never asked for the seclusion of women, but only for their veiling. Once clothes were designed that could safeguard their modesty, women thus had not only the right but even the religious duty to leave their houses and mingle with other women—though of course not with unrelated men.[31]

Women, especially those from the families of the north Indian bureaucrats, not only read what Muhibb Husain wrote for them but, in increasing numbers, also contributed to his journal and took up the topics he raised. While it can be safely assumed that not only courtesans but also respectable educated women had long since been in the habit of composing poetry, the extent and the genres in which they started to write and publish in Hyderabad were unprecedented. In the city of Hyderabad alone, one biographer identified no fewer than one hundred and fifty female writers working during the period from 1880 to 1940, taking into account only those writing in Urdu.[32] If we consider the fact that this author had himself migrated from the north and was most closely connected to the families of the migrant bureaucrats, it can be supposed that the actual number of women who were publishing was even greater. Their writings, ranging from poems to novels, from advice literature to journal articles, appeared not only in Hyderabad, but all over India.

If one read these texts only to look for traces of female resistance to a male civilizing project, one would be disappointed. Women writers most decidedly took their place at the side of the male reformers and, as sharply as any of them, condemned the old women's world as well as those men who helped to keep it up. At the top of their agenda was the fight against superstitions, against what was seen as the old slovenly habits. Women were exhorted by women no less than by men to manage the family resources carefully and to strive to create a clean and orderly home, with the threat that otherwise they might lose their husbands to some British "angel of the house," more proficient in housekeeping and able to be a true companion to him—a threat that was perhaps particular to Hyderabad and the princely states, where the racial boundaries were not quite as rigid as in British India.[33] Men had demanded education for girls and either stricter seclusion or, on the contrary, its replacement by some form of veiling only with a view of its effect on male comfort and the position of the community. Women certainly used these arguments, but added a concern for the wellbeing of women. For them, the development of a girl's mental and intellectual capacities was a God-given right, of which none was allowed to deprive them. Respectability certainly forbade women to mix freely with unrelated men, but "if all the joys of the world were made unlawful for women, except being obedient to the husband, I would prefer death immediately following birth."[34]

Above all, the first generation of educated women took up the call for an intensification of female social activities beyond the boundaries of their private houses. The fact that they received the support of the wives of the British officials in the state for their efforts and thus helped to build up a progressive and Anglophile image of their families certainly played a role in overcoming possible male opposition to their venture. Sometime between 1901 and 1903, the first female association, the Hyderabad Ladies Social Club, was founded. While here ladies of all communities—Muslims, Hindus, Parsis, and Christians—met, the Association for Islamic Ladies (*anjuman-e khawatin-e Islam*), founded in 1910, was from the beginning intended not only as a recreational club, but also as an association for the reform of Islam. Twice a month, ladies gathered to listen to lectures, most of which combined the teaching of Islam through episodes of the life of the Prophet and his family with moral exhortations and advice on how to lead a life that was both well organized and pious.

Right from the beginning, social work, too, was an important, if not the most important, aim of these associations. The terrible flood of the Musi river in 1908, which submerged large parts of the old city of Hyderabad and cost hundreds of lives, dramatized the fact that help for women could only be provided by other women, as many preferred to drown within their own walls rather than be rescued by men. A spontaneously founded committee to coordinate efforts to help women who had lost their houses and families included "European and Local Ladies."[35] It proved to be an initiating experience for many of them.

The activities of the early associations often began with founding schools for poor girls, an endeavor in which even the ladies observing stricter seclusion could join, as the new schools were often located within the houses of the women themselves, who also took an active part in their supervision and even in teaching. The associations also helped impoverished ladies from good families obtain legal advice—a great problem for women, who were not supposed to speak to unrelated men—or gain access to credit facilities if they wanted to set up home industries.[36] An even more basic problem than education was the provision of medical care for women living in seclusion. Here the ladies' associations aimed at both promulgating female health services by training female doctors and educating women to eradicate habits that were harmful for the physical well-being of their families. The establishment of a medical college for women and of hospitals and maternity wards owed much to their influence.[37]

While it is difficult to gauge the impact of this development on the social conditions of the poorer sections of the community, it certainly trained a whole generation of women in the organization of these new forms of social activities. These changes are exemplified in a highly didactic novel, *Sarguzisht-e Hajira* (The Story of Hajira), written by Sughra Humayun Begam and published in Hyderabad in 1926. The author was the wife of a north Indian medical doctor who had migrated to the princely state. While her husband was linked to the circle of men gathered around the editor of the journal *Mu'alim-e Niswan*, mentioned above, Sughra Humayun Begam belonged to, and often served as secretary of, almost every women's association that came up in Hyderabad. She was a prolific writer, publishing more than fourteen novels and editing two journals, all of them containing a very strong message.

Sarguzisht is the story of four women meeting for tea and taking turns in telling their life stories, quite a traditional genre in Urdu literature. The central character is a young woman spoiled by English education, which provided her with much bookish knowledge but no training of the heart. Therefore she is unable to either organize a household or to interact harmoniously with her in-laws; her home is on the brink of disruption. The stories her friends tell her, however, succeed in reconciling her to her husband and reforming her life. In order not to limit the success of their efforts to this one case—and it is here that the story takes an interesting turn—the women decide to publish their talks, found a girls' school that is not only to impart knowledge but also mold the hearts and manners of the students, and set up an association to promote the remarriage of widows and oppose polygamy.[38]

By the eve of the Great War, founding associations to remedy all kinds of social evils had become part of Indian women's cultural repertory, at least for the middle classes. This movement was by no means limited to Hyderabad. "Networks of reform" were spreading all over the country.[39] Although local in their origin, they kept close contact with each other and with the network of the male associations to which their husbands and fathers belonged. The All India Muslim Ladies' Conference was founded in 1914, followed by the Women's Indian Association in 1917 and the powerful All India Women's Conference in 1927. Women from Hyderabad who had received their first rhetorical and political training in the associations mentioned above were to be found in all of these organizations as well as in many of the political parties, but most prominently in the All India Muslim Ladies' Conference.[40]

At first glance, this development might tend to reinforce the idea that the concept of civil society based on an associational life as a form of political culture was one that was developed in the West and exported to India. Certainly these associations, with their annual meetings, elections and reports, looked very similar to their British counterparts and owed much to their influence. A closer look, however, reveals that the older form of a female civil society based on ties of family, patronage, and religious affiliation providing for regular gatherings at marriages and lifecycle celebrations had by no means disappeared, but rather constituted the underlying structure on which the new networks flourished.

This intertwining of the old and the new civil society took place at three levels. At the first, families provided the connections and social capital needed to establish associations in the local setting, but even more to link these associations in an all-India echelon. Here it is important to keep in mind that the families we are talking about were much more extensive not only than the European nuclear family, but also than the typical three-generation Indian household, even if including all its ramifications. The families of the upper-middle class and the nobility, in particular, were held together by genealogical knowledge extending over many generations, and they merged into descent groups that traced their origins to a real or fictive ancestor. For some of the families, their geographical range extended over many of the important townships of north India, possibly including branches in Calcutta, Bombay, and Hyderabad.

At the second level, nonfamilial networks were often included in the family networks within one or two generations. Thus the founder of one of the most prestigious girls' schools of north India, Shaikh Abdullah, who was linked to many of the leading Muslim educationists through his professional and reformist activities, became incorporated into their network by marrying into the higher ranks of the Muslim leaders of Delhi. His marriage procession was joined by most of his colleagues, many of whom were now to become his relatives. While the procession was traditionally a male preserve, the wedding festivities in the female quarters brought together many future leaders of the women's associational movement, and they introduced his bride into a network that later became crucial to her educational and philanthropic activities.[41] Similarly, the first girls to receive an education at the English-medium Mahbubia School at Hyderabad originally came from families that shared a similar background, but were not necessarily related. Two generations of shared associational life and social activities later, however, almost everyone among them was also linked to each other in family ties.[42]

At the third level, even those relations that could no longer be incorporated into the family networks once the circles became too extended and too socially heterogeneous were reinterpreted in kinship terms. This not only allowed the use of a language that was familiar to women, but also permitted the "expansion of women's realm" by blurring the boundaries between private and public.[43] Even while they participated in British-style associations, women were thus conscious of moving within the extended—the very extended—family.

Conclusion

How can these case studies help us to reconceptualize the notion of civil society? How can we think and write about civil society without perpetuating the exclusions of those white middle-class men who defined themselves as the apex of civilization and hence the center of civil society? First, situating civil society at the interstice between the private and the public has the great advantage of pointing out its orientation toward the common good, as opposed to the pursuit of particular interests in the private, and emphasizing its voluntary character as opposed to the force of the state.[44] However, this approach does not allow us to see that the boundary lines between the public and the private not only shift historically but are also intertwined at any given moment. A room in the female quarters is private, when viewed from the more public courtyard; this courtyard becomes private, when viewed from the male section of the house. The house in its entirety is situated within the private sphere when viewed from the lane, which again becomes private when viewed from the thoroughfare. Likewise, any place or event in which women were involved would—certainly under the conditions of female seclusion that prevailed in India but perhaps also in Europe—be considered more private than a similar place or event that involved only men. This conceptualization does not, however, preclude the existence of a mixed or purely feminine public sphere, in the sense the term is used in connection with civil society, that would be centered on family celebrations and religious events, and later on literature, journals, and associations.

Second, an approach oriented toward actors and their normative perceptions permits a solid historical grounding of the concept of civil society.[45] However, it does not in itself answer the question of which actors and whose perceptions are to be included in the discussion, and thus runs the risk of reproducing the exclusion mechanisms of civil society's most powerful actors. A focus on civil society's functions, its generation of social trust and horizontal solidarity, does, however, serve to move beyond the concept's narrow focus in European practices and formations and include its functional alternatives in other parts of the world.[46]

Third, the actor-oriented approach allows for the inclusion of new actors—in this case, South Asian women who were previously excluded as both "orientals" and women—a move which, in turn, leads to a shift of attention to areas previously considered to be outside of civil society's purview. As the chapter shows, this entails a re-evaluation of the role of the family, at least in this context. Unlike its European counterpart, the Indian extended family not only provided resources for a civil society located outside its confines, but was in itself an important institution of female civil society.[47] While this holds true for the precolonial and pre-reformist Muslim families, even the modern female public sphere is inconceivable without its familial underpinnings, which provided the associations with ready-made networks and a frame of reference.

A second area that can no longer be excluded from civil society is religion. According to Muslim tradition, philanthropy and a responsibility for the disadvantaged had been regarded not so much as a social duty, but rather as a religious one. The discourse that led Muslim middle-class women to value education, associational life, and social work thus emphasized piety, not citizenship. Transcultural comparative studies can no longer be seen as a one-way process in which European history provides the definitive conceptual framework for interpreting non-European societies. The empire writes back, not only in literature, but in history as well.[48] The result might well be that bringing back informal networks and families (both seen more clearly when societies are viewed through the lens of gender), and above all, religion will, even for Europe, lead to a truer picture of civil society, transcending the conceptual restrictions that white middle-class men imposed on it in the nineteenth century.

Notes

1. Heinz-Gerhard Haupt and Jürgen Kocka, eds., *Geschichte und Vergleich: Ansätze und Ergebnisse internationaler vergleichender Geschichtsschreibung* (Frankfurt/M., 1996).
2. John Hall, "Reflections on the Making of Civility in Society," in *Paradoxes of Civil Society: New Perspectives on Modern German and British History*, ed. Frank Trentmann (New York, 2000), 47–57. Helmut Dubiel, "Unzivile Gesellschaften," *Soziale Welt* 52 (2001): 133–150.
3. Catherine Hall, *White, Male and Middle Class: Explorations in Feminism and History* (Cambridge, 1992).
4. Harald Fischer-Tiné and Michael Mann, eds., *Colonialism as Civilizing Mission: Cultural Ideology in British India* (London, 2004).
5. Homi Bhabha, "Of mimicry and man: The ambivalence of colonial discourse," in *The Location of Culture* (London, 1994), 85–92.
6. Ibid.
7. Thomas Metcalf, *Ideologies of the Raj* (Cambridge, New York, 1994).
8. Janaki Nair, *Miners and Millhands: Work, Culture and Politics in Princely Mysore* (New Delhi, London, 1998).
9. Karen Hagemann, "Familie—Staat—Nation: Das aufklärerische Projekt der 'Bürgergesellschaft' in geschlechtergeschichtlicher Perspektive," in *Europäische Zivilgesellschaft in Ost und West: Begriff, Geschichte, Chancen*, ed. Manfred Hildermeier et al. (Frankfurt/M., 2000), 57–85; Gunilla Budde, "Das Öffentliche des Privaten: Die Familie als zivilgesellschaftliche Kerninstitution," in *Die Praxis der Zivilgesellschaft: Akteure, Handeln und Strukturen im internationalen Vergleich*, ed. Arnd Bauerkämper (Frankfurt/M., 2003), 57–77.
10. Jürgen Kocka, "Zivilgesellschaft als historisches Problem und Versprechen," in Hildermeier et al., *Europäische Zivilgesellschaft*, 13–41; Dieter Gosewinkel, *Zivilgesellschaft—eine Erschließung des Themas von seinen Grenzen her*, WZB Discussion Papers, SP IV 2003-505 (Berlin, 2003).
11. Kumkum Sangari, "Women against Women," in *Politics of the Possible: Essays on Gender, History, Narrative, Colonial English*, ed. Kumkum Sangari (London, 1999), 184–279.
12. For an introduction to the period see Barbara Metcalf and Thomas Metcalf, *A Concise History of India* (Cambridge, New York, 2002), with further references.
13. Dietmar Rothermund, "The Role of the State in South Asia," in *The Role of the State in South Asia and Other Essays*, ed. Dietmar Rothermund (New Delhi, 2000), 1–36.
14. This would also constitute the historical background for the analysis of Shalini Randeria, "Zivilgesellschaft in postkolonialer Sicht," in *Neues über Zivilgesellschaft aus historisch-sozialwissenschaftlichem Blickwinkel*, WZB Discussion Papers, P 01-801, ed. Jürgen Kocka et al. (Berlin, 2001), 81–104. The fact in itself, however, that certain tasks are taken care of by society and not by the state, tells nothing of the civility of civil society, and even much less about the enactment of gender justice.
15. James Mill, Horace Hayman Wilson, *The History of British India* (New York, 1968), 309–310.
16. Lata Mani, *Contentious Traditions: The Debate on Sati in Colonial India* (New Delhi, New York, 1998).
17. For the debate on when a state was an abode of Islam see Saiyid Athar Abbas Rizvi, *Shah Abd al-Aziz: Puritanism, Sectarian Polemics and Jihad* (Canberra, 1982).

18. Francis Robinson, *Islam and Muslim History in South Asia* (New Delhi, 2000).
19. For the concepts of "old" and "new" patriarchy see Partha Chatterjee, *The Nation and its Fragments: Colonial and Postcolonial Histories* (Delhi, 1993). For a critical discussion of his approach see Tanika Sarkar, *Hindu Wife, Hindu Nation: Community, Religion and Cultural Nationalism* (New Delhi, 2001) and Judith Walsh, *Domesticity in Colonial India: What Women Learned When Men Gave Them Advice* (Lanham, MD, 2004); see also: Margrit Pernau, "Family: A Gendering and Gendered Space," introduction to *Family and Gender: Changing Values in Germany and India*, ed. Margrit Pernau et al. (Delhi, 2003), 9–35.
20. Barbara Daly Metcalf, *Perfecting Women: Maulana Ashraf 'Ali Thanawi's Bihishti Zewar. A Partial Translation with Commentary* (Delhi, 1992).
21. Ashraf Ali Thanawi, *A Gift to the Husband and Wife* (New Delhi, 1998), 32–33.
22. Ibid., 40.
23. The most famous example is to be found in the wonderful novel (which has now been re-edited in translation) by Nazir Ahmad, *The Bride's Mirror* (New Delhi, 2001; 1st ed., 1869).
24. For a detailed description see Saiyid Ahmad Dehlawi, *Rusum-e Dihli* [The Customs of Delhi] (Delhi, 1986; 11th ed., 1900) and its female counterpart, S. Begam, *Rusum-e Delhi* (Lahore, 1906).
25. It is the introduction of the category of gender into the study of Indian history that enables us to deconstruct the neat and unambiguous opposition of a powerful Occident and an oppressed Orient; see the pathbreaking volume Kumkum Sangari and Sudesh Vaid, eds., *Recasting Women: Essays in Colonial History* (New Delhi, 1989).
26. Pernau, "From a 'Private' Public to a 'Public' Private Sphere: Old Delhi and the North Indian Muslims in Comparative Perspective," in *The Public and the Private: Issues of Democratic Citizenship*, ed. Gurpreet Mahajan, et al. (New Delhi, 2003), 103–130.
27. Gail Minault, *Secluded Scholars: Women's Education and Muslim Social Reform in Colonial India* (Delhi, New York, 1998).
28. Pernau, "Schools for Muslim Girls—a Colonial or an Indigenous Project? A Case Study of Hyderabad," *Oriente Moderno* 23, no. 1 (2004): 263–276.
29. *Mu'alim-e niswan* 8/9 (1894): 19.
30. Ibid; see also *Mu'alim* 8, no. 4 (1894): 4.
31. Ibid., 19.
32. Nasir ud Din Hashimi, *Khawatin-e Dekan ki Urdu Khidmat* [Service of the Ladies from the Dekan to the Urdu Language] (Hyderabad, 1940); Hashimi, *Khawatin-e Ahd Osmani* [Ladies from the Time of Osman Ali Khan, Ruler of Hyderabad, 1911–48] (Hyderabad, 1936).
33. Tayyaba Begam, "Aurten aur mulazimat" [Women and Service], in *Rasa'il-e Tayyaba* [Articles of Tayyaba], ed. Sakina Khediv Jang (Hyderabad, 1940), 85–96.
34. Tayyaba Begam, *Anwari Begam* (Hyderabad, 1905), 186.
35. *Mushir-e Dekan*, quoted in Rizwana Firdausi, *Emancipation of Women in Hyderabad with Special Reference to Muslim Women (1911–1948)*, (PhD diss., Osmania University, 1988), 141.
36. Hashimi, *Ahd-e Osmani*, 156–159.
37. N.R. Giridhar, *Health Service in Hyderabad City from 1853–1948*, (PhD diss., Osmania University, 1996).
38. Sughra Humayun Mirza, *Sarguzisht-e Hajira* (Hyderabad, 1926).
39. Minault, *Secluded Scholars*, 158.
40. For a detailed study of these institutions see Minault, *Secluded Scholars*; Geraldine Hancock Forbes, *Women in Modern India* (Cambridge and New York, 1996); for the later period some useful information is also contained in Azra Asghar Ali, *The Emergence of Feminism among Indian Muslim Women* (Karachi, 2000).

41. Minault, *Secluded Scholars*, 228–49.
42. Interviews with alumni of the Mahbubia Girls' School at Hyderabad, January 1999 and September 2001.
43. Gail Minault, "The Extended Family as Metaphor and the Expansion of Women's Realm," in *The Extended Family: Women and Political Participation in India and Pakistan*, ed. Gail Minault (Delhi, 1981), 3–19.
44. Jürgen Kocka, "Civil Society from a Historical Perspective," *European Review* 12, no. 1 (2004): 65–79.
45. Arnd Bauerkämper, "Einleitung. Die Praxis der Zivilgesellschaft: Akteure und ihr Handeln in historisch-sozialwissenschaftlicher Perspektive," in *Die Praxis der Zivilgesellschaft: Akteure, Handeln und Strukturen im internationalen Vergleich*, ed. Bauerkämper et al. (Frankfurt/M., 2003), 7–30; see also Gosewinkel, *Zivilgesellschaft—eine Erschließung des Themas*.
46. Ute Frevert, "Vertrauen—eine historische Spurensuche," in *Vertrauen: Historische Annäherungen*, ed. Frevert (Göttingen, 2003), 7–67, especially 35–48 with further references.
47. Gunilla Budde in this volume.
48. Bill Ashcroft, *The Empire Writes Back: Theory and Practice in Post-Colonial Literatures* (London, 1989).

Chapter 8

"ONLY CONNECT"
FAMILY, GENDER, AND CIVIL SOCIETY IN
TWENTIETH-CENTURY EUROPE AND NORTH AMERICA

Paul A. Ginsborg

"Only connect," as many readers will know, is the epigraph of Edward M. Forster's famous novel, *Howards End*. The invitation the epigraph contains can be read on a number of different levels: as the need to link different elements of human experience and memory; as a way to overcome barriers—whether social or intellectual; or, implicit in Forster's novel itself, as a means to reconcile opposites—the seen and the unseen, the practical mind and the intellectual, the outer life and the inner.[1] I use it here primarily for two purposes: to point out a major methodological area in civil society studies where there has been a clamorous lack of connection; and then to ask, in both theoretical and historical terms, how families have been, or could be, connected to civil societies in the countries of the "North" of the world. In this discussion I consider families as profoundly gendered entities, which very often limit or destroy the possibilities of connectedness for their female members, and nearly always offer to civil society male values and priorities.[2]

Let me begin with the methodological gap. What is extraordinary about most of the literature on civil society is that the family is simply left out. If we go into any great library's electronic catalog and tap in "civil society" in the keywords box, literally hundreds of entries come out, mostly from the last few years. If we enter "civil society and the state," we will still get a very long and recent list. But if we try "civil society and family," there are fewer than ten entries. The topic is clearly undertheorized and underresearched.[3] One of the few recent texts that tries to deal theoretically, but only then en passant, with the possible connections or lack thereof between families and civil society is that of political scientists Jean Cohen and Andrew Arato, *Civil Society and Political Theory*, first published in 1992.[4] Their argument is a very radical one. They write of the family as "the voluntary association par excellence," and as such the "first association of civil society." Theirs is an analytical suggestion, which stresses not *connectedness* but *inclusion*, yet I think it is a highly problematic solution. Families may be voluntary associations for adults, but they are certainly not so for children. We may choose to belong to Amnesty International, but we cannot choose our parents. Furthermore, viewing the family as the first association of civil society is to miss the specificity of close kinship ties, the unique daily (and nightly) continuities of family life, the nature of familial love, and the physical separateness of home living. It also distorts the shape of civil society in the terms that historian Jürgen Kocka has suggested, that is, as "a sphere connected to, but separate from, economy, state and the private sphere," in which a specific type of social action takes place.[5] Civil society's origins, continues Kocka, are in the European Enlightenment, and the project of civil society, however variegated and developed over time, is still an Enlightenment one. The same cannot be said for the history of the family.

In theoretical terms, I still find Hegel's concept of the relation between family and civil society, which he proposed in *Elements of the Philosophy of Right*, the most suggestive of all.[6] In this work, the moment of "dissolution" (*Auflösung*), of transition from family to civil society, is as revealing as it is neglected in current debates on civil society. Hegel's moment of transition bears the analytic weight of a triple-layered process—the passage from the family of origin to that of procreation, the entry of adult males into modern civil society, and the negation in civil society of the previous ethnicity of the family. Naturally, we would have considerable difficulties today accepting the terms in which Hegel describes this transition. We have no desire to share his version of gender relations—"woman has her substantial vocation (*Bestimmung*) in the family, and her ethical disposition consists in this [family] *piety*"; nor his famous definition of civil society as that which "affords a spectacle of extravagance and misery as well as of the physical and ethical corruption common to both."[7] However, what makes Hegel unique is the intensity and originality with which he invites us to concentrate on family–civil society relations, though this is confined to just a few pages. He alone, at a theoretical level, isolates the moment when family and civil society come into contact with each other. Instead of a simple private-public divide, his is a more complex treatment, with an explicit insistence on the connections, or lack of them, between individuals, families, civil society, and the state.

Finally, I would like to say a few introductory words about gender in relation to family–civil society relations. I think it would be fair to say that in gender studies as a whole, the need to study the connections between families and civil society has emerged very little. There are two reasons for this. The first is that feminist scholars have put a necessary emphasis upon gendered individuality rather than upon the family as an institution. With one or two recent exceptions, theirs has been a concentration upon individual, female liberation *from* the family (especially the patriarchal family) rather than upon families as collectives relating *to* civil society.[8] The second, closely linked to the first, is that there has been a tendency to subsume family studies into the general and all-embracing category of gender studies. Both these methodological inclinations, especially the second one, meant that the need to study the family from the aspect of its connections to civil society has emerged very little. The American philosopher Susan Moller Okin, in her outstanding *Justice, Gender and the Family*, was one of the very few feminist scholars who made explicit the family's centrality: "We refuse to give up on the institution of the family" she wrote in 1989, and not by chance she asked (although she did not answer) one of the key questions, which now concern us as civil society scholars: "unless the household is connected by a continuum of just associations to the larger communities within which people are supposed to develop fellow feelings for each other, how will they grow up with the capacity for enlarged sympathies such as are clearly required for the practice of justice?"[9]

In the pages that follow I will look first at some contemporary family forms in Europe and northern America. I will then examine family–civil society relations in historical terms, identifying four different versions of these relations as they have emerged in the twentieth century. From there, I shall elaborate upon two archetypes of families—the closed and the open—in order to analyze the factors, both internal and external, which facilitate or impede a constant and productive relationship between families and civil society.

Contemporary Family Forms

It is a commonplace in family studies to state there is no such thing as "*the* family," but rather an infinite variety of families, each one different from the other. It is certainly true that, in the course of the twentieth century, family forms have become more complex. An older vision of the family, one that was widespread but never entirely born out in reality, was of a nuclear unit composed of parents and children living under the same roof. It has come under increasingly severe pressure. Let me take a number of examples. There are so-called "postmodern" families, like those analyzed by Judith Stacey in Silicon Valley, California, the product of "the devastating economic effects on women and children of endemic marital instability."[10] Here in the 1980s men soaked up a fast-track individualist culture, heavily oriented to enrichment and social mobility. They became "workaholics" with sixty- to eighty-hour weeks, their family voices reduced to little more than whispers. Women, especially working-class women, struggled. They aspired to autonomy, but the market gave them few opportunities to realize it, and the frequency of divorce left them and their children disoriented and economically insecure. By the end of the century, mothers were fighting to defend their children from a rampant narcotics economy, and to reinvent kinship ties in an extended and often fictive way. The spaces left open to them for engagement in civil society were few indeed.

By way of contrast to this Californian and "postmodern" model, we can cite a more traditional one: the close-knit families of the villages and towns of the "industrialized countryside" of central and northern Italy. Here, too, in the 1980s and 1990s men often overworked in small, dynamic family firms and consequently spent little time with their children. However, solidarities in these families frequently extend across three generations, with grandparents looking after their grandchildren on a daily basis, and then themselves being cared for in advanced old age. Spatial and emotional proximity are the rule of the day. Children rarely move far away from their family of origin and "pop in" on a daily basis. Grown-up sons see their mothers with almost alarming regularity. These "long," loyal, generationally extended families, although not living under the same roof, form a single unit with regard to strategy and ambitions. They are important sites of saving, entrepreneurship, and investment. Gender relations are traditional ones, with mothers being the pivot around which family relationships revolve. Their daughters, however, are more emancipated and educated, and are often in the forefront of the active associational life of these regions.[11]

A third model, that of "reconstituted" families, is not tied to a single geographical area, but is ever more common in major urban conglomerations. These are highly complex groupings, often spatially spread, which try to put together pieces of families deriving from previous unions, sometimes successfully, often less so. Time is often a complicated business here. The habitual routine of everyday life is punctuated by children having two homes, visiting at holidays, having to deal with parents in different geographical locations and cope with stepparents who may well not be welcoming. Gender roles are often heavily modified, with fathers playing a very active role in childcare, and mothers having unexpected expanses of time for themselves. From the research so far available, it is not possible to tell how much of that time is oriented towards civil society activities.

In developed countries, as birth rates decline, the overwhelming tendency is for households to have an ever-smaller number of members.

There are heterosexual couples, who live together without having children, lone-parent families (often mother and child), and single-sex domestic groups, like gay and lesbian domestic couples. There are also increasing numbers of people, especially old people, who live alone, and are sometimes referred to in the statistics as "single-member families," a truly contradictory label.

Whichever of these family forms or groups we choose to study, we see that it cannot meaningfully be construed as "the first association of civil society." Each has its own rhythms and necessities, which have little or nothing to do with civil society. The latter is an appendage of family life for some of its members, and not an integral part of daily life. As the feminist scholar Anna Yeatman has written, to think in "inclusive" terms (the family as part of civil society) is to miss, at the very least, "the specificity of domestic sociality."[12] Some scholars, like Cohen and Arato, may wish for families to behave as the first associations of civil society, but that is very different from claiming that that is what they do. Here, there are important distinctions to be made between volition and cognition. I would suggest instead that both analytically and historically it makes sense to maintain a distinction between families and civil society. We must separate the two spheres, not necessarily in a traditional private-public way, and then see in what ways they connect, or fail to connect.

Historical Models of Family–Civil Society Relations

In historical terms, the twentieth century witnessed different versions and elaborations of family–civil society relations. Let me deal all too briefly with four contrasting versions of them. The first is a radical reading that comes and goes throughout the century: that of *the attempt to demote or even dissolve the family into a highly structured civil society.* We can find it strongly present in the writings of the Bolsheviks, especially those of Alexandra Kollontai: "the worker-mother," she wrote in 1920, "must raise herself up until she makes no distinction between *mine* and *yours*, she must remember that henceforth there are only *our* children … the common possession of all workers."[13] We can also find it with the theorists of the first and second waves of Jewish kibbutzim settlers in Palestine, at the end of the nineteenth and at the beginning of the twentieth century. They insisted on collective children's education and activities, the abolition of marriage, communal eating, and the sharing of rooms. On the original kibbutzim, family relations and the intimate sphere were demoted to a subordinate position, partly to foster a collective and pioneering spirit, but also in order to escape from the asphyxiating conformity of the family model of the Diaspora and the physical degeneration often associated with it.[14]

The radical model surfaced again in 1968 and the years after it, with the attempt to contest the family and all its relations. Psychiatrist David Cooper's *The Death of the Family*, first published in 1971, circulated widely among European and North American youth.[15] Among these alternative-oriented minorities of the 1970s, a new form of domestic sociality, the commune, was seen as superseding previous family forms and values. It was an idealized micro–civil society in the process of formation.[16] The basic thrust of all these three examples was to respond to the problem of connection by denying or demoting one of the elements, that of the family, and exalting instead different forms of collective sociality. In all three of them, formal gender equality became the order of the day. However, it was a strange sort of civil society that emerged in Russia in the post-revolutionary years—hyperactive, factory-based and increasingly dominated by the Communist Party. The Bolsheviks believed passionately in women's emancipation *from* the household and family. On the other hand, the new freedoms permitted to men by the Bolshevik Family Code of 1918 allowed them to behave irresponsibly towards their women and the children they sired, often deserting both in the quest for new adventures. This was not at all the scenario that Kollontai had envisaged.

Similarly, in the communes of the 1970s, sexual freedom, an integral part of the new civil society, was often theorized and practiced by men at the expense of women, and the emotional tensions deriving from these practices often accounted for the short-lived nature of the communes themselves. Only on the kibbutzim did an alternative model emerge that respected gender equality, if not gender difference. Young women and men worked in the fields, embracing a semimilitarized Zionist philosophy that was critical of both individualism and familism. All these three great experiments are failures, although of different sorts and with different consequences. The most moderate of them, the kibbutzim, was the longest lasting.

We can also find the opposite of the first model—not the substitution of civil society for the family, but rather *the substitution of the family for civil society*. This is the thrust of the Catholic integralism of Pius XI and Pius XII. For the highly influential popes of the mid-twentieth century, the family was the first "natural" society and as such took precedence over both civil society and the state. The *Enciclopedia Cattolica*, published in Rome in 1950, explained that this precedence was due to the fact that "the family was the first form of social organization, the first school and the first temple." In a hierarchy of values, society was subordinate to the family "because society is a means to assure to the family, and through it the individual, that which is indispensable for its [the family's] self-realization."[17] This concept of *"anteriorità,"* of the family coming first in all senses of the word, obviously imposed severe limitations upon the possible scope and flow of family–civil society relations, and indeed upon the very idea of civil society itself. Here is Pius XII in June 1940:

> Society is not formed of a conglomerate of individuals, sporadic beings who appear one moment and disappear the next. Rather it arises from the economic sharing and moral solidarities of families, which, by passing on from generation to generation the precious inheritance of the same ideal, the same civilization, the same religion, ensure the cohesion and continuity of social ties.[18]

Civil society simply becomes the agglomeration of like-minded families. Gender relations, both within and without the family, are clearly laid out in what is probably the most important document on the family in the twentieth century—Pius XI's encyclical *Casti Connubii* of 31 December 1930. Relations between men and women were to be governed by a precise hierarchy,

> which requires on the one hand the superiority of the husband over the wife and children, and on the other the prompt subjection and obedience of the wife, not for reasons of force, but for those recommended by the Apostle in the following way: "Let women be subject to the husbands as to the Lord, because the man is the head of the woman as Christ is head of the Church."[19]

A third model can be depicted which is neither imagined nor preached, but lived. There are long moments in the twentieth century, when *civil society finds its only refuge in the family*, survives only within the four walls of the household, if it survives at all. In other words, time and again under the regimes of the great dictators, it is the carefully guarded secrets of domestic sociality that keep alive any idea of a civil society. Though in a different context, the African-American activist bell hooks has much the same sort of thing in mind when she writes of the "subversive value of home-place, of having access to private space where we do not encounter white racist aggression" and where domestic space becomes "a crucial site for organizing, for forming political solidarity."[20] It is interesting to note that very often not only male but female voices make themselves heard in such circumstances. In the privacy of the home, in a sphere that historically has more naturally belonged to them, women attended meetings and conversations that would otherwise have been exclusively male. It was women who activated kinship networks in the face of the mass regimes of the 1930s, often in the first instance to protect their menfolk, but then in order to organize resistance, first passive and then active.[21]

A fourth model, perhaps that which comes to predominate most extensively in the last decades of the century, is that in which *family and civil society are clearly separated*. To understand the nature and implications of this model, so typical of modern democracies, is the purpose of the remaining sections of this article.

Closed and Open Families

I would like to suggest an initial dichotomy between *closed* and *open* families, between those that are basically inward-looking and those that, at least potentially, look outwards towards civil society. These can be considered as archetypes and I wish to illustrate them with two pieces of art. Dominant versions of modernity accentuate the privatization of family life, its separation from the public sphere, and its dedication to home-centered consumption. Rachel Whiteread's notable piece of sculpture *House* (1993) potently suggests this sort of family life. Her sculpture is a concrete cast of the interior of a house that has been demolished. It is an example of "negative space" which has been solidified. There are no real windows or doors, only their design on the concrete; no chance of looking in, let alone "popping in," and no way of getting out, let alone "popping out." Perhaps it is a refuge, but it looks more like a prison, a family prison, a site of neurosis and dysfunction, perhaps even of violence. In brutal fashion, Whiteread has captured one of the essentials of modern family life—its enclosedness, introspection, and preoccupation with itself.[22]

Mario Merz's *Igloos*, of which he made a long series, offer a rather different perspective. For Merz the *Igloo* is a home and a refuge, but, unlike Whiteread's *House*, it is not sealed up against the outside world. On the contrary, his igloos in one way or another are open, some even transparent. You can see inside them and from the inside you can see out. "This little construction, the mistress of space," writes Merz, "creates the inside by its definition of itself, as the measure of an anthropological space, and creates the outside by that same definition. IGLOO = HOME."[23] This home is of modest proportions, based one might say on "voluntary simplicity," and its very modesty and openness define its relation to the spaces outside it. Of course, taken literally, a transparent home would be a nightmare, a sort of permanent domestic "reality show" in which all privacy disappears. Yet I think the openness and sobriety that Merz has in mind are not of the literal sort, but rather an invitation to rethink the nature of home, and the relationship between internal and external.

How complex Merz considered such a relationship to be can be gleaned from the *Igloo* of 1985, now housed in the Tate Modern in London. It bears the enigmatic title, "Do we revolve around houses or do houses revolve around us?" I find it of particular significance because it has an illuminated walkway (perhaps "crawlway" would describe it better) that connects the *Igloo* to the outside. Connectedness is possible, Merz suggests, but it is not going to be easy. And as if to underline this point, he has placed shards of glass along the passage connecting the *Igloo* to the external world. Through the glass you can see the outside, but can you get there?

Evidence for the *closed* family can be found everywhere. In 1967 the British anthropologist Edmund Leach provoked wide discussion by stating in a well-known series of radio lectures that "today the domestic household is isolated.... The family with all its tawdry secrets and narrow privacy is the source of all discontents."[24] Many listeners objected and Leach had to apologize, reassuring them that he had not wished to speak out against the family. Privatism was a key theme of sociologist John H. Goldthorpe's sociological work on the Luton working class.[25] In Italy, ever since political scientist Edward C. Banfield's famous book *The Moral Basis of Backward Society* was published in 1958 the question of familism has never really gone away.[26] In America, the literature on gated communities has grown rapidly. "Walling out the world?" was the title of one recent article. In Australia, in the outer suburbia of Sydney and Melbourne, there is a new rage for what have come to be called "McMansions." The term was coined in the United States and describes huge new double-story houses with triple garages, porticos and columns, and big front doors with vaulted entries. They have been put up in record time and occupy almost the totality of the 400–600 square meters of the individual family's suburban plot. Gone is the traditional backyard with its trees, garden, vegetable patch, and room for the children to run around or build tree houses. Instead, they are taken by their parents in cars to organized sports activities. Above all, they find their entertainment inside, in the "rumpus room" and the big-screen media room.[27] All this, while the average number of persons in Australian households, as everywhere in the developed world, is constantly shrinking—from 3.7 persons in 1981 to 2.7 in 2001. In these examples, families are not only separate from civil society but hermetically sealed off from it by the nature of their daily activities and their model of home living.

The *open* family, by contrast, is much more difficult to locate and describe. To get some idea of it, we probably have to go back to traditional working-class quarters in major European cities in the second half of the nineteenth century or the first half of the twentieth, to realities like Bethnal Green in London or the Barriera San Paolo in Turin.[28] The memory and sometimes the history of these quarters are prey to idealization, but there are also clear recurring themes: the doors of houses left open, the constant "popping in," the internal crampedness that made for external sociability, the kids playing in the street.

It is symptomatic that in order to find modern examples of the same sort of fluidity we probably have to look outside the "developed" world. We can, for instance, follow the philosopher Martha Nussbaum in her exploration of the differences between the daily rhythms of family life in India and in the United States. For Nussbaum the Indian home, among all classes, "is simply more porous." Even in upper middle-class families, she writes, "visitors drop in unannounced and there is a constant ebb and flow of people through the house."[29] The out-of-doors and the other is in some sort of balanced relationship with the indoors and the familiar.

To sustain the thrust of my argument, I have intentionally posed the question of closedness and openness in terms of archetypes, art works, and binary categories. But family attitudes and actions in contemporary developed societies are, of course, infinitely graded between the two extremes I have described. Furthermore, different family members will behave in different ways, even if overall family culture and education exercise considerable hegemony over them. Generation and gender obviously make a difference. In the last part of this paper I want to look at the forces in contemporary society that work in favor of or against the connectedness of families with civil society. I will look first at family *interiors*, with particular attention to gender relations; and secondly at *exteriors*, especially new socioeconomic and cultural forces working upon and influencing families.

The Changing Nature of Gendered Interiors

The last decades of the twentieth century have witnessed startling developments in Western family life, so much so that the family, having occupied a subsidiary place on the political agenda for much of the century and having rarely been the object of animated discussion in parliaments, now enjoys a position of increasing preeminence. It is possible to single out a number of major trends, though in a schematic way. The first is the decline in fertility rates. This is a trend covering the whole century, only briefly interrupted by the baby boom after the Second World War. By the end of the century childlessness had reached about 20 percent in Britain, Australia, the US, and Germany.[30] A second trend, of great significance in historical terms, is the gradual liquefaction of the ancient institution of marriage. Couples have chosen to get married later and more rarely; cohabitation has become ever more popular. Divorces increased dramatically in European countries (especially in northwestern European countries) from the mid-1960s onwards, but have leveled off in the last fifteen years. Marriages, on the other hand, have continued to decline.[31] A third trend, in strong causal relation to the previous two, is the change of the position of women within the family. Increasing parity in gender relations, increased participation in the labor market, increased rights and protection under the law, and increased use of contraception have all contributed to a fundamental change in the perception and often the reality of women's family role.

How can we read these changes in relation to the question that we have in front of us—the connections between family and civil society? I would argue that there can be no single conclusion, and that any proper answer must recognize both positive and negative aspects in relation to the texture and expansion of civil society. Let me take first the relationship between civil society and fertility rates, which raises the important methodological question of the *family life cycle:* in what moment in the life of a family are the individuals that compose it most open to the sirens of civil society? Very many studies show, from Sweden to Portugal, that the moment of greatest opening of families is when they have school-age children, and that it is women, not men, who take the initiative. Mothers go to parks, meet other mothers, start chatting. Children sleep over, friendships are made between parents at nursery and primary school, and civil society battles are often waged around the school and public services.

The frequency of such moments is obviously put in jeopardy by the decline in fertility rates. In general, a society with a larger number of old people and a significantly smaller number of young and very young ones implies a structural constraint on civil society, even if it has been shown that certain generations, like that of the 1960s in Europe, have continued to contribute significantly to civil society as they have grown older.

Let us take another area. If we concentrate our attention on the changing role of women within the household, on their greater rights and liberty, on their exiting from Rachel Whiteread's *House* and entering into the labor market and civil society, then we see that there has been a strikingly positive change. All those who have experience working at length in civil society in developed countries have noted the presence of women in increasing numbers at meetings and associations. Furthermore, they are there as leading participants, not at the beck and call of men. In June 2004, a civil society list with the name *"Un' altra città/un altro mondo"* (Another city, another world) contested local elections in Florence for the first time. The first ten names on the list were all women, as was the candidate for mayor, Ornella De Zordo, an English literature professor, who received 12.4 percent of the vote.

Yet all this is at a price. Nearly always this greater presence of women in civil society is accompanied by the greater complication of their everyday life. Work outside the home, as has been noted time and again, is a double-edged sword. There is more opportunity, but less time. Women active in civil society find themselves having simultaneously to go to meetings in the evenings, carry out their family work of care and sustenance, and do regular paid work outside their homes. In societies like Italy and Spain, where the older generation is more rarely institutionalized than in northwestern Europe, the problem of aging parents constitutes a grave problem of daily responsibility for the central female figure of the family. At the end of a day a person in this sort of situation has very little energy left indeed. This has important consequences not only at a personal level, but for the texture of civil society, which is in any case quite fragile. Participation, as we all know, is subject to sudden highs and lows, and civil society associations are often of uncertain duration.

If too much time pressure is brought to bear on active women, there is a real danger of them abandoning civil society completely after a period of months or at most two or three years. The fragility of civil society is thus underscored by the vulnerability of the most recent and significant (female) figures in it.

And what of men? My impression is of men who nearly always put career first, often work very long hours, and consequently have little time left either to participate regularly in civil society themselves, support women in the home, or look after children when their companions are active in civil society. Attempted redefinitions of roles and arguments over each partner's time and availability remain sites of enormous tension. There is considerable evidence of a growing number of so-called new fathers, especially in northwestern Europe: fathers who assume much more responsibility for children, and who develop sensibilities that have been assumed to come with being a mother.[32] But it is still true in daily time terms that in southern European societies, as official statistics show, women are better off without husbands because the little they do to help is far outweighed by the amount of female care they both require and demand.[33]

My tentative conclusion would therefore be that changes in gender roles have opened up great possibilities for family–civil society relations. So, too, have some of the more recent transformations within the family. Yet although individuals, especially women, may be freer and more equal within the family, that does not guarantee their greater connectedness with civil society.

Home-oriented Exteriors

Part of the reason for this lies in the material and immaterial culture that surround and envelop modern family life. Here it is necessary, I think, to be less ambivalent and more categorically pessimistic. Let me just take two crucial elements—television and consumerism. Without wishing to become part of the "cataclysmic" school,[34] I would argue that, on balance, both television and consumerism exercise a negative influence on the question of family–civil society relations. In the ongoing, even raging debate about the effects of television upon everyday life, there is a profound division between those who stress what is called in cultural studies the *vertical dimension* of media power, and those who concentrate on the *horizontal dimension*. The members of the latter school, like media scholars Paddy Scannell and Joshua Meyrowitz, wish to stress the inclusive nature of television, even its democratic aspects.[35] A new "situational geography" of social life is created, where hierarchical senses of place and position are broken down: "Through television young and old, scholars and illiterates ... often share the same or very similar information at the same moment."[36] Those who stress the vertical dimension, by contrast, concentrate upon the ever-more-restricted nature of media ownership, the decline of public television (the abandonment of civic pedagogy, etc.) and its aping of the priorities of commercial television, i.e. audience ratings, advertising revenue, and profits.[37] The prime aim becomes not to produce television programs but to produce audiences, that is, the consumers required by the market of investors in publicity.

What does all this mean for connectedness? The single most important consequence of television, as political scientist Robert Putnam has rightly said, "has been to bring us home." American and European leisure time can increasingly be measured, as market consultants do, in terms of "eyeballs." Watching things, especially electronic screens, occupies more and more of our time, while doing things, especially with other people, occupies less and less.[38] Sometimes, a counterargument is couched in terms of the advantages that the Internet and e-mailing can play in disseminating information and bringing people together. There is little doubt about the first of these roles, considerably more about the second. For civil society, e-mailing is not at all the same thing as face-to-face contact. E-mail discussions are often brittle and unnecessarily divisive. It often needs just one "flamer," as they are called in e-mail jargon, one person to provoke and contest, for a "virtual" discussion to go rapidly downhill. Introducing a wide-ranging account of recent American associationism, Robert D. Putnam and Larry M. Feldstein note that the Internet and e-mail "play a surprisingly small role in most of our stories."[39] For them, local face-to-face contact, as time-consuming as it is, is irreplaceable. Civil society thrives on meeting, discussing, and taking action, but family leisure patterns are often diametrically opposed to these activities.

Finally, we need to consider the question of consumerism. It would be foolish indeed to deny the dignity of choice that buying confers upon us all. What drives modern consumption is not only economist Thorstein Veblen's classic theory of emulation, but also the elements that anthropologist Daniel Miller has stressed in *The Dialectics of Shopping*—love for oneself and for one's family and friends.[40] If we add to these Colin Campbell's "imaginative autonomous hedonism," which is pursued in the world of play, of emotion and romance, of dreaming and imagination, and which has become commodified on a mass scale, then we have an extraordinary, time-consuming realm of modern activity, conferring pleasure and promising self-fulfillment.[41]

But what does this realm offer on the question of family–civil society connections? Sociologist Juliet Schor's statistics, again from the US, are devastating in their own way. Shopping has become the most popular weekday evening "out-of-home" entertainment. Shopping malls are everywhere. Four billion square feet of American land has been converted into shopping centers—sixteen square feet for every man, woman, and child. In the five years between 1983 and 1987, Americans purchased 51 million microwaves, 44 million washers and dryers, 85 million color televisions, 36 million refrigerators and freezers, 48 million video cassette recorders, and 23 million cordless telephones—all for an adult population of only 180 million.[42] Consumerism has become the subject that occupies pride of place in family strategies and family conversation. Dignity of choice has given way to a form of dependency upon the world of goods. As Schor has written: "Work-and-spend has become a mutually reinforcing and powerful syndrome—a seamless web we somehow keep choosing, without even meaning to."[43]

In partial correction of this negative view, anthropologist Daniel Miller has underlined the role of supermarkets and shopping malls as "favored sites for meeting people and creating a public sphere."[44] He argues that the old sociability of working-class quarters, largely concentrated outside the home because of cramped living conditions, has been "transposed" to the new centers of acquisition. I think this is an overly benign view. Families may well go to hypermarkets and shopping malls for a "day out," and they will be encouraged to do so by unusual offers, like the possibility of sampling Swedish food at IKEA. But their sociality is family-based, not oriented towards the other shoppers, with whom they may well be in competition—for a table in a café on a crowded weekend, or for items on offer in a sale. People are not at all likely to talk to others that they do not know. There is little of a "public sphere," let alone a civil society, in these practices. And it is worth adding that such expeditions are often gender-based, with men reluctant to go, or making a great fuss once they are there.

In all this, what regular space or time or predilection are left for Mario Merz's illuminated passageway that might lead us towards civil society? People do join civil society associations in the contemporary "developed" world, in some countries in considerable numbers.[45] But they do so, I would suggest, against the grain of much of modernity, which pushes them gently but firmly back into the home, and towards the daily practices of "closed" rather than "open" families.

Conclusion

I have tried to show that a theoretical approach, one that derives from a Hegelian view of the necessary connectedness of family, civil society and the state, can open up entirely new vistas for contemporary civil society studies. The adoption of a tripartite analytical division of this sort, instead of a simple public-private divide, constitutes a clear invitation to scholars of civil society not just to confine their researches to a generic public sphere, but to confront specific questions concerning the linkages, or lack of them, between individuals, families, and civil society. It also presses us to look at family-state relations, although this is an area that—for reasons of space—I have here intentionally left largely unexamined. Hegel's own treatment of these themes is highly colored by the convictions and realities of his time. He was convinced that when the family "touched" civil society, it did so exclusively through its male members. In addition, civil society was for him not an Enlightenment project of associationism, containing Utopian elements that would be constantly reinterpreted over time, but rather the harsh and often destructive realities and values of early urban capitalism (*bürgerliche Gesellschaft* rather than *Zivilgesellschaft*). As such, civil society constituted for him the negation of family love, a "moment" when ethicity was all but lost.

To reexamine Hegel's categories of connection in the contemporary context of economically advanced societies in the North of the world is a challenging prospect. In gender terms much has changed since Hegel's time, but much has also remained the same. Women are not simply excluded a priori from civil society, but their participation in it, as I have tried to show, is undermined by a whole number of considerations—not least the weight of their commitments to families that have become far "longer" (i.e., tri-generational) than in Hegel's time. Women now enjoy greater freedom in nearly every sense of the word—in terms of mobility, educational opportunities, control of their own bodies, and rights within the family and outside of it, but these freedoms have not translated automatically into participation in civil society. The reasons for this are highly complex, and vary both by age group and by country, but at the heart of any explanation must lie the twin demands of participation in the labor force and commitment to family. At the end of the day, women, especially working-class women, have little time or energy left for the deliberative arenas of civil society. And their male partners are often of little aid, absorbed as they are by work or career demands which increasingly expand from the workplace to invade home spaces. For both genders, modern democratic states—with few, often Scandinavian, exceptions—do almost nothing to encourage countertendencies or culturally different approaches to the question of linking families to civil society. Most democratic states have not even posed the problem.

Modernity does not "dissolve" the family, but it tends to keep families and *Zivilgesellschaft* separate. Of the two archetypes that I have examined, "open" and "closed" families, in economically advanced societies it is the latter that dominates by far. Modern families take very many different forms, but they are nearly all permeated by what has become a highly dominant model of "family life"—that based on the exclusive joys of consumption and domesticity. The model does not imply immobility—quite the opposite—but connectedness at a more profound level, both local and global, remains a distant objective.

Notes

1. Oliver Stallybrass, "Editor's introduction," in Edward M. Forster, *Howards End* (London, 2000; 1st ed., 1910), 10.
2. See my "Individuals, Families, Civil Society and the State: Some General Considerations" in *The Golden Chain*, ed. Paul Ginsborg and Jürgen Nautz (forthcoming, London).
3. Ibid., for a more in-depth discussion of why this has been so.
4. Jean L. Cohen and Andrew Arato, *Civil Society and Political Theory* (Cambridge, MA, 1992), esp. 631 n. 48.
5. Jürgen Kocka, "Civil Society from a Historical Perspective," *European Review* 12, no. 1 (2004): 65–79, 74.
6. G.W.F.Hegel, *Elements of the Philosophy of Right*, ed. A.W. Wood, Cambridge, 1991.
7. Ibid., 206, paragraph 166, and 222, paragraph 185.
8. Sonya Michel, "Il 'ritorno alla famiglia' negli studi femministi" [The family turn in feminist studies], *Contemporanea: rivista di storia dell '800 e del '900* 2 (April 2004): 177–200.
9. Susan Moller Okin, *Justice, Gender and the Family* (New York, 1989), 100, 125. She asks this question in the context of her discussion of John Rawls's theory of moral development, which requires us, in his words, "to put ourselves into another's place and find out what we would do in his position." How, asks Moller Okin in another part of the same passage, are we likely to be able to do this in hierarchical families in which sex roles are rigidly assigned? See also John Rawls, *A Theory of Justice* (Cambridge, MA, 1971).
10. Judith Stacey, *Brave New Families: Stories of Domestic Upheaval in Late Twentieth-Century America* (New York, 1990), 13.
11. Giuseppe De Rita, "L'impresa familiare," in *La famiglia italiana dall'Ottocento ad oggi*, ed. Piero Melograni and Lucetta Scaraffia (Bari, 1998), 383–416. For a case study, see Paul Ginsborg, "I cambiamenti della famiglia in un distretto industriale italiano, 1965–1997," in *Un'Italia minore: Famiglia, istruzione e tradizioni civiche in Valdelsa*, ed. Ginsborg and Francesco Ramella (Florence, 1999), 109–154.
12. Anna Yeatman, "Gender and the Differentiation of Social Life into Public and Domestic Domains," *Social Analysis* 15 (1984): 32–50, 44. Of course, domestic sociality does not always coincide with the *Intimsphäre*, nor both with *family* life, but the overlapping of these three spheres is usually very great. For further discussion of the overlapping concepts of home, family, and the private sphere, see Paul Ginsborg, *The Politics of Everyday Life: Making Choices, Changing Lives* (London, New Haven, CT, 2005), 93f.
13. Alexandra Kollontai, *Communism and the Family* (London, 1973; 1st ed., 1920), 19. See also Elisabeth Waters, "The Bolsheviks and the Family," *Contemporary European History* 4, no. 3 (1995): 293–314; and Wendy Z. Goldman, *Women, the State and Revolution: Soviet Family Policy and Social Life, 1917–36* (Cambridge, 1993).
14. Marcella Simoni, "La costruzione di due nazioni: Famiglia e società civile in Palestina (1900–1948)," *Passato e Presente* 57 (2002): 125–146, 129–130. For Max Nordau's idea of the regeneration of the individual Jew after the experience of the Diaspora see Daniel Pick, *Faces of Degeneration: A European Disorder, 1848–1918* (Cambridge, 1989). Children's lives on the kibbutzim are memorably treated by Bruno Bettelheim, *The Children of the Dream* (London 1969).
15. David G. Cooper, *The Death of the Family* (New York, 1971).
16. See the very sensitive study by Philip Abrams and Andrew McCulloch, *Communes, Sociology and Society* (Cambridge, 1976).
17. "Famiglia," in *Enciclopedia Cattolica* 5 (Rome, 1950), 994.
18. *Insegnamenti pontifici*, vol. 1, *Il matrimonio* (Rome, 1964), 288f.

19. *Casti Connubii* is published in *Matrimonio e famiglia nel magistero della Chiesa. I documenti dal Concilio di Firenze a Giovanni Paolo II*, ed. Piero Barberi and Dionigi Tettamanzi (Milan, 1986), 107–154. For the quotation cited here, 147.
20. bell hooks, "Homeplace as site of resistance," in *Yearning: Race, Gender and Cultural Politics* (Boston, 1990), 47.
21. Luisa Passerini, *Fascism in Popular Memory: The Cultural Experience of the Turin Working Class* (Cambridge, 1987), 138–139.
22. For further details and comments, see James Lingwood, ed., *House* (London, 1995).
23. Mario Merz, *I Want to Write a Book Right Now* (Florence, 1986), 139.
24. Edmund Leach, *A Runaway World?* (London, 1968), 44.
25. John H. Goldthorpe et al., *The Affluent Worker*, 3 vols. (Cambridge, 1968–69).
26. Edward Banfield, *The Moral Basis of a Backward Society* (Glencoe, IL, 1958). Banfield coined the term *amoral familism* to describe the ethos of southern Italian rural life, and in particular of one village in Basilicata, Chiaromonte. Its extreme backwardness was caused by "the inability of the villagers to act together for their common good, or indeed for any good transcending the immediate, material interest of the nuclear family" (ibid.,10).
27. Janet Hawley, "Be it ever so humungous," *The Australian*, Good Weekend Supplement, 23 August 2003.
28. Michael Young and Peter Willmott, *Family and Kinship in East London* (London, 1957); Giovanni Levi et al., "Cultura operaia e vita quotidiana in Borgo San Paolo," in *Torino tra le due guerre: cultura operaia e vita quotidiana in borgo San Paolo, organizzazione del consenso e comunicazioni di massa, l'organizzazione del territorio urbano, le arti decorative e industriali, le arti figurative, la musica e il teatro: marzo–giugno 1978* (Turin, 1978), 2–45.
29. Martha Nussbaum, *Women and Human Development: The Capabilities Approach* (Cambridge, 2000), 259.
30. Catherine Hakim, "Models of the family, women's role and social policy," *European Societies* 1, no. 1 (1999): 33–58, 36.
31. Eurostat, *Eurostat Year Book 1998–99* (Luxembourg, 1999), 84.
32. Scott Coltrane, "The Future of Fatherhood: Social, Demographic and Economic Influences on Men's Family Involvements," in *Fatherhood: Contemporary Theory, Research and Social Policy*, ed. William Marsiglio (London, 1995), 255–274; Alois Herlth, "The New Fathers: What Does it Mean for Children, Marriage and for Family Policy?" in *Family Life and Family Policies in Europe*, ed. Franz-Xaver Kaufmann et al., vol. 2 (Oxford, 2002), 299–320.
33. ISTAT (Istituto Nazionale di Statistica), *Indagine multiscopo sulle famiglie: l'uso del tempo in Italia* (Rome, 1993).
34. See Karl Popper's last diatribe against television, which circulated very widely in Italy in the 1990s: Karl R. Popper and John Condry, *Cattiva maestra televisione* (Rome, 1994); as well as Giovanni Sartori, *Homo videns: Televisione e Post-pensiero* (Bari, Rome, 1997).
35. Paddy Scannell et al., eds., *Culture and Power: A Media, Culture and Society Reader* (London, 1992).
36. Joshua Meyrowitz, *No Sense of Place: The Impact of Electronic Media on Social Behavior* (Oxford, 1985), 90.
37. Informative about this world is Ronald V. Bettig and Jeanne L. Hall, *Big Media, Big Money: Cultural Texts and Political Economics* (Lanham, MD, 2003).
38. Robert D. Putnam, *Bowling Alone: The Collapse and Revival of American Community* (New York, 2000), 223, 245.
39. Robert D. Putnam and Larry M. Feldstein, *Better Together: Restoring the American Community* (New York, 2003), 9.

40. Thorstein Veblen, *The Theory of the Leisure Class: An Economic Study in the Evolution of Institutions* (New York, London, 1899; selections in reprint, New York, 2006); Daniel Miller, *The Dialectics of Shopping* (Chicago, 2001).
41. Colin Campbell, *The Romantic Ethic and the Spirit of Modern Consumerism* (Oxford, 1987), 77–95.
42. Juliet B. Schor, *The Overworked American* (New York), 1991, 107f.
43. Schor, *Overworked*, 112; also useful: Juliet B. Schor and Douglas B. Holt, eds., *The Consumer Society Reader* (New York, 2000).
44. Miller, *Dialectics*, 99.
45. Details of national membership and volunteering in "civil society" are to be found in Helmut Anheier and Sally Stares, "Introducing the Global Civil Society Index," in *Global Civil Society 2002*, ed. Marlies Glasius et al. (Oxford, 2002), 245, table 1.1, and 363, Record 28. They provide comparative figures, not only for Europe, relating to membership and volunteering in four different areas of activity: Community action, Third World/human rights, Environment, and Peace. Unfortunately, they do not give us the percentage of the adult population active in each country in such groups, nor do they offer a gender breakdown. In the year 2000, Sweden (1.00), Iceland (0.97), Holland (0.97) and Denmark (0.87) headed this league table.

CIVIL SOCIETY, GENDERED PROTEST, AND NONGOVERNMENTAL MOVEMENTS

Chapter 9

NECESSARY CONFRONTATIONS
GENDER, CIVIL SOCIETY, AND THE POLITICS OF FOOD IN EIGHTEENTH- TO TWENTIETH-CENTURY GERMANY

Manfred Gailus

Food riots have occurred frequently throughout much of modern German history, but do they belong under the rubric of civil society?[1] Certainly, subsistence protests may be considered a type of popular initiative, but they clearly lack the qualities of polite debate or deliberative procedures we associate with clubs and civic organizations. Rather, they are a form of "self-help" that emerges from the fears, worries, and needs of historical actors and materializes in direct, symbolic, and even violent action. If crowds had stopped to articulate their philosophy, it might have been something like, "Necessity knows no law." Such a rationale seems far removed from essential principles of civil society like the monopoly of physical force and the rule of law. To that extent, subsistence conflicts and civil society find themselves at loggerheads, facing mutual incompatibilities and exclusions. At the same time, however, under certain historical conditions, these widely separated spheres occasionally came into contact and sometimes even overlapped. This chapter identifies some of those historical conjunctures and analyzes the meanings of contentious food politics, in particular its gendered dimensions and its compatibility with the norms, modes of action, and aims of emerging civil societies.[2] I discuss the following three questions: First, to what extent do food riots, which were often violent, fit under the rubric of civil society actions, which are usually defined as nonviolent? Second, how and why were the older subsistence conflicts before 1850 gendered? Third, to what extent did alternative modes of public action and movement open up for nonbourgeois (*nichtbürgerliche*) women, when food conflicts allegedly or actually became marginalized after 1850, and what forms did these new activities take? I address these questions by focusing mainly on the German context, but I also integrate a comparative perspective on England and France.

Women and Food Riots in Early Modern Europe

Since the development of market societies in early modern Europe, subsistence and resource conflicts have ranked among the dominant forms of protest within a wide-ranging repertoire of contentious collective action.[3] For France, historian Cynthia Bouton has discovered some three thousand social eruptions of this kind from the sixteenth to the middle of the nineteenth centuries. It seems that during the ancien régime and later as well, French society was the European epicenter of these confrontations.[4] As for England, with its very early and extreme market radicalism, historian John Bohstedt has found more than one thousand food riots from the seventeenth to the early nineteenth centuries.[5] In the German-speaking regions, such outbreaks appear at first glance to have been less prevalent; on only very preliminary evidence, from four hundred to five hundred conflicts have been noted. But the German figures could doubtless easily be doubled by intense research, especially for the periods before 1800 and after 1850, including above all the First World War and its aftermath (1914–23), a time of many resource conflicts.[6] Taken together, these figures suggest that the protest movements represented a strong public voice—a political voice—that noble and middle-class market actors in their private transactions and governors or communities with their responsibility for the common good had to take into consideration.

The protagonists of contentious food politics consisted of mixed-gender crowds of different ages, often including children. They represented the working people—the ubiquitous crowds—who dominated the face-to-face publics of streets and open squares, and their actions can be read as an unwritten discourse of ritualized social practice that was highly inflected by emotion. Although their oral communications are recorded only indirectly and fragmentarily,[7] these conflicts appear to speak of uneven and asymmetric market relations, questionable and illegal commercial transactions, widespread rumor and suspicion, popular denunciations of profiteering, and collisions between the haves and the have-nots—where what was at stake was, for one side, a degree of commercial gain, while for the other, subsistence and sometimes even survival.

During the French Revolution, which was not only a liberal movement of the middle classes but also a large rebellion of the lower orders around subsistence issues, these confrontations played a crucial role.[8] Insofar as women participated in the revolution, they were involved predominantly in this way. It would be misleading, however, to assume that the more than one thousand known subsistence actions that occurred between 1788 and 1795 were conducted exclusively or even dominated by women.[9] John Bohstedt tried to deconstruct what he calls "the myth of the feminine food riot" by analyzing detailed protest statistics from England around 1800.[10] Surveying the whole body of research, it does not seem to me very fruitful to argue too much over the quantitative aspects of gender participation. A considerable number of empirical and quantitative case studies exist by now, suggesting that we should not overestimate women's participation. Women did not dominate these movements in general, but they took part in them to a very considerable degree, particularly when compared to other kinds of protests. Moreover, women's participation increased significantly in twentieth-century subsistence protests throughout the West.[11]

More interesting are the qualitative and gendered aspects of food protests. Were they primarily "women's work"? Historians like Olwen Hufton, Michelle Perrot, and Edward P. Thompson have noted that women very often initiated conflicts over food.[12] Presumably, according to some scholars, this was because they had gender-specific roles as "guardians of the market" (buying and preserving food, doing the housekeeping, cooking, childrearing, etc.), which made food protests a predominantly female terrain or genuine female occupation. Others, including Carola Lipp, have argued that although both sexes participated, they seemed to have different purposes. Women tended to be pragmatic (*gebrauchswertorientiert*), seizing and taking home contended foodstuffs, while men acted more violently, engaging in heavy destruction that may have expressed anger but served no practical purpose.[13]

Cynthia Bouton elaborates on gender, alongside neighborhood and work experiences, as a central criterion structuring behavior during the French Flour War of 1775. She argues that women did act separately, especially within the classic urban situation of market riots, while men (agricultural laborers) dominated the violent food raids in the countryside. Surprisingly, the high overall presence of men in more than three hundred single actions in 1775 has been interpreted as a "feminization" of male behavior, referring to the supposed background of previously predominantly female food rioting. This supposition, however, is far from proven.[14] Up to now, all these and further attempts to show that gender roles differed significantly in resource conflicts have not led to convincing generalizations. Rather, studies of classic food riots have demonstrated that, as far as this field of action by the lower orders is concerned, there was no strict polarization of gender roles. At most, differences concerning use of violence and physical strength emerged gradually, in parallel with long-lasting gender-specific differentiations in everyday life and work processes as well as within the context of the military and war.

All these collective actions included "violence" of many kinds.[15] For the protestors, this generally meant reactive violence, in response to the previously experienced violence of shortages and want, of empty markets—a kind of self-help in a time of crisis, acts of self-defense when governments, communities, or other institutions failed to intervene. At the same time, rioters conceived of their actions as retaliatory, justified by violations of established social norms resulting from neglect or profiteering. This reactive violence concentrated on property and symbolic punishments. Excessive violence against people such as "cornerers" and profiteers, who offended against the rules of the moral economy, was rare, although the often overwhelming physical superiority of large crowds would have made it possible. Using rituals of collective coercion, large crowds disposed of the property of others, forced owners to sell commodities below price, broke into private houses and storehouses to seize foodstuffs, and even destroyed houses or other symbols of questionable wealth. They also enacted rituals of threat, when charity was lacking, or given too late or too sparsely.[16]

All in all, there is no shortage of reports of female violence, most of them in the form of judicial inquiries. In such reports, we often find a notorious type of outraged woman, usually accompanied, often by male counterparts. One case may be cited here briefly. Judicial inquiries concerning the demolition of a food storehouse in Merseburg (a Prussian province of Saxony), in 1847, reported:

> Thirty-eight-year-old Johanne Friederike Hübner confessed to: throwing stones at the windows and the storehouse door of the Friedrich house, taking part in destroying the door, helping to destroy the counter, and tearing down the shop sign; later on she confessed to shouting loudly and walking to the Morgenroth house and finally, in front of another store, not only to agitating people by loud screaming but also taking away some quantities of grain from the granary.[17]

According to the reports, many other women took the same or similar actions. Here, as elsewhere, there were no significant gender-specific differences in the form of protest. Compared to the polarization of gender-specific characteristics in the middle classes that was taking shape far more explicitly at the same time, the modes of behavior and public roles of women and men of the lower classes in action tended to resemble each other more closely. In the public space of street politics, women acted together with men, alongside men, and also independently of men. But there was ultimately no single practice within such protests that was exclusive to either sex. In short, it is not possible to detect a gender-specific differentiation of roles in classic subsistence protests. Reports, however, always portrayed few extraordinary women as rebellious heroines who led attacks with rousing speeches and expressed a compelling readiness for violence. Even in those cases, though, men's and women's behavior seems to have been more or less similar. The caricatures of outrageous women that appeared in such reports can be explained by the gender expectations of bourgeois eyewitnesses (officials, journalists, or judicial examiners), who no doubt became nonplussed when women in revolt proved to lack the qualities of calmness, moderation, and decency they believed women should possess. "Attack, if you want to be real (proper) men!" women reportedly urged hesitant men, appealing to their sense of male honor during nightly meetings in 1801, before hundreds of inhabitants of the town of Havelberg (Prussian province of Brandenburg) looted ships transporting grain for export to Hamburg. One widow named Balckow, who participated in these meetings at her house and was put in prison, was set free by large crowds and led in triumphal procession through the streets.[18] In Halle in 1805, the thirty-eight-year-old wife of a day laborer declared that she had started the riot by pointing at the house of a usurer and shouting to the people, "that 'dirty dog' must be driven away, he is responsible for the calamity!" Later, it was reported, she ran through the streets shouting, "I started it! Citizens, come on, you are wretched curs (*Hundsfötter*) if you abandon me now!"[19] That same year in the neighborhood town Wettin, it was the wife of a greengrocer who shouted to the crowd, "Let's start it now! Will you come with me or won't you? Follow me, I will go ahead and pave the way!" Subsequently, "a woman," who had fetched an axe, broke down a warehouse door.[20]

Scores of such reports exist for the period until the middle of the nineteenth century in Germany, even more for England, France, and other countries.[21] In Germany, these rebellions culminated during the "hungry" 1840s, better characterized as the "angry forties," especially in the years before and during the Revolution of 1848–49.[22] They contributed indirectly to delegitimizing the old autocratic order and reforming pre-civil society. These self-help actions also initiated some short-term improvements by promoting a general increase in sensibility and responsibility for the social, a growth of public welfare activities and private charity, and a general improvement of living conditions through, for example, extended public work programs.

At the same time, however, these conflicts of redistribution created even sharper polarization between old elites and the secure middle classes on the one hand and the lower orders on the other. To be sure, the protest movements were quite removed from the sudden mushrooming of civil society through such means as the new freedoms of the press, assembly, public speech, and pluralities of opinion; the right to form clubs, parties, and associations of all kinds; and male suffrage. The two movements represented two distinct and opposed political cultures that hardly proved compatible during the extremely short period of revolutionary unrest. Mediations turned out to be difficult and required long-term learning processes on both sides. Mutual polarizations and a deep-rooted fear among elites and the middle classes regarding demands by the have-nots for a redistribution of wealth and power, for social or "Red Revolution," overshadowed any commonalities or alliances. Early labor associations tried to some extent to bridge the widening gap between the "social" and the "civil," but they continued to exclude women.[23]

Nineteenth-Century Society and Food Protest

The transition from preindustrial societies of want to modern industrial and consumer societies (thus runs the common thesis) marginalized or even eliminated these movements of traditional street politics. The end of old European subsistence crises, immediate increases in agrarian productivity, modern revolutions in transport including the growing transnational integration of food markets, the effects of social relief owing to mass emigration, full industrialization and an expanded supply of jobs, organized labor movements, increases in real wages, and the first steps toward a modern social security system beginning in the 1880s—all this, it is argued, helped to transform the old subsistence conflict and put a stop to old-fashioned negotiations of "bargaining by riot" in the streets. Such positions must be revised in the light of gender inquiry. The direct action-based self-help of mixed-gender crowds was not completely absorbed by the male labor movement. Rather, and parallel to organized labor, collective political conflict over food continued to expand and once again became relevant, especially under changing contexts of war, revolution, and inflation crises.

The first extended series of strikes during the founding period of imperial Germany was accompanied by a simultaneous wave of subsistence protests that has never been investigated in detail. Of course, these largely unknown actions were overshadowed by grand historical events such as the Wars of Unification and the founding of the empire in 1870–71, but even the early labor movement ignored or marginalized these conflicts.[24] A report in the local social democratic newspaper on the so-called butter revolution in Brunswig in July 1872 illustrates this attitude:

> Many market traders were put to flight, some others were forced to sell their products at reduced prices that had been dictated by angry men and women. "We, as the women, we will have to start it, otherwise it won't pay and the results will be practically nothing!"—thus were the cries of one of the market heroines. Indeed, there were many agitating female talents in petticoats and they really took the lead when the doors of houses where dealers were hiding their products were attacked. We hope and wish that regrettable and childish events such as these will finally cease; however, considering our numerous policemen, we are very surprised that riots of such scope could occur at all.

When assemblies of social democrats, which are very orderly and perfectly peaceful, are dissolved by police, this is said to happen for the reason of preserving the state; how then is it possible that the police should not be able to take measures against two days of heavy rioting on the marketplace? Or don't they have the courage to face these women?[25]

The malicious denigration of consumer protests in the local labor press was no coincidence. Early social democratic male workers, who had entered the sphere of organized politics by joining clubs, trade unions, and the party, withdrew from traditional market and price revolts. In any instance of old-style, violent self-help actions during the Wilhelmine Empire, which occurred much more often than has been assumed up to now, representatives of the labor movement distanced themselves sharply from what they viewed as an unworthy legacy. They threatened to expel from the party potential riot participants from their own ranks, as happened in the context of the Wiesbaden bread revolt of 1873 against a wealthy mill owner and baker—even though he was taken as a representative of the immoral capitalist nouveau riche.[26] While the male association and male club debate or—in regard to resource questions—the strike of male breadwinners had become appropriate means of articulation, the traditional food protest became verbally marginalized and feminized within the workers' club movement. According to the modern, enlightened worldview of the clubs, the old community-based moral economy protest was regarded as a wrong-headed revolution, a misleading and childish rebellion of the female "petticoats," foolish young boys, and the "rabble" (*Pöbel* or *Janhagel*). It challenged their claims to new social norms and privileges as male breadwinners, and undermined their attempts to gain respectability as citizens, to be recognized as *citoyens*, and participate in matters of high politics. These discourses on respectability within the workers' milieu placed a strict taboo on all kinds of spontaneous self-help and violent actions.[27]

There is no doubt that a certain transfer of resource conflicts from community or neighborhood action to the sphere of production, the realm of predominantly male industrial work and male strikes, occurred during the highly industrialized later German Empire. But consumer actions continued too; some thirty events during the years 1871–73—discovered by chance rather than systematic research—as well as numerous additional examples up to 1914, at least, attest to this fact.[28] As for France, the frequency of protests seem to have been even greater, including many demonstrations in the context of the *vie chère* movement after the turn of the century. The French protests were characterized by strong female participation.[29]

At the same time, however, the social and political spaces for action by nonbourgeois women were narrowing. Classic subsistence action became increasingly delegitimized as taboos were imposed from within their own social ranks. Those former female "guardians of the market," who had carefully managed restricted private household budgets, had no voice in the early labor movement. Participation in traditional action was discredited and criminalized; accounts repeatedly spoke of "women" and "the rabble" in the same breath. In the male worker milieu, only one position was allowed: resource conflicts should be a matter of heroic strike action on the part of male workers and a matter for the great politics of "the party," of elections and parliamentary debate. As a result, spontaneous direct action came to be looked upon as an uncivil or anticivil mode of conduct. It is important to note that inclusion of the politics of food into "respectable" civil society went hand-in-hand with the feminization of former styles of protest. Public discourses increasingly described riots as "female" and portrayed cast them as an "archaic" form of behavior, a kind of pitiful redoubt of angry women, workers' wives, and housewives; as such, they became the object of disdain, mockery, and malice.[30] Civil society, by contrast, was clearly portrayed as a male reserve.

With the traditional spaces of the street public narrowed or closed up, it proved difficult for women to find new spaces for action. Eventually, however, avenues began to open up through the new consumer associations, political party campaigns, and mass meetings and demonstrations addressing the high prices of basic necessities that appeared across Western societies starting in the second half of the nineteenth century. As an organized form of long-term self-help, these associations and events effectively replaced traditional direct action, and the new networks that were formed became sites for the continuation of the culture and worldview of the older moral economy in associational form. Surprisingly, while German women—the "decent" housewives of the respectable worker elites—increasingly became active in the everyday life culture of these organizations, they had little representation in their leadership.[31]

By contrast, English cooperatives of the 1880s were far more integrated in terms of class as well as gender, and more independent of party politics. In England, the "women with the basket," married working-class women, played a much more crucial role in the club culture of the cooperatives and thus conquered new public spaces of action.[32] The Women's Cooperative Guild grew out of this consumer movement and became a long-lived women's rights' organization, providing married women with a public arena where not only social problems in a narrower sense but all kinds of injustices could be debated. As historian Gillian Scott has put it, "Guildswomen now exhibited an awareness of speaking not for themselves as individuals but as representatives of a wider constituency—tens of thousands of Co-operative women, who were themselves the organized expression of the interests of the millions of working-class housewives so long denied any public voice."[33] Christoph Nonn's study of consumer protests and the party system in imperial Germany has shown how problems of high food prices contributed to women's "mass self-mobilization" and general politicization after 1905, before and even more intensively than the campaign for universal suffrage. This self-mobilization created separate female assemblies and organizations, often against the protests of husbands and party comrades.[34] From the turn of the century on, numerous newly politicized consumer protests in the form of mass demonstrations and boycott movements against companies and shops, driven by a rise in food costs and the prevalence of poor products and carried out by women, created new civil societal structures and modes of protest for women.[35]

The First World War—A Turning Point?

In many ways, 1914 marked a fundamental turning point in the history of European political participation. In many European countries, it brought the rapid erosion of civil societal structures and values, while at the same time, protests increased dramatically.[36] The decade between 1914 to 1924, a period of catastrophic everyday experiences including war, political violence, and food shortages, signaled a startling renaissance of traditional subsistence conflicts in Germany as well as across the continent.[37] To be sure, conditions for food acquisition and consumption had changed. War-related strictures, namely increasing food rationing, led to a newly centralized food politics from above. Access to and the strategic distribution of resources became a matter of military importance and thus an affair of state. This was accompanied by a deep-rooted politicization of all matters of daily provision of basic foodstuffs. There were wide-ranging demands, especially from suffering urban consumers, for strict regulation of food distribution directed against all private so-called profiteers, usurers, and black marketers; many longed for something like a "food dictator" (*Ernährungsdiktator*) to take over. And doubtless, some old and deep-rooted rumors and hostile images of "market villains" were reactivated.[38] Not just Germany but a number of European states saw a resurgence of subsistence protests that had seemed to be a thing of the past.[39]

More than ever before, women dominated those actions on the home front. They began with consumer queues in front of shops and in market places, which became "crystallization centers for discontent and protest."[40] As early as 1915, large food riots and mass demonstrations were occurring in cities like Berlin, Aachen, Chemnitz, and Stuttgart.[41] On 17 August 1916, notable popular discontent began spreading in the town of Tangermünde. During the afternoon large crowds gathered in front of the town hall, and by evening the crowd had grown to some one thousand demonstrators, predominantly women. A contemporary account described the scene:

> People were screaming and shouting continuously; also, there were mocking and insulting cries against the authorities. Seemingly, their main motive was not only a better provision with butter, but pure desire for scandal and mischief. At 7 o'clock the vice-mayor appeared in front of the town hall and informed the women standing nearby that the distribution of butter ... will not be possible before Saturday [two days later].... From 7 to 8 o'clock the crowd was shrinking a little bit—probably people had their supper—while they reappeared at half past 8 in even larger numbers. They attacked the house of a board member of the dairy cooperative, where people supposed [there were] some eight hundredweights [*Zentner*] of butter. Large stones were broken from the pavement, some more stones had been fetched from other streets and thrown against the house. By 11 pm all windows of the house had been destroyed. Also, people tried to break down the door.... [Rumors about the arrival of military] increased the excitement of the crowd and attacks on the house became more and more heavy. Troops needed more than half an hour to disperse the crowds.... At the beginning the crowd consisted exclusively of working-class women, later in the evening there were mainly women and young girls and teenage boys and, unfortunately, schoolchildren in large numbers, too. Further on, some dubious elements [*lichtscheue Elemente*] joined in, using this opportunity for mischief. Although at the beginning this disorder was caused by want of butter, later on its character turned more and more to [that of] a political demonstration.[42]

Authorities and trade unions proved incapable of preventing such spontaneous mass actions, not least because most were women. Labor leaders lamented that they were losing control of their "own folks." And when women joined the demonstrations, as happened in Tangermünde, accusations like the following were to be heard: "You are belonging to the big ones, [i.e., the wealthy ones, who were able to buy food illegally on the black market], "you care only for yourself and you have no sympathy for the common people."[43] The number of women arrested for disturbing the peace (*Landfriedensbruch*) and similar offenses increased exorbitantly during war times. Often, however, authorities refrained from prosecuting female rioters out of political consideration; large-scale punishments would have threatened the officially decreed *Burgfrieden*, the agreement between the trade unions, the Social Democratic Party, and the government to stop all economic and political struggle during the times of war. With regard to these problems of law and order, here, too, the Great War proved to be an innovator: increasingly helpless in the face of protesting housewives and workers, authorities in 1918 resorted to greater use of tear gas on the streets and squares of the home front.

Precise numbers of resource conflicts during World War I are not available, largely because of strict press censorship. But it was exactly at these points, in daily queues before stores and on markets, where consumers became exasperated and their patriotic feelings vanished. And it was here, too, that a new food politics from below, largely associated with women, was constituted. Historian Belinda Davis, studying the predominantly female food politics of the streets in Berlin, has noted:

> Women who protested in the streets were not consciously radical in their demands for "fair" food policy, a policy that would guarantee the accessibility of sufficient basic foods.... But when the institution of limited state and municipal ordinances failed to alleviate the desperation of the population of lesser means, shoppers waiting before stores called for increasingly drastic measures. Women of lesser means turned to a rhetoric of customary right and to a moral economy founded on the attack on unfair privilege.... Thus by the end of 1915, this population of poorer women came to demand state confiscation of all foodstuffs . . . from private entrepreneurs and the equal distribution of the same at cost or even at subsidized prices for the poor.[44]

The politicization of basic necessities during wartime signified an important delegitimation of the government and elites, who represented the autocratic old regime. Indirectly, for many women, expressing their collective outrage in the public space of the streets meant reconstituting a political voice, even before official woman's suffrage was achieved.

We do not know, even approximately, the real extent of these subsistence protests, which lasted until the end of 1923, flooding crisis-ridden German postwar society.[45] The emotions that fueled those conflicts and their long-term consequences were many-layered, multidimensional, even problematic. In no way did they function as a preschool for democracy, the welfare state, and civil societal engagement. Rather, they offered fruitful resonance for radical political agitation and exaggerated political projects of dictatorial or totalitarian dimension, for utopian promises and disastrous politics of despair. Occasionally, actions were mixed with anti-Jewish resentment. These explosions of anti-Jewish emotions and collective violence against Jews reconfirm a pattern of coincidence between times of crisis and anti-Semitism that had recurred since the mid-nineteenth century.[46] Examples of disorders include: Berlin during spring and summer 1919, Karlsruhe in July 1920, Memmingen in August 1921, Dresden in November 1922, and the well-known Scheunenviertel riots of Berlin in November 1923.[47]

Doubtless, these social eruptions were symptoms of a deeply disturbed social order on the verge of complete collapse. Even then, "self-help" was a ubiquitous popular slogan, and the practice of looting and "confiscating" food was widespread. Where, according to the optimistic nineteenth-century middle-class notions of progress, "civil society" should have been emerging, "civil war" now seemed to have taken its place. Far from strengthening the structures of civil society, the desperately aggressive self-help efforts of a period deeply shaped by physical destruction, social and political upheaval, and mental disorder contributed to the dissolution of civil society in a universal "struggle of all against all for their daily bread" and, of course, for power.[48] Public life was shaped by conflicts between urban consumers and rural producers in the countryside, between regions competing for scarce resources, between natives (Germans) and so-called aliens, between classes, between opposing social milieus and hostile parties and groups of all kinds. The monopoly of physical force increasingly passed into the hands of self-legitimating substitute powers: military formations and paramilitary political organizations, strike committees, and self-proclaimed proletarian committees that controlled food markets and provisions. Thus, attitudes of "proletarian self-help" led to markets, farmers, shops, and store houses coming under scrutiny, and foodstuffs being "confiscated" or sold for "just prices." Against this backdrop of innumerable social protests, upheavals, political violence and assassinations, coup d'états, and extreme political radicalizations, historian Martin H. Geyer has rightly spoken of a "fundamental crisis of *Rechtsbewußtsein*," awareness of law.[49]

Conclusion

The mid-nineteenth century did not mark the end of contentious food politics, but rather a change in their character. Here, historiographical revisions are long overdue. Compared to older protest traditions, conflicts became more and more female, in terms of both public images, which could be distorting, and women's actual participation. But at the same time, this protest tradition entered a dead-end street, as a stricter monopoly of force and growing civil taboos concerning violence, processes of self-civilization, and discourses of respectability within popular-proletarian milieus themselves, intensified by public discrediting and general social marginalization, pushed subsistence actions onto the historical margins. This appears as a paradox: for nonbourgeois female protestors, the extension of civil society spaces after the mid-nineteenth century meant a temporary shrinking or even total loss of traditional spaces of public action and thus also a loss of public sociopolitical power. For them, as Karen Hagemann has emphasized, civil society progress resembled, at least for a time, a double exclusion: while the old means of direct action in street politics became historically obsolete, participation in the new spaces of public action of an emerging political mass market (elections, parties, clubs) remained more or less closed to them. Thus the transformation of subsistence conflicts into associations and party movements took place without women or with women almost fully marginalized.

Until 1908, women were legally prohibited from becoming members of any political organization, but they founded their own associations, and in the second half of the nineteenth century the middle-class and social-democratic women's movements became more and more active. After the turn of the century, new opportunities for joining cooperative clubs, boycott movements, and mass demonstrations also opened up for women as consumers. The renaissance of the old conflict pattern after 1914 was the product of extraordinary ruptures (the war economy, long-term food shortages, revolutionary crisis, the chaos of inflation). Women had greater representation in these new subsistence movements than ever before, and political contention over daily bread became more and more a female affair. Thus, women (re-)gained a public voice, even before they had the vote. But when they obtained the suffrage in 1919, they quickly learned how little this increased their influence in politics. In response, working-class women in particular quickly left the political organizations they had joined after the war and, during the inflation years, protested against shortages of food, resorting to food riots, a form they knew well from World War I.[50]

Looking beyond this predominantly German story of contentious food politics to a more global perspective, these conflicts were and remain a dominant form of protest.[51] Movements of this kind can be powerful interventions into political life, even capable of overthrowing inactive governments, as recent examples of northern African states or Argentina have shown.[52] As street politics, they represent forms of nonbourgeois publics, with women included. In terms of their impetus toward self-help, such movements contribute significantly to the development of the kinds of actions and values normally associated with civil society. Indeed, social networks and clubs engaged in mutual assistance and the spirit of conflict prevention emerge from these actions. But considering the fact that direct action like food riots are likely to include violence, can we subsume them under the rubric of civil society, which is by definition nonviolent? These forms of social protest appear to be ambiguous for the project of civil society: subsistence conflicts were and are difficult, uncomfortable allies. They are frequently characterized by oppositional provocations to and a general questioning of the very values of civil society. Time and time again, when such protests occur in large numbers, civil society has already failed. The analysis of food riots shows that we need to define civil society as broadly as possible. From a historical perspective we can see that economic, social, or political constraints often left protagonists with no alternative to violent riots and upheaval. These forms of protest were the only possibility of public articulation of their needs that was left to them.[53]

Notes

1. It is quite obvious that "civil society" and "protest" should not be considered in general as incompatible, see: Dieter Rucht, "Die konstruktive Funktion von Protesten in und für Zivilgesellschaften," in *Zivilgesellschaft als Geschichte: Studien zum 19. und 20. Jahrhundert*, ed. Ralf Jessen, Sven Reichardt, and Ansgar Klein (Wiesbaden, 2004), 135–52.
2. See, among others: Anthony James Coles, "The Moral Economy of the Crowd: Some Twentieth-century Food Riots," *Journal of British Studies* 17, no. 1 (1978–79): 157–76; Paula Hyman, "Immigrant Women and Consumer Protest: The New York City Kosher Meat Boycott of 1902," *American Jewish History* 70 (1980): 91–105; Temma Kaplan, "Female Consciousness and Collective Action: The Case of Barcelona, 1910–1918," *Signs: Journal of Women in Culture and Society* 7, no. 3 (1982): 545–66; Dana Frank, "Housewives, Socialists, and the Politics of Food: The 1917 New York Cost-of-Living Protests," *Feminist Studies* 11, no. 2 (1985): 255–85; Paul R. Hanson, "The *Vie Chère* Riots of 1911: Traditional Protests in Modern Garb," *Journal of Social History* 21 (1987–88): 463–81; Giovanna Procacci, "Popular Protest and Labor Conflict in Italy, 1915–1918," *Social History* 14, no. 1 (1989): 31–58; Martin H. Geyer, "Teuerungsprotest und Teuerungsunruhen 1914–1923: Selbsthilfegesellschaft und Geldentwertung," in *Der Kampf um das tägliche Brot: Nahrungsmangel, Versorgungspolitik und Protest 1770–1990*, ed. Manfred Gailus and Heinrich Volkmann (Opladen, 1994), 319–45; Lynne Taylor, "Food Riots Revisited," *Journal of Social History* 30, no. 2 (1996–97): 483–96; Belinda J. Davis, *Home Fires Burning: Food, Politics, and Everyday Life in World War I Berlin* (Chapel Hill, NC, 2000).
3. Cf. Louise A. Tilly, "Social Protests, History of," in *International Encyclopedia of the Social and Behavioral Sciences*, vol. 21 (Amsterdam, 2001), 14397–402; Charles Tilly, *Social Movements 1768–2004* (Boulder, CO, 2004); Tilly, *Contention and Democracy in Europe 1650–2000* (Cambridge, MA, 2004).
4. Cynthia Bouton, "Les mouvements de subsistance et le problème de l'économie morale sous l'Ancien Régime et la Révolution Française," *Annales historiques de la Révolution Française* (2000): 71–100; Bouton, *The Flour War: Gender, Class, and Community in Late Ancien Régime French Society* (University Park, PA, 1993); Jean Nicolas, *La rébellion française: mouvements populaires et conscience sociale, 1661–1789* (Paris, 2002).
5. See John Bohstedt, *Riots and Community Politics in England and Wales 1790–1810* (Cambridge, MA, 1983); Andrew Charlesworth, ed., *An Atlas of Rural Protest in Britain 1548–1900* (London, 1983); Charles Tilly, *Popular Contention in Great Britain, 1758–1834* (Cambridge, MA, 1995).
6. Manfred Gailus, *Strasse und Brot: Sozialer Protest in den deutschen Staaten unter besonderer Berücksichtigung Preußens 1847–1849* (Göttingen, 1990); for the early twentieth century: Geyer, "Teuerungsprotest."
7. For eighteenth-century Paris: Arlette Farge, *Dire et mal dire: L'opinion publique au XVIIIe siècle* (Paris 1992).
8. On subsistence movements and politics during the French Revolution: William Sewell, "The Sans-culottes Rhetoric of Subsistence," in *The Terror: The French Revolution and the Creation of Modern Political Culture*, ed. Kevin Baker (Oxford, 1994), 249–69; Jean-Pierre Gross, *Fair Shares For All: Jacobin Egalitarianism in Practice* (London, 1997); Bouton, "Mouvements de subsistence," 86ff.
9. This is still the tenor of many standard books on the revolution. Cf. for variations of women's roles during the revolution: Gisela Bock, *Women in European History* (Oxford, 2002), 32–81; for gender aspects of subsistence protests 1789–1795 see: Bouton, "Mouvements de subsistance."
10. John Bohstedt, "The Myth of the Feminine Food Riot: Women as Proto-Citizens in English Community Politics, 1790–1810," in *Women and Politics in the Age of the*

Democratic Revolution, ed. Harriet B. Applewhite and Darline G. Levy (Ann Arbor, MI, 1990), 21–60; see the criticism by Edward P. Thompson, "The Moral Economy Reviewed," in *Customs in Common* (New York, 1991), 305–36.

11. For women's participation see also Carola Lipp, "Frauenspezifische Partizipation an Hungerunruhen des 19. Jahrhunderts: Überlegungen zu strukturellen Differenzen im Protestverhalten," in Gailus and Volkmann, *Kampf*, 200–213; Taylor, "Food Riots Revisited"; Denis Béliveau, "Le droit à la rebellion: Les femmes, le pain et la justice en France (1816–1847)" in *Femmes dans la Cité, 1815–1871*, ed. Alain Corbin et al. (Grâne, 1997), 41–55.

12. See Olwen Hufton, "Women in Revolution, 1789–1796," *Past & Present* 53 (1971), 90–108; Michelle Perrot, "Rebellische Weiber: Die Frau in der französischen Stadt des 19. Jahrhunderts," in *Listen der Ohnmacht. Zur Sozialgeschichte weiblicher Widerstandsformen*, ed. Claudia Honegger and Bettina Heintz (Frankfurt/M., 1981), 71–98; Edward P. Thompson, "The Moral Economy of the English Crowd in the Eighteenth Century," in *Past & Present* 50 (1971): 76–136.

13. See Carola Lipp, ed., *Schimpfende Weiber und patriotische Jungfrauen: Frauen im Vormärz und in der Revolution 1848/49* (Bühl-Moos, 1986).

14. See Cynthia Bouton, "Gendered Behavior in Subsistence Riots: The Flour War of 1775," in *Journal of Social History* 23, no. 4 (1989–90): 735–54; Bouton, *Flour War*.

15. For more general debates on violence in history: Thomas Lindenberger and Alf Lüdtke, eds., *Physische Gewalt: Studien zur Geschichte der Neuzeit* (Frankfurt/M., 1995); Magnus Eriksson and Barbara Krug-Richter, eds., *Streitkulturen. Gewalt, Konflikt und Kommunikation in der ländlichen Gesellschaft (16.–19. Jahrhundert)* (Cologne, 2003).

16. For variations of violence in food riots see Thompson, "Moral Economy of the English Crowd"; Bohstedt, *Riots and Community Politics*; Gailus, *Strasse und Brot*; Bouton, *Flour War*.

17. Quoted from: Christina Benninghaus, "Sittliche Ökonomie, soziale Beziehungen und Geschlechterverhältnisse. Zur inneren Logik der Hungerunruhen," in *Region in Aufruhr: Hungerkrise und Teuerungsproteste in der preussischen Provinz Sachsen und Anhalt 1846/47*, ed. Benninghaus (Halle, 2000), 117–58, 149.

18. Manfred Gailus, "Moralische Ökonomie und Rebellion in Preussen vor 1806: Havelberg, Halle und Umgebung," in *Forschungen zur Brandenburgisch-Preussischen Geschichte* NF 11, no. 1 (2001): 78–100, 82f.

19. See Arno Herzig, *Unterschichtenprotest in Deutschland 1790–1870* (Göttingen, 1988), 84.

20. Ibid.

21. For England: Thompson, "Moral Economy of the English Crowd"; Bohstedt, *Riots and Community Politics*; for France: Bouton, *Flour War*; Nicolas Bourguinat, *Les grains du désordre: L'État face aux violences frumentaires dans la première moitié du XIXe siècle* (Paris, 2002).

22. Food riots in the 1840s: Gailus, *Strasse und Brot*; Gailus, "Food Riots in Germany in the Late 1840s," *Past & Present* 145 (1994): 157–93; Benninghaus, *Region in Aufruhr*; Michael Hecht, *Nahrungsmangel und Protest: Teuerungsunruhen in Frankreich und Preussen in den Jahren 1846/47* (Halle, 2004).

23. For opposing political cultures in the revolution: Gailus, *Strasse und Brot*; for early labor movements: Franziska Rogger, "*Wir helfen uns selbst!*" *Die kollektive Selbsthilfe der Arbeiterverbrüderung 1848/49 und die individuelle Selbsthilfe Stephan Borns* (Erlangen, 1986); Thomas Welskopp, *Das Banner der Brüderlichkeit: Die deutsche Sozialdemokratie vom Vormärz bis zum Sozialistengesetz* (Bonn, 2000).

24. A first account of these protests is in: Lothar Machtan and René Ott, "'Batzebier!' Überlegungen zur sozialen Protestbewegung in den Jahren nach der Reichsgründung am Beispiel der süddeutschen Bierkrawalle vom Frühjahr 1873," in *Sozialer Protest:*

Studien zu traditioneller Resistenz und kollektiver Gewalt in Deutschland vom Vormärz bis zur Reichsgründung, ed. Heinrich Volkmann and Jürgen Bergmann (Opladen, 1984), 128–66.
25. See *Braunschweiger Volksfreund*, no. 167, 19 July 1872.
26. See Horst Steffens, "Der Wiesbadener Brotkrawall von 1873. Ursachen und Hintergründe sozialer Protestbewegungen in den frühen 1870er Jahren," in *Nassauische Annalen* 100 (1989): 173–96.
27. For the distinction between social democrats and traditional "street politics": Thomas Lindenberger, *Strassenpolitik: Zur Sozialgeschichte der öffentlichen Ordnung in Berlin 1900 bis 1914* (Bonn, 1995), 334–403. See also for discourses on respectability in Great Britain, starting earlier: Simon Cordery, "Friendly Societies and the Discourse of Respectability in Britain, 1825–1875," in *Journal of British Studies* 34 (1995): 35–58.
28. See for more examples, Manfred Gailus, "Nahrungsmangel, Versorgungspolitik und Protest in Deutschland (1770–1873)," (unpublished manuscript, Berlin, 1996), 160–75.
29. Jean-Marie Flonneau, "Crise de vie chère et movement syndical 1910–1914," in *Le Mouvement Social* 72 (1970): 49–81; Hanson, "The *Vie Chère* Riots."
30. Bernd Jürgen Warneken ed., *Als die Deutschen demonstrieren lernten* (Tübingen, 1986), esp. 105–26; Lindenberger, *Strassenpolitik*.
31. See Michael Prinz, *Brot und Dividende: Konsumvereine in Deutschland und England vor 1914* (Göttingen, 1996); see on female activities in the German consumer organizations: Karen Hagemann, *Frauenalltag und Männerpolitik: Alltagsleben und gesellschaftliches Handeln von Arbeiterfrauen in der Weimarer Republik* (Bonn, 1990), 138–54.
32. Peter Gurney, *Co-operative Culture and the Politics of Consumption in England, 1870–1930* (Manchester, 1996), 58–87.
33. Gillian Scott, *Feminism and the Politics of Working Women: The Women's Co-operative Guild, 1880s to the Second World War* (London, 1998), 67–92, cit. 88.
34. Christoph Nonn, *Verbraucherprotest und Parteiensystem im Wilhelminischen Deutschland* (Düsseldorf, 1996), 41–57.
35. See Taylor, "Food Riots Revisited."
36. See for 1914 as a decisive turning point for the twentieth century: Hans Mommsen, ed., *Der Erste Weltkrieg und die europäische Nachkriegsordnung: Sozialer Wandel und Formveränderung der Politik* (Cologne, 2000); and recently the special issue: "Violence and Society after the First World War" of the *Journal of Modern European History* 1 (2004).
37. For international dimensions: Cole, "Moral Economy of the Crowd" (England 1916–17); Kaplan, "Female Consciousness" (Barcelona 1918); Frank, "Housewives" (New York 1917); Procacci, "Popular Protests" (Italy 1915–18); Judith Smart, "Feminists, Food and the Fair Price: The Cost of Living Demonstrations in Melbourne, August–September 1917," *Labor History* 50 (1986): 113–31.
38. See Ute Daniel, *Arbeiterfrauen in der Kriegsgesellschaft: Beruf, Familie und Politik im Ersten Weltkrieg* (Göttingen, 1989); Anne Roerkohl, *Hungerblockade und Heimatfront: Die kommunale Lebensmittelversorgung in Westfalen während des Ersten Weltkriegs* (Stuttgart, 1991); Gerald D. Feldman, *The Great Disorder: Politics, Economics, and Society in the German Inflation, 1914–1924* (New York, 1993); Martin H. Geyer, *Verkehrte Welt: Revolution, Inflation und Moderne, Munich 1914–1924* (Göttingen, 1998); Roger Chickering, *Das Deutsche Reich und der Erste Weltkrieg* (Munich, 2002).
39. Up to now, there is no general account on the German protest evidence; only some pages in Daniel, *Arbeiterfrauen*, 246 ff.; Geyer, *Teuerungsprotest*, 326–30.
40. Volker Ullrich, "Kriegsalltag. Zur inneren Revolutionierung der Wilhelminischen Gesellschaft," in *Der Erste Weltkrieg. Wirkung, Wahrnehmung, Analyse*, ed. Wolfgang Michalka (Munich, 1994), 603–21, 607.

41. Detailed evidence in: Manfred Gailus, *Contentious Food Politics: Sozialer Protest, Märkte und Zivilgesellschaft (18.–20. Jahrhundert)*, WZB discussion paper (Berlin, 2004); Gailus, "Das Politische des Sozialen. Anmerkungen zur Wiederkehr von Subsistenzprotesten im 'katastrophalen Jahrzehnt' (1914–1923)," in *Politischer Protest und Öffentlichkeit im 20. Jahrhundert*, ed. Sven Reichardt and Dieter Rucht (Wiesbaden, forthcoming).
42. Quoted in Daniel, *Arbeiterfrauen*, 246ff (my translation).
43. Ibid., 248.
44. Belinda Davis, "Reconsidering Habermas, Gender, and the Public Sphere: The Case of Wilhelmine Germany," in *Society, Culture and the State in Germany, 1870–1930*, ed. Geoff Eley (Ann Arbor, MI, 1996), 397–426, 425; cf. also Davis, *Home Fires Burning*.
45. See Robert Scholz, "Ein unruhiges Jahrzehnt: Lebensmittelunruhen, Massenstreiks und Arbeitslosenkrawalle in Berlin 1914–1923," in *Pöbelexzesse und Volkstumulte in Berlin: Zur Sozialgeschichte der Strasse (1830–1980)*, ed. Manfred Gailus (Berlin, 1984), 79–123; Geyer, *Teuerungsprotest*.
46. For this historical coincidence: Manfred Gailus, "Anti-Jewish Emotion and Violence in the 1848 Crisis of German Society," in *Exclusionary Violence: Antisemitic Riots in Modern German History*, ed. Christhard Hoffmann et al. (Ann Arbor, MI, 2002), 43–65; in general for postwar anti-Jewish violence: Dirk Walter, *Antisemitische Kriminalität und Gewalt: Judenfeindschaft in der Weimarer Republik* (Bonn, 1999).
47. See Geyer, *Teuerungsprotest*, 328ff.; for the Berlin Scheunenviertel riots, see David C. Large, "'Out with the Ostjuden': The Scheunenviertel Riots in Berlin, November 1923," in Hoffmann, *Exclusionary Violence*, 123–40; this chapter also provides more evidence on the anti-Jewish character of food riots in Karlsruhe, Erfurt, Nürnberg, Coburg, Bremen, Oldenburg, and Breslau. For the general context see also: Walter, *Antisemitische Kriminalität*.
48. Quoted from "Denkschrift zur Wirtschaftlichen Lage (27. Juli 1923)" in *Das Kabinett Cuno, 22. November 1922 bis 12. August 1923 (Akten der Reichskanzlei)*, ed. Karl-Heinz Harbeck (Boppard/Rh., 1968), Document no. 229.
49. Geyer, *Teuerungsprotest*, 337; see also: Karen Hagemann, "Men's Demonstrations and Women's Protest: Gender in Collective Action in the Urban Working-Class Milieu During the Weimar Republic," *Gender & History*, 5, no. 1 (1993): 101–19.
50. Hagemann, "Men's Demonstrations."
51. See John Walton and David Seddon, eds., *Free Markets and Food Riots: The Politics of Global Adjustment* (Oxford, 1994).
52. See David Seddon, *Hunger und Herrschaft: Zur politischen Ökonomie der 'Brotunruhen' in Nordafrika* (Berlin, 1988); Javier Auyero, "Glocal Riots," *International Sociology*, 16, no. 1 (2001), 33–53.
53. See Iris Marion Young, *Inclusion and Democracy* (Oxford, 2000).

Chapter 10

"GOOD" VS. "MILITANT" CITIZENS
MASCULINITY, CLASS PROTEST, AND THE "CIVIL" PUBLIC IN BRITAIN BETWEEN 1867 AND 1939

Sonya O. Rose

In October 1936, two hundred men set off from the town of Jarrow in the northeast of England and walked to London to present a petition to Parliament pleading for work for the town. At their head was Ellen Wilkinson, Member of Parliament for Jarrow. They went on their way with the support of the town's mayor and prominent members of both its Conservative and Labour Parties. As they walked south, the men were welcomed by various town and city councils, and the "Crusade," as they called it, received widespread publicity in newspapers across the country. At about the same time two thousand men protesting the hated means test—those harsh and intrusive measures to determine a family's eligibility for public assistance—also moved toward London to press their claims for social justice. But in contrast to the groundswell of support and extensive media coverage of the men from Jarrow, the two thousand members of the National Unemployed Workers' Movement, four hundred of whom began their journey in Glasgow and were joined by others from England and Wales along the way, received virtually no coverage in the press.

Now let us move back in time to the period between 1867 and 1918. In 1867, for the first time, some working-class men were given the Parliamentary franchise. Then in 1918 with the Representation of the People Act, all men along with women thirty and older were enfranchised. During the time between these two acts of Parliament, at least 40 to 45 percent of those men who would be able to vote after 1918 lacked the

Parliamentary franchise. Disenfranchisement was especially pronounced in urban, working-class areas. In the Whitechapel district of London to take an extreme example, the level of enfranchisement in 1911 was only 20 percent.[1]

I mention these two stories as a prelude to investigating the histories of civil society and the public sphere in Britain. During the period that I cover in this paper, civil society, an arena of activity composed of voluntary "private associations that are relatively autonomous from both state and economy," was not accessible to all men.[2] In fact, the men who were denied the Parliamentary franchise until 1918 were unlikely to participate in political associations or social movement groups to make claims on the state for political inclusion. Furthermore in Britain, especially after World War I, "the public" was popularly understood as a site for the performance of a particular form of "civility." This "civil" public was a dominant public that politically silenced or ignored those who were part of what political scientist Nancy Fraser has termed a "subaltern counter public."[3]

This essay raises the question of which men are heard in the public sphere, and interrogates the linkages between the meanings of masculinity, the languages of citizenship, prevailing definitions of civility, and participation in civil society. My focus is on men because it is important to understand that gender, as a "rule of difference," works not only to differentiate masculine and feminine, male and female, but also, in concert with other categories of difference, to privilege some men and to marginalize others.

Masculinity

As sociologist Robert W. Connell has proposed, masculinity is a hegemonic project by which he means that it is constructed through cultural practices that legitimate men's power vis-à-vis women in the gender order.[4] But it is also the means by which some men legitimate their subordination of other men. Furthermore, it is through these cultural practices that individuals come to identify themselves and others as members of the social category "men." This involves an ideology about manhood or manliness embodying a historically shifting field of dominant or preferred meanings that creates the appearance that its performance and perquisites are "natural."

In an important essay, historian John Tosh suggests that there are three components of masculine identity—home, work, and associations—and that the "precise character of masculine formation at any time is largely determined by the balance struck *between* these three components."[5] Rather than seeing home, work, and associations as components of masculine identity, I think it is more helpful to think of these as venues of masculine performance requiring specific styles of affect and activity that cohere uneasily in the creation of masculine subjectivity. I would further suggest that the category of "association" refers to participation in civil society, and also add a fourth venue of masculine performance—the military. It too has been crucial to the formation of hegemonic masculinity—at some times more so than at other times. These four venues, it may be argued, require different forms of masculine practice that produce and delineate "exemplary masculinities"—masculine cultural ideals. The production of exemplary masculinities, in turn, is integral to *how* claims for rights are heard in the public sphere, and *which* men are likely to participate in civil society.

Citizenship

Like masculinity, citizenship is also a complex and multifaceted concept. Perhaps most commonly, citizenship is understood to be a membership category—one that defines who does and who does not belong to a particular national community. In this sense, *citizenship* in contemporary parlance is a synonym for *nationality*—one freighted with the notion of rights (and certain obligations) that attach to members. Citizenship implies equality between and among persons who are endowed with that status. That promise of equality embedded in the notion of "the citizen," coupled with unequal entitlements, opportunities, and obligations, has led those who are disadvantaged to make claims for political equality and civic entitlements. These claims are articulated through associations in civil society and are promulgated in the public sphere.

I have found it useful to think of citizenship as a discursive framework—as a language. It is a multidimensional framework that provides the basis upon which people can make claims on the political community concerning juridical rights and duties, political and ethical practices, and criteria of membership. And it is on the basis of the discursive framework of citizenship that the state or community can expect or demand reciprocity from its members. Crucially important, the discursive framework of citizenship also produces political subjectivities. People enact these subjectivities as they join associations to contest meanings and make claims on the political community. Two great traditions of political thought have informed the languages of citizenship in modern Britain: *civic humanism* and *liberalism*. Civic humanism or civic republicanism, stretching back to ancient Greece and Rome through Renaissance Florence, stresses the idea that citizenship is a practice that citizens enact in the interest of the common good. The idea of virtue, central to civic humanism, was crucial to eighteenth-century English and Scottish political and moral theory. Conceptions of virtue, of course, shift and change over time. Importantly, the idea of citizenship as a practice in the interest of the common good suggests that civil society is a major arena in which citizenship is practiced. And if that is the case, we may ask on what grounds are people judged wanting in civic virtue and thus excluded from or marginalized within civil society?

The notion of "independence" also was crucial to political thought in this tradition, and the possession of landed property was believed to enable individuals to exercise their political judgment independently. The civic humanist idea of citizenship was masculine because it linked virtue and military service, and it also insisted that only men of property could be trusted with power. Thus, it was particular men, not all men, who possessed civic virtue. The story of franchise reform in nineteenth- and twentieth-century Britain may be told as one concerned with changing notions of who would be independent and responsible members of the political community, and thus could be trusted to choose their political representatives and/or hold power.

The second tradition of political thought, and the one that has most influenced modern conceptions of citizenship is, of course, liberalism. If the emphasis in civic republican citizenship is on practice and obligation, the emphasis of liberal citizenship is on rights. Liberalism prioritizes the rights of individual citizens, and citizenship involves the guarantee that those whose status is that of citizen are accorded the formal civil, political, and, in sociologist T. H. Marshall's terms, social rights necessary to participate in civil society and so to protect their individual freedom.[6] One of the fundamental characteristics of liberal citizenship is that it produces, in theory, a universal subject. Liberal citizenship promises to apply universally to all, and offers a vision of being inclusive. But its history, of course, is marked by exclusions based on gender, race, and economic standing and in some cases ethnic, religious, and/or national ancestry. The promise of equality and inclusion in the abstract idea of the universal citizen, coupled with the legal and substantive inequalities and social, political, and economic incapacities that deny some people that status, historically have generated a great deal of political contestation. The language of liberal citizenship has been appropriated by the excluded, who capitalize on its implied universality to make claims that they should be included. In what follows, I sketch the history of franchise reform and the changing meaning of "good citizenship" to show the close connection between ideals of masculinity and fitness for citizenship.

Franchise Reform, Masculinity, and Civil Society

Parliament passed the Reform Act of 1832 in response to the political unrest of the early 1830s and the formation of numerous Political Unions among working and middle-class people in London and the industrial regions who were demanding the extension of the suffrage in one form or another. The resulting act enfranchised men in the boroughs who owned dwellings with an annual ratable worth of ten pounds, co-opting middle-class men of commercial, financial, and industrial wealth to defeat the radical working-class demand for universal male suffrage. Newly enfranchised voters were middle-class men who demonstrated their respectability and independence by their ownership of property and who, therefore, could be trusted with the vote.[7] Property stood as the measure of masculine independence and respectability, that is, trustworthiness or civic virtue.

It was not long after the bill had become law that domestic issues became central to the politics of citizenship. Under the banner of Chartism and in reaction to the draconian New Poor Law passed in 1834, Radicals began agitating for the suffrage. To counter their demands, conservatives justified having granted the suffrage to middle-class men because of their domestic virtues, and attacked working-class men as bad husbands.[8] Chartists responded to these claims of middle-class men's worthiness for political inclusion by arguing for manhood suffrage based upon the proposition that artisans and skilled workers possessed property—they had "property in their skill—in their labor."[9] Radicals drew upon the language of independence to broaden the meaning of property to make it more inclusive.[10] For the next two decades, those who opposed extending the franchise to working-class men claimed that they were unruly workers and bad husbands. Artisans and skilled workers active in civil society, in turn, used the ideology of domesticity to make claims for a breadwinner's wage so that they could support their families. And they emphasized the virtues of labor and self-improvement.[11]

Many prominent middle-class reformers who wished for a further extension of the suffrage but feared democracy presented household suffrage as an alternative to universal manhood suffrage. If working men, living as household heads, attained a breadwinner's wage and took care of their families, they would, as historian Anna Clark put it, "share middle-class masculinity."[12] The 1867 Reform Act enfranchised about one third of working-class men, and purposefully excluded those who were lower-waged and casually employed by restricting the vote to urban male householders and those lodgers paying more than ten pounds of rent annually. As historian Keith McClelland has written, the working-class man included in the franchise in 1867 "was a particular kind of man whose definition—the social, political and moral qualities he was thought to carry, his perceived relationship to the processes of government and politics—was crucial to the redefinition of what the political nation was and might become."[13] Men as fathers and workers who supported their families were now to be trusted with the vote. As John Bright argued in the House of Commons in March 1867:

> At this moment ... there is a small class which it would be much better for themselves if they were not enfranchised, because they have no independence whatsoever, and it would be much better for the constituency also that they should be excluded, and there is no class so much interested in having that small class excluded as the intelligent and honest working man. I call this class the residuum, which there is in almost every constituency, of almost helpless poverty and dependence.[14]

And it was this "residuum," those who were casually employed and residentially unstable as well as those men who were living in cheap lodging houses, or as "dependents" with their families or in army barracks, who were denied the franchise until 1918.

The 1867 Act excluded from the political nation not only all women and those men who could not qualify as "householders," but also agricultural laborers and miners. The Reform Bill of 1884 included them, but still about 40 percent of the adult male population remained purposefully disenfranchised either because they did not live in the kinds of dwellings that qualified them as householders, or by virtue of stringent residency requirements that required a minimum of one year of residence to be eligible. In actuality, because of the complexities of registration, the period of residential stability required for the vote was closer to eighteen months.[15] Debates about suffrage both in Parliament and in the public sphere were largely focused on the vital issue of enfranchising women.[16] Further reform of the parliamentary franchise for men was stymied, in part, because the large majority of those who were disenfranchised, like sons living at home, lodgers in humble dwellings, soldiers living in barracks, or those men who were residentially mobile, were unlikely to be engaged in or recruited to associations in civil society. The disenfranchised men tended to be unorganized and, therefore, to lack a political voice.[17] As John Garrard has written recently about the reforms of 1884–85, they excluded from the parliamentary vote those "whose needs, even if not demands, were most urgent. Indeed, they tended to exclude people at the precise point when those needs became urgent, and were thus a means of safeguarding the system against the potentially radicalizing effects of economic crisis."[18]

This brief overview of franchise reform in the nineteenth century demonstrates the close connection between the languages of ideal masculinity and the requirements for political citizenship. It also raises the issue of which people are likely to participate in civic associations and to form and/or join social movements dedicated to political reform. During this period the unemployed who were likely to be among the disenfranchised sporadically became mobilized to demand economic justice through the efforts of various political associations. The Land and Labour League, a short-lived organization that advocated a program by which the government would purchase land on which the unemployed could be put to work, organized a demonstration by people, dressed in scarlet sashes and caps of liberty, in August 1870, described by *The Times* as a "gathering, which, taken altogether, was of a most grotesque character."[19]

During the Great Depression of 1873 to 1896, unemployed men were brought together by various organizations, many of which were inspired or dominated by the Independent Labour Party, but as historian Richard Flanagan has suggested, the Independent Labour Party was not actually successful "in organizing the unemployed as a cohesive force: rather ... it introduced into the chaos of the casual labor market an occasional focus for feelings of rage and impotence."[20] It was precisely this casual labor force that epitomized the so-called residuum about which John Bright had spoken in 1867.[21] But during the late nineteenth-century depression, the ranks of the unemployed included those who had been in regular employment, but had lost their livelihoods. "Respectable artisans" including those associated with the Social Democrats, however, generally distanced themselves from the demonstrations of the unemployed. According to Richard Flanagan, "It was the unrespectable, the unskilled laborers and not the labor aristocrats, who formed the mass of demonstrations and meetings, and their desperate plight did not always find sufficient outlet in 'orderly' demonstrations."[22] They either were provoked by police into engaging in street battles or were, themselves, likely to express their demands through angry outbursts of destructive behavior. For a time the Social Democrats abandoned their efforts to organize the unemployed. The party itself distinguished between respectable workingmen temporarily out of a job and those it deemed unemployable. Thus, although the casually employed and "unemployable men" would occasionally demonstrate about their economic plight, they generally were not members of civic associations.

In the early years of the new century, the unemployed, many of whom were veterans of the Boer War, organized "hunger marches," providing a model for unemployed World War I veterans about whom we will learn later. But again, left-leaning political groups such as the Independent Labour Party attempted to recruit artisans, rather than members of the chronically unemployed, to their protests. In their eyes, "only the deserving unemployed were truly men."[23] Furthermore, those who lacked the parliamentary franchise were most likely to be among the chronically unemployed, the casually employed, and those who were geographically mobile. As I suggested earlier, these men were unlikely to engage in associations to press for political reform and their "disorderly" protests against unemployment failed to generate a sympathetic hearing.

Imperialism, New Meanings of Citizenship, and Masculinity

It was not long after some working-class men earned the right to the franchise if they were respectable householders that both the ideals of manliness and the languages of citizenship changed. During the period between 1867 and the end of the century, hegemonic masculinity became less domestic, and more imperial, less civil and more martial, less concerned with sentiment and more concerned with virility. Numerous scholars have documented this transformation of popular conceptions of masculinity and its consequences. John Tosh, for example, has written, "Two or three generations on from the spread of the new moralized domesticity of the early nineteenth century, men were signaling a growing irritation with the rigid and exclusive association of domestic space with femininity."[24] Masculinity, according to Tosh, implied a public destiny and men were to be self-possessed and self-controlled. Home, in contrast, was a feminine space in which women displayed warmth and affection. Importantly the public culture of imperialism fuelled men's anxieties about associating too closely with the female sphere of domesticity. In the 1880s, empire was portrayed as a quintessentially masculine arena—an arena absent of women (except for those "other" women who satisfied male sexual desire).[25]

Contributing to this transformation of exemplary masculinity were journalistic accounts of the heroic exploits of British soldiers in imperial battles and skirmishes—"small wars" that stretched the margins of the Empire. These military exploits were "eagerly featured in an increasingly fervent popular press driven by competition to secure the quickest reports, the most exciting descriptions, the most vivid visual images of the 'glamorous or tragic spectacle' of war."[26] As a Christian civilizing mission came to be replaced by "the spirit of imperialism," the number of heroes celebrated in the public culture of the time expanded, but their "adventures became illustrative of a single, uniform masculine type."[27]

Juvenile periodicals, purchased primarily by boys of the lower middle and middle classes, were instrumental in dramatizing the soldier-hero as an exemplary figure for boys to emulate.[28] In addition to an outpouring of adventure literature aimed at boys and men, the Boys Brigade, and later after the Boer War, the Boy Scouts, emphasized the virtues of heroic manliness—Spartan virtues of duty, obedience, and discipline.

From the 1880s onward "good citizenship" was increasingly a value to be inculcated in working-class children at school. The language of citizenship during this period was focused less on rights and more on duty. As would be the case in the two World Wars of the twentieth century, the meaning of citizenship was informed by the long tradition of civic humanist discourse, and in the late nineteenth century was influenced as well by the British idealist philosophers and then by the new liberalism. Like the meanings of masculinity that became dominant after the mid-1870s, the term *good citizenship* emphasized manly sacrifice and national duty. Good citizenship was the modern-day equivalent of the civic republican notion of civic virtue. In the years before the First World War, according to historian Stephen Heathorn, "the good citizen was presumed to be male, and in large part 'good citizenship' was the civic code of an approved form of masculinity."[29] This transformed language of citizenship flourished in the context of heightened imperialism, threats to the industrial and military supremacy of the nation, and at century's end, a difficult war in South Africa and its aftermath that included persistent fears of invasion in the period leading to World War I.

At the end of the century and in the early years of the next one, educationalists, regardless of their political leanings, used this language about citizenship in their writings about curricula reform.[30] As Heathorn writes, "Loyalty to the sovereign, the glories of the empire, the welcome necessity of the armed services ... and above all, the duties of the individual citizen to the nation and race" dominated the lessons in the books that they wrote.[31] Conservative citizenship discourse stressed loyalty, duty, and obedience to authority. Liberals like James Bryce proposed that "the citizen must be able to understand the interests of the community, must be able to subordinate his own will to the general will, must feel his responsibility to the community and be prepared to serve it by voting, working or (if need be) fighting."[32] Bryce clearly saw "the citizen" as a male person who, in contrast to women, was entitled to the vote, and was expected to fight and to be a breadwinner. Bryce was articulating a conception of citizenship as a practice undertaken by men who would exemplify a newly revised version of masculine civic virtue.

Ironically, working-class soldiers, like women, were denied the franchise until 1918. But Conservatives who traditionally had defended the constitutional basis of the franchise as one related to independence and property had a change of heart during the war. Conservatives became convinced "that a war that turned workers into soldiers also had the power to transform soldiers into citizens and erstwhile laborers into loyal Tory electors."[33] It became difficult to speak out in opposition to enfranchising soldiers and reforming the registration rules to expand the electorate. And when the issue of enfranchising women entered the debate, it became difficult in the context of the war for opponents to restrict patriotic service to mean only being militarily useful. Thus the 1918 Representation of the People Act not only allowed women over thirty years of age to vote, but also made the dream of one man–one vote a reality (with the exception of conscientious objectors, who lost their right to the franchise until 1926).

Respectable Masculinity and Exclusions from "the Public"

As scholars of England in the period between the World Wars have noted, a refurbished construction of masculinity came into prominence—one with echoes of the mid-nineteenth-century middle-class manly ideal that emphasized domesticity. This new home-loving, family-oriented, quintessentially middle-class and conservative vision of masculinity promised to heal the dislocations of war and return the nation to normalcy.[34] The ideal of an unimpassioned, respectable, domestically oriented masculinity shaped the contours of the public sphere in which working-class men whose livelihoods had been threatened and/or devastated by unemployment in the years following the war and in the 1930s attempted to press their claims for economic rights.

Working-class militants during the interwar years who stridently protested their unemployment were those whom the bourgeois public defined as outsiders to the so-called constitutional classes. Here, then, was a new or modified discourse of masculine citizenship centered on a reimagined ideal of respectable manliness and a practice of citizenship now defined as following the institutionalized "political rules of the game." This language of citizenship focusing on the necessity to behave in a "constitutional" manner and to exercise citizenship "responsibly" shaped the definition of civility and thus influenced which voices in the public sphere would be heard. It developed in the context of universal male suffrage now being a fact and it flourished in a period that was marked by rising fears of Bolshevism, especially with civil unrest across Europe and labor strife at home. It was promulgated with extraordinary effectiveness by Stanley Baldwin, Conservative Prime Minister for much of the period, who continually reminded his audiences of the disaster of war and the need to avert conflict and "elided in his speeches the violence of the trenches with the violence of domestic social conflict."[35]

Large-scale unemployment especially devastated the livelihoods of men in mining and in heavy industry—unionized men with a history of active and radical associational life. While some of the unemployed dealt with their plight by lapsing into forlorn apathy, others joined associations in order to protest their situation. As after the Boer War, it was especially veterans who became mobilized. The largest and most prominent of the organizations to lead their effort was the National Unemployed Workers' Movement formed in April 1921. It was an organization heavily dominated by Communists whose major weapons in protesting the plight of the unemployed and the inadequacy of relief were to be national hunger marches as well as other dramatic enactments of protest and dissent.

Such marches and demonstrations by the unemployed continued through the 1920s and the 1930s right up through the winter of 1939 and the eve of World War II. Thus, in decided contrast to the ideal of bourgeois domestic masculinity stood a militant "in your face" working-class masculinity. The hunger marchers portrayed themselves as saviors of working-class manhood. One of the leaders of the National Unemployed Workers' Movement claimed, for example, that "militant action" was necessary to preserve their "spirit of manhood."[36] Furthermore, to emphasize the manliness of their cause, women, when they participated in demonstrations at all, did so separately from the men.[37]

The public sphere was both the site and the target of the militancy of the workingmen's protests. As historian Ross McKibbin has suggested, in the interwar years the middle class and elite defined "the public" as "what remained after the manual working class had been subtracted."[38] Their "public" was made up of "the constitutional classes"—the "good citizens" who followed "agreed upon rules" of politics and worked through established institutions. The "constitutional classes" opposed the militant tactics of organized labor and the organizations of the unemployed. In their eyes, strikes, marches, and demonstrations were "extra-constitutional"— they were the tactics of those who were sympathetic to Bolshevism.

There are numerous examples of expressions by public figures that distinguished militant working-class men from "the public." Sir Francis Joseph, president of the North Staffordshire Chamber of Commerce, for example, was quoted in *The Times* in July 1925 distinguishing between "the public" and striking workers, saying, "The public were always greater in numbers than the strikers."[39] Such partitioning of the "public sphere" by those representing the opinion of the more powerful segments of society provides evidence supporting the arguments of political theorists and historians who have maintained that in a society characterized by substantial social and economic inequalities, the public sphere is dominated by those with privilege who monopolize public discussion, while those who lack economic, social, and cultural capital are politically marginalized.[40] If, as political theorist Iris Marion Young argues, the "public sphere is the primary connector between people and power," in the interwar period, those who appealed to the powerful for political and social transformation—especially for "social rights"—but were excluded from "the public" formed what Nancy Fraser has termed "subaltern counterpublics."[41] There they enacted a masculinized, militant street politics of working-class radicalism (and on the other extreme, of Oswald Moseley's fascism)—a politics that those in the halls of power denigrated and to which they denied legitimacy.

Jobless men proclaimed themselves to be men as they marched carrying banners that announced, "Only cowards starve in silence." In contrast to the domestic masculinity being preached by Prime Minister Stanley Baldwin, unemployed workers underscored their militant masculinity by referring to themselves using military references. The oath taken by the first hunger marchers was prefaced by the phrase "I, a member of the great army of the unemployed...."[42] The placard announcing the 1934 national hunger march called for working-class unity and heralded the working class, both employed and unemployed, as "continuously and heroically fighting."[43]

The Government's response to the 1926 General Strike, called by the Trades Union Council in support of striking coal miners, crystallized the distinctions between those who were to be considered "the constitutional classes" and those who were not. Prime Minister Baldwin's cabinet was anxious to declare, even before the strike began, that a general strike would be regarded "as a challenge to the constitutional rights and freedom of the nation."[44] In an effort to rally middle-class public opinion against the impending strike, *The Morning Post* (closely associated with one of Britain's largest coal owners), portraying the unions as threatening revolution, proclaimed that the Trades Union Council had "exchanged an industrial dispute for a political coup d'etat."[45] And in Parliament the day prior to the start of the strike, Stanley Baldwin claimed that the legitimate Government "found itself challenged with an alternative Government."[46] Winston Churchill, who was to be editor of the *British Gazette*, the Government-run newspaper during the strike, accused the General Council of the Trade Unions of challenging the British constitution. At least one Labour member of Parliament, James H. Thomas (leader of the National Union of Railway men), tried to counter such portraits of the unions, saying "This is not only not revolution, it is not something which says, 'we want to overthrow everything.' It is merely a plain, economic, industrial dispute where the workers say, 'We want justice'."[47] The attempt to define "industrial disputes" as not political, however, did little to convince "the public"—the "constitutional classes"—that such militancy was not revolutionary in intent or aim. Throughout the period of the strike, Government propaganda played up the idea that it was a "constitutional challenge." The belief on the part of many in Britain that the General Strike endangered social and political stability prevailed in spite of the fact that most of the union leaders were in actuality fiercely opposed to an overthrow of legitimate government.

In the end, the Trades Union Council called off the strike to the disgust of the miners, who steadfastly refused to accept a wage cut, and more generally to those on the left in the labor movement. The defeat of the General Strike further marginalized and alienated those who favored industrial and political militancy.[48] As historian James Cronin has written, "the outcome of the contest created a sanitized system of free collective bargaining between well-organized employers and responsible and cautious trade unions."[49]

The "responsible and cautious trade unions" kept up their guard against any possible association with the Communists and continued throughout the late 1920s and 1930s to refuse support to the Communist-led National Unemployed Workers' Movement, their marches, and their seemingly militant tactics of protest. Indeed from the movement's beginnings in the early 1920s, there was hostility between the National Unemployed Workers' Movement on one side and the Trades Union Council and the

Labour Party on the other, and little if any cooperation. After the General Strike, the Trade Unions' General Council formally ended what cooperation had existed. In 1930 and 1932 local Labour Parties and trades councils were ordered not to give the marchers any assistance. The Trades Union Council and the Parliamentary Labour Party gave no formal support, either, to the Jarrow Crusade that launched its own march to London beginning in October 1936.

Unlike the hunger marches, the Jarrow Crusade received enormous publicity—far more publicity than was given to previous hunger marches sponsored by the National Unemployed Workers' Movement. In fact, its organizers, headed by Ellen Wilkinson, member of Parliament for Jarrow, did not want it to be known as a "hunger march" in order to distance their movement from the National Unemployed Workers' Movement (perceived as it was to be militant, radical, and Communist), and so, they called it a "Crusade." To underscore that the participants were orderly and responsible citizens walking to London to present a petition to the Government pleading for work for the town, Wilkinson and other town dignitaries attended a church service the day before the march was scheduled to begin in which all the town's clergymen and ministers took part. The service, covered by the national press, included a blessing given by the Bishop of Jarrow, Dr. Gordon.[50] And when the marchers set out the next day, they took with them the blessing of the Bishop of Ripon. As the *Manchester Guardian* described the Crusade, "it is an example of civic spirit probably without parallel anywhere else in the country."[51] The news coverage of the march involving just two hundred men was unparalleled, and it repeatedly emphasized the orderliness of the marchers and how well organized was the Crusade itself.

Significantly, what was to be the last of the national hunger marches organized by the National Unemployed Workers' Movement, made up of two thousand men, also was moving toward London at about the same time. When the Government attempted to blur the differences between the two groups with its suggestion that "processions to London cannot claim to have any constitutional influence on policy," there were protests from people like the Bishop of Sheffield and the Chairman of the Leeds Conservative Party. *The Times* went so far as to defend the right to march and petition Parliament as "an ancient, a valuable, a well-recognized right."[52]

To assure the respectability of the Jarrow men only two hundred, 62 percent of whom were veterans, were selected from the five hundred volunteers who were vetted through questions "concerning their domestic affairs, their army service and their health."[53] Furthermore the volunteers had to pledge that they would follow instructions including remaining "sober at all times."[54] While the previous hunger marches by the National Unemployed Workers' Movement probably paved the way for the "moderate protest" of the Jarrow marchers, it was the Jarrow Crusade, not the hunger marches, "that lived on as the symbol of unemployed action in the 1930s as the officially approved motif of 'peaceful protest'," according to Richard Croucher.[55] Public approval was granted to a form of social protest that its organizers self-consciously fashioned in opposition to the more militant, aggressive, and decidedly more "red" masculinist demonstrations of the hunger marchers.

Arguably the Jarrow Crusade marked a turning point after which respectable and respectful working-class men and women could press the government for economic rights without risking that they would be excluded from the "constitutional classes" by their immoderate behavior. This was then a renewed claim for social rights. And Jarrow legitimated a certain way of making such claims—one that maintained a temperate tone.

From a mass movement involving tens of thousands, after 1936 the National Unemployed Workers' Movement became a much smaller group of hardcore activists that carried out what one historian describes as "propaganda and publicity 'stunts' on behalf of the unemployed."[56] Preparations for the possibility of a new war and the subsequent growth of armaments industries reduced unemployment among the skilled engineers who had been the backbone of the movement earlier. From 1938 on, small cadres of men carried out minor, but dramatic demonstrations to protest unemployment. Several days before Christmas of that year, for example, a group of men lay down in the middle of Oxford Street during a break in traffic and covered themselves with posters protesting unemployment. The following day fifty unemployed men engaged in a "sit in" of sorts at the Ritz where they ordered tea and explained that they could not pay. On New Year's Eve men chained themselves to railings outside the Unemployment Assistance Board while others paraded around Piccadilly Circus with a coffin marked, "He did not get winter relief."[57] The National Unemployed Workers' Movement discontinued its activities with the outbreak of World War II in September 1939. But the hungry thirties, with the Jarrow Crusade as its emblem, lived on in public memory.

Conclusion

This history raises several questions about civil society and the public sphere. By examining how prevalent ideals of masculinity shaped the languages of citizenship, I have sought to show that these ideals not only discriminated against or excluded all women, but also were defined against and marginalized some men who did not or could not conform to the preferred masculine ideal. In thinking about civil society we cannot restrict "gender" to a sexual binary. Feminists and others for some time have suggested that, for example, the so-called universal citizen of liberal thought was gendered in a particular kind of way. He was not only male, but also white and European, and he was of a particular social and economic stratum as well. Furthermore, gender is not just about male and female people. It is also about the kinds of behavior and styles of political communication that are considered to be normative.

In addition I want to highlight two points. First, civil society by itself will not create a democratic society without the recognition that it is only those people who see themselves as having a stake in the community who engage in the associations of civil society or participate in social movements. As philosopher Michael Walzer writes,

> The greatest danger of civil society is often realized: namely, exclusion from it. The danger is that the benefits of association will be captured by middle- and upper-class citizens, who already possess the time and money necessary to form strong organizations and the education and skill necessary to run them effectively. Sometimes when this happens, lower-class citizens are simply reduced to anonymity and silence; they become invisible men and women.[58]

The men who were likely to have been excluded from the franchise between 1884 and 1918 in Britain were invisible. They did not join associations to claim political rights.

The second point concerns the definitions of "good citizenship," which I have understood as a modern-day equivalent of "civic virtue"—or of the practice of citizenship in civil society. I have showed how changing ideals of masculinity and its appropriate performance shaped those definitions. Civility, or the appropriate form of deliberation and communication within civil society, generally has been gendered masculine—but it has been gendered by a specific ideal of masculine performance—one based on a form of rational argument and orderly protest that has marginalized other men as well as women. In thinking about this I have found the work of Iris Marion Young to be helpful. In discussing the problem she terms "internal exclusions," she writes:

> Having obtained a presence in the public, citizens sometimes find that those still more powerful in the process exercise, often unconsciously, a new form of exclusion: they ignore or dismiss or patronize their statements and expressions. ... People may find that their claims are not taken seriously and may believe that they are not treated with equal respect.[59]

She suggests that a singular focus on rational argument denigrates other forms of communication. As we have seen, unemployed men in the interwar years who used a militant style of political communication were excluded from the "respectable public"—the public that was seen as producing legitimate or "constitutional" public opinion. As Young has written:

A norm of dispassionateness dismisses ... embodied forms of expression, emotion, and figurative expressions. People's contributions to a discussion tend to be excluded from serious consideration not because of what is said, but how it is said. Norms of orderliness sometimes exclude disruptive or emotional forms of expression that can be very effective in getting people's attention and making important points.[60]

The historical instances of exclusion that I have analyzed in this essay suggest that Young's analysis of style of political communication adds a significant performative dimension to Walzer's more structural analysis. The hunger marchers engaged in civil society by forming protest groups to make claims for social rights, but their militant and masculinist tone, an aspect of their radical left politics, resulted in their marginalization. Political theorist Simone Chambers has made the following interesting observation:

> Voting-centric democratic theory is being replaced by talk-centric democratic theory.... While nineteenth- and early twentieth-century democracy focused on expanding the vote to include everybody, today democracy focuses on expanding the public sphere to give everyone a say. Voice, rather than votes, is the vehicle of empowerment.[61]

This essay suggests that "voice" has always been important in the development of civil society and its contribution to democracy.

Antonio Gramsci's ideas about civil society are important in this context. He envisioned it as the sphere in which consensus or hegemony is organized. We saw an example of that in Stanley Baldwin's England. But civil society, according to Gramsci, is also the "site of rebellion against the orthodox as well as the construction of cultural and ideological hegemony."[62] Inclusion is key to this contestation. And, in the end, it is the potential or opportunity to struggle for social justice that is the promise of a democratic civil society.

Notes

1. Ross McKibbin, "The Franchise Factor in the Rise of the Labour Party," in McKibbin, ed., *The Ideologies of Class, Social Relations in Britain 1880–1950* (Oxford, 1994), 72.
2. Iris Marion Young, *Inclusion and Democracy* (New York, 2000), 158.
3. Nancy Fraser, *Justice Interruptus: Critical Reflections on the "Postsocialist" Condition* (London, 1997), 81.
4. Robert W. Connell, *Masculinities* (Berkeley, CA, 1995), 77f.
5. John Tosh, "What Should Historians do with Masculinity? Reflections on Nineteenth-Century Britain," *History Workshop Journal* 38 (1994): 179–202,187f. Also see his more recent discussion in John Tosh, *Manliness and Masculinities in Nineteenth-Century Britain* (London, 2005), 36–41.
6. Thomas H. Marshall, *Citizenship and Social Class, and Other Essays* (Cambridge, 1950).

7. Susan Kingsley Kent, *Gender and Power in Britain, 1640–1990* (London, 1999), 166; Dror Wahrman, *Imagining the Middle Class: The Political Representation of Class in Britain, c. 1780–1840* (Cambridge, 1995); McKibbin, "The Franchise Factor," 72.
8. Anna Clark, "Gender, Class and the Constitution: Franchise Reform in England, 1832–1928," in *Re-Reading the Constitution: New Narratives in the Political History of England's Long Nineteenth Century*, ed. James Vernon (Cambridge, 1996), 230–53, 235.
9. For this tradition of argument see, for example, James Epstein, "The Constitutional Idiom: Radical Reasoning, Rhetoric and Action in Early Nineteenth-Century England," *Journal of Social History* 23 (1990): 552–78, 562.
10. James Vernon, *Politics and the People: A Study in English Political Culture, c. 1815–1867* (Cambridge, New York, 1993), 310–35.
11. Ibid., 313.
12. Clark, "Gender, Class," 236.
13. Keith McClelland, "'England's Greatness, the Working Man,'" in *Defining the Victorian Nation: Class, Race, Gender and the Reform Act of 1867*, ed. Catherine Hall et al. (Cambridge, 2000), 71–118, 71.
14. Quoted in Catherine Hall, *Civilizing Subjects: Colony and Metropole in the English Imagination, 1830–1867* (Chicago, 2002), 425.
15. Neal Blewett, "Franchise Reform in the United Kingdom, 1885–1918," *Past and Present* 32 (1965): 27–56, 35.
16. Radicals associated with the National Liberal Federation, and at Trade Union Congresses and Labour Party conferences, continued to make the case for male franchise reform. See Blewett, "Franchise Reform," 51.
17. Ibid., 52.
18. John Garrard, *Democratization in Britain Since 1880* (Houndsmill, UK, 2002), 65.
19. *The Times*, 16 April 1870, 6. See Richard Flanagan, *"Parish-fed Bastards": A History of the Politics of the Unemployed in Britain, 1884–1939* (New York, 1991), 17ff.
20. Flanagan, *"Parish-fed Bastards,"* 22.
21. A classic history of the reactions to and perceptions of this residuum is Gareth Stedman Jones, *Outcast London: A Study in the Relationship Between Classes In Victorian Society* (Oxford, 1971).
22. Flanagan, *"Parish-fed Bastards,"* 40.
23. Ibid., 74.
24. John Tosh, *A Man's Place: Masculinities and the Middle-Class Home in Victorian England* (New Haven, CT, 1999), 182.
25. Ibid., 177. Tosh has recently argued that not only did anxieties about Britain's imperial stature shape masculinity in the metropole, but that anxieties about masculinity in the domestic arena were displaced onto imperial concerns. See Tosh, *Manliness*, 173–92.
26. Graham Dawson, *Soldier Heroes: British Adventure, Empire and the Imagining of Masculinities* (London, 1994), 145.
27. Ibid., 149.
28. John Springhall, "Building Character in the British Boy: The Attempt to Extend Christian Manliness to Working-Class Adolescents, 1880–1914," in *Manliness and Morality, Middle-Class Masculinity in Britain and America, 1800–1940*, ed. J. A. Mangan and James Walvin (Manchester, 1987), 53–74, 65.
29. Stephen Heathorn, *For Home, Country, and Race: Constructing Gender, Class, and Englishness in the Elementary School, 1880–1914* (Toronto, 2000), 25.
30. Heathorn, *For Home*, 32.
31. Ibid., 37–38.
32. Ibid., 29.
33. Nicoletta F. Gullace, *"The Blood of Our Sons": Men, Women, and the Renegotiation of British Citizenship During the Great War* (New York, 2002), 173.

34. Alison Light, *Forever England: Femininity, Literature and Conservatism Between the Wars* (London, 1991). For a discussion of the effects of the First World War and the turbulence of the immediate postwar period see Jon Lawrence, "Forging a Peaceable Kingdom: War, Violence and the Fear of Brutalization in Post First World War Britain," *Journal of Modern History* 75 (2004): 557–89.
35. Bill Schwarz, "The Language of Constitutionalism: Baldwinite Conservatism," introduction to *Formations of Nation and People*, ed. Mary Langan and Bill Schwarz (London, 1984), 7.
36. Wal Hannington as quoted in Flanagan, "*Parish-fed Bastards*," 70.
37. Ibid., 61.
38. McKibbin, *Ideologies*, 284.
39. *The Times*, 11 July 1925, 8.
40. See especially Nancy Fraser, "Rethinking the Public Sphere," in *Habermas and the Public Sphere*, ed. Craig Calhoun (Cambridge, MA, 1992), 109–42; Geoff Eley, "Nations, Publics, and Political Cultures: Placing Habermas in the Nineteenth Century," in ibid., 289–339; Young, *Inclusion*, 170–73.
41. Ibid., 173; Fraser, "Rethinking," 123.
42. Wal Hannington, *Unemployed Struggles: My Life and Struggles amongst the Unemployed* (New York, 1936; reprint, 1973), 81.
43. Ibid., 97.
44. As quoted in Margaret Morris, *The General Strike* (Harmondsworth, UK, 1976), 224. See her discussion of cabinet debates about issuing a public statement to this effect, ibid., 224–27.
45. As quoted in ibid., 236.
46. Ibid.
47. Ibid., 237.
48. Richard Price, *Labour in British Society* (London, 1986), 167.
49. James E. Cronin, *Labour and Society in Britain, 1918–1979* (London, 1984), 42.
50. See, for example, *The Times*, 6 October 1936, 11.
51. *Manchester Guardian*, 13 October 1936.
52. James Vernon, "Hungry Citizens," in *Memories of Hunger*, chapter 3, 36. I am deeply grateful to James for sharing his unpublished work with me, and for his advice and help with this paper.
53. Ibid.
54. Ibid., 35.
55. Richard Croucher, *We Refuse to Starve in Silence: A History of the National Unemployed Workers' Movement, 1920–46* (London, 1987), 182.
56. Ibid.
57. Ibid., 191.
58. Michael Walzer, "Equality and Civil Society," in *Alternative Conceptions of Civil Society*, ed., Simone Chambers and Will Kymlicka (Princeton, NJ, 2002), 34–49, 39.
59. Young, *Inclusion*, 55.
60. Ibid., 56.
61. Simone Chambers, "A Critical Theory of Civil Society," in *Alternative Conceptions*, ed. Chambers and Kymlicka, 90–110, 98f.
62. Michael Edwards, *Civil Society* (Cambridge, 2004), 8.

Chapter 11

CIVIL SOCIETY IN A NEW KEY?
FEMINIST AND ALTERNATIVE GROUPS IN 1960s–1970s WEST GERMANY

Belinda Davis

In the 1960s and 1970s, West Germany witnessed the burgeoning of two kinds of politics. The first was an intentionally provocative set of practices that deployed "theater" (visual as well as verbal communications), humor, and emotionally charged language to push beyond the more restrained, "reasoned" interventions putatively supported by the postfascist Western German state. The second has been described as "kitchen table" politics, that is, subcultural processes in non- or semipublic realms, often treated as representing a kind of retreat from politics. These practices were not necessarily specific to men or women, but they bore significant gendered aspects; in turn, they affected gender relations because they disturbed existing hierarchies of power and perceptions of difference. Historians have provided useful models for understanding "kitchen table" politics in the context of civil society, particularly with reference to women in nineteenth-century Europe.[1] Social scientists have also addressed these "informal" politics, particularly in the context of Eastern and Central Europe during the 1980s, and they have examined the politics of provocation.[2] This chapter draws on these models in order to look at the ways in which such politics constituted attempts to create the "pluralist and free community of communications"[3] that helps define civil society, using the example of gendered informal politics in postwar West Germany.

Seminal thinkers have challenged the idea that civil society can serve as a locus for effective political change, but their estimations may reflect unnecessarily limited views of both the concept and of change. The term *civil society*, as a locus of social interaction, lends itself to the consideration of a multiplicity of sites and voices. While some political theorists have warned of the potential totalitarianism of the notion of a "common good," through civil society we can identify communitarian politics that leave space for recognition of variable "goods" among different populations. Antonio Gramsci questioned civil society's remove from the state and warned of its potential as a sphere for hegemonic cooptation, in which differing views could be easily neutralized. This anticipates Michel Foucault's assessment that civil society allowed self-expression while nonetheless controlling its power to produce change. In this sense, both Gramsci and Foucault might be said to regard civil society as a kind of safety valve. These critiques are surely important to consider, but it is still worth tracing the activities within civil society that did transform notions of where and how politics takes place. Moreover, while many scholars remind us that in practice there is no necessary link between civil society and democratization, formal or otherwise, attending to civil society allows us to see acts of "radical democracy" alongside the kinds of active participation, communication, commitment, responsibility, and "teamwork" with which the term has commonly been associated.[4] Further, understanding civil society as a sphere independent of formal legal rights, and one in which there are no firm boundaries between public and private, allows us to consider politics in a broad sense, perhaps above all gendered politics. For some, "provo" (provocation) politics may seem an ill fit with the concept of civil society. Others may argue that the politics of the kitchen table did more to make participants feel as though they were participating politically than to actually change things. In this examination of 1960s–1970s West Germany, I argue for a less dubious assessment of both of these types of acts, and, thereby, of the potential of civil society itself.

Out in Civil Society: Provo Politics

How should we use the sphere of civil society to understand the role of provo politics? Analysts of civil society, primarily social scientists, identify four basic views of the concept: communitarian; democratic and participatory; liberal; and defined by communicative action.[5] They point to four rudimentary modes of democratic engagement, as explicitly related to civil society, including representative liberal, participatory liberal, discursive, and constructionist.[6] These scholars have suggested that "participatory" engagement can include attention-getting and even provocative forms,[7] a range of styles that emphasizes not only the communicative effects of participants' acts but also the "empowerment" individuals draw from participation, which in turn validates for them their continued contribution. These styles are not limited to the "reason" and "detached civility" typically associated with, for example, liberal participation. Emotion often plays an important role in both the appeal to and effect upon the participant. Indeed the definition of "civility" itself can be challenged in this context. I would argue for a notion of "deep civility," that is, one that includes the potential to act with a surface incivility (minor destruction of property, ridicule of one's "opponent") that may appear to dismiss the value of communicative interaction but can in fact undergird it. It is vital to recognize that those deploying such forms in the 1970s, who often saw themselves as revolutionary (not always without merit) and opposed to "liberalism," overwhelmingly adopted strategies intended to *convince* others (rather than, say, shooting them) to get them to think about things differently.[8] While acts of provocation may seem to fall outside many definitions of civil society, in the West Germany of the 1960s and 1970s, I argue that they helped deepen democratic participation and political communication, opening spaces for minority viewpoints.

The activists of this period held free and open communication in high regard. One of the premier symbols of the "'68ers" throughout Western Europe was the image of a person (gender indistinguishable, indeed without individual features) with his or her mouth pinned closed. Produced in one key iteration by the Parisian *atelier populaire* in 1968, the picture communicated the degree to which youth felt closed off from "the public discussion."[9] It was adopted by West German New Left activists in the late 1960s and appeared with increasing frequency throughout the 1970s, above all in response to the 1972 *Radikalenerlass*, the Radical Decree. This draconian measure threatened the employment of all present and prospective public sector employees—professors, teachers, civil servants, clerks, and workers—who were perceived as "hostile" to the existing state, and by extension it brought pressure on those employed in the private sphere as well. Officials and sectors of the media used this and other means to tar the entire New Left movement, including the relatively few violent activists, with the same brush, in order to marginalize, discredit, and repress their voices.[10] Although photographic evidence shows that it was common for both men and women to tape up their mouths or wrap them in scarves during demonstrations (sometimes simultaneously to conceal their identities from officials), in West Germany, the face rendered speechless on posters and leaflets was most often female. This very gendering emphasized the impotence of men and women alike; feminizing the image powerfully communicated the sense of voicelessness experienced by both sexes.[11]

While provo actions have been characterized by some as fatuous distractions at best, prospective or actual violence at worst, they were extremely effective in introducing new ideas into public discourse. The violence associated with a minority of instances should not prevent us from considering the positive impact these practices generally had.[12] Certainly they angered many, but this was the point: they were a way of attracting attention when more conventional means had failed. Those engaging in provo acts most often drew negative attention from the larger society (though not as universally negative as is often described). Nonetheless, they did succeed in bringing issues they found important—from university reform to the Vietnam War and beyond—to broader discussion and making their voices heard.

Provo politics also played an empowering role for the activists themselves, and again, one with an important gender dimension. Some West German activists described their practices as a kind of "masculinist" intervention, as much a bullying insistence on one's own presence as a demonstration of serious political intent. Dagmar Seehuber, a member of the (in)famous *Kommune I*, a small group of activists living and working together in 1967 and 1968 who led the way with provocative strategies, described such acts as a "men's thing" (*Männergeschichte*).[13] Yet, she joined in with these acts, as a way of combating the silencing effects of prevailing gendered political-cultural practices. Robert A., a student at the University of Heidelberg during the same period, recalls feeling freed from a narrow, private world; engaging in "small provocative acts" allowed him "to emerge out of [his] own background, to come out of the shelter of [his] own family, and to liberate [him]self," as well as to communicate a public message he found important.[14] Women spoke even more of this sense of coming to feel as though they "existed," that they were a part of the scene—or some scene. These feelings, in turn, encouraged them to become further engaged, ultimately offering a range of rewards beyond remedying a "feminizing" silencing.

This kind of intervention informed efforts in the new feminist movement to rethink self-expression. Because it enabled a few to capture the attention of the many as well as ridicule those with power, provo action could be practiced effectively by a minority against the majority (numerically and in terms of power), and by socially "lower" individuals against elites (including those within organizations). It could challenge dogmatic, hierarchical, authoritarian, and totalitarian practices. Whether "masculinist" in terms of traditional practices, the arrogation of power, or otherwise, women as well as men used such means to gain visibility and convey their points within the larger society throughout this era, marking the birth of the West German second-wave women's movement; they betokened the assumption of a right to a voice and to a response. In 1969, the male and female leadership of the West Berlin antiauthoritarian *Kinderladenbewegung* (a movement for state-independent child care, collectively organized and controlled by parents), one of the earliest West German feminist projects, staged a "dirty diaper attack" on the editor of the popular weekly magazine *Stern*. They wanted to convey their dissatisfaction with the "shock" coverage the magazine had given them, which in their view diminished their efforts. In this instance, registering their anger was in itself a key goal, but the participants also showed that, like the magazine itself, they could communicate through tactics of surprise. The participants expressed considerable satisfaction with their efforts, which resulted in an acknowledgement of their concerns by *Stern*'s editor, who was otherwise unlikely to have taken time to talk to them directly.[15]

Indeed it was media outlets such as *Stern* that contributed to informing activists' provocative practices; activists attempted to use these means to spur critical thinking as well as find a voice for themselves. Certainly such press organs enabled activists to make themselves heard (albeit in mediated fashion). In 1971, West German feminist Alice Schwarzer and others, inspired by the French example, wrote an article for *Stern* entitled, "I've had an abortion," in order to force West Germans to confront this reality. It featured the stories of nearly four hundred women, several of them prominent, who had had illegal procedures.

Many women practiced provocative strategies of protest throughout this period despite, or indeed because of, the strategies' perceived masculinist bravado and assertion of confidence. In a 1973 "Go-In," feminists in Frankfurt decorated anti–reproductive-choice church leaders with baby powder and formula to dramatize not just the theory but the everyday realities of caring for children. Others carried banners graphically suggesting that criminalization of abortion would not be an issue if priests could become pregnant. While the history of abortion rights in (West) Germany has been rocky, the West German women's movement won considerable general support for this issue, resulting in an initial major parliamentary success in 1974.[16] In an ironic mimesis of the media's practice of featuring bare-breasted women on the front page of newspapers, women used their own disrobed bodies in several public actions.[17] This was intended to comment cynically on the use of naked women to "sell news" and on the culturally-conditioned attention given to women's bodies rather than to their words.[18] Activists made a verifiable impact, influencing national (or at least public) opinion against such media practices. At the same time, they felt that as women, as young people, and as activists, they were being listened to rather than being ignored or vilified.

Women also directed provocative forms of politics toward the men within activist ranks. As was the case with feminists elsewhere, it was largely their frustration with male fellow protesters that led them to form a West German women's movement. At the 1968 national assembly of the West German Socialist Students organization (SDS), female delegate Sigrid Rüger famously threw a tomato at the pontificating Hans-Jürgen Krahl, a leading theorist of the group. Krahl's speech followed the impassioned address by early feminist and filmmaker Helke Sander in which she had identified the oppressiveness of patriarchy within the SDS.

He continued as if she had not spoken. Men in the audience, insofar as they responded at all to Sander, did so largely with sniggers and dismissive comments. Though Krahl's practice was to some degree the standard—that is, that leaders offered their pre-rehearsed speeches without reference to those that came directly before—Sigrid Rüger and others insisted that Sander's message be heard, acknowledged, taken seriously, and responded to directly. The tomato certainly stopped the proceedings dead in their tracks, and the act took on iconic status, emphasizing the need to listen to women's voices and to unheard voices more broadly, as as was illustrated by the "speechless woman" figure.[19]

Instead of characterizing provo activists as irresponsible and irrelevant if not dangerous, one could argue that, by insisting on being heard and working to open up the sphere of public participation to others, they espoused the principle of "responsibility"—the responsibility to participate—often regarded as an aspect of "mature" civil society.[20] Practitioners described provo acts as also offering a particular kind of satisfaction in themselves that cannot be dismissed, one that inspired participants to continue their efforts. Their satisfaction lay precisely in the linkage between "public" and "private," a linkage not only of issues (from abortion rights to everyday violence) but also between the parts of people's experience, so that participation in public life as such could be joyous, gratifying, thrilling, socially enjoyable, and empowering.[21]

There was indeed a significant emotional component to these strategies, a characteristic contemporaneously dismissed as inappropriate to politics—and as feminine.[22] Both men and women who engaged in such acts described them as "fun," "inspiring," and "exciting." Activist Susanne Kleemann remembered, "it was fabulous to throw eggs at Amerika Haus" in West Berlin—which in turn unquestionably captured considerable public notice, drawing attention to the war in Vietnam and West Germany's close relationship with America.[23] Robert A. found such small-level provocation directed at the university in provincial Heidelberg "crazily, crazily exciting"; it seemed to put him "in contact with the wider world." This emotional appeal was gendered in another way as well: it was about embracing fantasy and desire and casting off close constraints and expectations, including the highly gender-specific expectations of the early postwar decades. Provo acts reflected "disobedience" (*Ungehorsam*) in both the "familial" and "political" context (the two often closely related), and the challenge of existing limits. Peter Schneider, a leading activist in West Berlin, described such politics in retrospect as "organized self-liberation" constituted by "misbehavior," "insubordination, civil courage, and self-organization."[24]

Provo action also drew on the desire to be and act with other people. One might claim that this had nothing to do with politics, that it was somehow responding to a far more fundamental instinct that should hardly be elevated to the political. But this shows once more the flexibility of the concept of civil society: that it is predicated on the need for and value of people coming together, in smaller and larger arenas beyond the family circle, to communicate with one another (sometimes to startle others into listening) and create a broad sense of community, even as it reinforced a kind of individuation and individual development. This satisfaction in turn motivated many activists to remain involved over many years rather than withdrawing in frustration and alienation. A broadened concept of civil society thus offers us a way of reading provo action in this period as a means of contributing to the building of a democratic and participatory society through a wide range of communicative means.

Back in Civil Society? The "Politics of the Kitchen Table"

Civil society emerged as a significant term for feminist historians in the 1980s in the context of activities "behind the scenes," outside of formal decision-making spheres. Catherine Hall and Leonore Davidoff used this concept to describe the ways in which women in nineteenth-century England participated in political discussions and collective associations on the local level beyond the family circle, to create for themselves a community identity, and to participate in decision-making within their communities.[25] Their approach provides a vital tool for understanding participation and the practice of influence in the overlaps between "private" and "public" life in West Germany more than a century later. It helps us view political expression among those who had not yet reached majority status in that country,[26] as well as among women and others who, despite bearing formal political rights did not feel able to exercise them satisfactorily. In the 1960s, sites such as schools and universities, neighborhood pubs, and churches, and by the 1970s, self-established loci such as women's and youth centers, the common rooms of non-familial shared residences (*Wohngemeinschaften* or *WGs*), and the developing alternative press were vital to these individuals' efforts to situate and express themselves among others. The concept of civil society enables us to understand the acts that took place at these sites as political. Moreover, they were often politically successful in a variety of ways.[27]

The "politics of the kitchen table" emerged, once more, out of perceived necessity, in part as a response to the repression associated with the Radical Decree and corresponding increasing physical violence by police against protesters throughout the 1970s. But they were not, as some have suggested, a retreat from politics. New Left activists added new forms of activity to actions in the streets, creating lively, alternative spaces of sociopolitical interaction and communication. Although these sites often existed away from broad public view, partly because of the growing police restriction on more open civil society practices, they became ubiquitous throughout the decade, with the women's movement leading the proliferation. The impact of this development can be seen inter alia in the proliferation of citizens' initiatives and the broader, new social movements, as well as in the peace movement of the early 1980s, and the Green Party. These developments helped build vast alternative communication networks that gave voice to women and to others who felt themselves unheard and even unable to speak.

As several activists have described, the alternative communication networks fostered a critical conjuncture and even transcendence of the dichotomy between "public" (and "political") and "private." Christiane W. emphasized that she met regularly with clusters of people of different ages and classes who found one another in a pub in Hof, the provinicial Bavarian city where she lived. To be sure, there was nothing new about meeting and talking with others about politics in a pub. What was different was Christiane's commitment to seeking out those who were "different," precisely those who were not likely to agree or see things from the same perspective. Not only pubs but also private dwellings increasingly served as "semipublic" meeting sites. Christiane remembers that after moving to Regensburg, she and her friends used their apartments, though tiny, to host meetings for many purposes, including, for example, forming a women's group. Soon her new group house (WG), with its "open-door policy," served this function even better; in addition, the women's center she co-founded offered a site for many types of interaction and organizing, connecting the public and private within its walls.

Alongside the acts most closely associated with provo politics, the "politics of the kitchen table" also became important to fulfilling specific needs; women in this era (and many men too) often found a greater comfort with political discourse in more informal and secluded settings. Typical of many, Katrin B. described how central it was for both her personal politicization and ongoing political engagement to have discussions every evening at dinner with the members of her all-women WG about politics at every level, and how these discussions directly concerned her smaller community. This was so important that when many members of the WG went on diets in the late 1970s and refused the collective meals, the WG was ultimately destroyed, its social and political functioning eroded. Such venues expanded well beyond the literal kitchen table, offering a combination of "publicness" and intimacy, creating an atmosphere of ease for speaking one's mind as well as for listening, and a sense that one had interlocutors, that one's thoughts reached others—ultimately, perhaps, many others. New living forms generally both emphasized this transcendence of public and private and allowed individuals to feel "whole" (*ganzheitlich*), as they saw it: living and eating with the same people with whom they planned and attended public events and engaged in political actions. Women's centers, which mushroomed in West Germany in the 1970s, were another major site, one that was especially effective for connecting women in smaller and more dispersed communities to one another. Hosting a constantly transforming congregation of women, they provided permanent space for the exchange of thoughts at every level. This space was vitally important both for women of all sexual orientations who were also involved in many other groupings and for those who were culturally, socially, and politically separatist.[28]

Such efforts were not limited to more controlled spaces like women's centers,[29] however, nor were they restricted to women-only spaces, although their initial development in such communities bespeaks not only the impact of official repression but also the limits of opportunities to speak and be heard even among one's peers in mixed-gendered settings. (Certainly individuals also could and did feel silenced and subjected to hierarchies of power in single-gender settings.) Women-only settings established a model for alternative public spaces and civil societies, one that was widely and effectively adopted by a range of citizens' initiatives and new social movements in the 1970s, and that provided space for a range of voices while offering a level of comfort for participants. Ultimately such alternative sites for discussion not only resulted in policy changes and a shift in priorities on a broad range of issues, but they also challenged understandings of a unitary, hegemonic "civil society."

Indeed, in many ways the model of discussion that emerged in these intimate settings approaches conventional ideals of civil society. To some, such settings may suggest a lack of the transparency and openness that are deemed so important in democratic political engagement; but insofar as they allowed individuals to participate directly in communicative processes and thereby permitted so many different voices to be heard directly, they represented a summa of these values, in principle at least. These contexts contributed to building trust as well as responsibility, elements also regarded as central to civil society.[30] To be sure, already in the 1970s, some feminists criticized what one termed "women sitting around drinking tea together." This might have been the most "comfortable" form of activism, she went on, but "we needed to get out there in the 'male society' (*Männergesellschaft*) to make our voices heard."[31] Yet, for hundreds of thousands of women (as well as men), "kitchen table politics" led to other, more conventionally public forms of activism as well. Despite the democratic impulses and other appealing attributes of the practices emerging from these settings, social scientists have questioned activists' ultimate efficacy, as have some contemporaries speaking in retrospect.[32] But in the event these practices were no less efficacious than other forms of popular politics and public self-expression of the period, such as demonstrations, boycotts, or strikes. The successes women and others achieved through this type of engagement—ranging from changes in abortion and family law, to the transformation of urban housing policy, to public awareness and new policy concerning nuclear energy—must be acknowledged.[33]

At least as important: all these forms of alternative activities provided space for "one's own voice," a remedy for the voicelessness perceived as feminine. Former activists emphasize that they felt encouraged to speak out and define and refine their own views against the sounding board of others; that they appreciated the broad spectrum of views these various settings offered; and that they saw these more intimate settings as being closely connected to larger networks of debate and discussion that moved across large populations, in turn linking them to other forms of action and to results. Without exaggerating the breadth of this openness, it must be emphasized that in the 1970s, the West German "New Left" was by no means dominated by the simpleminded orthodoxy it is sometimes claimed to have adopted.[34] Rather, alternative political spaces, situated as they were at the nexus of public and private, allowed marginalized voices of many types both to instigate discussions and enter a larger set of debates.

From Modernism to Postmodernism

Ideas about civil society in the last three centuries emerge from a modernist episteme that emphasizes individuation and independent thinking, education, and civic interchange and participation. Because provo actions and kitchen table politics also supported these qualities, they merit inclusion under the rubric of civil society. The process of individuation, as these participants described it—finding one's own voice and having a chance to test it out against others—was central to their participation in civil society. Robert A. described the "incredible feeling of self-possession and of strength" afforded by joining in both regular provo acts and evening meetings in local university pubs. These experiences forced him to define himself and speak his own positions clearly, thereby allowing him to find himself beyond the space of his family. This transformation did not always come easily. Anna J. described her shock after leaving school and heading to university to find that her comments were systematically ignored by members of the predominantly male political discussion group she joined. But she credits her earlier experience in small groups and with provo acts during high school with enabling her to fight back successfully—through communicative means. Gaby M. recalls her sense of inadequacy during her first year at the University of Cologne as a young woman coming from a poor family in a farm village: "I felt completely out of place," she commented, "naïve, stupid, and ignorant.... [I] couldn't even talk to anyone." For more than a year, she ceased speaking altogether. But eventually she joined small group discussions and found both her voice and good reason to speak. Along with other recently joined members, "we found ourselves much better informed, [more] unorthodox and critical" than presumed New Left leaders in West Berlin, who would speak for her. A sense of being silenced led many who felt disenfranchised to find their own means of being part of the conversation. The sense was often associated with characteristics of gender, if not necessarily related to specifically gendered bodies.

Reading these experiences through the concept of civil society, we might consider that the practices emerging in the 1970s can also be labeled postmodernist, or as introducing postmodern thinking.[35] Postmodernism is characterized by a rejection of grand theory and totalizing ideologies; it challenges ideas such as a linear and progressive human history and development, universal truths and values, and other notions associated with Enlightenment thought. Postmodernism is often associated with more and less widely-read political theorists, from Jacques Lyotard to Frantz Fanon to Jean Baudrillard. Yet it was the activists discussed here who through their political acts advanced the notions these thinkers described in their writings, communicating them to a broad audience. Moreover, the activists' de facto challenge to binaries such as "public vs. private" and "reason vs. emotion" also signaled the shift to postmodernism. Thus, it should come as no surprise to discover that some of the most compelling recent models of civil society, such as the "participatory model," precisely reflect political understandings that emerged from the politics of the 1960s and 1970s.

Contemporary (and some later) critics of provo protesters claimed that they represented a particularist view, hijacking a broader agenda and range of issues that "truly" represented West German interests (such as the growing stature of West Germany in the Cold War world order and an emphasis on societal order at home). But it was provo activists who demanded respect for minority views, for multivocality (in contrast to the simple acceptance of "majority rule"), and for the idea of going beyond mere "toleration" of difference. By insisting on the need and possibility to attend to these different voices, provo and kitchen table political actors questioned the notion of a common good, that is, the concept that political decisions should be made solely on the basis of the greatest good for the greatest number. In this sense, the more recent philosophical view that communitarianism requires consideration of "minority" interests must be seen, in part, as stemming from the activism of these years in West Germany and elsewhere.[36] The demand for attention to different voices representing various particular experiences defied notions of a unitary "truth" in favor of recognition of a range of perspectives emerging from quite varied needs and desires.[37] At the same time, the assumption that the views advanced by popular activists at any moment were those of only a tiny minority must itself be challenged. By looking at the full panoply of sites that we can describe as civil society, we discover that the activists represented a range of demographic characteristics in terms of age, class origin and, above all, life experience—far broader than is often acknowledged.[38]

Conclusion

While to be sure the popular political forms and impulses described here had counterparts outside of West Germany in this era, their emergence in West Germany has to be seen as both a direct and indirect response to the Nazi past. The modernist civil society ideal in early West Germany reflected reasoned discourse among educated participants, conducted in close concert with official sanction, in specified settings and forms, and manifested a clear division between the public and private. Yet many contemporary activists argued that this sober model, which distinguished so resolutely between the public and private, failed to permit a flourishing and vigorous civil society; instead, it represented a kind of deep self-censorship that perpetuated the effects of the Nazi era rather than transcending its politics. This was, once more, a gendered argument. Christiane W. noted in retrospect, "'Big Politics' and private life could no longer be divided for the entire postwar generation, and certainly for women still less than for men." Contemporaries speak uniformly of the "excitement" and "satisfaction" this civil participation engendered, beyond building self-confidence and a sense of one's right to participate. Emotion and personal needs and desires, still often discounted in discussion of politics, were significant in maintaining active participation in civil society, in itself a contribution to democratization.

The hierarchy of gender has long inflected institutionalized political processes, even when such differentiation has been legally and constitutionally prohibited. The concept of civil society allows us to see both how women without formal legal rights have participated politically with considerable efficacy and how women endowed with rights still encounter limits to fully exercising their voices. The concept offers a means of viewing the practice of politics in a highly complex form, transcending presumed boundaries of public and private and other "ideal" definitional features, with direct implications for our understanding of gender and power.

Examining a broad terrain of civil society helps us to read political participation as being of a piece with participants' desires, something that explains why so many gravitated toward politics and wanted to frequent existing sites in fresh ways and create new places for themselves. The concept also helps us to recognize the significant and lasting transformations in German political culture that took place in this era, characterized in part by the legitimation of a wide range of forms of political participation. While these transformations do not overturn the idea that civil society may, as Gramsci and Foucault implied, operate merely as a "safety valve," they do offer evidence of meaningful political change from the inside out and thereby also challenge how we measure meaningful change. As scholars have described civil society in practice, its functionality has been predicated on the ability of many to enter into discussions of broad significance, whether directly or indirectly. The forms of expression and communication that proliferated so expansively in the 1960s and 1970s overwhelmingly represented not, as some have assumed, a violation of the ideals of civil society, but rather an expansion of it. In turn, consideration of such activity adds new life to the notion of civil society.

Notes

1. Among European examples, including those looking specifically at gender, see Leonore Davidoff and Catherine Hall, *Family Fortunes: Men and Women of the English Middle Class, 1780–1850* (London, 1987); Ute Frevert, ed., *Bürgerinnen und Bürger: Geschlechterverhältnisse im 19. Jahrhundert* (Göttingen, 1988); Marion A. Kaplan, *The Making of the Jewish Middle Class: Women, Family, and Identity in Imperial Germany* (New York, 1991); Karen Hagemann, "Familie—Staat—Nation: Das aufklärerische Projekt der 'Bürgergesellschaft' in geschlechtergeschichtlicher Perspektive," in *Europäische Zivilgesellschaft in Ost und West, Begriff, Geschichte, Chancen*, ed. Hildermeier et al., 57–84; Gunilla Budde, "Das Öffentliche des Privaten: Die Familie als zivilgesellschaftliche Kerninstitution," in *Die Praxis der Zivilgesellschaft: Akteure, Handeln und Strukturen im internationalen Vergleich*, ed. Arnd Bauerkämper (Frankfurt/M., 2003), 56–76. More generally among historians, see James van Horn Melton, *The Rise of the Public in Enlightenment Europe* (Cambridge, 2001); Jürgen Kocka, "Zivilgesellschaft in historischer Perspektive," in *Forschungsjournal Neue Soziale Bewegungen* 16, no. 2 (2003): 29–37; Stefan-Ludwig Hoffmann et al., eds., *Geselligkeit und Demokratie: Vereine und zivile Gesellschaft im transnationalen Vergleich, 1750–1914* (Göttingen, 2003); Ralph Jessen et al., eds., *Zivilgesellschaft als Geschichte: Studien zum 19. und 20. Jahrhundert* (Opladen, 2004). As a still relatively rare historical application of the term in postwar Europe, see Paul Ginsborg, *Italy and Its Discontents 1980–2001: Family, Civil Society, State* (London, 2003). Thanks to Frank Trentmann and Sven Reichardt for their comments; also thanks to Jan Kubik and Philip Nord for discussion of civil society over the years.
2. Within this extremely rich literature, see from just the last years focusing on Europe: John Keane, *Civil Society: Old Images, New Visions* (Cambridge, 1998); Thomas R. Rochon, *Culture Moves: Ideas, Activism, and Changing Values* (Princeton, NJ, 1998); Roland Roth and Dieter Rucht, eds., *Jugendkulturen, Politik und Protest: Vom Widerstand zum Kommerz?* (Opladen, 2000); Grzegorz Ekiert and Jan Kubik, *Rebellious Civil Society: Popular Protest and Democratic Consolidation in Poland, 1989–1993* (Ann Arbor, MI, 2001); Matthias Freise, *Externe Demokratieförderung in postsozialistischen Transformationsstaaten* (Münster, 2004); Michael Edwards, *Civil Society* (London, 2004); Frank Adloff, *Zivilgesellschaft: Theorie und politische Praxis* (Frankfurt/M., 2005); Sven Eliason, ed., *Building Democracy and Civil Society East of the Elbe: Essays*

in *Honour of Edmund Mokrzycki* (London, 2006); also Ernest Gellner, *Conditions of Liberty: Civil Society and Its Rivals* (New York, 1994). The term has been used to be sure in some social scientific discussions of Western Europe; see Myra Marx Ferree et al., eds., *Shaping Abortion Discourse: Democracy and the Public Sphere in Germany and the United States* (Cambridge, 2002); Hanspeter Kriesi and Ruud Koopmans, eds., *New Social Movements in Western Europe: A Comparative Analysis* (London, 2003). Among recent efforts to bring together historical and social scientific perspectives, uses, and objects of understanding, Nancy Bermeo and Philip Nord, eds., *Civil Society Before Democracy: Lessons from Nineteenth-Century Europe* (Lanham, MD, 2000); John Hall and Frank Trentmann, eds., *Civil Society: A Reader in History, Theory, and International Politics* (London, 2005); Dieter Gosewinkel et al., eds., *Zivilgesellschaft—national und transnational. WZB-Jahrbuch 2003* (Berlin 2003).
3. Sven Reichardt, "Civil Society: A Concept for Comparative Historical Research," in *The Future of Civil Society: Making Central European Nonprofit-Organizations Work*, ed. Annette Zimmer and Eckhard Priller (Wiesbaden, 2004), 45.
4. See Benjamin Barber, *Strong Democracy: Participatory Politics for New Age* (Berkeley, CA, 1984); Ulrich Rödel et al., eds., *Die demokratische Frage* (Frankfurt/M., 1989).
5. This is Sven Reichardt's formulation in "Civil Society," 43–46.
6. This schematization is the work of Myra Marx Ferree et al., "Four Models of the Public Sphere in Modern Democracies," *Theory and Society* 31 (2002): 289–324.
7. See among others Paul Hirst, *Associative Democracy: New Forms of Economic and Social Government* (Cambridge, MA, 1994); Barber, *Strong Democracy*; John Gaventa, *Power and Powerlessness* (Urbana, IL, 1980). The forms discussed here do not fit exclusively into this category of democratic participation, but the characteristics marking the category are particularly critical here.
8. Naturally many revolutionary traditions rely on the notion of some number of people convincing others through argument or example. On the notion of violence in civil society: see Sheri Berman, "Civil Society and the Collapse of the Weimar Republic," *World Politics* 3 (1997): 401–29; Sven Reichardt, *Faschistische Kampfbünde: Gewalt und Gemeinschaft im italienschen Squadrismus und in der deutschen SA* (Cologne, 2002).
9. See Greil Marcus, *Lipstick Traces: A Secret History of the Twentieth Century* (Cambridge, MA, 1989), 35–36. Marcus's discussion of the Dadaist and Situationist roots of British Punk is equally relevant to the provo activism of the European New Left.
10. For officials' habit of lumping together all on "the left," see Belinda Davis, "From Starbuck to Starbucks, or, Terror: What's in a Name?" *Radical History Review* 85 (December 2002): 37–57; Davis, "Jenseits von Terror und Rückzug: Politischen Raum und Verhandlungsstrategien in der BRD der 70er Jahre," in *Innere Sicherheit und Terrorismus in der Bundesrepublik der 1970er Jahre*, ed. Heinz-Gerhardt Haupt et al. (Frankfurt/M., 2006), 154–86.
11. On the impact of this image, see Belinda Davis, *The Internal Life of Politics: The New Left in West Germany, 1962–1983* (forthcoming), chap. 3.
12. I would argue that even the violent activism of the RAF represented, initially at least, a kind of "extreme" (if not necessarily useful or successful) communication, until the violence degenerated into signs devoid of meaningful signification, when not simple revenge. Compare Belinda Davis, "Violence and Memory of the Nazi past in 1960s–70s West German Protest," in *Coming to Terms with the Past in West Germany: The 1960s*, ed. Philip Gassert and Alan E. Steinweis (New York, 2006), 210–37.
13. See Dagmar (Seehuber) Przytulla, "'Niemand ahnte, daß wir ein ziemlich verklemmter Haufen waren,'" in *Die 68erinnen*, ed. Ute Kätzel (Berlin, 2002), 210–.
14. Author's interview, "Robert A.," July 2004. (Many of these interviews are, at the request of the informants, referenced with pseudonyms.) My sources for this project

include contemporary documents, memoirs, and oral interviews. Though I cite relatively few interviews in this chapter, its arguments are based on themes that emerge in the interviews I have carried out with over fifty contemporary activists born between 1937 and 1957, as well as in research in archival and published sources.
15. Annette Schwarzenau, "Nicht diese theoretische Dinger, etwas Praktisches unternehmen," in Kätzel, *Die 68erinnen*, 41–59.
16. The West German law of 1974 allowed abortion on demand during the first trimester of pregnancy. The law was successfully challenged, however, and, in 1976, a range of restrictions were (re-)introduced. The issue came to the fore again in 1990, when East German activists battled to save that country's more liberal abortion law, as the German Democratic Republic was dissolved and subsumed under the Federal Republic; they ultimately achieved a partial success in the prevailing 1995 law.
17. Compare *CheShahShit: Die Sechziger Jahre zwischen Cocktail und Molotow* (Berlin, 1984), 170.
18. Indeed Alice Schwarzer and other feminists brought *Stern* to court over this regular practice in 1978, charging that these images incited violence and hatred against women. Compare "Die Stern-Klage," *Emma* (July 1978), reprinted in Alice Schwarzer, *Alice in Männerland* (Munich, 2004), 109–11.
19. Compare Halina Bendkowski, et al., eds., *Wie weit flog die Tomate?. Eine 68erinnen-Gala der Reflexion* (Berlin, 1999).
20. Kocka, "Zivilgesellschaft."
21. This feeling was emphasized in virtually all of my interviews.
22. On the link between provocation, emotion, and emancipation, see Belinda Davis, "Provokation als Emanzipation: 1968 und die Emotionen," *vorgänge* 164 (December 2003): 41–49
23. Susanne Schunter-Kleemann, "Wir waren Akteurinnen und nicht etwa die Anhängsel," in Kätzel, *Die 68erinnen*, 108.
24. Cited in Peter Mosler, *Was wir wollten, was wir wurden: Studentenrevolte, 10 Jahre danach* (Reinbek bei Hamburg, 1977), 26; see also the flyer "Organize Disobedience to the Nazi Generation!" reprinted in *Protest! Literatur um 1968* (Marbach, 2000), 43.
25. Davidoff and Hall, *Family Fortunes*.
26. The age of majority in West Germany was twenty-one until 1970, when it was lowered to eighteen, as elsewhere, specifically in response to protest.
27. Compare, e.g., Roland Roth, *Demokratie von unten: Neue soziale Bewegungen auf dem Wege zur politischen Institution* (Cologne, 1994); Ruud Koopmans, *Democracy from Below: New Social Movements and the Political System in West Germany* (Boulder, CO, 1995).
28. Some of those interviewed identified themselves as heterosexual separatists who had sex with men but chose to spend their time otherwise almost entirely in the company of women.
29. Author's interview, "Marianne H.," July 2004.
30. Kocka, "Zivilgesellschaft."
31. "Autonome Frauendemo in Bremerhaven am 14.10," *Oldenburger Frauenzeitung*, 9 November 1983, 4–6.
32. See Koopmans, *Democracy from Below*. In the West German context, compare Sibylla Flügge, "1968 und die Frauen—Ein Blick in die Beziehungskiste," in *Gender und Soziale Praxis*, ed. Margit Göttert and Karin Walser (Königstein/Taunus, 2002), 265–90. On East German women's disappointing confrontations with West German state and society (including West German feminists), see also Ingrid Miethe, "From 'Mothers of the Revolution' to 'Fathers of Unification': Concepts of Politics among Women Activists following German Unification," *Social Politics* 6, no. 1 (Spring 1999): 1–22; Myra Marx Ferree, "'The Time of Chaos was the Best': Feminist Mobilization and Demobilization

in East Germany," *Gender and Society* 6, no. 8 (1994): 597–623; Dorothy Rosenberg, "Women's Issues, Women's Politics, and Women's Studies in the Former German Democratic Republic," *Radical History Review* 54 (1992): 110–26; Lynn Kamenitsa, "East German Feminists in the New German Democracy: Opportunities, Obstacles, and Adaptation," *Women in Politics* 17, no. 3 (1997): 41–68; and Andrea Wuerth, "National Politics/Local Identities: Abortion Rights Activists in Post-Wall Berlin," *Feminist Studies* 25, no. 3 (Fall 1999): 601–31.

33. Compare variously Frankfurter Institut für Stadtgeschichte, Akte S6b/72, Bd. 2, Materialien zum Bürgerkampf und die Hausbesetzerbewegung der 70er Jahre im Frankfurter Westend, compiled by Til Schulz; Dieter Rucht, ed., *Von Wyhl nach Gorleben: Bürger gegen Atomprogramm und nukleare Entsorgung* (Munich, 1985); Rucht, ed., *Protest in der Bundesrepublik. Strukturen und Entwicklungen* (Frankfurt/M., 2001); Roger Karapin, *Protest Politics in Germany: Movements on the Left and Right since the 1960s* (University Park, Pa., 2007).
34. See Gerd Koenen, *Das rote Jahrzehnt: Unsere kleine deutsche Kulturrevolution, 1967–1977* (Cologne, 2001).
35. Many have claimed this era represented a major watershed of the postmodern turn. Scholars have looked to writings from Simone de Beauvoir to Frantz Fanon to Jean Baudrillard to make this case, cf. Jean-François Lyotard, *The Post-Modern Condition: A Report on Knowledge* (Minneapolis, 1984); Marianne DeKoven, *Utopia Limited: The Sixties and the Emergence of the Postmodern* (Durham, NC, 2004); Hans Bertens, *The Idea of the Postmodern: A History* (New York, 1995). Specifically on the West German case, seeAndreas Rödder, "Wertewandel und Postmoderne. Gesellschaft und Kultur in der Bundesrepublik Deutschland 1965–1990," *Stiftung-Bundespräsident-Theodor-Heuss-Haus, Kleine Reihe*, Heft 12 (Stuttgart, 2004).
36. On communitarianism, see Cohen and Arato, *Civil Society*, 20–23. On the ability of small numbers to make their voices heard, see such fearful characterizations as "Herzlich wilkommen!" *BILD*, 6 April 1967.
37. Author's interview with Wolf-Dieter Narr, July 2005.
38. Davis, *The Internal Life of Politics*, chap. 1.

Chapter 12

CIVIL SOCIETY-BY-DESIGN
EMERGING CAPITALISM, ESSENTIALIST FEMINISM, AND WOMEN'S NONGOVERNMENTAL ORGANIZATIONS IN POSTSOCIALIST EASTERN EUROPE

Kristen R. Ghodsee

In the first decade following the collapse of communism, one of the official goals of Western intervention in the countries of Eastern Europe was the creation and promotion of civil society. Since socialist states had monopolized all economic enterprises and citizen's organizations under the umbrella of the Communist Party, the dismantling of communism required the privatization and marketization of centralized economies as well as the establishment of an active voluntary or nonprofit sector that would be independent of both the state and the market. Historically, civil societies have been composed of private philanthropic and often religious associations and organizations that grew organically from the interests and needs of local populations. But as Marxist Leninism was opposed to both charity and religion, it might have taken many years for societies emerging from communism to develop their own indigenous civil society institutions. Instead, these institutions would be imported from the West in the form of nongovernmental organizations (NGOs), and it would be this form that would dominate the landscape of civil society in the former Eastern Bloc, a form that is rife with problems and has been largely ineffective at materially improving the conditions of people's lives.

Civil society has also served as an important arena for women's activism, providing a way for women to enter the public sphere and influence

---

I would like to thank *Signs* for allowing the editors to reprint this chapter in a shortened version.

politics and social policies. Although women in communist countries were more involved in the public sphere than their Western counterparts, this involvement was largely directed from above. Even so, the end of communism has seen a relative erosion of women's position in the polity and economy. The development of civil society in these countries after 1989 might have provided an important avenue for women to continue their influence and power in the public sphere. However, the very proliferation of Western-funded "feminist" NGOs may have ultimately undermined women's position in these societies even further.

Since 1989, billions of dollars have been lent and spent to aid the development of "civil society" and "free markets" in the former communist countries. Yet by 2000, only Poland's and Slovenia's citizens enjoyed a higher standard of living than they did at the end of the 1980s.[1] Similarly, after over a decade of attempts to create independent women's movements in Eastern Europe, feminism still has a bad name there, and an atmosphere of antifeminism persists, as women continue to resist a gendered analysis of their oppression.[2]

In this chapter, I will examine the impact of essentialist Western feminism and international aid on efforts to build "civil society" for women in postsocialist countries after 1989.[3] I will try to untangle how some Western feminists and their local counterparts have ignored the complex historical legacies of socialist versus what has been called "bourgeois feminism" in the East. It is important to note that I am not homogenizing all Western feminists in one indistinguishable group, but rather that I am examining the impact of "professional feminists" such as those who often work in the gender programs of the United States Agency for International Development (USAID), the World Bank, the European Union, and a variety of European and North American charitable foundations that focus on women's "issues." I argue that the specific type of essentialist feminism that these international organizations exported to Eastern Europe (and to many of the local NGOs that implement projects based on essentialist feminist assumptions) may be unwittingly complicit with the proponents of neoliberalism responsible for the very decline in general living standards that gave Western feminists their mandate to help East European women in the first place. The NGOs that privilege a gender-based analysis of oppression over one that is more sensitive to class issues may actually legitimize claims that women are somehow naturally less suited than men to free market economies. This has not only lowered their status, but perhaps perversely created a backlash that prevents them from building the kinds of independent women's organizations that would provide them with a voice in civil society.

Essentialist feminism refers to a specific package of discourses and practices that promote the idea that women and men are essentially different—either because of inherent biological differences or because of gendered socialization so deeply ingrained as to be irreversible. These differences between the two sexes transcend class, race, age, and ethnicity and supposedly unite all women in a common sisterhood. Whereas radical and socialist feminisms advocate for more comprehensive societal change in order to liberate women, essentialist feminism often aims at meeting women's special needs within the status quo. In other words, this type of feminism looks for ways to mitigate the worst offenses of male domination, while never challenging the social or economic relations within which it thrives. And while liberal feminists may reject the idea that there are innate differences between men and women, in practice their proposed solutions to social problems often rested on quite essentialist assumptions about "men's interests" and "women's interests" in postsocialist societies. Therefore, as a way of addressing women's concerns, essentialist feminism (often under the guise of liberal feminism) works well within the neoliberal ideological constraints of the large bilateral and multilateral aid institutions in the West, which prefer to target patriarchy rather than capitalism as the root of gender inequality. This is not to deny that strategic essentialism in the United States and Western Europe—and even in some instances in the developing world—has been responsible for gaining necessary and important rights and services for women.[4] However, this chapter focuses specifically on the applicability of essentialist feminism in the postsocialist context.

Capitalism-by-Design

After the unexpected collapse of communism in Eastern Europe, billions of dollars in aid and assistance flowed from the United States and Western Europe into the former Eastern Bloc. A virtual army of consultants and experts descended into capital cities to fashion the foundations of capitalism and liberal democracy from scratch.[5] These early years of the 1990s were characterized by what sociologist David Stark has called "capitalism-by-design."[6] Western experts advised local governments on how to create the institutions of democracy and capitalism. If the experts could create the proper institutions in a country, the rules of those new institutions would guide individual behavior, and one could create the conditions for the development of capitalism, literally by design. The capitalism-by-design paradigm still underlies the structural adjustment and stabilization practices of the World Bank and the International Monetary Fund in this region.

The problem with the capitalism-by-design thesis was that it duplicated the fallacy that society could be radically changed all at once, much as the socialists themselves had once believed that administrative decrees could instantaneously change property relations.[7] Early proponents of capitalism-by-design believed that 1989 represented a historical break with the past, creating a clear space in which a whole new society could be built.[8] But socialist (and in some cases presocialist) institutions, social practices, and ideologies were very slow to disappear despite the sweeping changes. Privileges under one economic system could be readily converted into privileges under new economic systems without regard to changing institutional imperatives.[9] The decades of experience that preceded the transformation process could not be swept away with the crumbling of a wall; memory and experience are embedded in the individual actors who have become the new capitalist subjects of Central and Eastern Europe.

Many Western donors and women's NGOs have failed to recognize exactly these historical legacies of socialist feminism (as distinct and separate from bourgeois feminism). Socialist women from Central and East European countries always prioritized resistance against class oppression above agitations based on any specific form of gendered subjugation. Proletarian men were seen as closer allies than bourgeois women, who then, as now, advocated for a kind of global sisterhood based on women's supposed biological and psychological similarities.

Feminism-by-Design

During the early transition period, Western feminists and women's organizations also jumped on the aid bandwagon. Money was abundant; studies were undertaken and reports were prepared to show that the economic transition from communism would disproportionately harm women. In fact, the overwhelming majority of Western scholars who have written about gender and economic transformation have tended to paint a very dark picture of women's position in the emerging postsocialist societies.[10] And while some disaggregated statistics do show that women as a whole have been the greater "losers" during the transformation, these analyses subsume important emerging class distinctions under their preoccupation with gender.

In many ways, the literature on gender and transformation fell into the trap of the capitalism-by-design paradigm. Institutions from advanced market economies in the West replaced the old socialist institutions. Since many scholars agreed that women are at a disadvantage in these Western institutions, there was an assumption that once these institutions were transplanted to postsocialist societies, they would produce the same effects on East European women. This argument seems to underlie many of the claims that were made about women very early in the economic transformation period. For example, in 1993 sociologist Nanette Funk observed: "Reducing women's paid work is a major instrument of economic quasi-privatization and the integration of post-communist societies into a capitalist market system. Past gender segregation of the work force under state socialism, in conjunction with new Western-style sex discrimination, help along that process."[11] If researchers such as Funk recognized any legacies from the socialist past, it was often in a negative way, assuming that any structural disadvantages women had under socialism would be reproduced under capitalism.[12] Although many disadvantages were ultimately reproduced, this was by no means an inevitable outcome of the transition, and many scholars failed to consider the possibilities of positive legacies of women's experience under socialism. Thus, East European women would suffer from the structural constraints of both socialism and capitalism, even if capitalism was drastically reshaping the institutions around which society revolved.

The same capitalism-by-design model also guided the solutions to the "problems" of East European women. USAID, for instance, funded teams of Western consultants to carry out "gender assessments" and create "gender action plans."[13] Each country was encouraged to have some kind of "national machinery" in place to deal with women's issues. Sections and oversight committees to monitor and advocate for women's rights were formed within government ministries or in parliament, but these were rarely effective because they had been imposed from the outside. Other institutions of Western feminism—women's advocacy groups, gender think tanks, battered women's shelters, rape crisis hotlines, women's resource centers, and so forth—began springing up throughout the former communist countries. Most of these entities were attached to local NGOs either directly funded by large multilateral and bilateral donors or supported by Western women's organizations subcontracted by USAID or the European Union's Poland and Hungary: Action for Restructuring the Economy program to foster "civil society" in the region.[14] Thus, donors retained Western feminists to produce what I am calling "feminism-by-design," in much the same way as the World Bank retained consultants from big accounting firms such as Pricewaterhouse Coopers to create capitalism-by-design.

A Clash of Feminisms

As defined earlier, the particular brand of feminism that has been exported to the postsocialist countries since 1989 favors an essentialist concept of gender over any social explanation for women's growing inequality with men. The deradicalization of women's movements in Western Europe and the United States after the turbulent 1960s eventually led to the mainstreaming of women's concerns within both national and international institutions. Western feminists began working within the dominant capitalist structures of society in order to make the system more favorable to the unique needs and requirements of women.[15] These unique needs applied to all women and allegedly united them in their common struggle against male domination. Men were the main enemy. Issues of both class and race were subsumed under the primacy of gender oppression.[16]

The sudden import of essentialist feminism in Eastern Europe went against the established ideologies used to understand oppression. Since the late nineteenth century, Western and socialist feminists have been debating the relative importance of either class or gender as the primary category of analysis when discussing the oppression of women. Because of these differences, bourgeois women could not be counted on as allies in the socialist cause. Not much has changed since 1907 when the German socialist Clara Zetkin wrote: "There cannot be a unified struggle for the entire [female] sex.... No, it must be a class struggle of all of the exploited without differences of sex against all exploiters no matter what sex they belong to."[17]

Communism taught women not to distinguish their needs from the needs of men, but rather to struggle together in their class interests. Of course, this may not have been the best model for women, because their needs were constantly subsumed under class rhetoric by communist states dominated by male leaders. But until 1989, at least on an ideological level, many East European women still considered bourgeois feminism a tool of capitalism and, in the aftermath of the communist collapse, saw Western feminism as a foreign and unwelcome ideology—not only because they believed that all women's organizations were tools of the state.

This ideology was piggybacked into Eastern Europe by Western scholars and activists, who themselves were riding a tidal wave of grants made available for research on and projects in the countries undergoing transition. The Western feminists who imported the paradigm of "gender first" did not really understand the significance of the historical struggle between Eastern and Western women over the primacy of class or gender as the appropriate category of analysis. Their research and project proposals merely had this analytical preference built into them as the hegemonic and commonsense way of thinking about women's lives in times of great social, political, or economic upheaval.

All of the major international bilateral and multilateral aid agencies developed some form of women's program to combat the negative effects of transformation.[18] Well funded and also informed by the ideas of essentialist feminism, these programs set out to document the plight of postsocialist women.[19] National statistics disaggregated by gender for the first time began to show that women made up the majority of the registered unemployed. North American and Western European NGOs funded local subcontractors to produce reports on issues such as domestic violence and rape—topics rarely discussed in the public sphere prior to 1989.[20]

Publicized through both the local and international press, this research created an overwhelmingly negative picture of the situation of women in postsocialist countries. Activists argued that the sensationalism was necessary to call attention to the real problems that women faced. Indeed, high-profile issues such as reproductive rights and trafficking in women brought much-needed resources into the region. At the end of the day, however, the constant attention to the vulnerability of women in these economies may have done them more harm than good. The discourses produced by these scholars, activists, and international donors have constructed women as the natural and inevitable victims in the economic transformation period. Ironically, this category of "losers" appeared in a previously egalitarian society where there had been no such socially acceptable category—no one group of people whose social and economic exclusion could be justified or even explained simply by their own inability to participate in the system. This means that women now have to combat new stereotypes portraying them as less adaptable to the market economy. Furthermore, an excessive focus on the poor and disenfranchised woman may alienate "survivors" from their "failing" female compatriots. Women who are thriving in the postsocialist period may not want to associate themselves with the negative stereotypes and may distance themselves from any potential women's movement. Finally, the discourse that women are less flexible in adapting to the new economic system may actually convince women themselves that they are ill equipped to weather the storms of economic transformation.

Women's Self-Perceptions and the Potential for Building Feminist Organizations

Yet, many East European women do not believe they are oppressed—or more oppressed—because of their gender. They tend to perceive their role in the private sphere as the more emancipatory and therefore more desirable than men's more public role.[21] In Bulgaria, my own experience and interviews also revealed reluctance on the part of women to agree with the idea that they were more negatively affected by the changes than men.[22] One very high-ranking female politician told me emphatically that there was absolutely no discrimination against women in Bulgaria despite all the "data" and "NGO whining" that argued otherwise.[23] Thus, as anthropologists Susan Gal and Gail Kligman have argued, in the East European context "political solidarity cannot be assumed on the basis of shared 'womanhood.'"[24]

On the one hand, this refusal to accept their new disenfranchised position may reflect years of Marxist-Leninist teachings. Political plurality in Eastern Europe may also preclude the creation of a unified women's movement. A study by political scientists Vlasta Jalusic and Milica Antic found that women in Hungary, Poland, the Czech Republic, Slovakia, and Slovenia had "a singular rejection of collective action on the part of women holding different political views."[25] Yet another possibility is that women in Eastern Europe truly do not perceive that their situations are different from men's. Indeed, staggeringly high unemployment rates and declining living standards for both sexes make it difficult to decide who is really worse off.

Finally, women may not buy into the discourses of disadvantage because, in a handful of cases, women actually had significant advantages over men, at least in the early stages of transition. In some sectors of the new market economy, women (particularly members of the former *nomenklatura* or those with higher levels of general education) were able to exchange their cultural capital for economic capital.[26] In Hungary, Poland, and Slovakia, Eva Fodor found that women who had worked in the quasiprivate sector during communism had more advantages and were more flexible in the new market economy than men who were wholly employed in the public sector before 1989.[27] Sociologist Julia Szalai found similar patterns in Hungary, where men have made up the majority of the registered unemployed since 1989.[28] In Bulgaria, economist Lisa Giddings has shown that women with higher levels of general education had an advantage over men in the early transition period.[29] In my own research in Bulgaria, I found that women's cultural capital—foreign languages, general education, knowledge of the West, and so forth—translated into significant advantages in the dynamic tourism sector, where women occupy the highest managerial levels.[30] In almost all of these cases, however, the social class of a woman before 1989 is a more significant determinant of success in the market economy than gender alone.

It is not my intention to discredit the idea that many women have, in fact, been hurt by the transition from communism or to argue that gender is not a useful category of analysis when examining the situation in Eastern Europe. My main goal is to understand why essentialist feminist ideas are being imported into these countries at this particular historical moment and with so much support from international organizations and Western bilateral aid agencies. Why might it be politically important to construct women as disadvantaged despite the fact that there is a great deal of heterogeneity among women within and among East European countries? The production and perpetuation of certain discourses may be essential ideological building blocks in the construction of the new material reality of postsocialist nations.

Research in Eastern Europe has also shown that NGOs have been less than successful in creating a viable form of civil society. Anthropologist Janine Wedel, in her analysis of Western aid to Eastern Europe, is also highly critical of NGOs and claims that "with outside donors as chief constituents, local NGOs are sometimes more firmly rooted in transnational networks than in their own societies."[31] Political scientists Sarah Mendelson and John Glenn also found that the heavy reliance of East European NGOs on foreign assistance interfered with their ability to service their own populations.[32] Furthermore, competition for external grants breeds divisiveness and bitterness among organizations that might otherwise cooperate for the common good. Kevin Quigley has argued that US funds for NGOs under the Democracy Network program created a perception among many East Europeans that "democracy building grants for NGOs were politically motivated, their primary purpose being to promote specific US political objectives."[33] Other studies have also shown that Bulgarian NGOs have little legitimacy among the people.[34]

In nearby Romania, Laura Grunburg has specifically demonstrated that women's NGOs have no constituencies despite their claims of representing the Romanian woman. In Russia, political scientists Rebecca Kay and Valerie Sperling have argued that women's organizations do not always represent the needs of the majority of Russian women.[35] Gal and Kligman have pointed out that women's NGOs in Eastern Europe are often dependent entirely on foreign agencies for their survival and that they "quickly learn to produce whatever 'language' and 'interest' the foreign funders are willing to finance."[36] The 2001 National Human Development Report for Bulgaria by the United Nations Development Program found that "NGOs are the least desired mediator for the transmittal of citizens' opinions to the government" and that "the least desired citizen practice is participation in NGO projects."[37] The UN Development Program concluded that

> the NGO sector [in Bulgaria] is growing not only because of the availability of a solvent and low-risk market as represented by donors, but also because of the growing unemployment among intellectuals. From its very origin this market is an export of services. Therefore, the NGOs sector has not emerged in a natural way, as a result of internal citizen needs; it complies with an external demand, articulated in the donors' aspiration to stimulate civic society in Bulgaria.[38]

Women's NGOs in Bulgaria and Eastern Europe

If NGOs are perpetuating the discourses created by international agencies and foreign states in regard to women's issues, then it could be assumed that the ultimate beneficiaries of these truths may also lie outside the boundaries of the nation-state. The shift from a class-based analysis of oppression to a gender-based analysis of oppression, as created and perpetuated by NGOs in Bulgaria, may work in the interests of transnational capital looking to take root in the Bulgarian economy. Thus, more than being the representatives or forerunners of a civil society, the NGOs may be the unsuspecting allies of transnational corporations and international organizations in promoting what one political scientist has called the "New Policy Agenda," or the unbridled pursuit of free markets and liberal democracy at any expense.[39] This set of ideologies revolves around neoliberal economics and liberal democratic theory and supports the expansion of Western capital into the region.[40]

Women's NGOs may actually weaken grassroots opposition to neoliberalism and the dismantling of the social welfare state in Bulgaria in two key ways. First, they place the blame for the drastic reduction in living standards for women squarely on the shoulders of traditional Bulgarian patriarchy. They deflect attention away from the structural adjustment policies of the World Bank and the stabilization programs of the International Monetary Fund, which are primarily responsible for the disappearance of the social safety net that once supported women and their families. Second, NGOs in Bulgaria co-opt educated middle-class women who may otherwise have been able to organize a solid class-based opposition to secure women's rights in the post-1989 period.

Many women's NGOs are implicated in what political scientist James Ferguson has called the "anti-politics machine."[41] Along with international organizations, these NGOs focus on technical fixes for social problems, not on the structural conditions in society that create those problems in the first place or the political measures or state policies that might alleviate them. Although there are many different kinds of NGOs in the Central and Eastern Europe region and it is difficult to make generalizations, there is a tendency for East European NGOs and their donors to concentrate on issues that are independent of politics; that is, they avoid tackling larger issues of economic injustice and inequality in society.[42] Many NGOs tend to emphasize individual projects that address specific goals narrowly defined by the project's funders. Community-based self-help projects are encouraged over national mobilizations. And NGOs find it difficult to support social movements that challenge the status quo or implicate class differences in the ever-widening gap in living standards between the haves and have-nots.[43]

Political scientist James Petras is especially scathing in his critique of women's NGOs.[44] He attacks the emergence of identity politics, which erase the class differences between the "Chilean or Indian feminist living in a plush suburb drawing a salary 15–20 times that of her domestic servant who works six-and-a-half days a week."[45] By focusing exclusively on patriarchy at the micro–sociological level, women's NGOs and the middle-class women who often run them may not only be complicit in the exploitation of women in their own country, they may also indirectly benefit from it. These middle-class women make careers out of their civil-society-building activities by emphasizing the problems women in their country face in order to secure the grants to fix them. This is not to say that there are not real challenges that concern only women, nor that there is not gender-based discrimination all over the world. The point is that in Bulgaria:

1. Women outlive men.
2. Infant mortality for boys is higher than for girls.
3. Women have higher levels of education at almost all levels.
4. Women have the right to own property and assets in their own name (which they can keep in case of divorce).
5. Women still enjoy longer paid maternity leaves than in most Western nations in spite of recent cuts supported by the International Monetary Fund.
6. Between 2001–05, there were more female members of parliament than anywhere else in Central and Eastern Europe, and more than in many countries in Western Europe as well.
7. Bulgaria has had a female foreign minister, a female deputy prime minister, and even, briefly, a female prime minister.
8. In 2001, men, not women, made up the majority of the registered unemployed.[46]

Despite all this, Bulgarian women's NGOs in the 1990s incessantly focused on such stock phrases as the "feminization of poverty" in order to attract external donor funding.

One instance of the emergence of the new gender discourse and its foreignness in the Bulgarian context is the fact that the English word *gender* has no direct translation into Bulgarian, where it is the same word used for *sex* (as in male or female). Bulgarian feminists simply adopted the English word *gender* with a slight alteration in its pronunciation. As *gender* is a recently imported word, therefore, most Bulgarian women do not even know what it means. Many of the NGOs, however, make sure to include the word *gender* in their names (e.g., Gender Project for Bulgaria, Bulgarian Gender Research Foundation), despite the fact that they are supposed to be representing Bulgarian women.

An even better indicator of women's NGOs' bias toward their Western donors are the publications they produce and disseminate in Bulgaria. In one women's magazine funded by the Netherlands Organization for International Development Cooperation, the editorial content is overwhelmingly about women's antagonistic relationships with men in society. Articles revolve around issues of domestic violence, prostitution, trafficking in women, infidelity, sexual performance, alcoholism, divorce, single motherhood, and child support. Most focus on the struggle between men and women—the ways in which men lie, cheat, and exploit women for their own gain. Furthermore, although there was a Bulgarian version up until 1999, now the magazine is only published in English due to lack of funding and therefore is linguistically inaccessible to the vast majority of Bulgarian women.[47]

Another debate in Bulgaria that provides further insights surrounded the issue of child support after divorce. During communism, the state automatically deducted child support from the father's wages and transferred it to the mother for care of the child. The shrinking of the public sector and the relocation of many men into private-sector employment has undermined the efficacy of this system. The courts are considered inefficient and corrupt, and few women have faith in the legal system. As a result, many women no longer receive support from their husbands. Since 1997, the Bulgarian government and the multilateral lending institutions have vigorously promoted the independence of the market from state interference. Consequently, the government failed to pass new legislation to ensure that women could collect their child support. A handful of women's organizations, such as the Bulgarian Association for University Women, are lobbying to reintroduce the state into this process. Most women's organizations, however, absolve the state of responsibility and instead point the accusative finger at errant fathers, despite the fact that the system worked very well during communism. In many cases, NGOs' desire to help women is thus constrained by their necessary complicity with the neoliberal tendencies of their donors, and thus the creation of an organic and indigenous form of civil society is hampered by Western economic interests.

In addition, NGO efforts to promote women's political participation are deeply informed by an essentialist form of feminism. In the postsocialist era, nationalists often view capitalism as masculine and aggressive, whereas many now reimagine communism as a political system that favored women.[48] Although there were many inequalities between men and women before 1989, communism is believed to have unnaturally displaced men's inherent competitive instincts and created a society in which the state was responsible for everyone's needs.[49] Socialism was thus more beneficial to women because women are portrayed as more naturally preferring to be taken care of than men.[50] Essentialist feminism fuels these kinds of biologist arguments. Women are constructed as being more inclined to crave the stability of public-sector employment—they are more risk-averse than men. As a result, women are supposedly less inclined to start businesses in the private sector and more likely to be hurt by the shrinking of the public sector. Women's higher unemployment rates throughout the 1990s were blamed on women's "natural" aversion to working in the private sector, not on structural factors—the lack of private-sector jobs available. Even when men made up the majority of the registered unemployed in Bulgaria in 2001, women were still being presented as the more economically vulnerable sex by international donors and NGOs.

Similarly, women are imagined as being more morally inclined and less attracted to power and politics—"kinder and gentler" than their male companions.[51] (In this sense, women's lack of political participation is cast as a result of their intrinsic aversion to the dirty and corrupt realm of East European politics in general. Interestingly, however, Jalusic and Antic found that women in five postsocialist countries were more likely to be represented in centrist and leftist parties (i.e., Green, liberal, socialist, and communist) than they are in "right-wing parties (people's parties, Christian parties, parties of free enterprise, etc)."[52] Thus, Western feminist explanations of women's lack of political participation and the projects they propose to encourage women to run for office may be based on a fundamental misunderstanding of the problem. Women in postsocialist countries may not have a natural aversion to elected office per se, but they may have real political reasons for avoiding nationalist parties and parties that support a neoliberal economic agenda. This creates an interesting dilemma for the international organizations that fund projects to increase women's political participation. If women are more likely to be on the political center or left, initiatives sponsored by the World Bank or the United States to increase both the number of women candidates and the number of women at the polls could result in the election of an anti–World Bank or anti–US government (i.e., a socialist or neocommunist government).

In Bulgaria, as elsewhere in Central and Eastern Europe, many NGOs also promote microcredit schemes for women or support women's entrepreneurship. Such schemes extend small amounts of capital to groups of disadvantaged women, who can use the money either to meet immediate basic needs or invest in some small income-generating project that will allow them to repay the money after making a profit. The remaining profits are then used to pay for meeting basic needs or saved and put to use productively in some further income-generating scheme. Support for women's entrepreneurship picks up where microcredit schemes leave off. Once women have enough capital to move beyond meeting basic needs, they are given the training and encouragement to start their own businesses. The hope is that these businesses will be sustainable and will realize a continuous stream of profits that will allow the women to meet their basic needs, reinvest in their businesses and eventually be able to consume nonessential goods and luxury items. In other words, these kinds of projects help women become good entrepreneurs (i.e., capitalists) so that they can support themselves and ultimately get ahead (i.e., become consumers).

The problem with this model in Bulgaria is multifaceted. Microcredit schemes and microentrepreneurship promotion by NGOs assume that

Bulgarian women are willing to borrow or work to pay for basic needs that were once provided for by the socialist state. Under socialism, these goods and services once existed as the basic rights and entitlements of the communist citizen. Indeed, one of the most lauded achievements of the communist countries was the high standard of living that they achieved. This was particularly true for women; in Bulgaria, for example, women workers greatly benefited from generous maternity leaves, free education, free health care, free or subsidized childcare, communal kitchens and canteens, communal laundries, subsidized food and transport, subsidized holidays on the Black Sea, and so forth.

In the postsocialist period, these rights and entitlements have all but disappeared. The collapse of communism in Bulgaria has relegated these rights to the status of needs for the first time in many women's lives. It should be no surprise that microcredit and women's entrepreneurship projects may not be welcome or useful in this society, where many women (and men) have not fundamentally accepted that it is their responsibility to meet these basic needs in the first place. Women in Bulgaria might have incentives to work for consumer items or to save money to travel abroad, but many may be resistant to the idea of taking loans to start businesses to make money to pay for the very same things they once had without cost. Instead of self-help, Bulgarian women may prefer to seek political solutions, which could explain their political affiliations with leftist parties.

Microcredit and entrepreneurship programs can help women through the transition to capitalism by increasing their access to economic capital. At the same time, however, they legitimate a system that forces women to bear the responsibility of caring for their families either by finding ways to pay for health care, childcare, elder care, education, and so on through their own employment; by becoming dependent on men who "earn" these benefits through their employment, or by providing these services themselves for free (because it is in their "natural" capabilities to do so). This then allows the state (at the request of international financial institutions) to make deeper cuts into social spending (in the interest of macroeconomic stability) and exempts foreign investors and transnational corporations from providing the social services and employee benefits that were once an essential part of the socialist labor contract (in the interest of creating a business-friendly climate).

Finally, NGOs divert women from social movements and co-opt their potential leaders. Participation in NGOs that are entirely dependent on foreign funding breeds both cynicism and opportunism in the few committed women leaders who genuinely believe that free markets and liberal democracy are more desirable alternatives to communism. In informal conversations, Bulgarian women activists complained to me that capitalist civil society was really not too different from its communist counterpart. Being forced to digest the rhetoric of international organizations and propose only those projects that support American or European interests was really no different than being forced to regurgitate the Marxist propaganda once required under the old regime. Women's rights and women's issues were once again used as tools to support the dominant political and economic system.

Conclusion

In many ways, the creation of civil society in Eastern Europe was hijacked by the proliferation of professionalized NGOs funded by the West. At the historic juncture when former communist societies had an opportunity to develop their own vibrant and dynamic civil society sectors to respond to the unique circumstances of the postsocialist era, Western governments and transnational corporations—perhaps fearing a resurgence of class consciousness and anticapitalist social activism—co-opted local leaders and created a nonprofit sector that would be largely accountable to Western donors and their political and economic interests. It is important to understand that this process was not the inevitable result of the transition process, but rather that the development of civil society after communism might have taken any number of other forms. Therefore, it is necessary to historicize the creation of civil society after 1989 and examine the consequences of NGOs displacing other types of organizations or preventing their emergence as the building blocks of civil society.

This has been especially true for women's organizations, which should be actively advocating to improve women's lives rather than merely providing explanations for why women are supposedly not doing as well as men in a newly competitive free-market society. It is not surprising, then, that East European women have yet to embrace Western feminism, despite more than a decade's worth of Western feminist NGO activities in the region. It is possible that women's success or failure in the post-1989 period may have less to do with their gender per se than with the social class to which they belong, but this is not the message of the NGOs seeking to impose, more or less self-consciously, a neoliberal interpretation of women's situation, using essentialist feminism as a vehicle. As a result, however, a "women's civil society" has failed to take root.

It might be useful to begin imagining what a local, independent form of civil society would look like. Once the funding for all of the women's NGOs dries up and local women's activists are forced to respond to the needs of their compatriots, the contours of civil society in the former socialist world may change considerably, and hopefully this time around, its participants would be better able to advocate for real improvements in the material conditions of ordinary people's lives. Of course, there is no guarantee that more "organic" forms of civil society that evolve from within a country will better express the collective interests of marginalized groups. However, if they emerge from the bottom up rather than being coaxed into existence through policies and funds that promote a civil society-by-design, there is at least a better chance that they will be able to meet local people's needs by having more legitimacy in the eyes of their constituents, and perhaps better access to power and resources. Moreover, as the experience of women in capitalist economies and democratic polities has shown, it is important that local organizations have a chance to find their own path, because civil society can serve as an important seedbed for women's mobilization.

Notes

1. United Nations Development Program, *Human Development Report 2000* (Sofia, 2001).
2. Beth Holmgren, "Bug Inspectors and Beauty Queens: The Problems of Translating Feminism into Russian," in *Postcommunism and the Body Politic*, ed. Ellen E. Berry (New York, 1995), 15–31. See Vlasta Jalusic, Milica Antic, "Prospects for Gender Equality Policies in Central and Eastern Europe," SOCO Project Paper, no. 70 (Vienna, 2000); Susan Gal and Gail Kligman, *The Politics of Gender after Socialism: A Comparative-Historical Essay* (Princeton, NJ, 2000).
3. In an earlier version of this paper, published in *Signs* in 2004, I used the term *cultural feminism* instead of *essentialist feminism* in my attempt to mark the specific ideology of the Western feminist organizations that were responsible for setting up or funding many of the women's NGOs in Eastern Europe after 1989. I saw cultural feminism as the heir to the "radical feminism" of the Second Wave feminists in the US in the 1970s. These women viewed gender as an essentialist category of difference between men and women and believed that women's oppression was ultimately the result of their gender (which superseded race, class, sexuality, age, etc.). There is, however, a great deal of slippage in the terminology used to discuss feminist theory that is specific to different academic disciplines and different historical eras, so here I have chosen to use the term *essentialist feminism* even though I recognize that there are few women who would actually call themselves "essentialist feminists."
4. Gayatri Spivak, "Subaltern Studies: Deconstructing Historiography," in *The Spivak Reader: Selected Works of Gayatri Spivak* (New York, 1995), 203–36.
5. Janine Wedel, *Collision and Collusion: The Strange Case of Aid to Eastern Europe* (New York, 2001).
6. David Stark, "Path Dependence and Privatization Strategies in East Central Europe," *East European Politics and Societies* 6, no. 1 (1992): 17–54.
7. Victor Nee, "A Theory of Market Transition: From Redistribution to Markets in State Socialism," *American Sociological Review* 56, no. 5 (1989): 663–81.
8. Ibid.; Jeffrey Sachs, "Postcommunist Parties and the Politics of Entitlements," *Transition: The Newsletter about Reforming Economies* 6, no. 3 (1995): 1–4, published by the World Bank.
9. Stark, "Path Dependence"; Gil Eyal et al., *Making Capitalism without Capitalists: The New Ruling Elites in Eastern Europe* (London, 1999).

10. Chris Corrin, *Superwomen and the Double Burden: Women's Experience of Change in Central and Eastern Europe and the Former Soviet Union* (Toronto, 1992); Barbara Einhorn, *Cinderella Goes to Market: Citizenship, Gender, and Women's Movements in East Central Europe* (London, 1993); Nanette Funk and Magda Mueller, eds., *Gender Politics and Post-communism: Reflections from Eastern Europe and the Former Soviet Union* (New York, 1993); Valentine Moghadam, *Democratic Reform and the Position of Women in Transitional Economies* (Oxford, 1993); Nahid Aslanbeigui et al., *Women in the Age of Economic Transformation: Gender Impact of Reforms in Postsocialist and Developing Countries* (New York, 1994); Marilyn Rueschemeyer, *Women and the Politics of Postcommunist Eastern Europe* (Armonk, NY, 1994); Mary Buckley, ed., *Post-Soviet Women: From the Baltic to Central Asia* (Cambridge, 1997).
11. Funk and Mueller, eds., *Gender Politics*, 7.
12. Nanette Funk, "Feminism East and West," in Funk and Mueller, *Gender Politics*, 318–30.
13. Donna Nails and Julianna Arnold, *Gender Assessment and Plan of Action USAID/Bulgaria* (Washington, DC, 2001).
14. In December 1989, the Council of Ministers of the European Union established the Poland and Hungary: Action for Restructuring the Economy (PHARE) program; within two years the program was extended, and it now covers fourteen partner countries in Central and Eastern Europe.
15. For example, "equal pay for equal work." It does not matter if the jobs are lousy and the wages are low; men and women should have equal access to them.
16. Both women of color in the United States and "third-world" women have criticized the white, middle-class bias of Western feminism. For women of color see: bell hooks, *Ain't I a Woman: Black Women and Feminism* (Boston, 1981); Audre Lorde, *I Am Your Sister: Black Women Organizing across Sexualities* (New York, 1985). On "third-world" women see Chandra Talpade Mohanty et al., eds., *Third World Women and the Politics of Feminism* (Bloomington, IN, 1991); Uma Narayan, *Dislocating Cultures: Identities, Traditions, and Third-World Feminism* (New York, 1997); Chilla Bulbeck, *Re-Orienting Western Feminisms: Women's Diversity in a Postcolonial World* (Cambridge, 1998).
17. Clara Zetkin, "Women's Right to Vote," in *Clara Zetkin: Selected Writings*, ed. Philip S. Foner (New York, 1984), 101.
18. The World Bank, UN Development Program, Open Society/Soros Network, US Agency for International Development (USAID), and EU PHARE Program all have gender programs or components informed by essentialist feminist ideologies.
19. For example, the United Nations Development Program (1997) in Bulgaria put together an entire report on Women in Poverty in the transformation period. In 2000 the World Bank held a conference and published a discussion paper on "Making the Transition Work for Women in Europe and Central Asia," in spite of the fact that its own structural adjustment programs are responsible for much of the alleged damage to women's position.
20. For example, Minnesota Advocates for Human Rights funded controversial reports on domestic violence (1996) and sexual harassment (1999) in Bulgaria.
21. Gal and Kligman. *Politics of Gender*.
22. The research for this study included sixteen months of fieldwork in Bulgaria in 1999 and 2000. I also conducted interviews and had ongoing personal communications with the major women's NGOs in Bulgaria, USAID Bulgaria, UNDP Bulgaria, the Women's Program at the Open Society Institute, the Center for the Study of Democracy, the Global Fund for Women, and the World Bank Resident Mission in Sofia between 1998 and 2001.
23. Interview with Ms. Vera Tagarinska, the presidential liaison to NGOs, in August 1998 in Sofia, Bulgaria.
24. Gal and Kligman, *Politics of Gender*, 106.

25. Jalusic and Antic, "Prospects," 3.
26. Eyal, *Making Capitalism*, 14.
27. Eva Fodor, "Gender in Transition: Unemployment in Hungary, Poland and Slovakia," *East European Politics and Societies* 11, no. 3 (1997): 470–500.
28. Julia Szalai, "From Informal Labor to Paid Occupations: Marketization from Below in Hungarian Women's Work," in *Reproducing Gender: Politics, Publics, and Everyday Life after Socialism*, ed. Susan Gal and Gail Kligman (Princeton, NJ, 2000), 200–224.
29. Lisa Giddings, *Does the Shift to Markets Impose Greater Hardship on Women and Minorities? Three Essays on Gender and Ethnicity in Bulgarian Labor Markets* (PhD diss., American University, 2000).
30. Kristen Ghodsee, *The Red Riviera: Gender, Tourism and Postsocialism on the Black Sea* (Durham, NC, 2005); Ghodsee, "State Support in the Market: Women and Tourism Employment in Postsocialist Bulgaria," *International Journal of Politics, Culture and Society* 16, no. 3 (2003): 465–82.
31. Janine Wedel, *Collision and Collusion: The Strange Case of Aid to Eastern Europe* (New York, 2001), 114.
32. Sarah Mendelson and John Glenn, "Democracy Assistance and NGO Strategies in Post-Communist Societies," Carnegie Endowment Working Papers, Democracy and Rule of Law Project, no. 8 (Washington, D.C., 2000).
33. Kevin F. F. Quigley, "Lofty Goals, Modest Results: Assisting Civil Society in Eastern Europe," in *Funding Virtue: Civil Society Aid and Democracy Promotion*, ed. Marina Ottaway and Thomas Carothers (Washington, DC, 2000), 191–215, 203.
34. Keith Snavely and Uday Desai, "The Emergence and Development of Nonprofit Organizations in Bulgaria," *Working Paper Series* (Washington, DC, 1994); Krassimira Daskalova, "Women's Problems, Women's Discourses in Bulgaria," in Gal and Kligman, *Reproducing Gender*.
35. Rebecca Kay, *Russian Women and Their Organizations: Gender, Discrimination, and Grassroots Women's Organizations, 1991–1996* (New York, 2000). See also Valerie Sperling, *Organizing Women in Contemporary Russia: Engendering Transition* (Cambridge, 1999).
36. Gal and Kligman, *Politics of Gender*, 96.
37. United Nations Development Program, *National Human Development Report 2001: Citizen Participation in Governance, from Individuals to Citizens* (Sofia, 2001), 40.
38. Ibid., 41.
39. Mark Robinson, "Governance, Democracy and Conditionality: NGOs and the New Policy Agenda," in *Governance, Democracy and Conditionality: What Role for NGOs?* ed. Andrew Clayton (Oxford, 1993), 35–51.
40. Theodore H. Moran, *Foreign Direct Investment and Development: The New Policy Agenda for Developing Countries and Economies in Transition* (Washington, DC, 1998), 239.
41. James Ferguson, *The Anti-Politics Machine: "Development," Depoliticization, and Bureaucratic Power in Lesotho* (Cambridge, 1990).
42. Jenny Pearce, "NGOs and Social Change: Agents or Facilitators?" *Development Practice* 3, no. 3 (1993): 222–27; Gerard Clarke, "Nongovernmental Organizations (NGOs) and Politics in the Developing World," *Papers on International Development*, no. 20 (Swansea, UK, 1996); Kevin F.F. Quigley, "*Lofty Goals*," 191–215.
43. James Petras and Henry Veltmeyer, *Globalization Unmasked* (Halifax, Nova Scotia, 2001).
44. James Petras, "NGOs: In the Service of Imperialism," *Journal of Contemporary Asia* 29, no. 4 (1999): 429–41, 435.
45. Ibid., 435–36.
46. For comprehensive statistics on women in Bulgaria see UNDP, *National Human Development Report*.

47. *Zharava* was the Bulgarian version of the publication. The English-language magazine *Fair Play* has been resurrected with new funding. It now serves as the "Gender and Development Magazine" of the KARAT Coalition, a consortium of women's NGOs from across Central and Eastern Europe. To be fair, the new magazine is far more critical of globalization and capitalism than its earlier incarnation, but because it is only published in English it is inaccessible to most women in the countries of the KARAT Coalition. Interestingly, the magazine would be able to reach a much broader constituency of women if it were also published in Russian, but this is unlikely to happen for obvious political reasons (author's personal communication with Regina Indshewa in 1998, 1999, and 2000).
48. See Katherine Verdery, *What Was Socialism and What Comes Next?* (Princeton, NJ, 1996).
49. See Jacqueline Heinen, "Public/Private: Gender—Social and Political Citizenship in Eastern Europe," *Theory and Society* 26, no. 4 (1997): 577–97; Heinen, "Polish Democracy is a Masculine Democracy," *Women's Studies International Forum* 15, no. 1 (1992): 129–38; Funk and Mueller, *Gender Politics*.
50. Verdery, *What Was Socialism*.
51. Einhorn, *Cinderella*; Leslie Holmes, *Post-Communism: An Introduction* (Durham, NC, 1997); Jane Jaquette and Sharon Wolchik, *Women and Democracy: Latin America and Central and Eastern Europe* (Baltimore, 1998).

CIVIL SOCIETY, THE STATE, AND CITIZENSHIP

Chapter 13

THE RISE OF WELFARE STATES AND THE REGENDERING OF CIVIL SOCIETY
THE CASE OF THE UNITED STATES

Sonya Michel

Welfare provision has been one of the key building blocks of civil society. Civil society did not precede and allow the establishment of the myriad philanthropies and other voluntary organizations devoted to poor relief that have come to be regarded as one of the hallmarks of civil society; rather, the emergence of such associations helped to *produce* what came to be known as civil society. Here I echo historian Katherine Lynch, who writes, "Europeans did not somehow form communities and then, once they were established, go about the task of distributing various sorts of benefits. Providing relief to the poor ... proved essential to the formation of communities themselves."[1] The same might be said of the societies beyond Europe that are discussed in this volume, including the United States, the subject of this chapter.

While serving as building blocks, voluntary welfare provision also lay at the root of one of the central paradoxes of civil society.[2] Despite lofty statements of goals, most private associations devoted to poor relief and social welfare were based on principles of exclusivity, inequality, and discrimination with regard to both their members and their beneficiaries. These inequalities, in turn, drew on discourses of class, religion, ethnicity, race, and gender. While not all of those who were marginalized or excluded would have—or could have—voiced their objections, the tensions that crystallized in such organizations belie the notion of a unified, egalitarian civil society.

Gender in particular produced a further set of paradoxes. Since certain groups of women as well as men were centrally involved in creating institutions of poor relief, they must be counted among the chief architects of civil society, and as such, share responsibility for its discriminatory rhetoric and practices. Yet these women—mostly from the middle and upper classes—were themselves compelled to work within gender hierarchies that simultaneously praised their innate capacity for charity while restricting their scope, minimizing their contributions, and ultimately dismissing them as inefficient, irrelevant, or worse. Dictates of respectability circumscribed women's spatial movements as well as occupations and behavior, so that in many periods and locales simply appearing outside the home—widely regarded as the locus classicus of morality and civilization—rendered women suspect.[3] It was only by carefully navigating the gendered shoals of their societies that women could use their good works to gain a voice in the public sphere.

This chapter examines different ways in which health and welfare served as a political platform for American women over time. I begin by showing how, starting in the early nineteenth century, middle-class women mobilized contemporary discursive and material resources, often under the umbrella of maternalist ideologies, to fashion the charitable institutions that helped build civil society.[4] I then turn to the late nineteenth century, when the forces of modernization, including professionalization, bureaucratization, and the emphasis on scientific approaches to poverty, served to marginalize women reformers and philanthropists within the emerging US welfare state, thereby constricting their presence in civil society. I conclude by considering the ways that twentieth-century women, in Canada as well as the US, once again using health and welfare as a platform, developed modes of self-help and self-representation to resist their marginalization and make claims for gender justice, thereby pointing toward more egalitarian models for civil society.

Building Civil Society through Voluntary Associations

As several of the chapters in this volume illustrate, the same conditions of bourgeois society that gave rise to civil society and the public sphere often bound middle-class women closely to home and family.[5] In order to move from private to public, these women needed some sort of pretext. Typically, they invoked nationalist, patriotic, civic, or religious duty. In the United States, for example, both women's benevolence and their efforts to obtain civil and political rights were, from the early nineteenth century on, framed in moral terms and based on an assumption of women's equality with men in the eyes of God. In practice, however, churches continued to require women's subordination, and this gender inequality carried over to, and was reinforced by, the government, even though it rested on a rhetorical separation of church and state. Indeed, the law and Christianity proved to be mutually reinforcing; as historian Nancy Isenberg puts it, "the courts and the government forged a national and legal consensus on Christian morality."[6] Thus in following religious directives to engage in charity, women could not avoid reinforcing the power of both church and state over their autonomy.

Nevertheless, benevolent societies allowed women—at least those who were white and middle class—to become members of collectivities that, in turn, provided avenues into the public sphere.[7] Most antebellum women's organizations were composed of women from the same social circles or networks, enabling them to use their social contacts to gain influence. Moreover, Isenberg notes,

> by incorporating, benevolent societies also expanded women's ability to exercise certain legal rights, allowing them to own and manage property, to make legally binding contracts, and to control their finances. In essence, the benevolent society constituted a private association of educated citizens who shared common public interests. Such societies permitted married women to meet the requirement of the bourgeois public sphere as property owners. Finally, almost all of these societies engaged in the domain of letters by publishing their constitutions, reports of meetings, and circulars in an attempt to persuade the educated public to donate funds and to support their efforts.... The benevolent society was called a society because women served "the interests of civil society."[8]

Yet in their organizational publications and techniques, women often framed pleas for support in rhetoric that reinforced their dependency and vulnerability, implicitly paying obeisance to male-imposed restrictions. As Isenberg herself argues, fundraising fairs and bazaars, where women sold their own "fancy goods"—handwork—"allowed women to preserve [their] demeanor of respectability and modesty within the context of bourgeois publicity."[9] But whether such displays also served to raise women's status is open to question. US historian Mary Ryan, examining women's (self-) representations in public ceremonies in the decades following the Civil War, claims that they merely drew attention to domesticity and women's lack of rights. "As long as women represented some transcendent other and projected ideals of domestic seclusion onto public ceremony their civic actions had the dialectical effect of affirming exclusion from the sphere of democratic participation," she writes. The expansion of political rights in American cities in the second half of the nineteenth century was, in Ryan's view, a democratization of and for white men only.[10]

Ryan may be overstating the case, for though American women remained voteless during this period, they were not wholly confined to the private sphere. Their philanthropic and civic activities were at an all-time high, with many women belonging to more than one association at a time.[11] However, since their charitable work was based on the principle of "face-to-face" encounters and friendly visiting, much of it occurred outside of public view.[12] Susan B. Anthony acknowledged women's spatial marginalization when she called upon her fellow suffragists to denounce women's exclusion from observances of the one hundredth anniversary of American independence: "'in meetings, in parlors, in kitchens wherever they may be, unite with us in this declaration and protest.'"[13] Anthony was, in a sense, invoking a different kind of public—not the male-dominated public of streets and saloons, but a women's public that was physically situated in domestic space yet still clearly oriented beyond the home.

The Limits of a "Women's Public"

The notion of a gender-segregated civil society may not match the ideal set forth in classical liberal theory, but it fits the historical experience of men as well as women. At the same time, the women's public was itself a source of inequality. Because it was sited in domestic and associational space, admission to it was also restricted by class and race. Working-class women and women of color may have been visible in bourgeois white women's kitchens and parlors, but their presence—and their voices—would have been strictly delimited by their roles as domestic servants or slaves. It was not until late in the second half of the nineteenth century that African American, immigrant, and working-class women began to form their own organizations in the US.[14]

Over the course of the nineteenth century, however, even white middle-class women found it more, not less, difficult to negotiate public space, as American gender codes became ever more rigid in the face of rapid urban growth and immigration. Historian Sarah Deutsch, mapping what she calls the "moral geography" of late nineteenth-century Boston, found that racial and ethnic as well as gender mixing could compromise a woman's respectability; young, white, unmarried women were viewed as being at special risk.[15] At the same time, however, women were venturing further into public life, whether through work or social service. While women of all classes found the spatial restrictions irksome, working-class women were more likely to simply ignore them, a luxury that middle-class women could ill afford. Instead, this group used their philanthropic experience and expanding cache of "social knowledge" to expand their geographic sphere, deploying the tools of social categorization to legitimate their own movements while seeking to constrain those of lower-class women. According to Deutsch, middle-class and elite reformers, in the name of protecting single women (but also with an eye toward recruiting domestic servants for themselves), denigrated nondomestic worksites as well as working-class homes. As Deutsch explains,

> In the process, they helped construct an urban geography of sexual danger that left them captains of the only safe vessels.... [M]iddle-class and elite matrons interpreted the spaces [of working-class homes] differently [than did the working class]. In so doing they bolstered their own authority by participating in a larger project of creating institutions and spaces that demarcated the normal and the abnormal, the virtuous and the deviant. The middle-class and elite reformers' discourse on virtue reinforced their role as surveillers and as those who chose what got looked at and what got overlooked. It also affirmed their position as producers of "virtue" itself and co-producers of the discourse about it.[16]

Thus, while elite women gained a certain amount of public power at the expense of those beneath them in the social hierarchy, they nonetheless continually reaffirmed the gendered system of respectability that kept them tethered to home and family.

Modernization and the Decline of Women's Public Power

At the same time that female elites across Europe and North America were using their charitable duties to claim the right to venture into the public, certain trends were emerging that would undermine the very basis of those claims. The rise of the social and behavioral sciences in the last quarter of the nineteenth century held out the hope of not only understanding but also predicting and controlling human behavior; by the turn of the century, these new forms of social knowledge had gained hegemony in the fields of health and welfare. Concomitantly, many female-dominated organizations were either incorporated into or displaced by public services or, at the least, found themselves coming under state regulation. On the one hand, this allowed them to expand and become more stable, but on the other, it meant that laywomen could not continue to operate as they had before. The types of work they had once performed as volunteers now became professionalized, and they were no longer "in charge." To some extent, younger generations of middle-class women found places in these new professions, as well as in a new type of public sphere that emerged in the many conferences and publications they spawned. But as the basis for claims to authority within this sphere shifted from morality and motherhood to "scientific" expertise, the cohorts of women who lacked education and professional training became marginalized.

Female philanthropists, reformers, and social activists responded in various ways. Some resisted all attempts at rationalization, clinging to the notion that their work was based in Christian principles of love as well as charity. Others, however, self-consciously embraced "modern" methods, most prominently Josephine Shaw Lowell, one of the founders of the Charity Organization Society, who was a firm advocate of "scientific charity."[17] But practitioners of the young social and behavioral sciences, thirsty for their own legitimation, demanded more than the adoption of a label; they sought a thoroughgoing rethinking of the premises of philanthropy and social work.

Women such as Lowell had in fact been involved in establishing the social sciences in the US from the mid-nineteenth century on,[18] but by the early twentieth century, a split occurred among reform-minded intellectuals (and intellectually-minded reformers), with men hiving themselves off in the universities, and women continuing to pursue "applied" research that, while certainly useful for the purposes of social reform, was regarded (at least by male academics) as intellectually inferior.[19] Helen Thompson Woolley, an American psychologist and reformer, retorted that "there was 'no reason why science should not guide reform nor why reform should not direct the use of science.'"[20] According to feminist scholar Helene Silverberg, many female social scientists agreed, but still could not find suitable positions within the academy. Rebuffed by various universities in their attempts to set up separate departments of applied research on a par with strictly academic departments, some managed to establish schools of social work, but these were mostly either freestanding or affiliated with women's colleges (for example, Smith in Northampton, Massachusetts, and Hunter in New York City) rather than with more prestigious research universities. Intended to raise the profile of the field and turn it into a profession, the schools ended up ghettoizing social work and transforming it into what came to be regarded as a "semi-profession."[21]

The gender implications of this division were perhaps most glaring in the life and work of Jane Addams, the founder of Chicago's Hull House and a leading Progressive reformer, who, along with a number of less famous but equally determined colleagues such as Florence Kelley, Julia Lathrop, Sophonisba Breckinridge, Alice Hamilton, and the Abbott sisters—Grace and Edith—left a lasting mark on US social policy.[22] During many decades of dedicated activism at the municipal, national, and international level, Addams found the time to write dozens of articles and books—writings that, in the estimation of many recent scholars, firmly establish her credentials as a sociologist as well as an activist.[23] Yet, notes Mary Jo Deegan, one of Addams's biographers, despite winning the Nobel Peace Prize in 1931, "her intellectual stature is barely appreciated, and her contributions to sociology totally obscured."[24]

The main reason for this, according to intellectual historian Dorothy Ross, is that Addams's sociology did not fit the prevailing mold; it was "interpretive" and "relational," rather than seeking to be strictly objective or to discover the "laws" of human society. Acknowledging that individuals from different social positions could easily misperceive one another, she herself sought "the point of view of both parties."[25] Ross concedes that Addams, because of her own upbringing and values (her "middle-class domestic bias"), tended to value the social over the economic.[26] Nevertheless, Addams dedicated her knowledge to social action and practice, and "if her aims and methods were inherently problematic, so too were the universalistic aims and objectivist methods of the university sociologists."[27]

Addams's aim, Ross tells us, was to "empower educated women and their social democratic values."[28] Her approach was "gendered feminine" as a result of the nineteenth-century culture from which she emerged, but as she moved increasingly into a heterosocial sphere, Addams pulled back from her earlier essentialism, though she never abandoned it entirely. While university sociologists sought to influence policy by relying on "middle-class experts" to apply their more speculative knowledge of "social ideas" and "economic laws," Addams condoned those "who are incited to activity by their sympathies as well as their convictions"[29]—that is, she was unwilling to give up her emotions altogether.

Male sociologists, bent on raising their own status, either ignored Addams or granted her work only grudging praise. She was asked to deliver the convocation address at the University of Chicago in 1905 and in 1913 was offered a part-time faculty position there (which she turned down). Though her work influenced many "Chicago School" sociologists, few acknowledged her explicitly, with the result that her work largely stood outside the academic field.[30] Despite these snubs, Addams must be considered one of the more fortunate female reform intellectuals; others, like Mary Van Kleeck and Florence Kelley, were summarily dismissed as "amateurs" (despite holding advanced degrees), their solid investigative work passing unnoticed by contemporaries.[31] Not only were most female social scientists excluded from academic positions on the basis of gender, but the knowledge and discourses associated with their research were also ignored. As a result, male academic social scientists not only accrued the lion's share of prestige and privileges but also were well positioned to exert political influence.

Much of women's social scientific work remained anonymous until its presence and impact were revealed by feminist historians. It was, for example, the astute research of self-trained statistician Josephine Goldmark that provided the foundations for the famous 1908 "Brandeis Brief," which succeeded in carrying the day when women's rights to protective labor legislation were being tested in the Supreme Court—but since her brother-in-law, Louis Brandeis, was the one who argued the case, it is his name that became eponymous.[32] Goldmark's role remained more or less hidden until it was unearthed by US historian Alice Kessler-Harris in 1982.[33]

However indirectly, studies conducted by women under the aegis of advocacy organizations as well as federal agencies helped shape debates over social policy, social work, and governmental programs throughout the Progressive Era. From the mid-1920s on, however, private foundations began pouring money into the academic social sciences, and women's research lost ground. In 1920, the Chicago School of Civics and Philanthropy (founded by Sophonisba Breckinridge and Edith Abbott) merged with University of Chicago; renamed the School of Social Service Administration, it almost immediately became marginalized, as the "regular" faculty discouraged their graduate students (especially women) from taking courses there.[34]

A parallel shift occurred in social work, the very field that women had, in effect, invented through decades of "friendly visiting." As professionalization spread, organizations founded by women became absorbed into larger bureaucracies, both public and voluntary, which granted female workers titles and improved their salaries but at the price of considerable loss of autonomy. In the 1920s, for example, the freshly minted female products of the new schools of social work readily found jobs in the new "child guidance clinics." Trained in the methods of psychotherapy and counseling, they were placed at the bottom of a gendered hierarchy, with male PhD psychologists on the rank above, and psychiatrists with medical degrees, also mostly men, at the very top. The hierarchy was reversed when it came to the clinic's actual work with families: the social workers dealt with mothers (and occasionally fathers), the psychologists performed tests, and the psychiatrists treated the children, who were, after all, the main focus of the work.[35]

What do these examples tell us about the gendering of civil society during the late nineteenth and early twentieth centuries? As the fields of social knowledge became compartmentalized along gender lines, women no doubt found communities of discourse within their own disciplines, as the robust literature of social work, including numerous journals, conference proceedings, and published studies, attests.[36] But there is scant evidence that women were able to participate on an equal footing with men in a larger, heterosocial sphere of policy debate. Even after winning suffrage, American women seldom held public office at the federal or national level. Though several women headed agencies (the Children's Bureau and Women's Bureau) within the US federal government, these remained relatively small, with restricted budgets and little legislative muscle.[37]

Thus, women had little say over the shape of the emerging federal welfare state. Ironically, perhaps their greatest legislative success—the campaign for widows' or mothers' pension legislation across dozens of states throughout the Progressive Era—had occurred *before* they gained the vote.[38] But in the 1930s, as Franklin Roosevelt's New Deal got underway, even the most prominent female reformers were relegated to a back seat when major social policy initiatives concerning women, children, and families were being designed and implemented. Most notably, although a number of experienced female governmental operatives—including Grace Abbott, a former chief of the Children's Bureau—served as advisors to the Council on Economic Security, the body that designed the Social Security Act, they lacked the power to craft legislation that would be favorable to women and children, such as a measure to recognize the contributions of non-wage-earning housewives.[39] By the same token, when it came time to implement the new law, which to a large extent affected women and children as well as male wage-earners, the Roosevelt administration bypassed both the Women's and Children's Bureaus—both logical choices—in favor of a new, male-headed agency, the Social Security Administration.

The Emergence of Alternative Publics

It would be inaccurate to say that, as a result of professionalization and bureaucratization, middle-class laywomen became totally excluded from civil society in the US after the Progressive Era. Indeed, they remained active as fundraisers and in most communities continued to serve as the backbone of voluntary work through religious as well as secular organizations. They established a key civic association, the League of Women Voters and, through the Parent-Teacher Association, oversaw and supplemented the work of the public school system.[40] Many also moved into a kind of global civil society as activists within the emerging international women's movement.[41] To a great extent, however, the forces of modernization did spell the end of maternalism, preventing middle-class women from continuing to rely on the health and welfare of the "less fortunate" as platforms for their own entry into civil society.[42] But this had a salubrious effect: low-income women now began mobilizing in their own right, while the growing ranks of college-educated, middle-class women discovered that they had issues of their own to attend to. Sometimes organizing within their own classes, sometimes across class, these cohorts of women found that they shared a common goal: to challenge the male-dominated professions and policies that affected their health and welfare and take matters into their own hands. Notably, they were less successful in making permanent changes in policy than they were in opening up new political sites for themselves and devising unique ways to participate in civil society.

For examples of this shift, I examine what we might call women's "post-maternalist" mobilizations, first around health issues, then around welfare rights. Starting in the late nineteenth century with practices such as faith healing, a series of American women's health movements went on to promote breastfeeding and informed, critical medical consumerism. Whether implicitly or explicitly, all of these movements questioned professional authority and aimed at helping women (re)gain control over their own bodies and health.[43] Struggles over welfare rights led by poor and low-income women themselves did not emerge until the 1960s. Unlike the women's health movement, which focused on the medical profession, these activists challenged the government, at the local, state, and federal levels. Seeking adequate support for themselves and their families, they questioned public social workers' authority to control the minutiae of their daily existence and demanded that they be allowed to live their lives in dignity.

I begin with the late-nineteenth century faith healing movement. Disease, along with poverty and immorality, had long been one of the chief targets of maternalists' efforts to reform poor families,[44] but these same women tended to impose a strict silence on their own bodily complaints and ailments.[45] At the same time, women's health was the main target of the emerging medical profession populated by "regular" physicians, nearly all men, who were seeking to establish a monopoly on health care by displacing the "irregulars"—some undoubtedly charlatans, but others women who, as healers, midwives, and herbalists, had long looked after Americans' health.[46] The physicians' campaign not only succeeded in establishing their own legitimacy but also produced in many women a continuous sense of being ill, creating a strong cultural link between women, frailty, and poor health.[47]

Looking for ways to resist this infantilizing, enervating, and gender-based diagnosis,[48] women turned to faith healing, helping to build a movement that rose and fell across Protestant Canada and the US from about 1880 to 1930. This movement promoted a set of beliefs and practices that allowed women to eschew all doctors and medicines and reject the "dispassionate" gaze of the doctor, which they perceived as chilling rather than objective. Although most of the leading faith healers were male, the movement was initially centered in female space: the bedrooms and sickrooms of the afflicted, which became active sites for cures effected through solitude, contemplation of one's faith, and intensive prayer, often under the guidance of lay women prayer leaders. Women also ran "faith" or "healing homes," where the sickly could find an environment conducive to their pursuit of recovery through prayer.[49]

As in social work and medicine, locally based female lay practitioners were eventually displaced by men—not men of science, but flamboyant charismatic preachers like Charles Price and F.F. Bosworth. The private, personal, and contemplative structures and practices created by the largely female adherents of faith healing gave way to spectacular mass meetings held in public halls.⁵⁰ (There were a few women preachers, most notably Aimee Semple McPherson, perhaps one of the most famous evangelists of all, and Lilian Yeomans, a minister who gained particular notice because she had practiced as a physician before converting and taking up divine cures.)⁵¹ But for the few brief decades before it "went commercial" and became male-dominated, faith healing allowed laywomen to resist the impositions of the male-dominated "regular" medical establishment.

What is the relationship between such a movement and civil society? How could a set of practices centered in isolated private homes, often located in remote rural areas, constitute a kind of women's public? This occurred in several ways: through prayer meetings, exchanges of tracts and books through the mail, and most powerfully, by means of what historian James Opp calls "narrative networks."⁵² Starting in the late 1880s, enterprising publishers began issuing collections of "testimonials" of faith healing and started a number of weekly and monthly magazines filled with similar accounts. About 80 percent written by or about women, these narratives described both revelations that resulted from self-scrutiny and the comfort received from certain gifted women visitors who came to pray with them, One Toronto woman attested, "'a lady called on me, and told me she believed God had sent her, and that if I would accept Jesus as the Divine Healer, he would restore me to health.'"⁵³ Another Canadian author explained that she had recovered after following precisely the instructions sent to her by Sarah Mix, an African American healer. Mix told her to give up all medicines and other remedies and to pray at specific times when a women's prayer group would make her the subject of their attention.⁵⁴

The predominance of women in this early stage of the faith healing movement had much to do with the gendered norms that surrounded health and illness. As Opp argues, "the act of [publicly] narrating sickness crossed a number of gendered boundaries. To openly discuss illness was to admit to bodily weakness, a social construction that did not align with masculine ideals of health and vitality." Thus men tended to avoid recounting personal experiences of healing, though as ministers or lay evangelists, they might discuss them in abstract terms or from a theological perspective. By contrast, "it was women's personal experience in itself that granted them the authority, and the obligation, to witness publicly and carry forth the message of faith healing. This personal experience of the divine, an experience that required testimony to maintain it, provided women with a social space in which their voices could be heard."⁵⁵ Unlike the maternalist organizations of the day, this gender-based network aimed at helping women reclaim power over their *own* bodies, not those of "the less fortunate." In so doing, it created an alternative public, one based on communication among equals and resistance to the professionals who sought to stifle it.

There were at least two other early twentieth-century instances of US women's organization around health issues, but neither fits precisely the pattern I am trying to delineate here. One was the birth control movement, which was initiated by elite women such as Margaret Sanger, primarily on behalf of the poor and working class (though ultimately, of course, it would benefit women of all classes), and thus more in the maternalist mold.[56] The second was the National Negro Health Movement, which was active from 1915 to 1950. Although this movement emerged out of initiatives taken by African American clubwomen and much of its work was carried on by grassroots women, its leadership tended to be male, making it more of a mixed-gender than a women's public.[57]

Instead, let me move on to 1956, when a group of seven Roman Catholic mothers from a Chicago suburb founded La Leche League,[58] an organization whose goal was to promote breastfeeding in an era when bottle-feeding and infant formula were regarded as the gold standard by the medical profession.[59] League members spread their idea by running structured discussion groups covering a range of topics including pregnancy, childbirth, and childrearing as well as infant feeding, and by coaching new mothers and offering them individual support. The discussion groups were based on a model that several of the founders had learned in the Christian Family Movement. Initially, all of them were led by one of the founders, but as the demand increased, this core group trained more lay leaders, in most cases other women who had successfully breastfed for at least a year. By the 1980s, La Leche League boasted more than 4,000 support groups in 48 countries.

Much of its popularity no doubt derived from League's oft-reprinted manual, *The Womanly Art of Breastfeeding*, first published in 1958, which has sold by the millions in English and in translation. Through the book, group meetings, and other practices, the League explicitly challenged medical authority on infant feeding and offered a refuge for those whose commitment to breastfeeding made them feel uncomfortably "radical." By means of its "woman-to-woman" communications, which included a telephone hotline for mothers experiencing problems with breastfeeding as well as the various discussion groups, it established a model for unconstrained exchanges of information and peer support among women.

In later years, La Leche League came to be considered conservative by many feminists, since it consistently privileged breastfeeding and childrearing above any other ambitions or needs that women might have (such as pursuing a career). The organization did, however, serve as an important resource for women seeking to carve out their own path through motherhood, one that often also included "natural childbirth." Thus the league, along with a general turn toward consumer rights in the sixties, and, of course, feminism, must be considered one of the roots of the women's health movement that emerged in the late 1960s—the next in my series. Second-wave feminism gave rise to multiple forms of alternative or counterpublics around dozens of different issues and practices; within the women's health movement alone, one could identify several, including the spread of women's self-examinations and the abortion rights coalition.⁶⁰ Here, though, I have space to discuss in detail only one example, the Boston Women's Health Book Collective and its audience.

The collective began in the summer of 1969, when a group of Boston feminist activists decided to learn more about their own bodies. They started by conducting research on a wide range of questions and soon began offering a series of informal courses in community settings (a common countercultural practice). In 1971, an "alternative press" began publishing the curriculum the collective had developed in the form of a mimeographed pamphlet entitled *Our Bodies, Ourselves*. After eleven reprintings, which put nearly a quarter-million copies into circulation, demand had outstripped the press's capacity, so the collective decided to turn over distribution to Simon & Schuster, a trade publisher, while retaining key editorial controls. By 1976 the first trade edition had sold over a million copies, and a Spanish translation appeared a year later. Revised editions appeared every few years thereafter, most recently in 2005.⁶¹

"From the beginning ... personal stories were at the heart of this project," notes historian Wendy Kline:

> The stories did more than illustrate medical viewpoints on health and sexuality; they expanded, enriched, and challenged them. In this context, consciousness-raising [a major technique of the women's liberation movement] transformed medical knowledge by suggesting that personal experience offered a "truth" just as valid as textbook views. In doing so, it reduced the "knowledge differential between patient and practitioner: and thereby challenged medical hierarchy.⁶²

Accordingly, it became the collective's practice to solicit critiques of each edition and to take seriously readers' responses in making revisions. In her analysis of its voluminous correspondence with the public during the 1970s and 1980s, Kline uncovered a distinctive process whereby the books' multiple authors struggled to eschew professional authority and instead create a sense of respect for and mutuality with readers. While many readers praised the book, thanking the authors for bringing them much-needed information and pointing out remedies that doctors had failed to recommend, others expressed deep disappointment or frustration when topics were neglected or suggestions did not work. One told a collective member, "'Though you tried hard, ... it seems that the materials available to you are either out of date or weren't properly researched by someone!'"⁶³ Although this reader was critical, she clearly understood the process by which the collective worked. Even when readers became confrontational, authors sought to address them as peers, acknowledging their expertise, at least with regard to their own experiences and their own bodies. Typical was the response sent to a reader who had written in about the book's treatment of particular test used in pregnancy: "'I'm not sure how to fix it, but you can be sure we'll make some modification the next time around.'"[64] And indeed, in the next edition, they did.

Readers' most common complaint, according to Kline, was "their sense of exclusion. [They] expected to find themselves described within the pages [of the books] and expressed confusion, disappointment, frustration, or anger if they did not."[65] They felt—and the collective encouraged them to feel—that they had a proprietary interest in the book and what it said, not only because it helped them with personal health issues and interactions with the medical establishment, but because they regarded it as an extension of the women's movement—of *their* movement. With its commitment to mutuality and refusal of hierarchy and deference to professional "expertise," *Our Bodies, Ourselves* became a key site for the creation of a feminist counterpublic within American civil society. And when specific groups such as African American women, lesbians, and women with disabilities challenged the collective for excluding, marginalizing, or ghettoizing them, it grappled with the issues according to those same principles. The authors took these challenges seriously and sought to address them by modifying their approach, revising certain sections of the book or adding new ones, and even, in one case, simply turning pages over to an independent set of authors.[66]

Like faith healing, the larger women's health movement eventually became co-opted, though vestiges of it remain. Many of the practices feminists demanded, such as allowing women to gain control of childbirth through de-emphasis on anesthetics and the use of "natural" methods, have become standard practice in US hospitals. Most now routinely offer childbirth classes to help parturient women participate actively in the process and, by being informed, presumably avoid fear and excessive pain. In practice, however, not all women experience the blissful deliveries in homelike "delivery suites" portrayed in training films; too often, many hours of "natural" labor are followed with Caesarean sections if a woman is deemed to have made "inadequate progress" toward delivery according to a statistically determined curve. Brief hospital stays, regarded by feminists as one of the hallmarks of "de-medicalization," have become a convenient way for insurance companies to cut costs, with the result that many mothers are now compelled to undergo "drive-by" deliveries.

The Boston Women's Health Book Collective, however, has prevailed. It continues to publish new editions of its book on a regular basis and has branched out with volumes such as *Ourselves Growing Older* (1987) and *Changing Bodies, Changing Lives* (1998), for adolescents. Moreover, the collective, along with other feminist organizations, maintains vigilance over practices and research affecting women's health. The battle is an ongoing one. Recently, for example, demands for greater research attention to women's health issues such as breast cancer have succumbed to commercial exploitation; while appearing to align themselves with feminists in challenging the medical establishment, corporations such as the cosmetics giant Avon are in fact exploiting the "women's health market" for profit, turning research and healthcare into a "market-driven industry of survivorship" through widely promoted events such as "walkathons." Such practices are all the more galling to women's health activists since they exploit methods of publicity and fundraising that feminists pioneered.[67]

While often divided along the lines of race, ethnicity, and class, the feminist health movement nevertheless formed and continues to mobilize around many issues that, potentially, affect all women. The welfare rights movement of the 1960s, 1970s, and early 1980s was organized along narrower lines, interpellating women through issues stemming from poverty and public assistance. But here, too, the principle of self-representation has been important. With African American women composing a majority of its membership (though they were not a majority of the poor population overall), this movement built on decades of organizing around civil rights, beginning with the National Association for the Advancement of Colored People (the NAACP) and the Urban League.[68] But while these two cross-class organizations had focused on poverty as a symptom of the larger issue of discrimination, the welfare rights movement turned the tables by taking poverty as a starting point for their demands. This meant that, for the first time, poor American women were organizing on their own behalf, and they took the opportunity both to claim material benefits and to articulate their understanding of the linkage between satisfying material needs and participating in civil society.

Initially coming together in small groups to share complaints about local housing and welfare practices, poor and low-income women coalesced to form the National Welfare Rights Organization in 1967. The NWRO quickly became the most visible face of the movement, with members addressing national rallies across the country and in Washington, DC, and famously testifying before Congress in what were undoubtedly some of the most raucous, indecorous hearings ever held there.[69] There is not space here to do justice to the rich history of this movement that is just beginning to emerge.[70] Suffice it to say, the struggle for welfare rights rose and fell against a backdrop of New Left activism as well as federal efforts to address the problem of poverty after many decades of neglect. While the young leftists, mostly white, middle-class, and male, provided much critical assistance to welfare recipients, particularly when it came to legal matters, their claims to expertise meant that they sometimes impeded the efforts of poor women to represent themselves.[71] Nevertheless, as historian Premilla Nadasen puts it, "black female recipients were able to make their voices heard and their power felt. But they struggled on multiple fronts to do so."[72] Although the welfare rights movement allowed these women to enter civil society on their own terms, they were unable to stem the neoliberal tide that eventually led to the draconian welfare reforms of the 1990s.

Conclusion

Questions of health and welfare have long served women as a political platform, one deemed "appropriate to their sex." At the same time, the organizations and mobilizations women constructed around these issues became part of the foundation of civil society. But it was a shaky foundation. Throughout the nineteenth and well into the twentieth century, philanthropic work afforded American women of the middle and upper classes an avenue into the public sphere while denying a direct voice to those they sought to assist. As their organizations became incorporated into the emerging welfare state, however, female volunteers and philanthropists who remained "amateurs" became marginalized, while the poor, now relabeled as "clients," continued to be silenced. In order to avoid the twin pitfalls of maternalism and professionalization, women mobilizing around issues of health and welfare began moving toward self-help and self-representation. Even before second-wave feminism articulated mutuality and a rejection of hierarchy as core principles of women's politics, adherents of faith healing and promoters of a revival of breastfeeding had started to develop models of alternative, egalitarian publics. The feminist organizations that followed reconfirmed those principles while fashioning new models for self-help. Representing themselves for the first time, the poor women who made up the ranks of groups such as the NWRO linked material well-being with dignity and access to the public sphere, while the more heterogeneous group of women who participated in the women's health movement devised practices of gathering knowledge about women's bodies that challenged the authority of the medical establishment. To be sure, none of these movements fully achieved its goals; all of them ended, one way or another, in co-optation, marginalization, or outright defeat. Yet the history of their struggles must also be considered as part of the history of the establishment and development of civil society in the United States. Both the flawed practices of maternalism and the more egalitarian models of self-help and self-representation offer important lessons for all those who look to civil society as the site for working toward gender justice in health care and social provision.

Notes

1. Katherine Lynch, *Individuals, Families, and Communities in Europe, 1200–1800: The Urban Foundations of Western Society* (New York, 2003), 103.
2. Frank Trentmann, "Introduction: Paradoxes of Civil Society," in *Paradoxes of Civil Society: New Perspectives on Modern German and British History*, ed. Trentmann (New York, 2000), 1–46.
3. Sarah Deutsch, *Women and the City: Gender, Space and Power, 1870–1940* (New York, 2002), 72. See also George Mosse, *Nationalism and Sexuality: Middle-Class Morality and Sexual Norms in Modern Europe* (Madison, WI, 1985), chaps. 1, 5.
4. By "maternalist ideologies" I mean those that "exalted women's capacity to mother and applied to society as a whole the values they attached to that role: care, nurturance, and morality"; Seth Koven and Sonya Michel, "Introduction: 'Mother Worlds,'" in Koven and Michel eds., *Mothers of a New World: Maternalist Politics and the Origins of Welfare States* (New York and London, 1993), 4.
5. See, for example, the chapters by Gisela Mettele and Gunilla Budde, this volume. See also Jean Quataert, *Staging Philanthropy: Patriotic Women and the National Imagination in Dynastic Germany, 1813–1916* (Ann Arbor, MI, 2001).
6. Nancy Isenberg, *Sex and Citizenship in Antebellum America* (Chapel Hill, NC, 1998), 83.
7. Ibid., 41–48.
8. Ibid., 59.
9. Ibid., 60. See also Sonya Michel, "Dorothea Dix, or 'The Voice of the Maniac,'" *Discourse* 17, no. 2 (1994–1995), 48–66.
10. Mary Ryan, *Women in Public: Between Banners and Ballots, 1825–1880* (Baltimore, 1992), 251.
11. Historian Sara Evans has referred to this as a "maternal commonwealth"; see her *Bound for Liberty* (New York, 1997), chap. 6.
12. Even then, Ryan contends, in performing charitable work, women were representing religion more than gender; *Women in Public*, 251.
13. Quoted in ibid.
14. On African American women, see Deborah Gray White, *Too Heavy a Load: Black Women in Defense of Themselves, 1884–1994* (New York, 1998) and Susan L. Smith, *Sick and Tired of Being Sick and Tired: Black Women's Health Activism in America, 1890–1950* (Philadelphia, 1995); on working-class and immigrant women: Annelise Orleck, *Common Sense and a Little Fire: Women and Working-Class Politics in the U.S., 1900–1965* (Chapel Hill, NC, 1995).
15. Deutsch, *Women in the City*, 88–90; see also Mosse, *Nationalism and Sexuality*, chap. 5.
16. Deutsch, *Women in the City*, 76–77.
17. See Joan Waugh, *Unsentimental Reformer: The Life of Josephine Shaw Lowell* (Cambridge, MA, 1998).
18. Ibid., 114; see also *Gender and American Social Science: The Formative Years*, ed. Helene Silverberg (Princeton, NJ, 1998).
19. See Silverberg, *Gender and American Social Science*, Introduction; also Ellen Fitzpatrick, *Endless Crusade: Women Social Scientists and Progressive Reform*, (New York, 1990); and Rosalind Rosenberg, *Beyond Separate Spheres: The Intellectual Roots of Modern Feminism*, (New Haven, CT, 1982).
20. Quoted in Silverberg, *Gender and American Social Science*, 11.
21. Sonya Michel, "Children's Interests/ Mothers' Rights: Women, Professionals, and the American Family, 1920–1945" (PhD diss., Brown University, 1986); Roy Lubove, *The Professional Altruist: The Emergence of Social Work as a Career, 1880–1930* (Cambridge, MA, 1965).

22. Robyn Muncy, *Creating a Female Dominion in American Reform, 1890–1935* (New York, 1991); and Kathryn Kish Sklar, *Florence Kelley and the Nation's Work* (New Haven, CT, 1995).
23. See, for example, Dorothy Ross, "Social Science as Cultural Critique: Gendered Social Knowledge, Domestic Discourse, Jane Addams, and the Possibilities of Social Science," in Silverberg, *Gender and American Social Science*; Mary Jo Deegan, *Jane Addams and the Men of the Chicago School, 1892–1918* (New Brunswick, NJ, 1988); and Jean Bethke Elshtain, *Jane Addams and the Dream of American Democracy: A Life* (New York, 2002).
24. Deegan, *Jane Addams*, 7.
25. Ross, "Social Science," 250.
26. Here she differed from her close colleague Florence Kelley; see Sklar, *Florence Kelley*.
27. Ross, "Social Science," 251.
28. Ibid.
29. Ibid., 252.
30. Deegan, *Jane Addams*.
31. The one major exception to this pattern was Alice Hamilton, a trained physician who became the first female faculty member of the Harvard Medical School, and whose research on industrial health and safety issues earned her recognition as one of the pioneers of the field of public health. But even she faced considerable discrimination from her male academic peers; see Hamilton, *Exploring the Dangerous Trades: The Autobiography of Alice Hamilton, M.D.* (Boston, 1943) and Barbara Sicherman, *Alice Hamilton: A Life in Letters* (Cambridge, MA, 1984).
32. Goldmark, who had majored in English at Bryn Mawr College, developed her expertise with statistics while working with Florence Kelley at the National Consumers' League and in other positions, preparing reports on various forms of protective legislation. See Kathryn Kish Sklar, "Brain Work for Women," in *The Social Survey in Historical Perspective, 1880–1940*, ed. Martin Bulmer et al. (New York, 1991).
33. See her pathbreaking book *Out to Work: A History of Wage-Earning Women in the United States* (New York, 1982), 201–5.
34. Silverberg, *Gender and American Social Science*, 17.
35. Margo Horn, *Before It's Too Late: The Child Guidance Movement in the United States, 1922–1945* (Philadelphia, 1989).
36. Michel, "Children's Interests," chap. 2.
37. Muncy, *Female Dominion*; and Kriste Lindemeyer, *A Right to Childhood: The U.S. Children's Bureau and Child Welfare, 1912–46* (Urbana, IL, 1997).
38. On this campaign, see Theda Skocpol, *Protecting Soldiers and Mothers: The Political Origins of Social Policy in the United States* (Cambridge, MA, 1992), chap. 8.
39. Alice Kessler-Harris, *In Pursuit of Equity: Women, Men, and the Quest for Economic Citizenship in 20th-Century America* (New York, 2001), 125. This measure was omitted in the original legislation passed in 1935, but added in the amendments of 1939; see ibid., 142ff.
40. Christine Wayshiner, "Race, Gender, and the Early PTA: Civic Engagement and Public Education, 1897–1924," *Teachers College Record* 105, no. 3 (2003): 520–44.
41. Leila Rupp, *Worlds of Women: The Making of an International Women's Movement* (Princeton, NJ, 1997); for an important discussion of the racialized as well as gendered dynamics of global civil society, see Marilyn Lake's chapter in this volume.
42. Rebecca Plant, "The Repeal of Mother Love: Momism and the Reconstruction of Motherhood in Philip Wylie's America" (PhD diss., Johns Hopkins University, 2001).
43. Around the same time, a patients' rights organization also began in the field of mental health, prompted by the publication of Clifford Beers's startling account of his experiences in an asylum, *A Mind that Found Itself* (New York, 1910). While this organiza-

tion did not thematize women's issues, the disability rights movement that began 1980s was inspired in part by the strategies and rhetoric of the feminist women's health movement.
44. Regina Morantz, *Sympathy and Science: Women Physicians in American Medicine* (Chapel Hill, NC, 2000), chap. 8.
45. To be sure, throughout the nineteenth century, a handful of women fought for recognition as medical professionals; see ibid., chaps. 5–7.
46. On women healers, see Emily Abel, *Hearts of Wisdom: American Women Caring for Kin, 1850–1940* (Cambridge, MA, 2000).
47. Morantz, *Sympathy and Science*, chap. 8.
48. For a portrayal of the impact of such a diagnosis on one woman, see Charlotte Perkins Gilman's dramatic novella, *The Yellow Wallpaper* (1899; repr., New Brunswick, 1993).
49. James Opp, *The Lord for the Body: Religion, Medicine, and Protestant Faith Healing in Canada, 1880–1930* (Montreal, 2005), chap. 2.
50. Ibid., chap. 4.
51. Ibid., chap. 2.
52. Ibid., 37.
53. Ibid., 40.
54. Ibid., 46.
55. Ibid., 43.
56. The birth control movement was a complicated movement, with a rich historiography to match; see for example Linda Gordon, *Woman's Body, Woman's Right: Birth Control in America* (New York, 1990); Rosalind Petchesky, *Abortion and Woman's Choice: The State, Sexuality, and Reproductive Freedom* (Boston, 1990); Ellen Chesler, *Woman of Valor: Margaret Sanger and the Birth Control Movement in America* (New York, 1992); Joanna Schoen, *Choice and Coercion: Birth Control, Sterilization, and Abortion in Public Health and Welfare* (Chapel Hill, NC, 2005); and Carole McCann, *Birth Control Politics in the United States, 1916–1945* (Ithaca, NY, 1994).
57. Smith, *Sick and Tired*.
58. The following account is based on Lynn Y. Weiner, "Reconstructing Motherhood: The La Leche League in Postwar America," *Journal of American History* 80, no. 4 (1994): 1357–81.
59. Indeed, the field of pediatrics had been founded on the discovery of a substitute for mothers' milk that would not make infants ill but instead allow them to thrive; see Naomi Aronson, "Fuel for the Human Machine: The Industrialization of Eating in America" (Ph.D. diss., Brandeis University, 1978). Today, of course, the American Pediatric Association insists that breastfeeding is best for children; see Jodi Kantor, "On the Job, Nursing Mothers Are Finding a Two-Class System," *New York Times*, 1 September 2006, 1.
60. Michelle Murphy, "Immodest Witnessing: The Epistemology of Vaginal Self-Examination in the U.S. Feminist Movement," *Feminist Studies* 30, no. 1 (2004): 115–47; Gordon, *Woman's Body*; and Petchesky, *Abortion*.
61. This would be Boston Women's Health Book Collective, *Our Bodies, Ourselves: A New Edition for a New Era* (New York, 2005). For background on the origins and various early editions, see Sheryl Ruzek, *The Women's Health Movement: Feminist Alternatives to Medical Control* (New York, 1978), 32–33; and Sandra Morgen, *Into Our Own Hands: The Women's Health Movement* (New Brunswick, NJ, 2002), chap. 2.
62. Wendy Kline, "'Please Include This in Your Book': Readers Respond to *Our Bodies, Ourselves*," *Bulletin of the History of Medicine* 79 (2005): 81–110, 87.
63. Anonymous letter, 14 April 1980, quoted in ibid., 91.
64. Response from author Norma Swenson, quoted in ibid., 99.

65. Ibid., 101.
66. Ibid., 101–9.
67. Samantha King, *Pink Ribbons, Inc.: Breast Cancer and the Politics of Philanthropy* (Minneapolis, 2006).
68. Susan Smith notes that there was also overlap between civil rights and mobilization around health issues, particularly for women: "Focusing on health issues permitted black women an authoritative voice in the realm of political organizing" (*Sick and Tired*, 169).
69. Premilla Nadasen, *Welfare Warriors: The Welfare Rights Movement in the United States* (New York, 2005), 137, 178–86.
70. In addition to Nadasen, see Felicia Kornbluh, *The Battle for Welfare Rights: Politics and Poverty in Modern America* (Philadelphia, 2007); Annelise Orleck, *Storming Caesars Palace: How Black Mothers Fought Their Own War on Poverty* (Boston, 2005); Rhonda Y. Williams, *The Politics of Public Housing: Black Women's Struggle Against Urban Inequality* (New York, 2004); and Nancy Naples, *Grassroots Warriors: Activist Mothering, Community Work, and the War on Poverty* (New York, 1998). All of these scholars have built on Guida West's pioneering study *The National Welfare Rights Movement: The Social Protest of Poor Women* (New York 1982).
71. See Wini Breines, *Community and Organization in the New Left, 1962–1968: The Great Refusal* (New York, 1982).
72. Nadasen, *Welfare Warriors*, xv.

Chapter 14

FELLOW FEELING
A TRANSNATIONAL PERSPECTIVE ON CONCEPTIONS OF CIVIL SOCIETY AND CITIZENSHIP IN "WHITE MEN'S COUNTRIES," 1890–1910

Marilyn Lake

In an essay called "Fellow Feeling as a Political Factor" published in the collection *The Strenuous Life* in 1902, the United States president Theodore Roosevelt wrote:

> The fact remains that the only true solution of our political and social problems lies in cultivating everywhere the spirit of brotherhood, of fellow-feeling and understanding between man and man, and the willingness to treat a man as a man, which are the essential factors in American democracy.... The chief factor in producing such sympathy is simply association on a plane of equality.[1]

It was this association between "man and man" on "a plane of equality" that underpinned masculine conceptions of civil society in self-styled "white men's countries" in South Africa, North America and Australasia at the end of the nineteenth century and the beginning of the twentieth century—conceptions whose legacies are with us still. In this chapter, I suggest that between 1890 and 1910, the interrelated ideas of civilization, citizenship, and civil society rested on a sense of "fellow-feeling" that was racialized, as well as gendered, in conception. I suggest that civil society was itself a racialized domain, whose meaning depended on constructions of non-Europeans—whether Blacks, Chinese, Japanese, Hindoos, or Pacific Islanders—as uncivilized and as incapable of assimilation into civil and political society. The historians Gail Bederman and Matthew Jacobson have in different ways shown the ways in which the ideals of white manhood, civilization, and a capacity for self-government were mutually constitutive in the United States during this period, while Elsa Barkley Brown has written of the ways in which the perceived "uncivility" of Black men in the United States became grounds for their civil exclusion. More recently, Mae M. Ngai in her book *Impossible Subjects: Illegal Aliens and the Making of Modern America*, has written that the legal racialization of "Asian Americans" and "Mexican Americans" in the early twentieth century made them "permanently foreign and unassimilable" to the nation of the United States.[2]

However, the "white man" in whose name "white men's countries" were forged was a transnational figure—produced in global discourse and sustained by transnational identifications. In South Africa, Canada, the United States, Australia, and New Zealand, white men's countries followed each other's fortunes with keen interest and sympathy—indeed with fellow feeling. Thus, when President Roosevelt received a letter in early 1908 from the Australian prime minister, Alfred Deakin, inviting the American Fleet to extend its tour of the Pacific by visiting Sydney and Melbourne, he was pleased to go out of his way to accept, as he explained in his autobiography: "It was not originally my intention that the fleet should visit Australia, but the Australian Government sent a most cordial invitation, which I gladly accepted; for I have, as every American ought to have, a hearty admiration for, and fellow feeling with, Australia."[3]

What was the basis of this fellow feeling? When the fleet arrived in Sydney, the premier of New South Wales and Rear Admiral Sperry greeted each other effusively as "white men to white men."[4] Indeed, Admiral Sperry told his no doubt gratified hosts that he regarded Australians as "very white men."[5] In a report of the visit in the New York *Independent*, Sydney journalist W.R. Charlton recalled how Prime Minister Alfred Deakin "in fervid words and trembling with ecstatic passion" had announced the news of the arrival of the fleet to the Australian public. The "unexampled warmth" of the welcome offered to the American sailors was due, Charlton explained, to the fact that "the Americans are our kinsmen, blood of our blood, bone of our bone, and one with us in our ideals of the brotherhood of man."[6]

In analyzing the "public sphere" in which racialized and gendered understandings of citizenship and civil society were formed, we need to move beyond the national analytical frames usually favored by historians. At the same time, however, we must also keep national specificities in view. Citizenship is a state-based status; its reach, rights, and duties were (and are) defined within and by nation-states. To elucidate the different ways in which ideas about citizenship and civil society shaped and were shaped by the public sphere, I suggest we bring both analytical frames—the national and the transnational—into focus. In the first part of this paper, I will give some sense of the transnational conversations that produced and sustained white men's sense of fellow feeling;

in the second part, I will look more closely at the Commonwealth of Australia to suggest the ways in which national specificities produced particular forms of gendered, racialized citizenship. In Australia, with its tradition of "state socialism," the federal government enacted a series of policies designed to secure the status of the (white) male citizen as worker and the (white) woman citizen as mother. Enfranchised in 1902, white women in Australia became exemplary citizens, forming political organizations, leading community associations, holding public meetings, working as activists and lobbyists, and writing for journals of opinion and making radio broadcasts.[7] Increasingly, however, this activism seemed to express a new sexual division of labor, with women occupied in civil society, while men took control of the political sphere. Despite Australian women's early enfranchisement, men monopolized federal government until 1943; until that time women's exercise of citizenship was largely limited to the associations of civil society.[8]

White Men in International Solidarity

An imagined community of white men was produced in transnational conversation between leading intellectual and political figures such as Charles Pearson, James Bryce, Cecil Arthur Spring Rice, Theodore Roosevelt, Edward A. Ross, and Alfred Deakin. Charles Pearson's influential fin de siécle text, *National Life and Character: A Forecast*, published by Macmillan in London and New York in 1893, provided the discursive framework in which much subsequent discussion of changing "world-forces" (Roosevelt's phrase) unfolded.[9] The German Kaiser Wilhelm was so moved by the book he allegedly invented the phrase "the yellow peril."[10] Whereas Pearson's account of the "rise of the Black and Yellow races" challenged Roosevelt to argue for a "vigorous foreign policy" that saw the "cowboy militant" become the popular hero of the day, Australian political leaders, among whom Labor party men and their Liberal allies were prominent, took up a more defensive position, seeking to use the state to secure the status, "in their own homes," of white men as workers and white women as mothers of the race.[11]

In his essay on fellow feeling, Roosevelt was responding to political mobilizations along class lines, which he saw as destructive to the sentiment that sustained what he called "civic helpfulness."[12] The fact remains, however, that the "spirit of brotherhood" he invoked encompassed only white men. At the very time that Roosevelt proclaimed the imperative of treating a man as a man, he was also insisting on the necessity of American rule in the Philippines, where the United States was about to engage in a brutal war (their first Asian land war, as Matthew Jacobson has noted) to defeat Filipinos fighting for their political independence.[13]

The Filipino people, said Roosevelt, invoking Anglo-Saxonist discourse, were not fit for self-government. The population comprised

> half-caste and native Christians, warlike Moslems, and wild pagans. Many of their people are utterly unfit for self-government, and show no signs of becoming fit. Others may in time become fit, but at present can only take part in self-government under a wise supervision, at once firm and beneficent. We have driven Spanish tyranny from the islands. If we now let it be replaced by savage anarchy, our work has been for harm and not for good.[14]

In the Philippines, in other words, because the diverse peoples were deemed uncivilized and therefore unfit for citizenship, there could be no civil society, only "savage anarchy." Unable to govern themselves, Filipinos needed to be ruled by white men—there could be no association with them on a plane of equality.

The declaration of the Spanish-American War saw a spontaneous outburst of "fellow feeling" in Australia. Several hundred men attempted to enlist at American consulates, while women offered to serve as nurses.[15] Theater productions were interrupted by the announcement of hostilities. In Perth, the Cremorne Theater erupted into cheers for America, while the orchestra played "Yankee Doodle," a performance repeated in Adelaide during a production of *A Royal Divorce* when "the audience enthusiastically demonstrated sympathy with the United States."[16] In Sydney, during a production of *The White Squadron*—in which British and American powers combined to put down brigandage on the Brazilian coast—the unfurling of the American flag was "a signal for a great outburst of applause, which lasted several minutes."[17] In Brisbane, as in the other cities, crowds gathered outside newspaper offices, keen to see the latest developments.[18] "Self-government is not an art which comes by nature and instinct to any people," declared the newspaper *The Age* in Melbourne. "It requires training and preparation; and the interests of the world's civilization will demand that neither the Philippines nor Cuba shall be handed over to the unregulated passions of people only a few degrees removed from savagery."[19] The "utter unfitness of the natives for self-government" became a continuing theme of *Age* editorial commentary.[20]

Citizenship, in this Anglo-Saxonist discourse on self-government, was the prerogative of the white man. Civil society was a race-based achievement; the "unregulated passions" of "natives," "negroes," or "savages" could lead only to "savage anarchy."[21] Understandings of white men's and women's citizenship in the white men's countries of the New World were predicated on the racialized relations of colonial rule. Hence the particular character attributes required of white men—in Roosevelt's terms, a capacity for "wise supervision, at once firm and beneficent"—and of white women, fecundity and a capacity for maternal protection.[22]

In the figure of the white man in the New World, the imperialist became a democrat and the democrat an imperialist. For the white man as a New World citizen defined himself not just against "natives," "negroes," and "savages," but also in opposition to the aristocratic Englishman, whose sense of self was constituted in terms of inherited privilege and hierarchical divisions between white men. Theodore Roosevelt, like his counterparts in Australia, bristled at any suggestion of English condescension. When taking his second wife, Edith, on their honeymoon to London, in 1887 (when he met both Cecil Arthur Spring Rice and James Bryce), he was careful never to give any impression of deference to the English ruling class. He confided to his friend Henry Cabot Lodge: "Edith, thank Heaven, feels as I do, and is even more intensely anti-Anglomaniac; and I really think our utter indifference, and our standing sharply on our dignity, have been among the main causes that have procured us so hospitable a reception."[23] And when he met Rudyard Kipling at dinner parties in Washington in the early 1890s, he took offense at the imperial poet's superior attitude towards Americans: "Kipling is an underbred little fellow," Roosevelt wrote to his sister Anna in 1894, "with a tendency to criticize America to which I put a stop by giving him a very rough handling, since which he has not repeated the offense."[24]

White men of the New World—in South Africa, North America, and Australia—thus identified most strongly with one another and looked to each other for models of racial exclusion and segregation. In the United States, Canada, Australia, and New Zealand, policies of exclusion initially focused on the Chinese, who were depicted as incapable of assimilation as citizens. The joint committee investigating Chinese immigration in the United States in 1877 concluded that the Chinese didn't have "sufficient brain capacity ... to furnish the motive power for self-government."[25] The United States passed an Exclusion Act in 1882. Two years later, British Columbia passed a law "to regulate the Chinese population" in view of the fact that they were

> not disposed to be governed by our laws; are dissimilar in habits and occupation from our people; evade the payment of taxes justly due to the Government; are governed by pestilential habits; are useless in instances of emergency; habitually desecrate graveyards by the removal of bodies therefrom, and generally the laws governing the whites are found to be inapplicable to Chinese; and such Chinese are inclined to habits subversive of the comfort and well-being of the community.[26]

With their "pestilential" and subversive "habits" and uselessness in cases of emergency, Chinese were not considered capable of the duties of citizenship or participation in citizenship's domain, civil society.

American Blacks were also deemed incapable of citizenship, and in the decades following Reconstruction were all but excluded from the white public domain. Historian John Cell, in his study of the origins of segregation in South Africa, has pointed to the importance of the American example of segregation to South African nation builders. He has also noted the significance of James Bryce's book *The American Commonwealth*, first published in 1888, in circulating knowledge about race relations in the United States among English-speaking peoples everywhere.[27] Bryce had researched his book on trips to the United States in 1870, 1881, and 1883–84. Of freed Blacks, he wrote: "Emancipation found them utterly ignorant; and the grant of the suffrage found them as unfit for political rights as any population could be."[28]

Certainly *The American Commonwealth* was a key text for the Australian Convention delegates meeting throughout the 1890s to frame a constitution for the proposed Commonwealth of Australia, a name chosen, according to the first prime minister Edmund Barton, in honor of Bryce's book. The first edition, published in 1888, dealt at length with the legacy of racial violence that had followed the Civil War in the United States, and in the second edition, which appeared in 1895, he added four new chapters including "The Present and Future of the Negro" and "The South Since the War."[29] In the later edition of his book, Bryce gave more emphasis to white racial hatred and lynchings "accompanied by revolting cruelty." "There can be no doubt," he wrote, "that the practice of lynching has a pernicious effect on the whites themselves, accustoming them to cruelty and fostering a spirit of lawlessness which tells for evil on every branch of government and public life."[30] Bryce's account drew on the emergent historiography on the "failed experiment" of Radical Reconstruction. One of his main sources was John W. Burgess, founder of the political science department at Columbia University and author of the influential text, *Political Science and Comparative Constitutional Law*, who argued famously that nations had a right to expel "ethnically hostile elements."[31] Citizenship and civil society, the authorities agreed, rested on racial homogeneity.

Australian radicals and liberals, such as Andrew I. Clark, Henry B. Higgins, and Alfred Deakin, were vocal in their admiration for what they saw as the manly republic of the United States, even as they deplored its racial problems. But because their own sense of independent manhood was compromised by their continuing status as colonial subjects, Australians felt a particular need to emphasize their racial identity as white men and thus as members of the "ruling race." In 1906, Alfred Deakin in an article on "White Australia" endorsed New Zealand Prime Minister Richard Seddon's view that the British empire, "though united in one whole, is, nevertheless, divided broadly into two parts, one occupied wholly or mainly by a white ruling race, the other principally occupied by colored races who are ruled. Australia and New Zealand are determined to keep their place in the first class. And in order to secure their pride of place agree in putting racial purity before economic gain."[32] To further secure their "pride of place," white men's countries all emphasized (white) women's primary vocation as mothers of the race. In the United States, Roosevelt became a convert to the importance of fertility rates—and thus motherhood—for racial vigor after reading Charles Pearson's *National Life and Character: A Forecast*, which he reviewed at length in the *Sewanee Review* in 1894, an essay republished in 1897 as the chapter "National Life and Character" in his collection *American Ideals*, dedicated to his friend and ardent Anglo-Saxonist, Henry Cabot Lodge. In his review, Roosevelt hailed *National Life and Character* as

> one of the most notable books of the end of the century. ... No one can read this book without feeling his thinking powers greatly stimulated; without being forced to ponder problems of which he was previously wholly ignorant, or which he but half understood; and without realizing that he is dealing with the work of a man of ... deep and philosophic insight into the world-forces of the present.[33]

One of those "world-forces" was the decline of the European birthrate, a problem that greatly stimulated Roosevelt's "thinking powers."

Charles Pearson was a former professor of modern history at King's College, London, who in the early 1870s migrated to the Australian colonies. Initially, he took up a lectureship at the University of Melbourne, where he formed a debating society that recruited two future political leaders and architects of the White Australia policy, Alfred Deakin and Henry B. Higgins. Pearson played a leading role in the colony of Victoria as a radical reformer, journalist, and headmaster of a progressive girls' school, Presbyterian Ladies College. Elected as a Liberal member to the Victorian parliament, he entered the cabinet as minister for education.

As Pearson noted in the introduction to *National Life and Character,* "twenty years' residence under the Southern Cross" had afforded him a new historical perspective on world events. His assessment of "world forces" caused a sensation, in particular his twin predictions that English-speaking peoples were entering a "stationary state," while the "Black and Yellow races" were coming into their own as the dynamic agents of world history. "With civilization equally diffused," wrote Pearson, "the most populous country must ultimately be the most powerful; and the preponderance of China over any rival—even over the United States of America—is likely to be overwhelming."[34] The future would see China take "its inevitable position as one of the great powers of the world."[35]

Pearson was a prophet of decolonization, imagining a future in which once colonized and subordinated peoples would form independent nations, build their own navies, control their own commerce, and be accepted as equals in international relations. "The day will come," he wrote in a passage quoted by the first Australian prime minister, Edmund Barton, in the federal parliament in 1901, and perhaps is not far distant, when the European observer will look round to see the globe girdled with a continuous zone of the black and yellow races, no longer too weak for aggression or under tutelage, but independent, or practically so, in government, monopolizing the trade of their own regions, and circumscribing the industry of the Europeans; ... represented by fleets in the European seas, invited to international conferences and welcomed as allies in quarrels of the civilized world....We shall wake to find ourselves elbowed and hustled, and perhaps even thrust aside by peoples whom we looked down upon as servile and thought of as bound always to minister to our needs. The solitary consolation will be that the changes have been inevitable.[36]

As a radical liberal who advocated democratic reform, free secular education, state socialism, and women's emancipation, Pearson regarded these developments as "inevitable." But as a white colonial, whose subjective sense of self was constituted through "feelings of caste," Pearson also thought that white men's "pride of place" in the world would be "humiliated."[37] For the "Englishman," he noted, "enjoys the prestige of a dominant race."[38]

Pearson's argument about the future power of India and China shocked readers everywhere. He asked his readers to imagine "a condition of political society" in which the peoples of "China, Malaysia, India, Central Africa and Tropical America" were "teeming with life, developed by industrial enterprise, fairly well administered by native governments, and owning the better part of the carrying trade of the world."[39] The Chinese, like the British, were taking advantage of the technologies of modern mobility. The cheapness of steamship travel meant that they had long been engaged in a process of peaceful expansion into Southeast Asia, Australasia, the Americas, and the islands of the Pacific. Chinese and Indians, Pearson suggested, should be regarded as dynamic historical agents, actively engaged in transforming the modern world.

Clearly, the novelty of Pearson's perspective on world history owed much to his residence in the Australian colonies, twelve thousand miles from Britain, but close to Southeast Asia. One of the more perceptive reviews of *National Life and Character*, in the *Athenaeum*, noted the significance of Pearson's migration to the New World:

> The forecast will take many by surprise, because the view it presents is not only not fashionable, but is fundamentally different from that to which we have been accustomed since "progress" became a catchword among us.... In another respect, too, he quits the beaten track of anticipation. His view is not purely or mainly European, nor does he regard the inferior races as hopelessly beaten in the struggle with Western civilization. The reader can indeed discern that Mr. Pearson's point of view is not London or Paris, but Melbourne. He regards the march of affairs from the Australian point of view, and next to Australia what he seems to see most clearly is the growth of Chinese power and of the native populations of Africa. In this forecast, in fact, Europe loses altogether the precedence it has always enjoyed. It appears here as not only the smallest, but as the least important continent.[40]

From Pearson's standpoint in the South Pacific, Europe had, indeed, become marginal to key developments in world history. China, on the other hand, contrary to its conventional image as despotic and decadent, was a dynamic, expansive, and industrious nation of four hundred million people.

When Roosevelt read *National Life and Character*, he wrote personally to Pearson to tell him of the "great effect" of his work on men in Washington: "All our men here in Washington … were greatly interested in what you said. In fact, I don't suppose that any book recently, unless it is Mahan's *Influence of Sea Power* has excited anything like as much interest or has caused so many men to feel that they had to revise their mental estimates of facts."[41] Many of those facts concerned relative birth rates, tracked by Pearson with census figures, which showed stagnating European populations, the expansion of the Chinese, and the fact that in Natal and the Cape Colony, Blacks were gaining on whites. With "competition between the races reducing itself to the warfare of the cradle," Roosevelt wrote in his review, "no race has any chance to win a great place unless it consists of good breeders as well as of good fighters."[42]

Roosevelt would thereafter become a leading champion of "good breeders." "The woman must be the housewife, the helpmeet of the homemaker, the wise and fearless mother of many healthy children," he wrote in *The Strenuous Life*. "When men fear work or fear righteous war, when women fear motherhood, they tremble on the brink of doom."[43] It was the noted American sociologist Edward A. Ross, however, also influenced by Pearson, who, in his address to the annual meeting of the American Academy of Social and Political Science in 1901, would give a name to the problem of declining birth rates: "race suicide."[44]

Roosevelt saw Australian and American destinies as intertwined. In his own work of history, *The Winning of the West*, he had argued that Australia and the United States shared the same "race history" and drew parallels between American and Australian processes of settlement in the New World. As an ardent spokesperson for English-speaking peoples, and following English historian Edward A. Freeman, he located their common origins in the "great Teutonic wanderings" of many centuries before. The settlement of Australia and America were, he argued, key events in world history: "When these continents were settled they contained the largest tracts of fertile, temperate, thinly peopled country on the face of the globe. We cannot rate too highly the importance of their acquisition. Their successful settlement was a feat, which by comparison utterly dwarfs all the European wars of the last two centuries."[45]

Roosevelt would return to the significance of the white settlement of Australia in his review of Pearson's book: "Nineteenth century democracy needs no more complete vindication for its existence than the fact that is has kept for the white race the best portions of the new worlds' surface, temperate America and Australia."[46] British historians, he charged, had for the most part not grasped the importance of Australia, thinking the acquisition of India more important, "yet, from the standpoint of the ages, the peopling of the great island-continent with men of the English stock is a thousand fold more important than the holding [sic] Hindoostan for a few centuries."[47]

English-speaking peoples, he wrote in *The Winning of the West*, were especially gifted as colonizers: "The kind of colonizing conquest, whereby the people of the United States have extended their borders, has much in common with similar movements in Canada and Australia, all of them standing in sharp contrast to what has gone on in Spanish-American lands." The Spanish, Roosevelt would later charge, when determining to eject them from Cuba, were fit only to exercise "medieval tyranny," lacking the manly qualities such as honor, probity, and restraint necessary to self-government and the government of others.[48]

In letters to his friend, the English diplomat, Cecil Arthur Spring Rice at the end of the 1890s, Roosevelt reiterated his view of Australia as the world's great white hope. In 1899, responding to Spring Rice's concern about the British losing India, he wrote:

> To you India seems larger than Australia. In the life history of the English-speaking peoples I think it will show very much smaller. The Australians are building up a giant commonwealth, the very existence of which, like the existence of the United States, means an alteration in the balance of the world & goes a long way towards ensuring the supremacy of the men who speak our tongue & have our ideas of social, political & religious freedom & morality.[49]

And in 1901, the year of the inauguration of the Commonwealth of Australia as a nation-state and, as it happened, his own inauguration as United States president, Roosevelt reiterated his faith in Australian vigor. "I do not wonder that you sometimes feel depressed over the future both of our race & of our civilization," he wrote to Spring Rice.

> There are many reasons why one should be, although I think there are also many reasons why one should not be.... Still I should be a fool if I did not see grave cause for anxiety in some of the social tendencies of the day: the growth of luxury throughout the English speaking world; & especially the gradual diminishing birth rate.... Nevertheless, the settlement of North America & of Australasia goes on & the remaining waste places of the two continents will be practically occupied in our lifetime.... In spite of all the unhealthy signs in this country, I still see ample evidence of abounding vigor. There is certainly such vigor in Australia.[50]

The main lesson Roosevelt, Bryce, and Ross and their counterparts in Australia took from Pearson was the necessity to defend the temperate lands of South Africa, North America, and Australasia as "white man's country." Both white men's land and labor needed to be defended against expansionist "Asiatics" because, as Ross noted, they were not disposed to "assimilate to us or adopt our standards."[51] Or as the first Australian prime minister, Edmund Barton, said, when justifying the expulsion of Pacific Islanders from Australia, they did not understand the contracts that underpinned civil society and thus white men could not deal with them man to man. There could be no association on a plane of equality.

American History Lessons Down Under: The Inauguration of White Australia

In 1901, the Commonwealth of Australia was inaugurated in an act of racial expulsion, when the first federal parliament legislated to expel Pacific Islanders, who had been brought to labor in the sugar cane fields of north Queensland during the preceding decades. Both James Bryce and Charles Pearson in their commentaries on the United States had reported discussions there about the feasibility of deporting Blacks—numbering more than eight million people by the late nineteenth century—to Africa. There were two fatal objections to the proposal according to Bryce: "One is that they will not go; the other that the whites cannot afford to let them go."[52] In *National Life and Character,* Pearson had written: "The most reasonable proposal yet made for [solving the Negro problem] has been to remove the blacks in a body, and plant them again in Central Africa. To carry out this proposal, however, in an equitable and humane way, would mean an expenditure of many hundred millions; a sum so vast that ... even the United States might well demur to the cost."[53]

In deporting the few thousand Islanders back to the Pacific islands, Australians would do what the United States could not. The Australian Commonwealth determined to learn from the American republic, and the main lesson they imbibed was the impossibility of a multiracial democracy. Bryce had called the "race problem" in the United States "a new one in history, for the relations of the ruling and subject races of Europe and Asia supply no parallel to it."[54] In the first Australian parliament, Henry B. Higgins, Liberal "friend of labor" and future president of the Australian Court of Conciliation and Arbitration, echoed these sentiments and emphasized the importance of heeding American experience: "We have only to look at the great difficulty which is being experienced in America in connexion with the greatest racial trouble ever known in the history of the world, in order to take warning and guard ourselves against similar complications."[55]

The legislation to deport Pacific Islanders was, Higgins declared, "the most vitally important measure on the program which the government has put before us." Its significance lay in the fact that it addressed the question of whether "northern Australia should be peopled by white men or not. I feel convinced that people who are used to a high standard of life—to good wages and good conditions—will not consent to labor alongside men who receive a miserable pittance and who are dealt with very much in the same way as slaves."[56] In speaking in support of the legislation, Prime Minister Barton spoke of the impossibility of bridging the gulf between the "white man" and the Pacific Islander:

> The difference in intellectual level and the difference in knowledge of the ways of the world between the white man and the Pacific Islander is one, which cannot be bridged by acts or regulations about agreements. The level of the one is above that of the other, the difference being one in human mental stature—of character as well as mind—which cannot be put aside by passing 50 laws or 1000 regulations.[57]

Pacific Islanders did not have the capacity to enter into contracts, declared Barton, and thus could not participate as equals in civil society and democratic government.

The complement to the Pacific Islands Laborers Act was the Immigration Restriction Act: "The two things go hand in hand," declared Attorney General Alfred Deakin, "and are the necessary complement of a single policy—the policy of securing a 'white Australia.'" The matter caused Deakin "so much anxiety" because it spoke to "the profoundest instinct of individual or nation—the instinct of self-preservation for it is nothing less than the national manhood, the national character and the national future that are at stake."[58] The Immigration Restriction Act provided for a dictation test as a ruse for excluding nonwhites from settling in Australia. Many Australian politicians would have preferred to name racial origin explicitly as the basis for exclusion, but were persuaded against this by the Colonial Office, which argued that the desired object could be achieved without giving offence to other British subjects, such as Indians and Chinese. The "Natal precedent" was cited by Joseph Chamberlain in his advice to the Australian premiers, and by many historians since, but in fact the idea of an education or literacy test as a means of effecting racial exclusion was first enacted in Mississippi in 1890, to disenfranchise Blacks, and subsequently, in United States immigration legislation (ultimately vetoed) in 1896. Natal's legislation of 1897 was, the South Africans said, "founded on the American Act."[59]

Mississippi set the precedent for white men around the world by introducing an education test—specifically a literacy test—to disenfranchise Blacks. The legislation stated that a voter "shall be able to read any section of the Constitution, or be able to understand the same when read to him, or to give a reasonable interpretation thereof." In *The American Commonwealth*, Bryce remarked of the American example: "The advantages of such a method are obvious, and have suggested its adoption in a British colony where the presence of a large colored population has raised a problem not dissimilar to that we have been examining" and referred to the Cape Colony Franchise and Ballot Act of 1892.[60]

Alfred Deakin, attorney-general and chief architect of the White Australia Act, also made explicit reference in the first federal parliament of 1901 to American history "lessons": "We should be false to the lessons taught us in the great republic of the west; we should be false to the never-to-be-forgotten teachings from the experience of the United States, of difficulties only partially conquered by the blood of their best and bravest; we should be absolutely blind to and unpardonable neglectful of our obligations, if we fail to lay those lessons to heart."[61] And congratulating the "federal fathers" (of whom he was one) for making constitutional provision to deal with the "difficulty in all its aspects," Deakin advised the federal parliament:

> Our Constitution marks a distinct advance upon and difference from that of the United States, in that it contains within itself the amplest powers to deal with this difficulty in all its aspects. It is not merely a question of invasion from the exterior. It may be a question of difficulties within our borders, already created, or a question of possible contamination of another kind. I doubt if there can be found in the list of powers with which this Parliament, on behalf of the people, is endowed—powers of legislation—a cluster more important and more far reaching in their prospect than the provisions contained in subsections (26) to (30) of section 51, in which the bold outline of the authority of the people of Australia for their self-protection is laid down.[62]

In their commentary on section 51, constitutional authorities Quick and Garran pointed out that whereas the United States in dealing with the "race problem" had to take into account the "special inhibitions" of the Fourteenth Amendment, which offered its citizens "equal protection," Australia had armed itself with the power to pass "special laws" against particular racial groups.[63]

Workers as "Civilized Beings," Women as Mothers of the Race

Conceptions of citizenship and civil society in White Australia—and the sexual differentiation of citizenship that saw men positioned as workers and women as mothers of the race—were crucially shaped by the racialized formation of Australia as a white man's country. Central to the project of White Australia was the goal of securing the status of the white working man as a "civilized being" living in "a civilized community," and the key figure in articulating and achieving this goal was Henry B. Higgins, Liberal member of parliament in 1901, and from 1906, president of the Commonwealth Court of Conciliation and Arbitration. An ardent supporter of the Pacific Islands Laborers Act and the Immigration Restriction Act, Higgins accepted the appointment as attorney general in the first and short-lived Labor government of 1904, and then as judge on the Conciliation and Arbitration Court in 1907, was called upon to define what constituted a "fair and reasonable wage" for Australian workers. The decision arose from an application by H. V. McKay, a manufacturer of agricultural machinery, including the Sunshine Harvester (after which the judgment would be known) for exemption from excise duties under the Excise Tariff Act of 1906 on the ground that the employer paid his employees a "fair and reasonable wage."[64]

In Australia, tariff protection for manufacturers was linked to the requirement that they pay their workers a prescribed level of wages, an arrangement known as the New Protection. It fell to Higgins, in 1907, to determine the meaning of a "fair and reasonable" wage, which he did by invoking the standards of "civilized" men. In 1901, he had told parliament: "We do not want men beside us who are not as exacting in their demands on civilization as ourselves."[65] In the 1907 Harvester judgment, Justice Higgins laid down that in determining what constituted a "fair and reasonable" wage, the "first and dominant factor" was the cost of living of "a civilized being" "living in a civilized community"—redefining civilization in terms of the white standard of living.[66]

After surveying a range of evidence, some of it submitted by workers' wives, Higgins determined that the minimum living wage for an unskilled laborer should be set at seven shillings a day or two pounds, two shillings a week for a six-day week. He also made it clear, in this and subsequent judgments, that life as a civilized man entailed marriage and children, hence the male worker would need to be paid sufficient to maintain his dependents—his ability to support a wife and children also defined his white manhood. Higgins based his calculation of the worker's needs on the cost of living for a household of "about five people." As dependents, women workers would be paid a lesser wage—set at 54 percent of the male wage—thus ensuring their continued dependence.

The determination of a minimum wage did not just reward manhood, however; it empowered *white* manhood. Aboriginal men were not awarded equal pay until the 1960s, while federal and state legislation and industrial awards barred Chinese, Afghan, Indian, and Islander men from entering a range of designated occupations. In defining the Australian worker as "a civilized being" "living in a civilized community," the Harvester judgment both signaled that Australia was to be a "white man's country" and offered a new definition of civilization centered not on antiquity, culture, or heritage, but on the white working man's standard of living. This judgment was the hallmark of Australia's version of a civil society. The Harvester judgment represented a radical rebuff to employers and the champions of business, who argued that wages should be determined by productivity or industry's capacity to pay. Defining human need as the central wage-fixing criterion, they predicted, would bring the country to economic ruin. The importance of Higgins' intervention has been widely recognized in Australian historiography. As leading historian F. K. Crowley wrote: "No judicial decision roused greater interest in the first decade of federation.... None had such long-term significance." The principles of Higgins' Harvester judgment, wrote historian Stuart Macintyre, "became a fundamental feature of national life."[67]

A range of racial discriminations affecting political, civil, and economic rights permeated the Australian public sphere. In 1901, the Federal Post and Telegraph Act specified that only "white" labor could be employed in the carriage of mails across the seas. The Commonwealth Franchise Act of 1902, which extended the federal vote to all white women, specifically denied it to the majority of Aboriginal Australians. It also excluded "natives" of Asia, Africa, and the Pacific Islands, unless they were already enfranchised under earlier colonial legislation. The Naturalization Act of 1903 said that no aboriginal native of Asia, Africa, or the Islands of the Pacific, except New Zealand, could apply for a certificate of naturalization. Queensland state legislation prevented Asians, Africans, and Polynesians from holding mining licenses or land leases. Factory legislation in all states specifically discriminated against Chinese.[68]

Social security legislation was also explicitly discriminatory. The Old Age and Invalid Pensions Act of 1908 excluded "Asiatics" unless they were born in Australia, as well as Aboriginal natives of Australia, Africa, the Islands of the Pacific, and New Zealand. The Maternity Allowance Act of 1912, which shocked conservative opinion by including unmarried mothers, confirmed the general trend toward the racialization of citizenship by denying the allowance to "women who are Asiatics, or who are aboriginal natives of Australia, Papua, or the islands of the Pacific."[69] While white motherhood was encouraged by public discourse and economic support, Aboriginal mothers were considered ineligible for motherhood and had their children systematically removed by state authorities under legislation that remained in place for several decades.

Australian feminists, enfranchised in 1902, mobilized with considerable success to claim economic and social rights for white mothers as maternal citizens and secured appointment to the whole range of civic offices as doctors, police officers, magistrates, welfare workers, factory inspectors, prison wardens, and justices of the peace. The Maternity Allowance was introduced by a Labor government in response to lobbying by Labor women. They were proud of their achievement—especially the extension of the payment to include unmarried mothers—which they interpreted as an "installment of the mother's maternal rights." Labor women, like the men in their party, supported the racial discrimination in the act, but some nonparty feminists were critical and opposed racial discrimination, invoking motherhood as a universal condition. "This exclusion is supposed to be part of the White Australia policy," said the Women's Political Association in Melbourne, "but surely it is the White Australia policy gone mad. Maternity is maternity whatever the race."[70]

It is nevertheless clear that it was the racial significance of motherhood that enabled feminists to speak with a powerful political voice in the early decades of the twentieth century and to win a number of significant reforms in the name of their maternal citizenship.[71] Significantly, however, they were unsuccessful in their most radical goal of securing an independent income for mothers in the form of motherhood endowments paid by the state. The challenge to men's economic and domestic power posed by the claim for an individual income for mothers was seen to be "revolutionary" and ultimately rejected as such.[72] The discourse on maternal citizenship empowered women, but it also locked them more firmly into an identity as mothers, which made it harder for them to realize professional careers of the sort envisaged in the 1880s by Charles Pearson, as headmaster of Presbyterian Ladies College and champion of higher education for women. In alerting people to a declining birth rate, Pearson had unwittingly prepared the ground for an alarmist campaign about "race suicide," one of whose leaders in Australia was the New South Wales politician, Dr Richard Arthur, who, in an ironic example of the global circulation of knowledge, took his cue from the tirades issuing from across the Pacific from Theodore Roosevelt, who had first been alerted to the "warfare of the cradle" in 1894 when he read Pearson's account in *National Life and Character*. And it was Richard Arthur who suggested to Prime Minister Deakin in 1907 that he should invite the American Fleet to visit Australia.

Conclusion

As a derivative of the concept of "civilization," the idea of civil society was shaped in the race relations of colonialism and reshaped by "white men's countries" intent on preserving the white male standard of living and white men's rule. In the immigrant countries of South Africa, North America, and Australasia, claimed as "white men's countries" in the wake of Pearson's "epoch-making book" *National Life and Character*, those peoples deemed nonwhite—Chinese, Blacks, Indians, Japanese, and Pacific Islanders—were excluded on the grounds that they did not share the attitudes, customs, habits, and traditions of civilized peoples necessary for engagement in civil society. When the Chinese, Indians, and Japanese pointed to their own proud civilizations, the Anglo-Saxonists of the New World insisted that civilization be understood in terms of a tradition of self-government and increasingly, a commitment to a "civilized" standard of living. In the name of civilization and the requirements of civil society, other races were excluded, expelled, marginalized, or segregated.

The racialized requirements of civil society also saw the gendering of citizenship, with white women positioned as mothers of the race (and nonwhite mothers deemed ineligible for motherhood allowances) and white men positioned as soldiers and workers. In Australia, enfranchised women mobilized in their capacity as mothers—as active participants in civil society—to achieve recognition for their rights as maternal citizens.

When Australian men mobilized in their capacity as workers, they achieved direct representation in politics, through their own Labor party, in the state and federal governments. In the Commonwealth of Australia, with its tradition of "state socialism" and its valorization of the working man, White Australia worked primarily to secure white men's status as workers, defined significantly as "civilized beings living in a civilized community," in terms that excluded nonwhite working men. In this sense, the Harvester judgment that enshrined the living wage was at once the keystone of the White Australia policy and of white working men's status as citizens.

Notes

1. Theodore Roosevelt, "Fellow Feeling as a Political Factor," in *The Strenuous Life* (London, 1902), 71.
2. Gail Bederman, *Manliness and Civilization: A Cultural History of Gender and Race in the United States, 1880–1917* (Chicago, 1995); Matthew Frye Jacobson, *Whiteness of a Different Color: European Immigrants and the Alchemy of Race* (Cambridge, MA, 1998); Elsa Barkley Brown, "Negotiating and Transforming the Public Sphere: African American Political Life in the Transition from Slavery to Freedom," in *The Black Public Sphere*, ed. The Black Public Sphere Collective (Chicago, London, 1995), 144; Mae M. Ngai, *Impossible Subjects: Illegal Aliens and the Making of Modern America* (Princeton, NJ and London, 2004), 8.
3. Theodore Roosevelt, *An Autobiography* (New York, 1913), 598.
4. *Age*, 27 August 1908, Melbourne, Australia.
5. Ibid.
6. W. R. Charlton, "The Australian Welcome to the Fleet," *Independent*, 8 October 1908: 813, 815.
7. Marilyn Lake, *Getting Equal: The History of Australian Feminism* (Sydney, 1999), 139–42.
8. Australian women were elected to state legislatures from 1921, when Edith Cowan won a seat in the Western Australian parliament.
9. See Theodore Roosevelt, "National Life and Character" in *American Ideals and Other Essays Social and Political* (New York, 1897); Edward A. Ross, "The Causes of Race Superiority," *Annals of the American Academy of Political and Social Science* 18 (1901); Lawrence E. Neame, *The Asiatic Danger in the Colonies* (London, 1907); "Viator" (Anon.), "Asia Contra Mundum," *Fortnightly Review* 1 (February 1908); Seetsele Molema, *The Bantu: Past and Present. An Ethnographical and Historical Study of the*

Native Races of South Africa (Edinburgh, 1920); Lothrop Stoddard, *The Rising Tide of Color Against White World-Supremacy* (New York, 1923); Thomas G. Dyer, *Theodore Roosevelt and the Idea of Race* (Baton Rouge, LA, 1980), 11; Richard Hofstadter, *Social Darwinism in American Thought* (New York, 1965), 185–86; Akira Iriye, *Pacific Estrangement Japanese and American Expansionism, 1897–1911* (Cambridge, 1972), 29–31.
10. David Walker, "Race Building and the Disciplining of White Australia." in *Legacies of White Australia Race, Culture and Nation*, ed. Laksiri Jayasuriya et al. (Perth, 2003), 42, 45.
11. Charles Pearson, *National Life and Character: A Forecast* (London, 1893); for Roosevelt as "cowboy militant" see: *Age*, 18 November 1898; on men protecting themselves in "their own homes," see Roosevelt, "National Life and Character."
12. Theodore Roosevelt, "Civic Helpfulness" in *Strenuous Life*, 98–121.
13. Matthew Frye Jacobson, *Barbarian Virtues: The United States Encounters Foreign Peoples at Home and Abroad, 1876–1917* (New York, 2000), 264.
14. Roosevelt, "The Strenuous Life," in *The Strenuous Life* (London, 1902), 9.
15. *Age*, 22 April 1898.
16. Ibid., 25 April 1898.
17. Ibid., 25 April 1898.
18. Ibid., 25 April 1898.
19. *Age*, 25 July 1898.
20. See, for example, *Age*, 29 November and 6 December 1898.
21. Roosevelt, "The Strenuous Life," 9.
22. Ibid.
23. Theodore Roosevelt to Henry Cabot Lodge, 28 June 1898, in *The Letters of Theodore Roosevelt*, ed. Elting E. Morrison (Cambridge, 1951).
24. Roosevelt to Anna Roosevelt, 1 April 1894, in ibid.
25. Jacobson, *Whiteness of a Different Color*, 159.
26. Charles Lucas, "The Self-Governing Dominions and Coloured Immigration," CO 886/1/1, 7 UK National Archives. See also Robert H. Huttenback, *Racism and Empire: White Settlers and Colored Immigrants in the British Self-Governing Colonies 1830–1910* (Ithaca, NY, 1976), 130–36.
27. John W. Cell, *The Highest Stage of White Supremacy: The Origins of Segregation in South Africa and the American South* (New York, 1982), 23.
28. James Bryce, *The American Commonwealth*, 1st ed. (London, 1888), vol. 3: 92.
29. Ibid., 2nd ed. (London, 1895), vol. 1: 469–90, 491–521.
30. Ibid., 3rd ed. (London, 1900), vol. 2: 507.
31. See Hugh Tulloch, *James Bryce's American Commonwealth: The Anglo-American Background* (London, 1988); for Australian constitutional authorities' use of Burgess, see Marilyn Lake, "White Man's Country: The Trans-National History of a National Project," *Australian Historical Studies* 34, no. 122 (2003): 358.
32. Alfred Deakin, *Morning Post* 17 July 1906, in *Federated Australia: Selections from Letters to the Morning Post, 1900–1910*, ed. John. A. LaNauze (Melbourne, 1968), 185.
33. Roosevelt, "National Life and Character," 271. Thomas Dyer noted Pearson's impact on Roosevelt in *Theodore Roosevelt and the Idea of Race* (Baton Rouge, LA, London, 1980): "The Australian author's book was the rage in the intellectual circles during which Roosevelt moved during 1894 and 1895" (11). Other historians, such as Gail Bederman in *Manliness and Civilization* and Gary Gerstle in *American Crucible Race and Nation in the Twentieth Century* (Princeton, NJ, 2001), confining their analysis of Roosevelt to a national frame, have failed to recognize the transnational intellectual world—and the imagined community of white men—in which Roosevelt's preoccupation with virile manhood and imperial power took shape.

34. Pearson, *National Life and Character,* 137ff.
35. Ibid., 52.
36. Ibid., 89ff.
37. Ibid., 89ff.
38. Ibid., 219.
39. Ibid., 138
40. *Athenaeum,* 4 March 1893.
41. Roosevelt to Pearson, 11 May 1894, Pearson papers, Bodleian Library, Oxford, MS, English Letters, D 190. See also Marilyn Lake, "The White Man under Siege: New Histories of Race in the Nineteenth Century and the Advent of White Australia," *History Workshop Journal* 58 (2004): 41–62.
42. Roosevelt, *American Ideals,* 293–94.
43. Roosevelt, *Strenuous Life,* 2.
44. Ross, "The Causes of Race Superiority," 88.
45. Theodore Roosevelt, *The Winning of the West* (New York, 1888–99), vol. 1: 14.
46. Roosevelt, "National Life and Character," 289.
47. Ibid., 281.
48. Roosevelt, "The Strenuous Life," 9.
49. Roosevelt to Cecil Arthur Spring Rice, 11 August 1899, in Morrison, *Letters,* vol.2.
50. Roosevelt to Cecil Arthur Spring Rice, 16 March 1901, in Morrison, *Letters,* vol.2.
51. Ross, *Causes of Race Superiority,* 81.
52. Bryce, *American Commonwealth,* 3rd ed., vol. 2: 514f.
53. Pearson, *National Life and Character,* 11.
54. Bryce, *American Commonwealth,* 3rd ed., vol. 1: 514.
55. *Commonwealth Parliamentary Debates (CPD),* 6 September 1901, 4659.
56. Ibid., 3 October 1901, 6815–19.
57. Ibid., 6815. See also: Marilyn Lake, "On Being a White Man," in *Cultural History in Australia,* ed. Hsu Ming Teo and Richard White (Sydney, 2003).
58. *CPD,* House of Representatives, 12 September 1901, 4804, 4806.
59. Marilyn Lake, "From Mississippi to Melbourne: The Literacy Test as an Instrument of Racial Exclusion," in *Connected Worlds History in Trans-National Perspective,* ed. Lake and Ann Curthoys (Canberra, 2006).
60. Bryce, *American Commonwealth,* 3rd ed., vol. 2: 511.
61. *CPD,* 12 September 1901, 4806.
62. Ibid., 4806.
63. Lake, "White Man's Country," 358.
64. *Commonwealth Arbitration Courts* (CAR) vol. 11, 1907–08, Ex-Parte HV McKay, 3–4.
65. *CPD,* 20 September 1901.
66. *CAR,* vol. 11, 1907–08, Ex-Parte H.V. McKay, 3–4.
67. Francis K. Crowley, *A New History of Australia* (Melbourne, 1974), 284; Stuart Macintyre, *A Concise History of Australia* (Melbourne, 2002), 151.
68. "Discrimination against Persons of Non-European Race in Australia," paper prepared in the Pacific Branch, Prime Minister's Department, for First Assembly, League of Nations, 1920, 6, 7. National Archives of Australia, A 10356/1.
69. Marilyn Lake and Katie Holmes. eds., *Freedom Bound II: Documents on Women in Modern Australia* (Sydney, 1995), 5.
70. Ibid., 7.
71. Marilyn Lake, "Colonized and Colonizing: The White Australian Feminist Subject," *Women's History Review* 2, no. 3 (1993): 377–86; Lake, "Between Old Worlds and New: Feminist Citizenship, Nation and Race, the Destabilisation of Identity" in *Suffrage and Beyond International Feminist Perspectives,* ed. Caroline Daley and Mela-

nie Nolan (Auckland, 1994); Lake, "Between Old World 'Barbarism' and 'Stone Age Primitivism': The Double Difference of the White Australian Feminist Subject," in *Australian Women: Contemporary Feminist Thought*, ed. Norma Grieve and Alisa Burns (Melbourne, 1994); Patricia Grimshaw, "A White Woman's Suffrage," in *A Woman's Constitution? Gender and History in the Australian Commonwealth*, ed. Helen Irving (Sydney, 1996); Grimshaw, "Gender, Citizenship and Race in the Woman's Christian Temperance Union of Australia, 1890–1930s," *Australian Feminist Studies* 13, no. 28 (1998): 199–214; Grimshaw, "White Women as Nation Builders," in *Selective Democracy: Race, Gender and the Australian Vote*, ed. John Chesterman and David Phillips (Melbourne, 2003). For the United States, see Louise Newman, *White Women's Rights: The Racial Origins of Feminism in the United States* (New York, 1999).

72. Marilyn Lake, "'A Revolution in the Family': The Challenge and Contradiction of Maternal Citizenship," in *Mothers of a New World: Maternalist Politics and the Origins of Welfare States*, ed. Seth Koven and Sonya Michel (New York, 1993).

Chapter 15

"BRINGING THE STATE BACK IN"
CIVIL SOCIETY, WOMEN'S MOVEMENTS, AND THE STATE[1]

Birgit Sauer

In the last decade, European feminists have increasingly referred to civil society as a sphere that promises female autonomy and agency, self-organization without hierarchies, solidarity, gender democracy, and justice. These ideals are not new: feminists of the second-wave women's movement have promoted the ideal of autonomy from the state since the 1970s, but they did not use the term *civil society*. This has changed; nowadays, more and more feminist activists use the term and regard civil society as more promising for the feminist project than hierarchical, bureaucratic, androcentric state institutions or competitive, profit-oriented market relations. Civil society is seen, as political scientist Mary Kaldor phrased it in 2003, as based on "consent rather than coercion," on inclusion rather than exclusion, and as concerned with "individual empowerment" and "personal autonomy."[2] In the current discourse of social movements, the term expresses the demand for a "radical extension of democracy, for political as well as economic emancipation."[3]

If we look at the inter- and supranational level since the late 1990s, the term and project of civil society become even more attractive for feminist activists because of their global dimension; Kaldor, for example, frames the concept as a global "answer to war."[4] This development is caused by dramatic changes of political spaces and the style of politics. Nation-states are "uploading" power and responsibilities to higher state levels—to the EU and the UN, for instance.[5] "Governance without government" is the new structure of international deliberation and decision making, in which nation-states are no longer privileged actors but decide together with international civil society organizations.[6] These governance structures might open up political space for movement actors, who could then become actively integrated in decision-making processes. The European Women's Lobby is an example of civil society actors' meaningful participation in political decision making on the European level. Civil society therefore appears to offer a real chance for gender democracy, for equal participation of men and women, for responsiveness of state institutions to women's movement demands—in short, for the descriptive and substantial representation of women and full political citizenship for women on national as well as on international levels. And indeed, during the last decade an international women's movement has emerged and actively gendered policy issues such as human and women's rights.[7] These developments have given rise to the hope that gender democracy and gender justice can be realized through civil society better than in formal state institutions.

But the feminist propagandists of civil society tend to overlook the fact that civil society organizations are not open per se to feminist demands. Many such organizations are male-dominated. The experiences of feminist organizations show that domination, heteronomy, exclusion, and injustice—due to differences between women from different ethnicity, class, and cultural backgrounds—also make up the reality of women in civil society. Moreover, women's movements in state-centered societies like Germany and Austria developed tight connections with state institutions during the 1980s and 1990s and became part of the state. These examples cast a shadow on the positive image of a "woman-friendly" and democratic civil society *opposed* to the alienating male-dominated state. And of course, feminist theory and practice challenged the notion of the separation of social spheres on which the concept of civil society rests. Feminism conceptualized the private realm not only as a sphere of political agency and empowerment of women, but also one of political disempowerment and violence against women: the personal is political, and the political is (sometimes) private!

To add one more point to the skeptical view of civil society: the retrenchment of welfare states in Europe comes with changes in state-society relations and shifting boundaries between state, economy, society, and families/private economy.[8] State restructuring rests on the "offloading" of state power and responsibilities to nonstate actors like families, neighborhood organizations, and female volunteers (*Ehrenamt*).[9] These processes of state restructuring may also open political opportunities for women's groups and strengthen the influence of civil society actors on political decision making and the organization of society. However, the pessimistic version of the story of shifting state-society boundaries is that civil society and women's work may be instrumentalized for the smooth implementation of neoliberal politics and exploitation of unpaid labor. The marketization and privatization of care work, for instance, pre-empts the work and time of women in the so-called private sphere of the family in order to cut state budgets. Civil society actors and their resources are called upon to compensate for the retreat of the state and the marketization of social relations while at the same time state funding for women's organizations and projects is being cut sharply.

These examples reveal the "paradoxes of civil society" for gender democracy and gender justice.[10] Moreover, most of these concepts of civil society are gender-blind. This puzzling picture poses the questions of whether or not civil society is more inclusive than state institutions of liberal democracies, and whether or not civil society brings forward gender justice more effectively than state institutions. Or, to put it somewhat differently: How should civil society be conceptualized by social scientists and also by political actors in order to realize gender equality? And how should the concept of civil society be framed in order to criticize inequality between men and women? My argument is that civil society—the world of local, national, and global associations—is not per se the better locus for feminist politics and gender justice than state institutions. Civil society is not the woman-friendly sphere opposed to both the male-dominated state and the unjust arena of the economy. On the contrary: economy, state, and civil society work as channels of communication to one another. The state is as male-dominated as civil society and markets and vice versa. Therefore, the normative concept of civil society as a form of communication and deliberation without domination must be contested.[11] Heuristically, this norm can lead toward gender equality, but the norm can be realized only through a permanent struggle for gender democracy within civil society itself. This perspective is important for the assessment of the role, the success, and the failures of women's movements in liberal democracies. Moreover, it is useful for future strategies and struggles for gender justice in the era of globalization.

A gender-critical concept of civil society, which can explain the above-mentioned contradictions and ambivalences and avoids the danger of reproducing the paradoxes of the concept, should, on the one hand, be able to analyze the working of unequal gender relations in civil society, while on the other, explain the challenge to unjust gender relations mounted by the women's movement in liberal democracies. It should also be able to shed light on recent transformations of nation-states and state-society relations in a gender perspective. I argue that the normative concept of civil society simply as an interstice between state, market, and family/private sphere is analytically short-handed and problematic in terms of gender politics. In this chapter, I want to point out the intricate but dialectic connection and interplay between civil society, state, economy, and the private. I want to suggest a gender-sensitive conceptualization of civil society, state, economy, and family/private not as different spheres, but as different discourses and interactions among social actors—actors who have different resources and access to power. Unjust gender relations are developed—as well as challenged—in civil society and institutionalized in state policies, norms, and political organizations. Thus, "bringing the state back in" refers to the need to analyze how the different societal spheres overlap, how they are connected, and how unjust gender relations are interwoven in these overlapping, reinforcing societal relations and spheres.

To state it differently, the state is an arena and form of power that organizes the sphere of the economy as well as civil society. The women's movement thus contributes to the production and reproduction of state power and economic relations. But, at the same time, the women's movement is an actor involved in state and market struggles and therefore has the opportunity to overcome unjust gender regimens in all societal spheres. However, compared to state administration and companies, women's movements, like other nongovernmental organizations (NGOs), are weak actors with few resources.

The first section of this chapter elaborates a gender-sensitive concept of civil society that seeks to overcome the male-centered bias of civil society concepts. This section will also point out how the relation of women's movement actors and the state might be conceptualized. The second section analyzes the interplay between women's movements and state institutions in Western democracies since the 1970s. I ask if and when women's associations and women's movement actors in civil society have effectively changed state policies and state institutions by discussing the findings of the Research Network on Gender Politics and the State (RNGS), which examine how "state feminism" developed in liberal democracies and advanced the aims of the women's movement.[12] The third section turns to structures of domination and exclusion within women's movements and shows how women's movement actors can become responsible for excluding specific issues and actors from policy debates by creating an exclusive hegemonic discourse within civil society. The concluding section explains the "revival" of the concept of civil society in the process of state restructuring and asks for the feminist trajectory in this process.

"Bringing the State Back In": A Gender-Sensitive Concept of Civil Society

A critical concept of civil society, one that is able to analyze gender relations, conceptualizes civil society not as an interstice between the market and the state, but as part of a broader concept of statehood. The Gramscian idea of civil society is useful for conceptualizing power and domination within civil society and state institutions based on unequal relations in the economy. It can also explain the relation between women's political underrepresentation and discrimination at work as well as domination within women's movements and in state institutions. As Antonio Gramsci understood it, civil society is not a separate social sphere, but a social *relation*, characterized by social differences and inequalities.[13] Civil society is not the democratic paradise but a field of conflict, a contested social site of struggles between different actors with different interests—and women's movements are one of them. Actors in civil society are located in economic, political, social, and cultural structures. They are equipped with different economic, social, political, cultural, and symbolic capitals and have differential access to power. Struggles within civil society occur over legitimate views and frames of social relations, social order, and social problems—for instance, definitions of work and life, public and private, production and reproduction, and legitimate identities and interests. Gramsci differentiates the *società borghese*—the sphere of the economy—from the *società civile*, the strategic field of distribution of power and of the production of a hegemonic consensus. NGOs, women's movements, and the media, for instance, are part of civil society. Moreover, he defines the state in "a narrow sense" as *società politica*, comprising parties, unions, and political institutions like parliament.[14] An "integral" concept of the state in the Gramscian sense defines it as "hegemony plus force."[15] Thus, civil society is not a sphere in between society and the state but is *part of* the state, the arena where common sense and hegemony are produced, both legitimizing state power.

The outcome of struggles in civil society is a hegemonic compromise—the legitimate or "common-sense" view of social relations, such as those between the genders and the definition of the political. Modern civil society has been the terrain of the elaboration of a male hegemony, and the modern state, the institutionalization of this male compromise. Since the nineteenth century women and men have been defined as opposed gender groups with different roles and tasks, identities, and status. The hegemonic gender compromise in civil society legitimizes the sexual division of labor and the exclusion of so-called private relations from the public sphere by normalizing and naturalizing sexual differences in a polarized gender order. The hierarchical gender order is one of the most powerful of the compromises that structure civil society, states, and the market sphere.

The common sense view of gender relations becomes institutionalized in norms, images, frames, and social institutions such as the family, work contracts, labor market structures, and political institutions like male-dominated state bureaucracy and the military. In the past, these norms and institutions legitimized the disenfranchisement of women and the denial of their political citizenship, and they continue to restrict their social and economic citizenship. The power to frame social relations and render these frames as "common sense" depends on the resources of actors within civil society. Dominant actors—bourgeois men, for instance—have been able to transform their particularistic norms, ideas, and frames into universal views and forge a hegemonic compromise within civil society. Inequality and domination are, therefore, originally located in civil society and not in states and markets alone.

In this schema, civil society is not a norm or a utopia, but an empty signifier that has to be filled in specific contexts. Civil society is a powerful discourse and practice, a practice of domination and of violence. But of course, civil society is also the sphere of political activism to overcome domination and injustice.[16] In civil society, counterhegemony is also developed. Since the nineteenth century, women's movement actors have fought to change the male-dominated compromise about women's intellectual and political inferiority and gain civic, political, and social citizenship rights for women.

Conceptualized in this way, civil society shifts the view to empirical analysis and to the social and economic foundations of civil society action. This perception of the private, civil society and the state opens a critical perspective on gender relations: on the one hand, gender inequality is located in the economic sphere and the sexual division of labor, but on the other, these economic differences and different (economic) resources are reinforced and legitimized in civil society. Dominant views, frames, and mindsets lend specific meanings to sexual differences and the hierarchical division of labor. Gender, therefore, can be seen as signifying meaning and knowledge about sexual differences—the hegemonic gender compromise. Gender is also a practice of reproducing this knowledge, and gendering is a conflicting strategy of self-definition and definition by others in civil society struggles.[17]

The representational regimes of modern democracies—parliaments, elections, parties and NGOs, and laws and norms—are also grounded in the hegemonic compromise in civil society. They are designed in social conflicts, in and through struggles within civil society. In nineteenth-century Europe, parties, trade unions, and the organizations of the first women's movement were among the civil society actors that shaped state institutions, namely, the welfare state. But male-dominated welfare-state institutions, established to overcome class inequalities, reproduced inequality between men and women.[18] Parties and trade unions then became part of state institutions through social partnership and corporatist models of decision making, while women's movements were not been able to form quasi-state organizations until the 1980s, when the first women's policy agencies were established.

Struggles in civil society also *disarticulate* social actors and groups—and women's organizations for a long time have been such a disarticulated political group, constructed either as unpolitical, their interests framed as nonpolitical, or as marginal and therefore unable to influence and shape state policies. The idea of shared violence between states and male heads of families, which is institutionalized in the liberal discourse of the private sphere, legitimized violence against women in the family and has been stabilized by a gender compromise that presents women as inferior. Powerful actors in civil and in political society—parties, trade unions, employers' associations, churches, and media—occupied the political space and formed a hegemonic compromise that excluded women's organizations from political debate and decision making. Throughout most of German history, for instance, women have had little opportunity to influence state policies, but at the end of the nineteenth and the beginning of the twentieth century, the first women's movements in Germany and elsewhere were able to intervene in the process of state and nation building and inscribe at least some women's interests in the negotiations of Western welfare states.[19] Suffrage for women in the first half of the twentieth century was also a result of struggles within civil society and the engagement of women's movements.

State power and state institutions are not therefore separable from the hegemonic compromise in civil society—to the contrary: the hegemonic view of social relations is institutionalized in state institutions and state policies. The state is an effect of social relations, power relations, and struggles within civil society. And civil society is as patriarchal as the "patriarchal state." Civil society is the locus of the development, preparation, and legitimation of male state power and unjust gender relations. State institutions, state policies, and the gender regime originate in social differences; they are developed within civil society as a gendered hegemonic compromise, mediated through and institutionalized by the political society of parties, unions, and parliaments. State and civil society cannot be separated in a such a way that the state is presented as patriarchal and male-dominated while civil society associations are women-friendly and the (only) realm of autonomy and gender justice. Unjust gender relations and the hegemonic gender compromise are inscribed in political regulation and state institutions, for instance, in marital laws and welfare-state regulations. Thus, the gender compromise either opens or closes accessibility to resources—money, power, and time. It defines women's citizenship status and their opportunities to participate in political decision making.

Hegemonic ideas also shape the identities of people. Sociologist Louis Althusser calls this "interpellation."[20] Gender relations and gender roles are results of a process of subjectivization and interpellation of individuals by state agencies. Gendering is a strategy of interpellation and, of course, of segregation and domination of certain groups of people. Therefore, gender has the dimension of both institution and identities.

But this conceptualization of civil society and state also includes the possibility of change. Civil society and the male-dominated state are not monolithic structures but have to be reformulated and practiced by people. Civil society and the state are not fixed entities but arenas where the struggle over political representation, over inclusion and exclusion, over the distribution of goods and resources takes place. Change occurs in this practice of reformulation and compromising. State regulation, the development of the welfare state, and affirmative action policies, for instance, were negotiated in civil society; the women's movement took part in these bargaining processes and has been able to codify some of its claims as state norms. Struggles, conflict, and the fight for hegemony and counterhegemony are part of civil society. Counterhegemonic discourses of gender relations challenge the boundaries between state, economy, and family, between the public and the private.

Gender justice thus needs the transformation of unequal processes of gendering, of the male hegemonic gender discourse in civil society. It also needs the transformation of: state norms and institutions, the distribution of social resources, the unequal distribution of labor, and blocked access to power. Gender justice has to be actively fought for in civil society—against male dominance, but also against structures of domination between women. Moreover, gender justice has to be transformed into state institutions by the actors of political society and by women's groups and their allies. Because the struggle over meaning takes place in civil society, this is an important locus for changing the process and discourse of gendering and transforming unjust gendered state institutions and policies.

Or, put differently: gender justice needs the transformation of state institutions and the economy, in, for example, the gendered division of labor in capitalist market structures as well as the hegemonic gender compromise. I would therefore claim that gender justice can only be achieved by social equality. Moreover, a concept of civil society and public sphere that entails gender justice and includes "the Other" must reintegrate issues, ideas, and strategies that are labeled as private (for instance emotions).[21]

A Mésalliance? State, Women's Movements, and Civil Society

After World War II, Fordist regimes of production and reproduction were established in most West European polities. The regimes of representative democracy with strong parties, unions, and associations that excluded women and women's organizations from the political society became part of postwar social and political arrangements. These regimes were based—of course, with national differences—on a male-dominated gender compromise with a strict division between public and private and a hierarchical sexual division of labor. Since the 1970s, the crisis of Fordism has been accompanied by the delegitimation of representational regimes—mainly, through de-alignment, of the parties and unions that had been the principal actors in political society—that were responsible for the underrepresentation of women. New actors were able to organize and mobilize constituencies, among them the second-wave women's movements. Not only did the emergence of "new" women's movements in the 1970s indicate changes in the hegemonic gender compromise, but women's movements successfully challenged the established patterns of gender compromise and male-dominated states, although the movements tended to be hostile toward the state and displayed "a distaste for male-dominated national politics."[22]

Second-wave women's movements in Western democracies have participated in the struggle over hegemony; they have been the main actors to transform civil society discourse on gender relations. Women's associations had the power to delegitimize unjust gender regimes and mobilized antihegemonic interpretations of gender. Compared to rule-of-law and welfare-state democracy, the participation of citizens—men and women—has been weak in state-centered democracies such as Germany and Austria. Civil society thus became a "battle term" of the women's movement in order to establish new representational forms—for instance, direct democracy versus representational or party democracy—and put new issues on the political agenda such as gender inequality at work, violence against women, and reproductive rights.

Women's movements scandalized the exclusive and male-dominated structures of state institutions and challenged the outcome of politics that privilege men. The aim of tearing down the boundaries between the so-called private and the public, between civil society and the state, was to politicize women's issues and to politicize women "in their homes." The movements organized and mobilized women in order to question the idea that women are unpolitical and undo the hegemonic compromise in civil society over issues such as abortion, domestic violence, discrimination in the labor market and welfare-state regulations. Women's projects and feminist countercultures were successfully implanted in the fields of body politics, reproduction and women's health, violence against women, and education. Moreover, they have been able to establish new state institutions for equal-opportunity policies—women's policy agencies. The concept of gender mainstreaming is the latest tool for improving the situation of women in and through state institutions, policies, laws, and norms. One could conclude that despite skepticism toward the state, some women's groups have become "state authorities or agents" and became involved "in state reform projects."[23]

The antihegemonic struggle of women's movements in Western societies has had two important results: First, the movements have changed the procedures of politics and succeeded in bringing women into the political process, into positions of decision making within parties and within state institutions, and representing women as a group (either descriptively or procedurally). Second, women's movements in Western societies have been able to change the hegemonic gender compromise in civil society. They have, for example, denormalized the female caregiver/male breadwinner model, identified restrictive abortion laws, and violence against women as violations of human rights. These have brought about new gender compromises that either regulate formerly "private" relations (through anti-domestic violence laws and affirmative action to address discrimination against women in the labor force) or deregulate them (for instance abortion, substantive representation, and policy change). Women's movement organizations have been able to change and transform states, making them more "feminist" and open to women's demands and interests. "State feminism"—the descriptive and substantial representation of women—is a success story of civil society.[24]

The findings of Research Network on Gender Politics and the State show that "women's movements in democratic states have tended to be successful in increasing both substantive representation, as demonstrated by policy content, and descriptive representation, as demonstrated by women's participation in policy making processes."[25] How can these changes be explained? Of course women's movement actors in civil society were the most important actors in the field. Interestingly, the characteristics and resources of the women's movements that were analyzed—for instance, the stage of the movement (growth or decline), closeness to leftist parties, cohesiveness around an issue, and the priority of an issue on the movement's agenda—are not the most important factors for the women's movement success.[26] The most significant factor is the policy environment—its approach or frame, the extent to which it is open or closed to movement actors, and the parties in power. If the policy environment is open to women's movement demands and the framing of an issue is compatible, a policy change is likely to occur. This was, for instance, the case in the Austrian abortion policies in the 1970s; since then, Austria has had a liberal abortion law.[27] But if the policy environment is closed and the women's movement frame challenges the hegemonic compromise, policy change is quite improbable. This was the case with prostitution policies in Austria in the 1970s and 1980s.[28] Moreover, women's policy agencies are rather important for women's movement success: if "femocrats" mediate between ordinary policymakers, the state administration, and the women's movement, success is much more likely than in cases where women's policy agencies are not involved in the policy process. Again, abortion and prostitution policies are examples for these constellations.

These results show the importance of conceptualizing civil society groups and action not as separate from the state but as cogenerating; as political scientists Lee Ann Banaszak, Karen Beckwith, and Dieter Rucht put it, "Given the central role of the modern interventionist state, women's movements must engage the state to bring about political and societal changes."[29] To summarize: struggles over gender justice in civil society since the 1970s have led to new forms of women's movement organizations, to new state institutions, and to policy change. Women's movements' success in turn affected civil society organizations: second-wave women's movements transformed their strategies, structures, and forms of action; the movement moved "from the streets" to institutions; project workers, femocrats, and feminist policy entrepreneurs became engaged in the struggle for gender justice.

Struggles for Hegemony: Domination and Exclusion within Women's Movements

The history of the women's movement is characterized by struggles between different women's groups (also between antifeminist groups and countermovements) over adequate representation in civil society. The fight for female suffrage at the end of the nineteenth and the beginning of the twentieth century in Germany and Austria, for instance, was marked by conflicts between the so-called bourgeois and socialist women's movements. A coalition was nearly impossible, and only some movement activists from the two branches cooperated. In addition to the struggle over representation, women's movements reproduce divisions, exclusions, and power relations, as well as legitimize hegemonic structures of power and domination within civil society. In this respect, the exclusiveness of the white middle-class women's movements in Western industrialized democracies has been criticized by Black and queer feminisms.[30] We do not need to refer to poststructuralist attempts to diversify the women's movements or question the notion of "the" women to see exclusive structures within a feminist civil society: the struggle of women's movements since the 1970s mainly represent the interests of middle-class and well-educated women. Equal-opportunity policies, for example, mainly target these groups. Working-class women were marginalized in this discourse and had no voice or agency within civil society associations, nor did migrant women.

Those women's associations that had the infrastructures, resources, and strategic frames to interact with state institutions became hegemonic, while other women's organizations became marginalized and failed to gain a voice or agency in civil society or in state institutions. Some women's issues have been legitimized, while others have received only restricted acceptance or been eliminated from the public agenda.³¹ According to Banaszak, Beckwith and Rucht, a "moderate feminist discourse has gained legitimate place within the political debate," and this moderate movement has limited itself to policy discourses that "resonated with a wider public."³²

To give an example: the project on prostitution by the Research Network on Gender Politics and the State shows that women's movements have been rather ambivalent and divided on this issue. Within Western women's movements, "prostitution was never an issue where consensus has been reached, with often sharp controversy between warring factions."³³ For a long time the movements saw prostitutes as "the Other"—as victims of patriarchal structures or even as a threat to the feminist project. Therefore, they concluded, prostitution should be contained but not supported. While women's movements have never been cohesive around this issue, there was little cooperation between feminist groups and organizations of prostitutes. Prostitutes had no voice in women's movements, and, moreover, abolitionist attempts on the part of the movements ignored the working conditions of women in the sex business and ran the risk of reproducing discrimination against female sex workers.

Another example of power struggle and hegemonic domination within the women's movement is the German debate about Muslim headscarves. The debate shows how divided feminists can be on a given issue. Although no single feminist view became hegemonic, some women's movement groups contributed to the hegemonic view of women with headscarves as oppressed and as victims. Some formed policy coalitions with conservative actors; for example, the German feminist leader Alice Schwarzer joined the former Christian Democratic minister for cultural affairs in the province of Baden-Württemberg, Annette Schavan. Once legitimated, the view of female headscarves as symbols of female oppression led to a prohibitive approach that not only excluded women with headscarves from civil service but also silenced their voices in civil society.

Conclusion

Why is the concept of civil society so attractive for social movements as well as for governments in the recent era of global social and political transformation? How can we explain the career of this term? What is the context in which the concept traveled from the state-socialist and Latin American countries to Western democracies at the end of the twentieth century? My argument is that debates about civil society constitute part of the global transformation of state-society relations that is occurring through a discourse of state restructuring. A discursive rearticulation of the boundaries between states, markets and civil society claims that the welfare state is overtaxed with responsibilities for citizens, or that the state curbs the freedom and activity of the citizens, and therefore the burden between state and society must be redistributed.[34] This discursive reconstruction shifts state responsibilities to society—to families or even to women's organizations, driving a restructuring of national (welfare) states.[35]

Three dimensions of this discourse about civil society at the beginning of the twenty-first century have an impact on gender relations and on women's movements. First, the transformation of state-society relations challenges traditional forms of political representation and participation, such as weariness and boredom with political parties, rapid party dealignment, and mistrust in political institutions. The discourse on civil society indicates a crisis and reorganization of political representational regimes. Civil society organizations are used and created actively to form a new hegemonic compromise. The concept of civil society is adopted to renew political integration, organize new forms of participation, and discuss new forms of political representation. The buzzword for this reorganization is "governance."[36] In governance structures, civil society organizations are integrated into political decision making to legitimize the retreat of the state and replace "old" institutions of the political society; these organizations should mediate the new hegemonic compromise in civil society. The multilevel governance polity of the European Union is a perfect example: the concept of civil society is adopted to organize new forms of participation and decision making in multilevel polities. Of course this restructuring process extends the field for political debate and opens up windows of opportunity to rearrange gender relations and reorganize gender regimes. NGOs like the European Women's Lobby have been able to influence policy decisions, for instance, in the constitutional process, although in the beginning women were excluded from the negotiation processes.

Second, transformation of statehood—the restructuring of state apparatus—is accompanied by a tremendous transformation of the hegemonic state project. A new hegemonic compromise has to be elaborated and developed in a civil society that fits with the new relations of economy, house economy, and state. The retreat of the state and the dominance of free-market forces are part of this neoliberal project. The new design of the boundaries between economy, state, and family/household economy needs new social arrangements, which have to be elaborated in civil society. Important aspects of this compromise are competitiveness, effectiveness, and individualism. Inequality and differences between people are stressed, and citizens are seen as individual consumers, not as participants in a common endeavor. State restructuring results in new interpellations of citizens, in a fundamental reconstitution of the role of citizens—and of course of the role of civil society. "Each person is the proprietor of his own person and capacities and does not owe society," is the credo of neoliberal restructuring of state, economy, and civil society.[37] The neoliberal discourse has shifted the perception of the citizen from a state subject to the master of his or her own fate: the *"Ich-AG"* (Me-Inc.) in German labor-market policy symbolizes this shift.[38] The vivid debate about civil society, then, can be seen as a new "technology" for governing society, as a strategy of the "governmentalization" of the state--making the individual responsible for his or her life, and implementing societal governance *within* the individual, no longer as a cooperative endeavor of societal groups.[39] This discourse is designing a hegemonic gender compromise that is not based on equality between men and women but draws gender lines differently, rearticulating ethnicity and class. While well-educated women in Western societies might have an opportunity to get well-paid jobs, they still carry the burden of care work. The emergence of "care chains" from southern Asian and former state-socialist countries to Western ones are examples of the differentiation between women: affluent women in Western societies employ women from less affluent societies and from different ethnic background to perform care work in their households. These developments dramatically change the notion of women as a group opposed to men, and new inequalities between women emerge.

Third, changes in state-society relations have consequences for the notion of civil society and women's movement organizations. The "cooperative state" uses civil society both as a resource and as compensation. Marketization runs the danger of instrumentalizing civil society actors in order to achieve cuts in state budgets.[40] The "offloading" of state responsibilities onto families and civil society associations may result in cutting off the "democratic surplus" of civil society. While civil society organizations are used to compensate for a lack of state services—for instance, shelters for battered women—they are the first victims of welfare state downsizing. In Germany, for example, some women's policy agencies at the community and provincial levels have been dissolved over the last two years, and public funding for women's projects has been reduced or transformed into project-based funds, disrupting the continuity of their work. The ambivalence of the relation between women's movements and state institutions highlights the fact that civil society will not grow and flourish automatically if the state is retreating. Nor will democratic deliberation and decision making be more woman-friendly if the state retreats. Democratization does not simply mean less state, but needs a different state—and another civil society compromise. Of course, the feminist project of gender justice has to target and challenge male dominance in civil society; it must create antipatriarchal hegemony and transform it into state institutions.

To escape the neoliberal trap of instrumentalizing the concept of civil society for antiemancipatory projects, one must take the following aspects into account: First, the "women's question" has to be repoliticized. This means to politicize the contradictions within women's lives in the process of state restructuring and show that the private sphere is being used as a resource for state restructuring and that social inequality according to class and ethnicity is deepening. Second, an antipatriarchal counterhegemony has to be developed in civil society as well as in political society and in the state. The feminist project must criticize power and domination in all societal spheres, design equal social relations, and work for the institutionalization of new gender relations. The feminist project also has the task of criticizing power relations between women, and should be open to different framings of problems from different women's groups. Third, mobilization within civil society towards gender justice has to be part of the transformation of states and state institutions, the institutionalized gender regime, and the economy. The economic relations that shape gender relations must be re-regulated to produce a new organization of paid labor and care work. Struggles for basic income are as important as women's health centers, shelters in the countryside, emergency apartments for trafficked women, citizenship rights for migrant women, the re-regulation of part-time work and the pension system, quotas in political bodies, and changes in the international sexual division of labor.

To realize this project, women's movements need allies in political society, the economy, the media, and the sciences. They must also form coalitions with special groups inside states—for instance, women's policy agencies. As the results of the Research Network on Gender Politics and the State project show, the struggle for more gender justice is a paradoxical task—with and against the state, with groups in the political society against hegemonic frames and interpretations within civil society.

Notes

1. The title refers to Peter B. Evans et al., eds., *Bringing the State Back In* (Cambridge, UK, and New York, 1985).
2. Mary Kaldor, *Global Civil Society: An Answer to War* (Cambridge, UK, 2003), 1, 6.
3. Ibid., 4.
4. Ibid.; see also John Keane, *Global Civil Society?* (Cambridge, UK, 2003).
5. Lee Ann Banaszak, Karen Beckwith, and Dieter Rucht, "When Power Relocates: Interactive Changes in Women's Movements and States," in *Women's Movements Facing the Reconfigured State*, ed. Banaszak et al. (Cambridge and New York, 2003), 1–29, 7.
6. James N. Rosenau and Ernst-Otto Czempiel, eds., *Governance without Government* (Cambridge, UK, and New York, 1992).
7. Mary K. Meyer and Elisabeth Prügl, eds., *Gender Politics in Global Governance* (Lanham, MD, 1999).
8. Ralph Jessen and Sven Reichardt, "Einleitung," in *Zivilgesellschaft als Geschichte: Studien zum 19. und 20. Jahrhundert*, ed. Ralph Jessen et al. (Wiesbaden, 2004), 29–42, 7.

9. Banaszak et al., "When Power Relocates," 7.
10. Dieter Gosewinkel and Dieter Rucht, "History meets Sociology: Zivilgesellschaft als Prozess," in *Zivilgesellschaft—national und transnational, WZB-Jahrbuch 2003*, ed. Gosewinkel et al. (Berlin, 2004), 29–60, 32.
11. Jürgen Habermas, *Strukturwandel der Öffentlichkeit* (Frankfurt/M., 1990); Jürgen Kocka, "Civil Society from a Historical Perspective," *European Review* 1 (2004): 65–79.
12. Dorothy McBride Stetson and Amy Mazur, eds., *Comparative State Feminism* (London, 1996); Mazur, ed., *State Feminism, Women's Movements and Job Training: Making Democracies Work in a Global Economy* (New York, 2001); Stetson, ed., *Abortion Politics, Women's Movements, and the Democratic State: A Comparative Study of State Feminism* (Oxford and New York, 2001); Joyce Outshoorn, ed., *The Politics of Prostitution: Women's Movements, Democratic States and the Globalisation of Sex Commerce* (Cambridge, UK, 2004); Joni Lovenduski, ed., *State Feminism and Political Representation* (Cambridge, UK, 2005).
13. Antonio Gramsci, *Gefängnishefte. Kritische Gesamtausgabe*, vol. 1, ed. Wolfgang F. Haug (Hamburg, 1991).
14. Gramsci, *Gefängnishefte*, 783.
15. Ibid., 783.
16. Kaldor, *Global*, 21.
17. Joan W. Scott, "Gender: A Useful Category of Historical Analysis," in *Coming to Terms: Feminism, Theory, Politics*, ed. Elizabeth Weed (New York and London, 1989), 81–100.
18. Carole Pateman, "The Patriarchal Welfare State," in *The Disorder of Women: Democracy, Feminism, and Political Theory* (Stanford, 1989), 179–209.
19. See, for example, Gisela Bock and Pat Thane, eds., *Maternity and Gender Policies: Women and the Rise of European Welfare States, 1880–1950s* (London and New York, 1991); and Seth Koven and Sonya Michel, eds., *Mothers of a New World: Maternalist Politics and the Origins of Welfare States* (New York and London, 1993).
20. Louis Althusser, *Ideologie und ideologische Staatsapparate: Skizzen für eine Untersuchung* (Berlin, 1969).
21. Iris Marion Young, "Communication and the Other: Beyond Deliberative Democracy," in *Democracy and Difference: Contesting the Boundaries of the Political*, ed. Seyla Benhabib (Princeton, NJ, 1996), 120–35.
22. Banaszak et al., "When Power Relocates," 24.
23. Ibid., 24.
24. Stetson and Mazur, *Comparative State Feminism*.
25. Joyce Outshoorn, "Comparative Prostitution Politics and the Case for State Feminism," in Outshoorn, *Politics of Prostitution*, 265–92, 280; Mazur, *State Feminism*; Stetson, *Abortion Politics*.
26. Outshoorn, "Comparative Prostitution," 285ff.
27. Regina Köpl, "State Feminism and Policy Debates on Abortion in Austria," in Stetson, *Abortion Politics*, 17–38.
28. Birgit Sauer, "Taxes, Rights and Regimentation: Discourses on Prostitution in Austria," in Outshoorn, *Politics of Prostitution*, 41–61.
29. Banaszak et al., "When Power Relocates," 24.
30. bell hooks, *Feminist Theory: From Margin to Center* (Boston, 1984).
31. Banaszak et al., "When Power Relocates," 24.
32. Ibid., 23.
33. Outshoorn, "Comparative Prostitution," 277.
34. Jürgen Kocka, "Zivilgesellschaft in historischer Perspektive," in *Forschungsjournal Neue Soziale Bewegungen* 2 (2003): 29–37, 34.

35. Banaszak et al., "When Power Relocates," 8.
36. Jon Pierre and Guy B. Peters, *Governance, Politics and the State* (New York, 2000).
37. Isabella Bakker, "Who Built the Pyramids? Engendering the New International Economic and Financial Architecture," *femina politica* 1 (2002): 13–25, 17.
38. The "Ich-AG" policy was instituted by the German government in 2005 to encourage the unemployed to become self-employed.
39. Michel Foucault, *Geschichte der Gouvernementalität*, vols. 1 and 2 (Frankfurt/M., 2004).
40. Eckhard Priller, "Mehr Zivilgesellschaft wagen: Gemeinnützige Organisationen im gesellschaftlichen Wandel," *WZB-Mitteilungen* 103 (2004): 23–26, 24.

CIVIL SOCIETY, PUBLIC SPACE, AND GENDER JUSTICE: A SELECTED BIBLIOGRAPHY

The following selection includes the most important publications on the subject in English, French, and German. It is intended to introduce the theme of public space and gender justice into the international discussion on civil society.

Adam, Thomas, ed. *Philanthropy, Patronage, and Civil Society: Experiences from Germany, Great Britain, and North America*, Bloomington, IN, 2004.
Akkermann, Tjitske and Siep Stuurman, eds. *Perspectives on Feminist Political Thought in European History, From Middle Ages to Present*. London and New York, 1998.
Alexander, Jeffrey. "The Paradoxes of Civil Society," *International Sociology* 12, no. 2 (1998): 115–133.
Appel, Margit et al., eds. *Zivilgesellschaft - ein Konzept für Frauen?* Frankfurt/M, 2003.
Banaszak, Lee Ann, Karen Beck, and Dieter Rucht. "When Power Relocates: Interactive Changes in Women's Movements and States." In *Women's Movements Facing the Reconfigured State*, edited by idem., 1–29. Cambridge, 2003.
Bermeo, Nancy and Philip Nord, eds. *Civil Society before Democracy: Lessons from Nineteenth-Century Europe*. Lanham, MD, 2000.
Biagini, Eugenio F., ed. *Citizenship and Community: Liberals, Radicals and Collective Identities in the British Isles 1865–1931*. Cambridge and New York, 1996.
Budde, Gunilla. "Das Öffentliche des Privaten: Die Familie als zivilgesellschaftliche Kerninstitution." In *Die Praxis der Zivilgesellschaft: Akteure, Handeln und Strukturen im internationalen Vergleich*, edited by Arnd Bauerkämper, 57–77. Frankfurt/M., 2003.
———. "Harriet und ihre Schwestern: Frauen und Zivilgesellschaft im 19. Jahrhundert." In *Zivilgesellschaft und historischer Wandel, Studien zum 19. und 20. Jahrhundert*, edited by Ralph Jessen and Sven Reichardt. Berlin, 2004.
Butler, Judith, and Joan W. Scott, eds. *Feminists Theorize the Political*. London and New York, 1992.
Calhoun, Craig, ed. *Habermas and the Public Sphere*. Cambridge, MA, 1992.
———. "Civil Society/Public Sphere: History of the Concept." *International Encyclopedia of the Social and Behavioral Sciences* 3 (2001): 1897–1903.

Canning, Kathleen and Sonya O. Rose. "Gender, Citizenship and Subjectivity: Some Historical and Theoretical Considerations," *Gender & History* 13, no. 3 (2001): 427–43.

Chambers, Simone and Will Kymlicka, eds. *Alternative Conceptions of Civil Society.* Princeton, NJ, 2002.

Christidoulidis, Emilios A., ed. *Communitarianism and Citizenship.* Aldershot, UK, 1998.

Clarke, Eric O. *Virtuous Vice: Homoeroticism and the Public Sphere.* Durham, NC, 2000.

Cohen, Jean and Andrew Arato. *Civil Society and Political Theory.* Cambridge, MA, 1992

Cohen, Yolande and Françoise Thébaud, eds. *Féminisme et identités nationales: Les processus d'intégration des femmes au politique.* Lyon, 1998.

Curthoys, Ann and Marilyn Lake, eds. *Connected Worlds History in Transnational Perspective.* Canberra, 2006.

Davidoff, Leonore. "Regarding Some 'Old Husbands' Tales': Public and Private in Feminist History." In *Feminism, the Public and the Private*, edited by Joan B. Landes, 164–93. Oxford, 1998.

Davis, Belinda J, "Reconsidering Habermas, Gender, and the Public Sphere: The Case of Wilhelmine Germany." In *Society, Culture and the State in Germany, 1870–1930*, edited by Geoff Eley, 397–426. Ann Arbor, MI, 1996.

Dean, Jody. *Solidarity of Strangers: Feminism after Identity Politics.* Berkeley, CA, 1996.

———. "Including Women: The Consequences and Side Effects of Feminist Critiques of Civil Society." *Philosophy and Social Criticism* 18, nos. 3–4 (1995): 378–406.

Deutsch, Sarah. *Women and the City: Gender, Space and Power in Boston 1870–1940.* Oxford, 2000.

Dietz, Mary D. "Context is All: Feminism and Theories of Citizenship." In *Feminism and Politics*, edited by Anne Philips, 378–400. Oxford, 1998.

Edwards, Michael. *Civil Society.* Cambridge, UK, 2004.

Eger, Elizabeth and Charlotte Grant, eds. *Women, Writing and the Public Sphere 1700–1830.* Cambridge, UK and New York, 2001.

Ehrenberg, John. *Civil Society: The Critical History of an Idea.* New York, 1999.

Einhorn, Barbara and Charlotte Sever. "Gender and Civil Society in Central and Eastern Europe." *International Feminist Journal of Politics* 5, no. 2 (2003): 163–91.

Elshtain, Jean B. *Public Man, Private Women: Women in Social and Political Thought.* Princeton, NJ, 1981, 1993.

———. *Power Trips and Other Journeys, Essays in Feminism as Civic Discourse.* Madison, WI, 1990.

Farge, Arlette. *Dire et mal dire: L'opinion publique au XVIIIe siècle.* Paris, 1992.

Fauré, Christine. *Democracy without Women: Feminism and the Rise of Liberal Individualism in France.* Bloomington, IN, 1991.

Ferguson, Adam. *An Essay on the History of Civil Society*, edited by Fania Oz-Salzberger. Cambridge and New York, 1995.

Fischer-Tiné, Harald, and Michael Mann, eds. *Colonialism as Civilizing Mission: Cultural Ideology in British India.* London, 2004.

François, Etienne. *Sociabilité et Société Bourgeoise en France, en Allemagne et en Suisse, 1750–1850*. Paris, 1986.
Fraser, Nancy, "Rethinking the Public Sphere." In *Habermas and the Public Sphere*, edited by Craig Calhoun, 109–42. Cambridge, MA, 1992.
———. "Sex, Lies, and the Public Sphere: Some Reflections on the Confirmation of Clarence Thomas." *Critical Inquiry* 18 (1992): 595–612.
———. *Justice Interruptus: Critical Reflections on the "Postsocialist" Condition*. London and New York, 1997.
Freeden, Michael. "Civil Society and the Good Citizen: Competing Conceptions of Citizenship in Twentieth-century Britain." In *Civil Society in British History: Paradigm or Peculiarity?* edited by José Harris, 295–91. Oxford, 2003.
Gal, Susan and Gail Kligman. *The Politics of Gender after Socialism: A Comparative-Historical Essay*. Princeton, NJ, 2000.
Gellner, Ernest. *Conditions of Liberty: Civil Society and its Rivals*. London, 1994.
Gerhard, Ute. "Bürgerrechte und Geschlecht: Herausforderung für ein soziales Europa." In *Staatsbürgerschaft in Europa, Historische Erfahrungen und aktuelle Debatten*, edited by Christoph Conrad and Jürgen Kocka, 63–91. Hamburg, 2001.
———. "Geschlechterdifferenz, soziale Bewegungen und Recht: Der Beitrag feministischer Rechtskritik zu einer Theorie sozialer Staatsbürgerrechte." In *Differenz und Integration: Die Zukunft moderner Gesellschaften*, edited by Stefan Hradil, 402–19. Frankfurt/M,, 1997.
———. "Atempause: die aktuelle Bedeutung der Frauenbewegung für eine zivile Gesellschaft." In *Feministische Perspektiven der Politikwissenschaft*, edited by Kathrin Braun et al., 293–314. Munich, 2000.
———. *Debating Women's Equality: Toward a Feminist Theory of Law from a European Perspective*. New Brunswick, NJ, 2001.
Giddens, Anthony. "Risk, Trust, Reflexivity." In *Reflexive Modernization: Politics, Tradition and Aesthetics in the Modern Social Order*, edited by Ulrich Beck et al., 184–97. Cambridge, MA, 1994.
Ginsborg, Paul. "Family, Civil Society and the State in Contemporary European History: Some Methodological Considerations." *Contemporary European History* 4 (1995): 249–73.
———. *The Politics of Everyday Life*. London and New Haven, CT, 2005.
Glasius, Robe Marlies and Helmut K, Anheier, eds. *Global Civil Society*. Oxford, 2002.
Godel, Brigitta. *Auf dem Weg zur Zivilgesellschaft: Frauenbewegung und Wertewandel in Rußland*. Frankfurt/M. and New York, 2002.
Goodman, Dena. *The Republic of Letters: A Cultural History of the French Enlightenment*. Ithaca, NY, 1994.
Gordon, Daniel. *Citizens Without Sovereignty: Equality and Sociability in French Thought 1670–1789*. Princeton, NJ, 1994.
Gosewinkel, Dieter. *Zivilgesellschaft—eine Erschließung des Themas von seinen Grenzen her*. WZB Discussion Paper. Berlin, 2003.
Gosewinkel, Dieter et al., eds. *Zivilgesellschaft—national und transnational*. WZB-Jahrbuch 2003. Berlin, 2004.
Gosewinkel, Dieter and Dieter Rucht. "'History meets Sociology': Zivilgesell-

schaft als Prozess." In *Zivilgesellschaft—national und transnational, WZB-Jahrbuch 2003.* 29–60. Berlin, 2004.
Gramsci, Antonio. *Prison Notebooks.* New York, 1991.
Habermas, Jürgen. *The Structural Transformation of the Public Sphere: An Inquiry into a Category of Bourgeois Society.* Cambridge, MA, 1989 (1st German ed., 1962).
Hagemann, Karen. "Familie—Staat—Nation: Das aufklärerische Projekt der 'Bürgergesellschaft' in geschlechtergeschichtlicher Perspektive." In *Europäische Zivilgesellschaft in Ost und West: Begriff, Geschichte, Chancen,* edited by Manfred Hildermeier et al., 57–85. Frankfurt/M., 2000.
Hall, John A. *Civil Society: Theory, History, Comparision.* Cambridge, 1995.
Hall, John. "Reflections on the Making of Civility in Society." In *Paradoxes of Civil Society: New Perspectives on Modern German and British History,* edited by Frank Trentmann, 47–57. New York, 2000.
Hann, Chris and Elizabeth Dunn, eds. *Civil Society: Challenging Western Models.* London, 1996.
Harris, José, ed. *Civil Society in British History: Ideas, Identities, Institutions.* Oxford, 2003.
Hausen, Karin. "Öffentlichkeit und Privatheit: Gesellschaftspolitische Konstruktionen und die Geschichte der Geschlechterbeziehungen." In *Frauengeschichte—Geschlechtergeschichte,* edited by Karin Hausen and Heide Wunder, 81–88. Frankfurt/M., 1992.
Hemment, Julie. "Global Civil Society and the Local Costs of Belonging: Defining Violence against Women in Russia." *Signs* 29, no. 1 (2004): 840–66.
Hobson, Barbara, ed. *Gender and Citizenship in Transition.* New York, 2000.
Ishkanian, Armine. "Importing Civil Society? The Emergence of Armenia's NGO Sector and the Impact of Western Aid on Its Development." *Armenian Forum: A Journal of Contemporary Affairs* 3, no. 1 (2003): 7–36.
Islamoglu, Huricihan. "Civil Society, History and the Idea of." *International Encyclopedia of the Social and Behavioral Sciences* 3 (2001): 1891–97.
Jessen, Ralph and Sven Reichardt. "Einleitung." In *Zivilgesellschaft als Geschichte, Studien zum 19. und 20. Jahrhundert,* 29–42. Wiesbaden, 2004.
Kaldor, Mary. *Global Civil Society: An Answer to War.* Cambridge, UK, 2003.
Kaviraaj, Sudipta and Sunil Khilnani, eds. *Civil Society: History and Possibilities.* Cambridge, UK and New York, 2001.
Kay, Rebecca. *Russian Women and Their Organizations: Gender, Discrimination, and Grassroots Women's Organizations, 1991–1996.* New York, 2000.
Keane, John, ed. *Civil Society and the State: New European Perspectives.* London, 1988.
———. *Civil Society: Old Images, New Visions.* London, 1999.
———. *Global Civil Society?* Cambridge, UK, 2003.
———. ed. *Civil Society: Berlin Perspectives.* Oxford, 2006.
Kershaw, Paul W. *Carefair: Rethinking the Responsibilities and Rights of Citizenship.* Vancouver, 2005.
Klein-Hessling, Ruth. *Zivilgesellschaft, Frauenorganisationen und Netzwerke.* Bielefeld, 1999.
Knott, Sarah and Barbara Taylor, eds. *Women, Gender and Enlightenment.* New York, 2005.

Kocka, Jürgen. "Civil Society from a Historical Perspective." *European Review* 1 (2004): 65–79.
Lake, Marilyn. *Getting Equal: The History of Australia Feminism.* Sydney, 1999.
Landes, Joan B. *Women and the Public Sphere in the Age of the French Revolution.* Ithaca, NY, 1988.
———. "Jürgen Habermas, The Structural Transformation of the Public Sphere: A Feminist Inquiry." *Praxis International* 12 (1992): 106–27.
———, ed. *Feminism, the Public and the Private.* Oxford, 1998.
Lister, Ruth. *Citizenship: Feminist Perspectives.* 2nd edition, New York, 2003.
Lovenduski, Joni, ed. *State Feminism and Political Representation.* Cambridge, UK, 2005.
Marshall, Thomas H. *Citizenship and Social Class, and Other Essays.* Cambridge, UK, 1950. Reprint. London, 1992.
Meeks, Chet. "Civil Society and Sexual Politics of Difference." *Sociological Theory* 19, no. 3 (2001): 325–44.
Miller, Melanie L. "Male and Female Civility: Towards Gender Justice." *Sociological Inquiry* 72, no. 3 (2002): 456–66.
Moghadam, Valentine M. "Engendering Citizenship, Feminizing Civil Society: The Case of the Middle East and North Africa." *Women and Politics,* 25, nos. 1–2 (2003): 63–87.
Offen, Karen. *European Feminisms, 1700–1950: A Political History.* Stanford, CA, 2000.
Okin, Susan Moller. "Gender, the Public, and the Private." In *Feminism, the Public and the Private,* edited by Joan B. Landes, 116–41. Oxford, 1998.
Ostner, Ilona. "Familie und Zivilgesellschaft." In *Zivile Gesellschaft: Entwicklung, Defizite und Potentiale,* edited by Klaus M, Schmals and Hubert Heinelt, 369–83. Opladen, 1997.
Paletschek, Sylvia and Bianka Pietrow-Ennker, eds. *Women's Emancipation Movements in the Nineteenth Century.* Stanford, CA, 2004.
Pateman, Carol. *The Sexual Contract.* Cambridge, MA, 1988.
———. *The Disorder of Women: Democracy, Feminism and Political Theory.* Oxford, 1989.
———. "Democratizing Citizenship: Some Advantages of a Basic Income." *Politics and Society* 1 (2004): 89–105.
Pernau, Margrit. "From a 'Private' Public to a 'Public' Private Sphere: Old Delhi and the North Indian Muslims in Comparative Perspective." In *The Public and the Private: Issues of Democratic Citizenship,* edited by Gurpreet Mahajan et al., 103–30. New Delhi, 2003.
Phillips, Anne. "Who Needs Civil Society? A Feminist Perspective." *Dissent* 46, no. 1 (1999): 56–61.
———. "Does Feminism need a Conception of Civil Society?" In *Alternative Conceptions of Civil Society,* edited by Simone Chambers and Will Kymlicka, 71–89. Princeton, NJ, 2002.
———, ed. *Feminism and Politics.* Oxford, New York, 1998.
Rabinovitch, Eyal. "Gender and the Public Sphere: Alternative Forms of Integration in Nineteenth-Century America." *Sociological Theory* 19, no. 3 (2001): 344–70.

Randeria, Shalini. "Zivilgesellschaft in postkolonialer Sicht." In *Neues über Zivilgesellschaft aus historisch-sozialwissenschaftlichem Blickwinkel*. WZB Discussion Paper. Berlin, 2004.

———. "Kastensolidarität als Modus zivilgesellschaftlicher Bindungen, Gemeinschaftliche Selbstorganisation und Rechtspluralismus im (post)kolonialen Indien." In Gosewinkel and Rucht, *Zivilgesellschaft–national und transnational*, 223–43.

Reichardt, Sven. "Civil Society and Violence: Some Conceptual Reflections from Historical Perspective." In *Civil Society: Berlin Perspectives*, edited by John Keane, 139–68. Oxford, 2006.

———. "Gewalt und Zivilität im Wandel, Konzeptionelle Überlegungen zur Zivilgesellschaft aus historischer Sicht." In Gosewinkel and Rucht, *Zivilgesellschaft–national und transnational*, 61–81.

Rendall, Jane. "Women and the Public Sphere." *Gender & History* 11, no. 3 (1999): 475–88.

Ritter, Martina, ed. *Zivilgesellschaft und Gender-Politik in Rußland*. Frankfurt/M, 2001.

Rosenvallon, Pierre. *Le modèle politique français: la société civile contre le jacobinisme de 1789 à nos jours*. Paris, 2004.

Rossteutscher, Sigrid, ed. *Democracy and the Role of Voluntary Associations: Political, Organizational and Social Contexts*. London, 2005.

Ryan, Mary P. *Civic Wars: Democracy and Public Life in the American City during the Nineteenth Century*. Berkeley, CA, 1997.

———. *Women in Public: Between Banners and Ballots, 1825–1880*. Baltimore, 1990.

Sauer, Birgit. "Zivilgesellschaft versus Staat: Geschlechterkritische Anmerkungen zu einer problematischen Dichotomie." In *Zivilgesellschaft—ein Konzept für Frauen?* edited by Margit Appel and Luise Gubitzer, 117–36. Frankfurt/M., 2003.

Schmitt, Britta. *Zivilgesellschaft, Frauenpolitik und Frauenbewegung in Rußland: von 1917 bis zur Gegenwar.* Königstein/Taunus, 1997.

Scott, Joan W. and Debra Keates, eds. *Going Public: Feminism and the Shifting Boundaries of the Private Sphere*. Urbana and Champaign, IL, 2004.

Seligman, Adam B. *The Idea of Civil Society*. Princeton, NJ, 1992.

Shils, Edwards. "Nation, Nationality, Nationalism and Civil Society." *Nations and Nationalism* 1 (1995): 93–118.

Silliman, Jael. "Expanding Civil Society: Shrinking Political Spaces—The Case of Women's Nongovermental Organisations." *Social Politics* 6, no. 1 (1999): 23–54.

Stetson, Dorothy M. and Amy Mazur, eds. *Comparative State Feminism*. London, 1995.

Tester, Keith. *Civil Society*. London, 1992.

Tomaselli, Sylvana. "The Enlightenment Debate on Women." *History Workshop* 20 (1985): 101–25.

Trentmann, Frank ed. *Paradoxes of Civil Society, New Perspectives on Modern German and British History*. 2nd edition. New York, 2003.

Veauvy, Christiane, ed. *Les Femmes dans l'espace public: Itinéraires français et italiens*. Paris, 2004.

Vernon, James. *Re-Reading the Constitution: New Narratives in the Political History of England's Long Nineteenth Century.* Cambridge, 1996.
Walzer, Michael, ed. *Toward a Global Civil Society.* Providence, RI, 1995.
Young, Iris Marion. "Communication and the Other: Beyond Deliberative Democracy." In *Democracy and Difference: Contesting the Boundaries of the Political,* edited by Seyla Benhabib, 120–35. Princeton, NJ, 1996.
———. "Polity and Group Difference: A Critique of the Ideal of Universal Citizenship." In *Feminism and Politics,* edited by Anne Phillips, 401–29. Oxford, 1998.
———. "State, Civil Society, and Social Justice." In *Democracy's Value,* edited by Ian Shapiro and Casiano Hacker-Cordón, 141–62. Cambridge, 1999.
———. *Inclusion and Democracy.* New York, 2000.
Yuval-Davis, Nira, and Pnina Werbner, eds. *Women, Citizenship and Difference.* London, 1999.

CONTRIBUTORS

Gunilla Budde is Professor of Modern German and European History at the Carl von Ossietzky Universität of Oldenburg. Her research focuses on the history of the European middle classes, gender history, the history of the German Democratic Republic, political scandals and music and politics in history. Her publications include: *In Träumen war ich immer wach: Die Erinnerungen des Dienstmädchens Sophia von ihr selbst erzählt*, editor (Bonn, 1990); *Auf dem Weg ins Bürgerleben: Kindheit und Erziehung in deutschen und englischen Bürgerfamilien, 1840–1914* (Göttingen, 1994); *Frauen arbeiten: Weibliche Erwerbstätigkeit in Ost- und Westdeutschland nach 1945*, editor (Göttingen, 1997); and *Transnationale Geschicht: Themen, Tendenzen und Theorien*, co-edited with Sebastian Conrad and Oliver Janz (Göttingen, 2006).

Belinda Davis is Associate Professor of Modern German and European History at Rutgers University. Her research focuses on popular protest and political culture, particularly in twentieth-century Germany. The results of her current research project will be published under the title *The Internal Life of Politics: The New Left in West Germany, 1962–1983*. Her publications include: *Home Fires Burning: Food, Politics, and Everyday Life in World War I Berlin* (Chapel Hill, NC, 2000); and *Changing the World, Changing Oneself: Political Protest and Collective Identities in the 1960s/70s West Germany and U.S.*, co-edited with Wilfried Mausbach, Martin Klimke, and Carla MacDougall (forthcoming).

Manfred Gailus is Professor of Modern German History at the Technical University of Berlin. His research focuses on the history of social protest and political violence, anti-Semitism and the relationships between Protestantism, nationalism, and Nazism. His publications include: *Straße und Brot: Sozialer Protest in den deutschen Staaten unter besonderer Berücksichtigung Preußens, 1847–1849* (Göttingen, 1990); *Der Kampf um das tägliche Brot: Nahrungsmangel, Versorgungspolitik und Protest 1770–1990*, co-edited with Heinrich Volkmann (Opladen, 1994); *Protestantismus und Nationalsozialismus: Studien zur nationalsozialistischen Durchdringung des protestantischen Sozialmilieus in Berlin* (Cologne, 2001); *National-*

protestantische Mentalitäten in Deutschland (1870–1970): Konturen, Entwicklungslinien und Umbrüche eines Weltbildes, co-edited with Hartmut Lehmann (Göttingen, 2005); and *Von der babylonischen Gefangenschaft der Kirche im Nationalen: Regionalstudien zu Protestantismus, Nationalsozialismus und Nachkriegsgeschichte 1930 bis 2000,* co-edited with Wolfgang Krogel (Berlin, 2006).

Kristen R. Ghodsee is Associate Professor of Gender and Women's Studies at Bowdoin College. In 2006–7 she was a fellow at the Princeton Institute for Advanced Study, where she completed her second monograph, *The Miniskirt and the Veil: Gender, Eastern Aid and Islamic Revivalism on the Edge of Europe.* Her articles on gender in Bulgaria have been published in journals such as *Signs, Gender and Women's Studies Quarterly, The International Journal of Politics, Culture and Society, L'Homme,* and *Human Rights Dialogue.* Her first book is *The Red Riviera: Gender, Tourism and Postsocialism on the Black Sea* (Durham, NC, 2005).

Paul A. Ginsborg is Professor of Contemporary European History at the University of Florence. His research focuses on nineteenth- and twentieth-century Italian history and politics, and the history of the family in Europe. His publications include: *A History of Contemporary Italy: Society and Politics, 1943–1988* (London and New York, 1990); *Italy and Its Discontents: Family, Civil Society and State* (London, 2001); *Silvio Berlusconi: Television, Power and Patrimony* (London and New York, 2004); and *The Politics of Everyday Life: Making Choices, Changing Lives* (New Haven, CT and London, 2005). Two of his long essays on the theme of the European family have appeared in *Contemporary European History,* one theoretical (1995, no. 3) and one more empirical (2000, no. 3). See also *Thesis Eleven* (2002, no. 68) for his work on 1968, communes, and the family.

Karen Hagemann is James G. Kenan Distinguished Professor of History at the University of North Carolina at Chapel Hill. Her research focuses on the history of eighteenth- to twentieth-century Germany and Europe; women's and gender history, in particular the history of welfare states, labor culture, and women's movements; as well as the history of the nation, the military, and war. Her most recent books include: *Gendered Nations: Nationalisms and Gender Order in the Long Nineteenth Century,* co-edited with Ida Blom and Catherine Hall (Oxford and New York, 2000); *Home/Front: Military and Gender in Twentieth Century Germany,* co-edited with Stefanie Schüler-Springorum (Oxford and New York, 2002); *"Mannlicher Muth und Teutsche Ehre": Nation, Militär und Geschlecht zur Zeit der Antinapoleonischen Kriege Preußens* (Paderborn, 2002); *Masculinities in Politics and War: Gendering Modern History,* co-edited with Stefan Dudink and John Tosh (Manchester and New York,

2004); and *Frieden—Gewalt—Geschlecht: Friedens- und Konfliktforschung als Geschlechterforschung*, co-edited with Jennifer Davy and Ute Kätzel (Essen, 2005).

Marilyn Lake, based at La Trobe University in Melbourne and the Australian National University in Canberra, currently holds an Australian Professorial Research Fellowship. Her research focuses on citizenship, gender, sexuality, nationalism, and feminism. Essays on these subjects have appeared in the international collections *Feminism and History*, edited by Joan Scott (Oxford, 1996) and *Feminism: The Public and the Private*, edited by Joan Landes (Oxford, 1998). Recent books include *Getting Equal: The History of Feminism in Australia* (St. Leonards, 1999); *Women's Rights and Human Rights: International Historical Perspectives*, co-edited with Patricia Grimshaw and Katie Holmes (New York, 2001); *FAITH: Faith Bandler: Gentle Activist* (Crows Nest, 2002); and *Connected Worlds: History in Transnational Perspective* (Canberra, 2006); and, with Henry Reynolds, *Drawing the Global Colour Line: White Men's Countries and the International Challenge of Racial Equality* (Cambridge, New York, and Melbourne, 2008). •

Gisela Mettele is a "New Blood Lecturer" in the School of Historical Studies at the University of Leicester. Previously she served as acting director of the German Historical Institute in Washington, DC., where she was also a Research Fellow. Her research focuses on social and cultural history of the eighteenth to the mid-twentieth century, religion and society in the eighteenth and nineteenth century in a transnational perspective, the history of urbanization, theory of biographical narratives, the history of the middle classes, and gender history. Her publications include: *Bürgertum in Köln 1775–1870: Gemeinsinn und freie Association* (Munich, 1998); and *Weltbürgertum oder Gottesreich? Die Herrnhuter Brüdergemeine als transnationale Gemeinschaft 1760–1857* (Göttingen, 2006).

Sonya Michel is Professor of History and Director of the Miller Center for Historical Studies at the University of Maryland, College Park. She is a founding editor of the journal *Social Politics: International Studies in Gender, State and Society*. Her research focuses on the history of women, men and gender, and the history of social policy in the US and in comparative perspective. Her publications include: *Behind the Lines: Gender and the Two World Wars*, co-edited with Margaret Higonnet, Jane Jenson, and Margaret Weitz (New Haven, CT, 1987); *Mothers of a New World: Maternalist Politics and the Origins of Welfare States*, co-edited with Seth Koven (New York, 1993); *Children's Interests/Mothers' Rights: The Shaping of America's Child Care Policy* (New Haven, CT, 1999); and *Child*

Care Policy at the Crossroads: Gender and Welfare State Restructuring, co-edited with Rianne Mahon (New York, 2002). She is currently writing a book with the working title "The Benefits of Race and Gender: Old Age (In)Security in America's Public/Private Welfare State."

Karen Offen, a historian and independent scholar, is a Senior Scholar with the Institute for Research on Women and Gender, Stanford University. Her research focuses on the history of European feminism and French women's and gender history in the nineteenth and twentieth centuries. Her publications include: *Paul de Cassagnac and the Authoritarian Tradition in Nineteenth-Century France* (Berkeley, CA, 1991); *Writing Women's History: International Perspectives*, co-edited with Ruth Roach Pierson and Jane Rendall (Bloomington, IN, 1991); *European Feminisms, 1700–1950: A Political History* (Berkeley, CA, 2000). She is completing a book on the "woman question" debate in modern France and an edited volume on global feminism between 1789 and 1945.

Margrit Pernau is Research Fellow at the Social Science Research Center Berlin (WZB). Her research focuses on modern Indian history, the history of indirect rule, and comparative studies. She is currently working on a study entitled "Muslims at the Cross Road of Identities: Delhi 1803–1922." Her publications include: *Verfassung und politische Kultur im Wandel: Der indische Fürstenstaat Hyderabad 1911–48* (Stuttgart, 1992), translated as *The Passing of Patrimonialism: Politics and Political Culture in Hyderabad 1911–48* (New Delhi, 2000); *Family and Gender: Changing Patterns of Family and Gender Values in Europe and India*, co-edited with Helmut Reifeld and Imtiaz Ahmad (New Delhi, 2002); *C.F. Andrews: Zaka Ullah of Delhi*, co-edited with Mushirul Hasan (New Delhi, 2003); and *Regionalizing Pan-Islam: Documents on the Khilafat Movement*, co-edited with Mushirul Hasan (New Delhi, 2005).

Jane Rendall is an Honorary Fellow in the History Department at the University of York. Her research focuses on eighteenth- and nineteenth-century British and comparative women's history, particularly Scottish women's history and the Scottish Enlightenment. Her publications include: *The Origins of Modern Feminism: Women in Britain, France, and the United States, 1780–1860* (Basingstoke, UK, 1985); *Equal or Different: Women's Politics 1800–1914*, editor (Oxford, 1987); *Writing Women's History: International Perspectives*, co-edited with Karen Offen and Ruth Roach Pierson (Basingstoke, UK, 1991); *Defining the Victorian Nation: Class, Race, Gender and the British Reform Act of 1867*, co-authored with Catherine Hall and Keith McClelland (Cambridge, UK, 2000); *Eighteenth-Century York: Culture, Space and Society*, co-edited with Mark Hallett (York, 2003).

Sonya O. Rose is Professor Emerita of History, Sociology and Women's Studies at the University of Michigan, Ann Arbor and Honorary Professor at the University of Warwick. Her main field of research is British nineteenth- and twentieth-century gender history with a focus on labor, citizenship, and war. Her publications include: *Limited Livelihoods: Gender and Class in Nineteenth-Century England* (Berkeley, CA, 1993); *Which People's War? National Identity and Citizenship in Wartime Britain, 1939–45* (Oxford, 2003); *Gender and Class in Modern Europe*, co-edited with Laura Frader (Ithaca, NY, 1996); and *Gender, Citizenship and Subjectivities*, co-edited with Kathleen Canning (Oxford, 2002). Most recently she has been interested in questions of citizenship, masculinity, and empire, especially during and in the aftermath of war in twentieth-century Britain.

Birgit Sauer is Professor of Political Science at the University of Vienna. Her main fields of research are state transformation, comparative state feminism, globalization, and governance in gender perspective. Her publications include: *Die Asche des Souveräns. Staat und Demokratie in der Geschlechterdebatte* (Frankfurt/M., 2001); *Zivilgesellschaft: Eine geschlechterkritische Perspektive*, co-edited with Margit Appel and Luise Gubitzer (Frankfurt/M., 2003); *Geschlecht und Politik: Institutionelle Verhältnisse, Verhinderungen und Chancen* (Berlin, 2004); *Politikwissenschaft und Geschlecht. Konzepte—Verknüpfungen—Perspektiven*, co-edited with Sieglinde Rosenberger (Vienna, 2004); *Was bewirkt Gender Mainstreaming? Ansätze der Evaluierung durch Policy-Analysen*, co-edited with Ute Behning (Frankfurt/M., 2005).

Regina Wecker is Professor of Women's and Gender History at the University of Basel and director of the Swiss Doctoral Program in Gender Studies. Her main research focuses on women's work and on citizenship in nineteenth- and twentieth-century Central Europe, in particular in Switzerland. Her current research projects focus on the on the history of eugenics and genetics in Switzerland. Her publications include: *Zwischen Ökonomie und Ideologie: Arbeit im Lebenszusammenhang von Frauen im Kanton Basel-Stadt 1870–1910* (Zurich, 1997); *"Die schutzbedürftige Frau": Zur Konstruktion von Geschlecht durch Mutterschaftsversicherung, Nachtarbeitsverbot und Sonderschutzgesetzgebung im 20. Jahrhundert*, co-author with Brigitte Studer and Gaby Sutter (Zurich, 2001); *Wissen, Gender, Professionalisierung: Historisch-soziologische Studien*, co-edited with Claudia Honegger and Brigitte Liebig (Zurich, 2003); and several articles on eugenics in Switzerland.

INDEX

A

Aberdeen, Lady Ishbel, 110
Abbott, Edith, 250, 252
Abbott, Grace, 250, 253
Abdullah, Shaikh, 148
abortion, 33, 212, 257
Addams, Jane, 250–251, 262nn23–24, 262n30
Alexander, William, 64
All India Muslim Ladies' Conference, 147
All India Women's Conference, 147
alternative publics, 191, 200, 255, 257–8, 260
Althusser, Louis, 291, 300n20
American Academy of Social and Political Science, 273
"amoral familism," 169n26
Anglo-Saxonism, 268
Anthony, Susan B., 248
Antic, Milica, 231, 236, 239n2, 241n25
Arato, Andrew, 34–35, 42nn72–73, 123, 133n14, 154, 157, 168n4
Aristotle, 47, 98–9, 100, 106
Arthur, Richard, 267, 269, 274, 280, 283nn49–50, 280
Association of German Women's Organizations. See *Bund Deutscher Frauenvereine*, 130
Association of Islamic Ladies (*anjuman-e khawatin-e Islam*), 145
Astell, Mary, 100, 113n12
Augspurg, Anita, 110
Australia: Commonwealth of, 267, 270, 274–75, 281; Federal Post and Telegraph Act, 279; Immigration Restriction Act, 276, 278; Old Age and Invalid Act, 279; Pacific Islands Laborers Act, 276, 278; White Australia policy, 271, 277

B

Baldwin, Stanley, 199–201, 205, 207n34
Ballard, George, 71
Banfield, Edward C., 161, 169n26
Barton, Edmund, 270–271, 275, 276
Baumgartner, Ida, 128–129
Bederman, Gail, 265, 281n2, 282n33
Begam, Sughra Humayun, 146, 151n24
Bhabha, Homi, 136, 150n5
Blair, Hugh, 68
Boer War, 196–97, 199
Bohstedt, John, 174–75, 186n5, 186n10, 187n16, 187n21
Bolshevik Family Code (1918), 158
Bolshevism, 157–58, 168n13, 199–200
Boston Women's Health Book Collective (BWHBC), 257–258, 263n61
Bouton, Cynthia, 174–75, 186n4, 186nn8–9, 187n14, 187n16, 187n21
Boy Scouts (England), 197
Boys Brigade (England), 197
Brandeis, Louis, 251, 263n59
Breckinridge, Sophonisba, 250, 252

Bright, John, 195, 196
Britain, 59, 60, 61, 70, 72, 73–74, 77n49, 77n51; Boy Scouts, 197; Boys Brigade 197; campaign for women's property rights, 107; Chartism, 194; Church of England, 60; Hunger Marches, 199–200, 203, 205; Independent Labour Party, 196; Land and Labour League, 195–6; National Unemployed Workers' Movement, 190, 199, 201–203, 207n55; New Poor Law (1834), 194; Reform Acts, 108, 193–95; Reform Act (1832), 193, 206n8; Reform Act (1867), 194–95, 206n13; Representation of the People Act (1918), 190, 198; Society for Bettering the Condition of the Poor, 73; Women's Cooperative Guild, 173; Women's Social and Political Union (WSPU), 108.
Brodbeck, Paul, 43, 54n1
Brown, Elsa Barkley, 266, 281n2
Bryce, James, 198, 267, 269–270, 274–276, 282n28, 282n31, 283n52, 283n54, 283n60
Budde, Elisabeth, 128, 130, 134n43, 134n46
Bulgarian Association for University Women, 235
Bund Deutscher Frauenvereine (BDF, Association of Women's Organizations), 130
Bürgerliche Gesellschaft (middle-class society), 2, 18–19, 40n29, 60, 71, 82–3, 120, 167
Burgess, John W., 270, 282n31
Burke, Edmund, 71–2
Burlamaqui, Jean-Jacques, 61, 75n
Butler, Josephine, 111, 115n45

C

Campbell, Colin, 165, 170n41
"capitalism-by-design," 226–7
caring, work of, 2, 27, 29, 35–6
Carlsbad Decrees (Germany), 87, 96n43

Catholic integralism, 158
Catt, Carrie Chapman, 109–10, 115n44
Cell, John, 270, 282n27
Cercle Sociale (France), 106
Chaix-Chaponnière, Pauline, 110
Chamberlain, Joseph, 276
Chambers, Simone, 205, 207n58, 207n61
Charity Organization Society, 250
Charlton, W.R., 266, 281n6
Chartism, 194
Chicago School of Civics and Philanthropy, 252
Christian Family Movement, 256
Christianity, 62, 72, 247, 250
Church of England, 60
citizenship, 81–82, 90–91, 92n6, 92n10, 93n13, 93n14, 93n18, 94n21, 95n26–27, 96n55, 97, 100–101, 105, 108, 109, 110, 114n21, 116n48, 190–99, 200, 202–204, 205n6, 206n33; active, 137, 143; female, 122–123; gendered, 265–67; individual, 102–103, 107, 110; male, 19, 36; maternal, 279–81, 284n72; political, 195; racialized, 265–67, 277; of *Staatsbürger* (male citizen), 19, 38n2, 41n62
civic humanism, 192
civic motherhood, 90
civic republicanism, 192
civic spirit (*Bürgersinn*), 82, 85
civil society: democratic, 31; *societas civilis*, 60, 98; *société civile*, 18, 60; modern, 289; racialized, 23; Western model of, 21–22, 39n17. *See also Bürgerliche Gesellschaft; Zivilgesellschaft*
civil society models, 153, 166; action-logical, 6, 20–21, 191, 200; actor-oriented, 149; field-logical, 20, 29; functional, 137, 149; normative, 20–23; participatory, 218; social relations, 289
civility, 18, 22, 42n66, 60–62, 66, 75n13

civilization, 5, 18, 59–95 passim, 265, 268, 271–72, 247, 278, 280–81, 281n2, 282n33
Clark, Andrew I., 270
Clark, Anna, 194, 206n8, 206n12
Clarke, Eric O., 13, n5, 35, 42n79
class, 225–27, 229, 231–33, 238, 239n3, 240n16, 267, 269–270; bourgeois, 28–30, 35, 39n9; *Bürgertum*, 80, 92n9, 94n23, 94n27, 95n31, 95n32, 96n56; gentry, 61; lower, 24, 30, 31; middle ,19, 61, 72–74, 119–20, 122–126, 128–131, 133, 133n17, 134n50, 135–137, 139, 141, 143–44, 147–150, 150n3, 246; nobility, 146–49, 251, 253, 259, 261n3; polarization of, 177–8
Cohen, Jean, 34–35, 42nn72–73, 123, 133n14, 154, 157, 168n4
Cold War (1945–1989), 218
Cologne Association for Poor Girls' Schools (Germany), 79, 85, 86
Cologne Freemasons' Lodge (Germany), 86
colonialism, 136, 150; Australian, 271–2, 275; defense of, 274
common good, 192–93, 209, 218
communism, 225, 229, 231, 235
Communist Party, 224, 239n8
de Condorcet, Marquis, 74, 104
Connell, R. W., 191, 205n4
Conseil National des Femmes Françaises (National Council of French Women, France), 110
conservatism, 207nn34–35
consumer movements, 180–1, 185, 188n31, 254
counter-publics. *See* alternative publics
Cooper, David, 158, 168n15
Cronin, James, 201, 207n49
Croucher, Richard, 203, 207n55
Crowley, F. K., 279, 283n67

D

Davidoff, Leonore, 129, 132n4, 134n50, 214, 220, 222n25
Davis, Belinda, 183, 186n2, 189n44

Deakin, Alfred, 266–267, 270–271, 276–277, 280, 282n32
Dean, Jodi, 17, 38n2,
Declaration of Sentiments (United States), 46
Declaration of the Rights of Man (France), 105, 107
Declaration of the Rights of Women (France), 46, 105
decolonization, 271
Deegan, Mary Jo, 250, 262nn23–24, 262n30
democracy, 285–97, 292–93, 300n18
Diderot, Denis, 18, 69–70
Deutsch, Sarah, 248–9, 261n3
double burden, 47
Dunn, Elizabeth, 21, 22, 39n17

E

Ehrenberg, John, 19, 39n9
Eley, Geoff, 29, 41n50, 41n52
Elshtain, Jean B., 17, 34, 38n2, 41n47, 42n76
emancipation, 100–101, 111, 113n10, 112n37
Enlightenment, 20, 27–29, 32, 122; Scottish, 60, 62–64, 67–70, 75nn5, 15, 76n17, 76n27, 76n30, 76n37, 77n41, 77n55; European, 154
d'Épinay, Mme. Louise, 70
equality, 99–101, 103, 105, 109, 113n10
Estates-General of Feminism, 111
European Union, 225, 228, 240n14, 297, 297
European Women's Lobby, 286, 297
Exclusion Act (1882, United States), 269
Eyck, Helene, 123–27, 131, 133n17, 133n19, 133n33, 134n38

F

faith healing, 254–5
Fanon, Frantz, 218, 223n35
family, 18, 20–21, 23–37, 40n41, 41n42, 97–99, 101, 104, 112n2,

113n7, 113n14, 113n18, 113n19, 114n34, 117, 119–29, 131–32, 132n7, 133n15, 133n17, 134n50, 246, 249, 256, 261n21, 287–89, 291–92, 297; and civil society, 154–5, 157–9; as constraint on civil society participation, 162–4, 167; closed and open, 160, 166; life cycle of, 163; materfamilias, 90; paterfamilias, 81, 90; postmodern, 155; varieties of, 155–7
Febvre, Lucien, 64, 76n25, 77n48
Feldstein, Larry M., 165, 169n39
feminism, 97, 100–101, 103, 104, 111, 112n1, 112n4, 113n14, 113n16, 114n22, 114n25, 114n28, 114n30, 114n32, 115n37, 115n41, 115n45, 231, 233, 235, 237–238, 239nn2–3, 240n12; as critique, 26, 28, 31, 37, 38n2; "by design," 227–8; clashes within, 228–30, 295; essentialist, 224–29; in nongovernmental organizations (NGOs), 224–25, 227–38, 239n3, 240nn22–23, 241n32, 241n39, 241n42, 241n44, 242n47; politics of, 51–52; protests, 99; state, 288, 294, 300n12, 300n24–25, 300n27; Western, 9; as movement, 51, 25, 53, 54. *See also* women's movements
femocrats, 294–5
Ferguson, Adam, 18, 25, 59, 62, 63–64, 68, 71, 75n16, 76nn17–18, 76n23, 126, 133n37
Fichte, Johann Gottlieb, 101
Flanagan, Richard, 196, 206nn19–20, 206n22, 207n36
Fletcher of Saltoun, Andrew, 63
Flour War (France), 175
Fodor, Eva, 231, 241n27
food riots, 173–75, 178–9,181, 185, 186n2, 187n11, 187n16, 187n22, 187n35, 187n47, 187n51; and anti-Semitism, 183; reactions against, 178–80, 184
Fordism, 292–3
Fordyce, James, 68
Foucault, Michel, 209, 220

France: Ancien Régime, 174, 186n4; campaign for women's property rights, 107; *Cercle Sociale*, 106; *Conseil National des Femmes Françaises* (National Council of French Women), 110; Declaration of the Rights of Man, 105, 107; Declaration of the Rights of Women, 46, 105; feminists, 98, 100–1; Flour War, 175; French Revolution, 32, 41n54, 46, 71–4, 100–102, 105, 114n31, 114n34, 174, 186n8; Jacobins, 106, 113n18; Paris Commune (1870/71), 108; Saint-Simonianism, 102; secular women's clubs, 106; Society of Revolutionary Republican Women, 106; women's political rights, 46
franchise: Australian, racial restrictions on, 276; British, 190–1, 194–6, 198
Fraser, Nancy, 17, 30, 38n2, 41n47, 41n55, 42n66, 49, 50– 52, 55nn28–29, 55n31, 55n33 55n36, 55n37, 120, 125, 191, 200, 205n2, 207n40, 207n40
French Revolution, 32, 41n54, 46, 71–4, 100–102, 105, 114n31, 114n34, 174, 186n8
La Fronde (feminist newspaper), 110
Funk, Nanette, 227–28, 240nn10–12, 242n49

G

Gal, Susan, 230, 232, 239n2, 240n21, 240n24, 241n28, 241n34, 241n36
Gall, Lothar, 81, 92n8, 92n11
Garrard, John, 195, 206n18
Gaskell, Elizabeth, 124
Gellner, Ernest, 19, 39n9
gender, 136, 140, 143, 149, 150n11, 150n14, 151n19, 151n25, 153–159, 162, 164, 166–67, 168n9, 169n20, 170n45; bourgeois, 122; equality, 287; justice, 3, 36, 37, 40n32, 42n68, 45, 49, 52, 53, 54, 292; norms, 30, 126; relations, 154, 156, 159, 162; studies, 18, 26; theory, 49

General German Female Teachers Association (*Allgemeiner Deutscher Lehrerinnenverband*), 128
Gerhardt, Ute, 17
Germany: Carlsbad Decrees, 7, 96n43; BDF, 130; Cologne Association for Poor Girls' Schools, 79, 85, 86; Cologne Freemasons' Lodge, 86; General German Female Teachers Association, 128; Green Party (*Die Grünen*), 215; Hausarbeitstag (housekeeping day), 47; *Kinderladenbewegung* (movement for independent child care), 211; *Militärgesellschaft* (military society), 21; *geistige Mütterlichkeit* (spiritual motherhood), 129; Music-Lovers' Society, 86; Northern German Federation, 82; *Normalfamilie*, 27; Patriotic Women's Association, 79, 84, 91n3; philhellenic movement, 87–89; Prussian Law of Associations (*Preußisches Vereinsgesetz*), 80; Radical Decree (*Radikalenerlass*), 210, 214; '68ers, 210; Socialist German Students Organization (SDS), 212; *Stern* (magazine), 211–12; Weimar Republic (1919–1933), 46; welfare state, 44; West German Labor Court, 47; *Wohngemeinschaften* (WGs, communes), 214–15
Geyer, Martin H., 184, 186n2, 186n6, 188nn38–39, 189n45, 189n47, 189n49
Giddens, Anthony, 126, 133n36
Giddings, Lisa, 231, 241n29
Ginsborg, Paul, 34, 40n38, 41n42, 42n78
Glenn, John, 232, 241n32
globalization, 1
Godwin, William, 73
Goldmark, Josephine, 251, 262n32
Goldthorpe, John H., 161, 169n25
Goodman, Dena, 70, 77n43, 77n49
Gordon, Daniel, 69, 77n42, 77n45, 77n48
Gosewinkel, Dieter, 19, 38n1, 39n10, 39n14, 39n22, 40nn25–26

de Gouges, Olympe, 46, 105
Gourd, Emilie, 110
Gramsci, Antonio, 30, 41n56, 85, 288, 289, 300n13, 300n14
grassroots movements, 36, 256
Green Party (*Die Grünen*, Germany), 215
Gregory, John, 68–69, 76n37, 76, 38, 77n39
Grotius, Hugo, 61, 75n9, 76n27
Grunburg, Laura, 232

H

Habermas, Jürgen, 19, 27, 28, 30, 32, 39n9, 41nn42–44, 41nn45–46, 41n50, 59, 64, 75n1; *Structural Transformation of the Public Sphere*, 27
Hagemann, Karen, 87, 92n11, 95n39, 96n41, 184, 188n31, 189nn49–50
Hainisch, Marianne, 110
Hall, Catherine, 129, 134, 214, 220n1, 222n25
Hall, John A., 19, 39n9
Hamilton, Alice, 250, 262n31
Hanley, Sarah, 100, 113n11
Hann, Chris, 17, 23
Hardtwig, Wolfgang, 88, 93n15, 96n50
Harris, Jose, 74, 75nn6–8, 75n14, 77n58, 78n69
Harvester Judgment (Australia), 278–9
Hausarbeitstag (housekeeping day, Germany), 47
Hauser, Christoph, 87, 96n42, 96n44
Hegel, Georg Wilhelm Friedrich, 19, 25–26, 28, 40n37, 99, 101, 123, 133n13, 154, 166– 67, 168n6
Heineccius, Johann, 61, 77n9
Herder, Friedrich, 121, 132n10
Hesselgren, Kirsten, 110
Heymann, Lida-Gustava, 110
Higgins, Henry B., 270–271, 275, 277, 278–279
von Hippel, Theodor, 74, 78n68
Hobbes, Thomas, 60, 99
Honneth, Axel, 50, 55nn31–32

Hooker, Richard, 60, 75n7, 77n58, 77n69
hooks, bell, 159
Hübner, Johanne Friederike, 176
Hufton, Olwen, 175, 187n12
Hull-House (Chicago, United States), 250
Hume, David, 62, 64–67, 71, 76n26, 76nn28–29, 76n31
Hunger Marches (England), 199–200, 203, 205
Husain, Muhibb, 143–44
Hutcheson, Francis, 63
Hyderabad Ladies Social Club (India), 145

I

identity, 23, 25, 34
imperialism, 196–98
Independent Labour Party (England), 196
International Abolitionist Federation, 111
International Council of Women, 111
International Labour Organization, 43
International Monetary Fund, 226, 233–34
interpellation, 291
Isenberg, Nancy, 90, 96n55, 247, 261n6
Islam, 138–40, 143–46, 150n17, 151n18

J

Jacobins (France), 106, 113n18
Jacobs, Aletta, 109, 110, 115n44
Jacobson, Matthew Frye, 265, 267, 281n2, 282n13
Jalusic, Vlasta, 231, 236, 239n2, 241n25
Jarrow Crusade (England), 202–3
Jodin, Marie-Madeleine, 100, 105, 113n13
Joseph, Francis, 200
Joseph, Suad, 13n3, 22, 39n18
justice, 43–49, 52, 53–54, 97, 100–101, 105, 111, 113n17, 116n46; equality, 45–51, 53; gender, 43, 45, 49, 52–54
justitia communitiva, 47
justitia distributive, 47

K

Kaldor, Mary, 285, 299n2, 300n16
Kames, Lord (Henry Home), 64, 67–69
Kant, Immanuel, 18, 25, 81, 92n7, 99
Kätzel, Ute, 221n13, 222n15, 222n23
Kay, Rebecca, 232, 241n35
Keane, John, 19, 23, 39n9, 40n25, 40n27
Kelley, Florence, 250–251, 262n22, 262n26, 262n32
Kessler-Harris, Alice, 47, 55n19, 55n28, 252, 262n39
kibbutzim, 157–158, 168n14
Kinderladenbewegung (movement for independent child care, West Germany), 211
kitchen-table politics, 208–9, 214–18
Kipling, Rudyard, 269
Van Kleeck, Mary 251
Kleemann, Susanne, 213, 222n23
Kligman, Gail, 230,232, 239n2, 240n21, 240n24, 241n28, 241n34, 241n36
Kline, Wendy, 257, 258, 263n62
Kocka, Jürgen, 13n2, 18–20, 38n1, 39nn4–5, 39nn11–12, 39n15, 39n20, 41n49, 42n68, 42n70 42n83, 45–46, 52, 54n4, 54n8, 54n15, 56n41, 98, 112n4, 119, 132nn1–3, 132n8 133n35, 154, 168n5
Kollontai, Alexandra, 157–58, 168n13
Krahl, Hans-Jürgen, 212–13
Kreisky, Eva, 44, 54n7
Krug, Wilhelm Traugott, 87

L

La Leche League, 256, 263n58
labor, gender division of, 24, 26, 33, 35–6, 101

Land and Labour League (England), 195–6
Landes, Joan, 27, 30, 41n43, 41n45, 41n48, 41n54, 42n86
Lange, Helene, 91, 128, 130, 134n54, 134n55
Lathrop, Julia, 250
Leach, Edmund, 160–61, 169n24
League of Nations, 111
League of Women Voters (United States), 253
liberalism, 192–93, 197
liberty, 39n9, 64, 86, 93n14, 100, 105, 163, 196, 220–221n2, 261n11
Lipp, Carola, 175, 187n11, 187n13
Lister, Ruth, 82, 93n13
Locke, John, 18, 25, 59, 60, 75n5, 99, 100, 113n12
Lodge, Henry Cabot, 269, 271, 282n23
Lowell, Josephine Shaw, 250
Lynch, Katherine, 245, 261n1

M

McClelland, Keith, 194, 206n13
Macintyre, Stuart, 279, 283n67
Mackenzie, Henry, 69, 77n40
McKibbin, Ross, 200, 205n1, 206n7, 207n38
McPherson, Aimee Semple, 255
Macpherson, James, 68
Mäder, Rudolf, 43
Maihofer, Andrea, 48, 55n22
male breadwinner ideal, 278
de Mandeville, Bernard, 62
manhood, 265, 271, 176, 282n33; white, 278
manliness, 200; middle-class, 206; heroic, 197; respectable, 199
masculinity, 191–205 passim, 211–12
Manus, Rosa, 110
market, 34, 37, 19, 20, 21, 23, 25
market societies, 174
Marshall, Thomas H., 31, 41n61, 193, 205n6
Marx, Karl, 19, 99
Marxist-Leninism, 230

maternalism, 9–10, 32, 246, 253–56, 260
Mendelson, Sarah, 232, 241n32
Merz, Mario, 160, 166, 169n23
Meyrowitz, Joshua, 164, 169n36
microcredit, 236–7
Militärgesellschaft (military society, Germany), 21
Mill, Harriet Taylor, 129, 134nn52–53
Mill, James, 139, 143, 150n15
Mill, John Stuart, 102, 129, 135nn52–53
Millar, John, 65, 67–7, 71, 76nn32, 35
Miller, Daniel, 165–66, 170n40, 170n44
Mix, Sarah, 255
modernization, 249–53
Moghadam, Valentine, 111, 116n48
Montagu, Elizabeth, 62
de Montesquieu, Baron, 18, 62–63, 69, 99, 100
Moore, Barrington, 45–46, 50, 54nn10–12
More, Hannah, 72–73, 77n59
Morellet, Abbé, 70, 77n44
Moseley, Oswald, 200
motherhood, 272, 273, 279–80
Music-Lovers' Society (Cologne, Germany), 86
Mütterlichkeit, geistige (spiritual motherhood), 129

N

Nadasen, Premilla, 259, 264n69, 264n70, 264n72
National Association for the Advancement of Colored People (NAACP, United States), 259
National Council of French Women (*Conseil National des Femmes Françaises*), 110–111
National Unemployed Workers' Movement (England), 190, 199, 201–203, 207n55
National Welfare Rights Organization (NWRO, United States), 259, 264n70

National Women's Party (United States), 108
natural law, 60–62, 65, 71, 75n9, 76n27
Nazism, responses to, 219
neoliberalism, 2, 19, 37, 225–26, 233, 235–36, 287, 298
New Left, 214, 217–18, 259
Ngai, Mae M., 266, 281n2
Nipperdey, Thomas, 83, 88, 93nn15–16, 96n49
nongovermental organizations (NGOs), 1, 9, 17, 288; in Bulgaria and Eastern Europe, 232–4, 236; critiques of, 230, 232, 236–7; feminist, 225, 227, 232–3, 235–7; and neo-liberalism, 233–5, 238; North American-West European, 229, 238
Nonn, Christoph, 180, 188n43
Normalfamilie, 27
Nussbaum, Martha, 161, 169n29

O

Oeuvre Libératrice (Liberation through Work), 110
Ogilvie, Sheilagh, 104, 114n26
Okin, Susan Moller, 17, 24, 28, 41n48, 99, 113n6, 155, 168n9
Opp, James, 255, 263n49
Organization for Economic Cooperation and Development (OECD), 234
Ossian, 68
Ostner, Ilona, 17, 34, 38n2, 42n75, 42n77
Oz-Salzburger, Fania, 64, 76n17

P

Paine, Thomas, 72
Paris Commune (France 1870/71), 108
Pateman, Carole, 17, 25–26, 38n2, 40nn36–37, 40n39, 42n86, 99, 103, 113n6
Patriotic Women's Association (Germany), 79, 84, 91n3

Paul, Alice, 108
Pearson, Charles, 267, 271, 275, 280, 282n11
Performativity, 191–92, 204–5
Pernau, Margrit, 22, 39n18, 42n67, 42n69,
Perrot, Michelle, 175, 187n12
Petras, James, 233, 241n43, 241n44
Philhellenic movement (Germany), 87–89
Phillips, Anne, 17, 25, 36, 38n2, 41n59, 42n84
physician philosophers, 108
Plato, 99
pluralism, 30
Plymley of Shropshire, Katherine, 62
political rights, 82, 85, 91
Pope Pius XI, 158–59
Pope Pius XII, 158–59
postcolonial studies, 22
post-maternalism, 253
postmodernism, 217–19
post-socialist societies, 9, 49–50, 226–27, 230,235–36, 238
Poullain de la Barre, François, 100, 104
Print culture, 59, 61, 74
Private life, 26, 35; personal life, 26, 28, 35; privacy, 27, 29, 33, 35; *Privatleben*, 26–27; *vie privée*, 26;
Private sphere, 2–3, 119–120, 123, 131, 136–138, 140, 149, 151n26, 136–138, 140, 149, 151n26
privatism, 161
professionalization, 246, 249, 252–53, 260
prostitution, 294, 296, 300n12, 300n25, 300n26, 300n28, 300n33
protest, 21, 30, 99, 173–86, 86nn1–3, 86n4, 86n6, 186n9, 187n22, 187n24, 188n28, 188n37, 188n39, 189n41, 189n49, 190, 196, 199, 200–205, 212, 241, 218, 220n2, 221n12, 222n24, 222n26, 223n33, 248, 264n70
Protestantism, 254
provo politics, 8, 208–14, 217–18
Prudhomme, Louis-Marie, 106

Prussian Law of Associations (*Preußisches Vereinsgesetz*, Germany), 80
Public space, 21, 23, 30, 137–39, 143–44, 149
Public sphere, 27–30, 32–33, 35, 38n2, 39n9 41n43, 41n47, 41n54, 41n55, 42n79, 191–92, 195, 197, 199, 200, 203, 207n40; *Öffentlichkeit*, 26, 103, 113n18, 115n36
Putnam, Robert, 165, 169nn38–39

Q

Quataert, Jean H., 88, 91n3, 95n39, 96n47, 96n51
Quigley, Kevin, 232, 241n33, 241n42

R

Race, 10, 43, 50, 68–69, 136, 267–8, 270–77, 280–1
race suicide, 273, 280
Randeria, Shalini, 22, 39n20, 39n22, 40n24
Rathbone, Eleanor, 97
Reagin, Nancy R., 89, 95n32, 96n51
refamilialization, 2
Reform Acts (Britain), 108, 193–95
Reichardt, Sven, 23, 40n26
religion, 149–50, 224, 245–6, 261n12. *See also* Catholic integralism; Christianity; faith-healing; Islam; Protestantism
Research Network on Gender and State (RNGS), 288, 294, 296, 299
respectability, 178–79, 184,194, 196,198–99, 202–4, 246–49
Revolution of 1848/49, 84, 96n43, 177
Rice, Cecil Arthur Spring, 267, 269, 274, 283nn49–50
Richardson, Samuel, 61
Robertson, William, 64, 67–68, 70, 76n34
Roosevelt, Franklin, 253
Roosevelt, Theodore, 265–69, 271, 273–74, 280, 281n1, 281n3, 281n9, 281–82n9, 282nn11–12, 282n21, 282nn23–24, 282n33, 283nn41–43, 283nn45–46, 283n48–50
Ross, Edward A., 267, 273–75, 281n9, 283n14, 283n51
de Roumier, Marie-Anne (Dame Robert), 104, 114n28
Rousseau, Jean-Jacques, 62, 69, 72, 99, 100, 104, 106, 113n18
Roy, Raja Ram Mohan, 139
Rüger, Sigrid, 212, 213
Russell, William, 70, 77n51
Rutherforth, Thomas, 61, 75nn9–10
Ryan, Mary, 30, 41n54, 247, 261n10, 261n12

S

Sachse, Carola, 47, 55nn16–18
de Sainte-Croix, Ghénia Avril, 110–111, 115n45
Saint-Simonianism (France), 102
Salomon, Alice, 110
Sander, Helke, 212–213
Sauer, Birgit, 17, 24, 37, 38n2, 40n32, 42n87
Scannell, Paddy, 164, 169n35
Schaaffhausen, Abraham, 79, 91n1, 95n35
Schaaffhausen, Therese, 79, 86, 91n9, 95n35
Schavan, Annette, 296
Schor, Juliet, 165–66, 170nn42–43
Schwarzer, Alice, 212, 222n18, 296
Scott, Gillian, 180, 188n33
Scott, Joan W., 47–49, 51, 55nn19–20, 55n24
Scott, Sarah, 62
Scottish Enlightenment. *See* Enlightenment
de Scudéry, Madeleine, 100
Sears case (United States), 47–49
de Secondat, Charles, 18
Seddon, Richard, 270
Seehuber, Dagmar, 211, 221n13
segregation, 270
self-help, 173–m 176–80, 183–84, 246, 260

sex, 98–103, 105–106, 109, 112,
   113n6, 114n20, 115n40
Shackleton of Lancashire, Elizabeth,
   61–62
Silverberg, Helene, 250, 261nn19–20,
   262n23, 262n34
'68ers (Germany), 210
Smith, Adam, 18, 62, 64–67, 73,
   76n27, 76n30,
social democracy, 179,188n7, 196
social knowledge, 248–9, 252
Socialist German Students
   Organization (SDS, Germany), 212
Society for Bettering the Condition of
   the Poor (Britain), 73
society of citizens, 2
Society of Revolutionary Republican
   Women (France), 106
Spanish-American War (1898), 268
Sperling, Valerie, 232, 241n35
Sperry, Admiral, 266
Stacey, Judith, 155, 168n10
Stark, David, 226, 239n6, 239n9
Stern (magazine, Germany), 211–12
street politics, 185, 188n27
Stuurman, Siep, 104, 113n10,
   114n23, 114n25
Suard, Jean-Baptiste, 70
suffrage, 177, 181, 183, 185;
   universal,181, 184
Swanwick, Helena, 110
Switzerland, 44, 46, 47, 53; National
   Council, 43; parliament, 43–44,
   54n2; women's political rights, 46;
   women's suffrage, 43, 54n2
Szalai, Julia, 231, 241n28

T

Talleyrand, 107
Taylor, Charles, 19, 50
Teachers of Women (*Mu'alim-e
   Niswam*), 144, 146
Tennyson, Lord Alfred, 109, 115n43
Tester, Keith, 23, 119, 132n1
Thanawi, Ashraf Ali, 140–41, 143–44,
   151nn20–21
Thomas, Antoine-Léonard, 70

Thomas, James H., 201, 205n6
Thompson, Edward P., 175, 186–
   87n10, 187n12, 187n16, 187n21
de Tocqueville, Alexis, 19
Tosh, John, 191, 197, 205n5,
   206nn24–25
Trentmann, Frank, 22, 39n19, 40n26
Turgot, Anne-Robert-Jacques, 70,
   77n47

U

unemployment, 199–204, 229, 231
United Nations, 232
United States: Chicago School of
   Civics and Philanthropy, 252;
   Declaration of Independence,
   46; Declaration of Sentiments,
   46; Exclusion Act (1882), 269;
   Hull-House (Chicago), 250;
   National Association for the
   Advancement of Colored People
   (NAACP), 259; National Welfare
   Rights Organization (NWRO),
   259, 264n70; National Women's
   Party, 108; Sears case, 47–49;
   Social Security Act, 253; United
   States Agency for International
   Development (USAID), 225,
   228, 240n13, 240n18, 240n22;
   Urban League, 259; welfare rights
   movement, 254, 259–60; welfare
   state, 245–46, 252, 260, 261n4;
   women's political rights, 46
United States Agency for International
   Development (USAID), 225, 228,
   240n13, 240n18, 240n22
Urban League (United States), 259

V

Veblen, Thorstein, 165, 170n40
Vickery, Amanda, 61, 75n3, 75n12
Vietnam War (1959–1975), 211
violence, 3, 8, 20–21, 23, 33, 40n25,
   108, 110, 138, 160, 175, 176, 177,
   181, 183–85, 187nn15–16, 187n21,
   188n36, 189nn46–47, 199, 207n34,

210, 213–14, 221n8, 221n12, 222n18, 229, 234, 240n20, 270, 286, 290–91, 293–94

W

Wakefield, Priscilla, 73, 78n65
Walzer, Michael, 19, 34, 39n9, 42n72, 204–205, 207n58
Wars of Unification (1870/71), 178
Weber, Helene, 128–29, 134n48, 1324n51
Wedel, Janine, 231, 239n5, 241n31
welfare associations, 91
welfare rights movement (United States), 254, 259–60
welfare state, 2, 9, 24, 31, 36–37, 41–42n65, 42n86, 44, 45, 49, 53, 94n26, 95n28, 115n42, 183, 284n72, 286, 290–93, 296–98, 300nn18–19; post-communist, 233, 237; United States, 245–46, 252, 260, 261n4
West German Labor Court, 47
White Australia policy, 271
"white men's countries," 10, 265–66, 268, 271, 280
Whiteread, Rachel, 160, 163
Wilkinson, Ellen, 190, 202
Wohngemeinschaften (WGs, communes, Germany), 214–15
Wollstonecraft, Mary, 72–73, 77n57, 78nn62–64, 101, 104, 114, 114n24
Woman's Leader and the Common Cause, 97, 109, 112n1

woman question, 99, 104, 138–39, 143
women's centers, 215–216
Women's Cooperative Guild (England), 173
Women's Indian Association, 147
women's health movement, 254, 256–60
women's movements, 212, 285–86, 288, 293, 298–99
Woolley, Helen Thompson, 250
World Bank, 225–26, 228, 233, 236, 239n8, 240n18, 240n19, 240n22
World War I (1914–1918), 174, 181–84, 188n36, 191, 196–98, 207, 207n34
World War II (1939–1945), 47, 199, 203
Women's Social and Political Union (WSPU, England), 108

Y

Yeatman, Anna, 157, 168n12
Young, Iris Marion, 17, 32–33, 38n2, 41n63, 42n68, 42n86, 200, 204, 205, 205n2, 205n40, 205n59

Z

Zetkin, Clara, 229, 240n17
de Zordo, Ornella, 163
Zivilgesellschaft (civil society), 2, 18–19, 21, 167